PRAISE FOR *THE SUM OF US*

"Illuminating and hopeful . . . [Heather McGhee] is compassionate but also clear-eyed, refusing to downplay the horrors of racism. . . . There is a striking clarity to this book; there is also a depth of kindness in it that all but the most churlish readers will find moving."

—*The New York Times*

"Required reading to move the country forward . . . Every so often a book comes along that seems perfectly timed to the moment and has the potential to radically shift our cultural conversation. [*The Sum of Us*] is one of those books."

—*Chicago Tribune*

"Supported by remarkable data-driven research and thoughtful interviews with those directly affected by these issues, McGhee paints a powerful picture of the societal shortfalls all around us. There is a greater, more just America available to us, and McGhee brings its potential to light."

—*BookPage*

"[McGhee] takes readers on an intimate odyssey across our country's racial divide to explore why some believe that progress for some comes at the expense of others. . . . A powerful, singular, and prescriptive blend of the macro and the intimate."

—*Oprah Daily*

"McGhee offers a mountain range of evidence that zero sum is a falsehood. . . . In actuality, the 'Solidarity Dividend' proves that everyone's lives are improved when anyone advances. McGhee's book is required reading, a true work of courage and intellectual rigor. Readers have likely asked: Why is this so hard for a country that has so much? By unearthing and exposing the faulty why, McGhee illuminates the path to actual change."

—*Booklist* (starred review)

"A head-on consideration of the costs of American racism . . . Compassionate but also candid about the tremendous challenges we face, the author clearly shows how Southern racism extends throughout the country today. Those most opposed to unions, public education, and integration are mostly those at the top of the financial ladder; those lower down, of whatever ethnicity, wind up paying richly. . . . An eye-opening, powerful argument for working ever harder for racial equity."

—*Kirkus Reviews* (starred review)

"Astute and persuasive . . . This sharp, thorough, and engrossing report casts America's racial divide in a new light."

—*Publishers Weekly* (starred review)

"*The Sum of Us* is a powerhouse of a book about the deep, enduring, cross-cultural, multigenerational, and real-life cost of racist policy-making in the United States. With intelligence and care (as well as with a trove of sometimes heartbreaking and sometimes heart-opening true stories) Heather McGhee shows us what racism has cost all of us, as a society. And that cost has been brutally high across the board. This is a book for every American, and I am grateful for McGhee's research, her humanity, and her never-more-important teachings."

—Elizabeth Gilbert, #1 *New York Times* bestselling author

"If everyone in America read this book, we'd be not only a more just country, but a more powerful, successful, and loving one. A vital, urgent, stirring, beautifully written book that offers a compassionate road map out of our present troubled moment."

—George Saunders, #1 *New York Times* bestselling and
Booker Prize–winning author of *Lincoln in the Bardo*

"Racism is not merely destructive to people of color. It is self-destructive to many white people. Racism is anti-American and anti-human, as Heather McGhee expertly and judiciously proves in *The Sum of Us*. This is the book I've been waiting for. *The Sum of Us* can help us come together to build a nation for us all, with policies that benefit us all."

—Ibram X. Kendi, #1 *New York Times* bestselling author
of *How to Be an Antiracist*

"Heather McGhee again slices through the rhetoric and the obfuscation right to the heart of what racism is costing us all. . . . A riveting read and a very fresh perspective!"

—Abigail Disney, activist and filmmaker

"*The Sum of Us* removes the cloak from this land of so-called innocents and brilliantly offers a path forward for the nation. . . . An extraordinary book for these difficult days."

—Eddie S. Glaude Jr., author of *Begin Again: James Baldwin's America and Its Urgent Lessons for Our Own*

"For those who still question the cost of systemic racism in America— and whether there is anything we can do about it—Heather McGhee has written a book you must read."

—David Axelrod, former senior advisor to President Barack Obama and CNN senior political commentator

"Heather McGhee has written a wonderful and engaging book that unpacks the work of racism in the lives of not only African Americans, but all Americans. Traveling across the country and talking to people from varying backgrounds, McGhee details how the work of white supremacy and racism continues today by promoting a zero-sum story in which white Americans are encouraged to view the world through an us-versus-them lens. *The Sum of Us* is a must-read."

—Cathy Cohen, David and Mary Winton Green Distinguished Service Professor at the University of Chicago and founder of the Black Youth Project

# THE
# SUM
# OF US

# THE
# SUM
# OF
# US

## What Racism Costs Everyone and How We Can Prosper Together

## HEATHER McGHEE

**ONE WORLD**

*New York*

2022 One World Trade Paperback Edition

Published in the United States by One World, an imprint of
Random House, a division of Penguin Random House LLC, New York.

ONE WORLD and colophon are registered trademarks of Penguin Random House LLC.

Originally published in hardcover in a slightly different form in the United States
by One World, an imprint of Random House, a division of
Penguin Random House LLC, in 2021.

An earlier version of the Discussion Guide appeared
on the author's website in 2021.

Library of Congress Cataloging-in-Publication Data
Names: McGhee, Heather C., author. Title: The sum of us: what racism costs
everyone and how we can prosper together / Heather C. McGhee.
Description: First edition. | New York: One World, 2021 | Includes index.
Identifiers: LCCN 2020044567 (print) | LCCN 2020044568 (ebook) |
ISBN 9780525509585 (paperback) | ISBN 9780525509578 (ebook)
Subjects: LCSH: Racism—United States. |
United States—Race relations—Economic aspects.
Classification: LCC E185.8 .M38 2021 (print) | LCC E185.8 (ebook) |
DDC 305.800073—dc23
LC record available at https://lccn.loc.gov/2020044567

Printed in the United States of America on acid-free paper

oneworldlit.com

6 8 9 7

*Design by Debbie Glasserman*

FOR MY MOTHER

# Contents

# Introduction

"Why can't we have nice things?"

Perhaps there's been a time when you've pondered exactly this question. And by nice things, you weren't thinking about hovercraft or laundry that does itself. You were thinking about more basic aspects of a high-functioning society, like adequately funded schools or reliable infrastructure, wages that keep workers out of poverty or a public health system to handle pandemics. The "we" who can't seem to have nice things is Americans, all Americans. This includes the white Americans who are the largest group of the uninsured and the impoverished as well as the Americans of color who are disproportionately so. "We" is all of us who have watched generations of American leadership struggle to solve big problems and reliably improve the quality of life for most people. We know what we need—why can't we have it?

"Why can't we have nice things?" was a question that struck me pretty early on in life—growing up as I did in an era of rising inequality, seeing the wealthy neighborhoods boom while the schools and parks where most of us lived fell into disrepair. When I was twenty-two years old, I applied for an entry-level job at Demos, a research and advocacy organization working on public policy solutions to inequality. There, I learned the tools of the policy advocacy trade: statistical research and white papers, congressional testimony, litigation, bill drafting, media outreach, and public campaigns.

It was exhilarating. I couldn't believe that I could use a spreadsheet to convince journalists to write about the ideas and lives of the people I cared most about: the ones living from paycheck to paycheck who needed a better deal from businesses and our government. And it actually worked: our research influenced members of Congress to introduce laws that helped real people and led to businesses changing their practices. I went off to get a law degree and came right back to Demos to continue the work. I fell in love with the idea that information, in the right hands, was power. I geeked out on the intricacies of the credit markets and a gracefully designed regulatory regime. My specialty was economic policy, and as indicators of economic inequality became starker year after year, I was convinced that I was fighting the good fight, for my people and everyone who struggled.

And that is how I saw it: part of my sense of urgency about the work was that my people, black people, are disproportionately ill served by bad economic policy decisions. I was going to help make better ones. I came to view the relationship between race and inequality as most people in my field do—linearly: structural racism accelerates inequality for communities of color. When our government made bad economic decisions for everyone, the results were even worse for people already saddled with discrimination and disadvantage.

Take the rise of household debt in working- and middle-class families, the first issue I worked on at Demos. The volume of credit card debt Americans owed had tripled over the course of the 1990s, and among cardholders, black and Latinx families were more likely to be in debt. In the early 2000s, when I began working on the issue, bankruptcies and foreclosures were rising and homeowners, particularly black and brown homeowners, were starting to take equity out of their houses through strange new mortgage loans—but the problem of burdensome debt and abusive lending wasn't registering on the radar of enough decision makers. Few politicians in Washington knew what it was like to have bill collectors incessantly ringing their phones about balances that kept growing every month. So, in 2003, Demos launched a project to get their attention: the first-ever comprehensive research report on the topic, with big, shocking numbers about the increase in debt. The report included policy recommendations about how to free families from debt and avoid a financial meltdown. Our data resulted in newspaper editorials, meetings with banks, congressional hearings, and legislation to limit credit card rates and fees.

Two years later, Congress took action—and made the problem of rising debt worse. Legislators passed a bankruptcy reform bill supported by the credit industry that made it harder for people ever to escape their debts, no matter how tapped out they were after a job loss, catastrophic medical illness, or divorce. The law wasn't good for consumers, did nothing to address the real problems in family finances, and actually made the problem worse. It was a bad economic policy decision that benefited only lenders and debt collectors, not the public. This was a classic example of the government not doing the simple thing that aligned with what most Americans wanted or what the data showed was necessary to solve a big problem. Instead, it did the opposite. Why?

Well, for one thing, our inability to stop bankruptcy reform made me realize the limits of research. The financial industry and other corporations had spent millions on lobbying and campaign donations to gin up a majority in Congress, and many of my fellow advocates walked away convinced that big money in politics was the reason we couldn't have nice things. And I couldn't disagree—of course money had influenced the outcome.

But I'll never forget something that happened on the last day I spent at the Capitol presenting Demos's debt research to members of Congress. I was walking down the marble hallway of the Russell Senate Office Building in my new "professional" shoes—I was twenty-five years old—when I stopped to adjust them because they kept slipping off. When I bent down, I was near the door of a Senate office; I honestly can't remember if it belonged to a Republican or a Democrat. I heard the bombastic voice of a man going on about the deadbeats who had babies with multiple women and then declared bankruptcy to dodge the child support, using the government to avoid personal responsibility. There was something in the senator's invective that made my heart rate speed up. I stood and kept moving, my mind racing. Had we advocates entirely missed something about the fight we were in? We had been thinking of it as a class issue (with racial disparities, of course), but was it possible that, at least for some of the folks on the other side of the issue, coded racial stereotypes were a more central player in the drama than we knew?

I left Capitol Hill, watching the rush hour crush of mostly white people in suits and sneakers heading home after a day's work in the halls of power, and felt stupid. Of course, it's not as if the credit card companies had made racial stereotypes an explicit part of their communications strategy on bankruptcy reform. But I'd had my political coming-of-age in the mid-1990s, when the drama of the day was "ending welfare as we know it," words that helped Bill Clinton hold on to the (white) political center by scapegoating (black) single mothers for not taking "personal responsibility" to escape poverty. There was nothing explicit or conclusive about what I'd overheard, but perhaps the bankruptcy reform fight—also, like welfare, about the deservingness and character of people with little money—was playing out in that same racialized theater, for at least one decision maker and likely more.

I felt frustrated with myself for being caught flat-footed (literally, shoe in hand!) and missing a potential strategic vulnerability of the campaign. I'd learned about research and advocacy and lobbying in the predominantly white world of nonprofit think tanks, but how could I have forgotten the first lessons I'd ever learned as a black person in America, about what they see when they see us? About how quick so many white people could be to assume the worst of us . . . to believe that we wanted to cheat at a game they were winning fair and square? I hadn't even thought to ask the question about this seemingly nonracial financial issue, but had racism helped defeat us?

Years later, I was on a conference call with three progressive economists, all white men. It was 2010, and we were plotting the research strategy for a huge project about the national debt and budget deficit. Both measures were on the rise, as the Great Recession had decimated tax revenue while requiring more public spending to restart the economy. The Tea Party had burst onto the political stage, and everyone, from conservative politicians to the kind of Democrats who had President Obama's ear, was saying that we needed a "grand bargain" to create a dramatically smaller government by 2040 or 2050, including cuts to Social Security, Medicaid, and Medicare. We were preparing the numbers to show that such a bargain would be the death blow to a middle class that was already on its knees, and to offer an alternative budget proposal that would include a second stimulus and investments to grow the middle class.

Toward the end of our planning call, I cleared my throat into the speakerphone. "So, when we're talking about the fiscal picture in 2040 or 2050, we're also talking about a demographic change tipping point, so where should we make the point that all these programs were created without concern for their cost when the goal was to build a white middle class, and they paid for themselves in economic growth . . . and now these guys are trying to fundamentally renege on the deal for a future middle class that would be majority people of color?" Nobody spoke. I checked to see if I'd been muted. No—the light on the phone was still green. Finally, one of the economists spoke into the awkward silence.

"Well, sure, Heather. We know that, and you know that, but let's not lead with our chin here. We are trying to be persuasive."

I found the Mute button again, pressed it, and screamed.

Then I laughed a little, and sighed. At least that economist had said the quiet part out loud for once. He was just expressing the unspoken conventional wisdom in my field: that we'd be less successful if we explicitly called out the racial unfairness or reminded people that the United States had deliberately created a white middle class through racially restricted government investments in homeownership and infrastructure and retirement security, and that it had only recently decided that keeping up those investments would be unaffordable and unwise. What was worse, I didn't have the confidence to tell my colleagues that they were wrong about the politics of it. They were probably right.

Nearly all the decision makers in our target audience were going to be white, from the journalists we wanted to cover our research to the legislative staff we'd meet with to the members of Congress who would vote on our proposal. Even under a black president, we were operating within a white power structure. Before long, the Tea Party movement used the language of fiscal responsibility but the cultural organizing of white grievance to force a debt ceiling showdown, mandate blunt cuts to public programs during a fragile recovery, and stall the legislative function of the federal government for the rest of Obama's presidency. Was it possible that even when we didn't bring up race, it didn't matter? That racism could strengthen the hand that beat us, even when we were advocating for policies that would help all Americans—including white people?

ON THE DAY Donald Trump was to take the oath of office in 2017, I'd been the president of Demos for three years. I was gearing up to fight against the onslaught that Trump's incoming administration portended for civil rights and liberties, for immigrants and Muslims, and for the Black Lives Matter movement that he had gleefully attacked in his campaign. But as an economic policy advocate, I also knew that the Trump agenda—from repealing the Affordable Care Act to cutting taxes for big corporations and the wealthy (apparently the concern about the national debt expired with the Obama presidency) to stopping action on climate change, which would have catastrophic economic and social costs for the country and the world—was going to do damage across the board. It would create more economic inequality. Why would white voters have rallied to the flag of a man whose agenda promised to wreak economic, social, and environmental havoc on them along with everyone else? It just didn't add up.

The inadequacy of the tool I was bringing to this question, economic policy research, felt painfully obvious. Contrary to how I was taught to think about economics, everybody wasn't operating in their own rational economic self-interest. The majority of white Americans had voted for a worldview supported not by a different set of numbers than I had, but by a fundamentally different story about how the economy works; about race and government; about who belongs and who deserves; about how we got here and what the future holds. That story was more powerful than cold economic calculations. And it was exactly what was keeping us from having nice things—to the contrary, it had brought us Donald Trump.

So, I made an unexpected decision. I decided to hand over the reins at Demos and start plotting a journey, one that would take me across the country and back again over the next three years. I began calling experts not on public policy but on public opinion, the psychology and the political proclivities of people: what makes us see the world in certain ways, what compels us to act, what drives us toward or against certain solutions to our big problems. Before I left, I had Demos partner with a critical race scholar and a linguist to develop our own public opinion research on race, class, and government. Most important, I leaned on the relationships I'd built over the years with grassroots and labor organizers, who introduced me to Americans of all backgrounds who were willing to talk to me about how they were making sense of one another and their futures. I remained guided by the same mission I had when I started at Demos nearly two decades prior: changing the rules to bring economic freedom to those who lack it today. But I wouldn't be treating the issues as cut-and-dried dollars-and-cents questions, but questions of belonging, competition, and status—questions that in this country keep returning to race.

In my gut, I've always known that laws are merely expressions of a society's dominant beliefs. It's the beliefs that must shift in order for outcomes to change. When policies change in advance of the underlying beliefs, we are often surprised to find the problem still with us. America ended the policy of enforced school segregation two generations ago, but with new justifications, the esteem in which many white parents hold black and brown children hasn't changed much, and today our schools are nearly as segregated as they were before *Brown v. Board of Education*. Beliefs matter.

So, what is the stubborn belief that needs to shift now for us to make progress against inequality? I found my first clues in a series of psychology studies. Psychologists Maureen Craig and Jennifer Richeson presented white Americans with news articles about people of color becoming the majority of the population by 2042. The study authors then asked the subjects to "indicate their agreement with the idea that increases in racial minorities' status will reduce white Americans' status." The people who agreed most strongly that demographic change threatened whites' status were most susceptible to shifting their policy views because of it, even on "race-neutral policies" like raising the minimum wage and expanding healthcare— even drilling in the Arctic. The authors concluded that "making the changing national racial demographics salient led white Americans (regardless of political affiliation) to endorse conservative policy positions more strongly."

I immediately thought of the deficit project and of my white colleagues' resistance to stating the obvious about demographic change for fear it would backfire and make austerity more popular. Six years later, there it was, that fear corroborated in a psychological experiment: thinking about a more diverse future changed white Americans' policy preferences about government.

It was a dramatic finding, but it still wasn't clear to me why white people would view the presence of more people of color as a threat to their status, as if racial groups were in a direct competition, where progress for one group was an automatic threat to another. And it was even more baffling to me how that threat could feel so menacing that these white people would resist policies that could benefit *them*, just because they might also benefit people of color. Why would they allow a false sense of group competition to become a self-defeating trap?

But then again, they weren't getting that idea out of nowhere. This zero-sum paradigm was the default framework for conservative media—"makers and takers," "taxpayers and freeloaders," "handouts," and "special favors"; "they're coming after your job, your safety, your way of life." Without the hostile intent, of course, aren't we all talking about race relations through a prism of competition, every advantage for one group mirrored by a disadvantage for another? When researching and writing about disparities, I was taught to focus on how white people benefited from systemic racism: their schools have more funding, they have less contact with the police, they have greater access to healthcare. Those of us seeking unity told that version of the zero-sum story; the politicians seeking division told the other version—is it any wonder that many white people saw race relations through the lens of competition?

But was that the real story? Black people and other people of color certainly lost out when we weren't able to invest more in the aftermath of the Great Recession, or tackle climate change more forcefully under President Obama, or address the household debt crisis before it spiraled out of control—in each case, at least partly because of racist stereotypes and dog whistles used by our opposition. But did white people win? No, for the most part they lost right along with the rest of us. Racism got in the way of all of us having nice things.

If I looked back at all the vexing problems I'd worked on in my career (student debt, workers' rights, money in politics, unfair taxes, predatory lending, low voter turnout), would I find the fingerprints of racism on all our setbacks and defeats? It is progressive economic conventional wisdom that racism accelerates inequality for communities of color, but what if racism is actually driving inequality for everyone?

**THIS BOOK RECOUNTS** my journey to tally the hidden costs of racism to us all. It starts where my own journey began, trying to understand how the rules of our economy became so tilted toward the already wealthy and powerful. The people of our country are so productive and generate so much wealth, but most of the gains go to a small number, while most families struggle to stay afloat. I traveled to Mississippi and sat with factory workers trying to unite a multiracial workforce to bargain collectively for better pay and benefits. I talked to white homeowners who had lost everything in a financial crisis that began with the predatory mortgages that banks first created to strip wealth from black and brown families. I heard from white parents and students who feared that segregated white schools would render them ill equipped for a diverse world. To understand when white America had turned against government, I traveled to one of the many places where the town had drained its public swimming pool rather than integrate it.

In each of these places, the white people's neighbors and co-workers of color struggled more because of racism: the Latinx factory worker is paid less for the same work; black homeownership rates are near thirty-year lows while white levels are on their way back; the black child in the segregated school has far more barriers to overcome; the loss of public goods at the time of integration means that families of color never got to enjoy that kind of government largesse.

As the descendant of enslaved Africans and of a line of black Americans who were denied housing, equal education, jobs, and even safety from white lynch mobs, I am well aware that the ledger of racial harms is nowhere near balanced. I know the risks I'm taking by widening the aperture to show the costs of white supremacy to our entire society. This book amasses evidence for a part of the story I believe we are neglecting at our peril, but rather than shift focus from racism's primary targets, I hope this story brings more people's eyes—and hearts—to the cause.

Black writers before me, from James Baldwin to Toni Morrison, have made the point that racism is a poison first consumed by its concocters. What's clearer now in our time of growing inequality is that the economic benefit of the racial bargain is shrinking for all but the richest. The logic that launched the zero-sum paradigm—I will profit at your expense—is no longer sparing millions of white Americans from the degradations of American economic life as people of color have always known it. As racist structures force people of color into the mines as the canary, racist indifference makes the warnings we give go unheeded—from the war on drugs to the financial crisis to climate disasters. The coronavirus pandemic is a tragic example of governments and corporations failing to protect black, brown, and Indigenous lives—though, if they had, everyone would have been safer.

I'll admit that my journey was deeply personal, too. At its best, this country brings together all the world's peoples and invites them to make something new. Collisions of cultures have stretched the branches of my black family over the years, so that it now includes white, Asian, and Latinx people, too. I started my journey when I was pregnant with a child whose grandparents would be black, white, and South Asian. I'm sure some part of me doesn't want to believe that oppression of people of color really is an unalloyed good for white people, making us truly separate and intrinsically at odds— because then the multiracial America that made my son possible is doomed.

The logical extension of the zero-sum story is that a future without racism is something white people should fear, because there will be nothing good for them in it. They should be arming themselves (as they have been in record numbers, "for protection," since the Obama presidency) because demographic change will end in a dog-eat-dog race war. Obviously, this isn't the story we want to tell. It's not even what we believe. The same research I found showing that white people increasingly see the world through a zero-sum prism showed that black people do not. African Americans just don't buy that our gain has to come at the expense of white people. And time and time again, history has shown that we're right. The civil rights victories that were so bitterly opposed in the South ended up being a boon for the region, resulting in stronger local economies and more investments in infrastructure and education.

The old zero-sum paradigm is not just counterproductive; it's a lie. I started my journey on the hunt for its source and discovered that it has only ever truly served a narrow group of people. To this day, the wealthy and the powerful are still selling the zero-sum story for their own profit, hoping to keep people with much in common from making common cause with one another. But not everyone is buying it. Everywhere I went, I found that the people who had replaced the zero sum with a new formula of cross-racial solidarity had found the key to unlocking what I began to call a "Solidarity Dividend," from higher wages to cleaner air, made possible through collective action. And the benefits weren't only external. I didn't set out to write about the moral costs of racism, but they kept showing themselves. There is a psychic and emotional cost to the tightrope white people walk, clutching their identity as good people when all around them is suffering they don't know how to stop, but that is done, it seems, in their name and for their benefit. The forces of division seek to harden this guilt into racial resentment, but I met people who had been liberated by facing the truth and working toward racial healing in their communities.

At the end of my journey to write this book, a multiracial coalition voted to end Donald Trump's presidency, with historic turnout levels despite a pandemic, and racial inequality topping the list of voter concerns. That coalition included millions of white voters, particularly the college-educated and the young. Yet the majority of white voters still supported an impeached president who lied to Americans on a daily basis, whose rhetoric and policies made him a hero of white supremacist terror groups, and who mismanaged and downplayed a pandemic that cost more than 200,000 American lives in less than a year. Rather than ending the soul-searching of the Trump era, the 2020 election raised new questions about how much suffering and dysfunction the country's white majority is willing to tolerate, and for how elusive a gain.

I'm fundamentally a hopeful person, because I know that decisions made the world as it is and that better decisions can change it. Nothing about our situation is inevitable or immutable, but you can't solve a problem with the consciousness that created it. The antiquated belief that some groups of people are better than others distorts our politics, drains our economy, and erodes everything Americans have in common, from our schools to our air to our infrastructure. And everything we believe comes from a story we've been told. I set out on this journey to piece together a new story of who we could be to one another, and to glimpse the new America we must create for the sum of us.

# THE
# SUM
# OF US

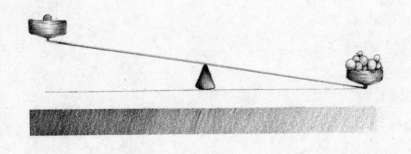

**Chapter 1**

# AN OLD STORY: THE ZERO-SUM HIERARCHY

Growing up, my family and my neighbors were always hustling. My mother had the fluctuating income of a person with an entrepreneur's mind and a social worker's heart. My dad, divorced from my mom since I was two, had his own up-and-down small business, too, and soon a new wife and kids to take care of. If we had a good year, my mom, my brother, and I moved into a bigger apartment. A bad spell, and I'd notice the mail going unopened in neat but worrisome piles on the hall table. I now know we were in what economists call "the fragile middle class," all income from volatile earnings and no inherited wealth or assets to fall back on. We were the kind of middle class in the kind of community that kept us proximate to real poverty, and I think this shaped the way I see the world. My mother took us with her to work in Chicago's notorious Robert Taylor public housing projects while she gave health lessons to young mothers, and some of my earliest playmates were kids with disabilities in a group home where she also worked. (It seemed she was always working.) We had cousins and neighbors who had more than we did, and some who had far less, but we never learned to peg that to their worth. It just wasn't part of our story.

I did learn, though, to ask "why," undoubtedly to an annoying degree. In the back seat of the station wagon facing the rear window, I asked why there were so many people sleeping on the grates on Lower Wacker Drive downtown, huddled together in that odd, unsunny yellow lamplight. Why did the big plant over on Kedzie have to close, and would another one open and hire everybody back? Why was Ralph's family's furniture out on the curb, and where did their landlord think Ralph was going to live now?

My father turned eighteen the year the Voting Rights Act was signed; my mother did when the Fair Housing Act was signed three years later. That meant that my parents were in the first generation of black Americans to live full adult lives with explicitly racist barriers lowered enough for them even to glimpse the so-called American Dream. And just as they did, the rules changed to dim the lights on it, for everyone. In the mid-1960s, the American Dream was as easy to achieve as it ever was or has been since, with good union jobs, subsidized home ownership, strong financial protections, a high minimum wage, and a high tax rate that funded American research, infrastructure, and education. But in the following decades, rapid changes to tax, labor, and trade laws meant that an economy that used to look like a football, fatter in the middle, was shaped like a bow tie by my own eighteenth birthday, with a narrow middle class and bulging ends of high- and low-income households.

This is the Inequality Era. Even in the supposedly good economic times before the COVID-19 pandemic that began in 2020, 40 percent of adults were not paid enough to reliably meet their needs for housing, food, healthcare, and utilities. Only about two out of three workers had jobs with basic benefits: health insurance, a retirement account (even one they had to fund themselves), or paid time off for illness or caregiving. Upward mobility, the very essence of the American idea, has become stagnant, and many of our global competitors are now performing far better on what we have long considered to be the American Dream. On the other end, money is still being made: the 350 biggest corporations pay their CEOs 278 times what they pay their average workers, up from a 58-to-1 ratio in 1989, and nearly two dozen companies have CEO-to-worker pay gaps of over 1,000 to 1. The richest 1 percent own as much wealth as the entire middle class.

I learned how to track these numbers in my early days working at a think tank, but what I was still asking when I decided to leave it fifteen years later was: Why? Why was there a constituency at all for policies that would make it harder for more people to have a decent life? And why did so many people seem to blame the last folks in line for the American Dream—black and brown people and new immigrants who had just started to glimpse it when it became harder to reach—for economic decisions they had no power to influence? When I came across a study by two Boston-based scholars, titled "Whites See Racism as a Zero-Sum Game That They Are Now Losing," something clicked. I decided to pay the study authors a visit.

It was a hot late-summer day when I walked into the inner courtyard at Harvard Business School to meet with Michael Norton and Samuel Sommers, two tall and lean professors of business and psychology, respectively. Harvard Business School is where some of the wealthiest people in America cemented their pedigrees and became indoctrinated in today's winner-take-all version of capitalism. It is an overwhelmingly white club, admittance to which all but guarantees admittance to all other elite clubs. Nonetheless, that's where we sat as these two academics explained to me how, according to the people they'd surveyed, whites were now the subjugated race in America.

Norton and Sommers had begun their research during the first Obama administration, when a white Tea Party movement drove a backlash against the first black president's policy agenda. They had been interested in why so many white Americans felt they were getting left behind, despite the reality of continued white dominance in U.S. life, from corporations to government. (Notwithstanding the black president, 90 percent of state, local, and federal elected officials were white in the mid-2010s.) What Norton and Sommers found in their research grabbed headlines: the white survey respondents rated anti-white bias as more prevalent in society than anti-black bias. On a scale of 1 to 10, the average white scoring of anti-black bias was 3.6, but whites rated anti-white bias as a 4.7, and opined that anti-white bias had accelerated sharply in the mid-1970s.

"We were shocked. It's so contrary to the facts, of course, but here we are, getting calls and emails from white people who saw the head-lines and thanked us for revealing the truth about racism in America!" said Norton with a dry laugh.

"It turns out that the average white person views racism as a zero-sum game," added Sommers. "If things are getting better for black people, it must be at the expense of white people."

"But that's not the way black people see it, right?" I asked.

"Exactly. For black respondents, better outcomes for them don't necessarily mean worse outcomes for white people. It's *not* a zero sum," said Norton.

As to why white Americans, who have thirteen times the median household wealth of black Americans, feel threatened by diminished discrimination against black people, neither Sommers nor Norton had an answer that was satisfying to any of us.

"There's not really an explanation," said Professor Sommers.

I NEEDED TO find out. I sensed that this core idea that's so resonant with many white Americans—there's an us and a them, and what's good for them is bad for us—was at the root of our country's dysfunc-tion. One might assume that this kind of competitiveness is human nature, but I don't buy it: for one thing, it's more prevalent among white people than other Americans. If it's not human nature, if it's an idea that we've chosen to adopt, that means it's one that we can choose to abandon. But if we are ever to uproot this zero-sum idea, we'll need first to understand when, and why, it was planted. So to begin my journey, I immersed myself in an unvarnished history of our country's birth.

———

THE STORY OF this country's rise from a starving colony to a world superpower is one that can't be told without the central character of race—specifically, the creation of a "racial" hierarchy to justify the theft of Indigenous land and the enslavement of African and Indigenous people. I use quotes around the word *racial* when referring to the earliest years of the European colonialization of the Americas, because back then, the illusory concept of race was just being formed. In the seventeenth century, influential Europeans were starting to create taxonomies of human beings based on skin color, religion, culture, and geography, aiming not just to differentiate but to rank humanity in terms of inherent worth. This hierarchy—backed by pseudo-scientists, explorers, and even clergy—gave Europeans moral permission to exploit and enslave. So, from the United States' colonial beginnings, progress for those considered white did come directly at the expense of people considered nonwhite. The U.S. economy depended on systems of exploitation—on literally taking land and labor from racialized others to enrich white colonizers and slaveholders. This made it easy for the powerful to sell the idea that the inverse was also true: that liberation or justice for people of color would necessarily require taking something away from white people.

European invaders of the New World believed that war was the only sure way to separate Indigenous people from the lands they coveted. Their version of settler colonialism set up a zero-sum competition for land that would shape the American economy to the present day, at an unforgivable cost. The death toll of South and North American Indigenous people in the century after first contact was so massive—an estimated 56 million lives, or 90 percent of all the lands' original inhabitants, through either war or disease—that it changed the amount of carbon in the atmosphere.

Such atrocities needed justification. The European invaders and their descendants used religious prejudices: the natives were incurable heathens and incompatible with the civilized peoples of Europe. Another stereotype that served the European profit motive was that Indigenous people wasted their land, so it would be better off if cultivated by productive settlers. Whatever form these rationales took, colonizers shaped their racist ideologies to fit the bill. The motive was greed; cultivated hatred followed. The result was a near genocide that laid waste to rich native cultures in order to fill European treasuries, particularly in Portugal, Spain, and England—and this later fed the individual wealth of white Americans who received the ill-gotten land for free.

Colonial slavery set up a zero-sum relationship between master and enslaved as well. The formula for profit is revenue minus costs, and American colonial slaveholders happened upon the world's most winning version of the formula to date. Land was cheap to free in the colonies, and although the initial cost of buying a captured African person was high, the lifetime of labor, of course, was free. Under slavery's formative capitalist logic, an enslaved man or woman was both a worker and an appreciating asset. Recounts economic historian Caitlin Rosenthal, "Thomas Jefferson described the appreciation of slaves as a 'silent profit' of between 5 and 10 percent annually, and he advised friends to invest accordingly."

With sexual violence, a white male owner could literally create even more free labor, indefinitely, even though that meant enslaving his own children. The ongoing costs of slave ownership were negligible: just food and shelter, and even these could be minimized. Take the record of Robert Carter of the Nomini Hall plantation in early 1700s Virginia: He fed his enslaved workers "less than they needed and required them to fill out their diet by keeping chickens and by working Sundays in small gardens attached to their cabins. Their cabins, too, he made them build and repair on Sundays." It stands to reason that the less the slaveholder expended making his bound laborers' lives sustainable, the more profit he had. The only limit to this zero-sum incentive to immiserate other human beings was total incapacity or death; at that point, theoretically, black pain was no longer profitable.

Then again, by the nineteenth century, owners could purchase life insurance on their slaves (from some of the most reputable insurance companies in the country) and be paid three-quarters of their market value upon their death. These insurance companies, including modern household names New York Life, Aetna, and U.S. Life, were just some of the many northern corporations whose fortunes were bound up with slavery. All the original thirteen colonies had slavery, and slavery legally persisted in the North all the way up to 1846, the year that New Jersey passed a formal emancipation law. Even after that, the North-South distinction meant little to the flow of profits and capital in and out of the slave economy. Wealth wrung from black hands launched the fortunes of northeastern port cities in Rhode Island; filled the Massachusetts textile mills with cotton; and capitalized the future Wall Street banks through loans that accepted enslaved people as collateral. In 1860, the four million human beings in the domestic slave trade had a market value of $3 billion. In fact, by the time war loomed, New York merchants had gotten so rich from the slave economy—40 percent of the city's exporting businesses through warehousing, shipping insurance, and sales were Southern cotton exports—that the mayor of New York advocated that his city secede along with the South.

In very stark and quantifiable terms, the exploitation, enslavement, and murder of African and Indigenous American people turned blood into wealth for the white power structure. Those who profited made no room for the oppressed to share in the rewards from their lands or labor; what others had, they took. The racial zero sum was crafted in the cradle of the New World.

**OF COURSE, CHATTEL** slavery is no longer our economic model. Today, the zero-sum paradigm lingers as more than a story justifying an economic order; it also animates many people's sense of who is an American, and whether more rights for other people will come at the expense of their own. It helped me understand our current moment when I learned that the zero sum was never solely material; it was also personal and social, shaping both colonists' notions of themselves and the young nation's ideas of citizenship and self-governance.

The zero sum was personal because the revolutionary ideal of being a free person (a radical, aspirational concept with no contemporary parallel) was abstract only until it was contrasted with what it meant to be absolutely unfree. According to historian Greg Grandin:

> At a time when most men and nearly all women lived in some form of unfreedom, tied to one thing or another, to an indenture, an apprentice contract, land rent, a mill, a work house or prison, a husband or father, saying what freedom was could be difficult. Saying what it wasn't, though, was easy: "a very Guinea slave."

The colonists in America created their concept of freedom largely by defining it against the bondage of the Africans among them. In the early colonial years, most European newcomers were people at the bottom of the social hierarchy back home, sent to these shores as servants from orphanages, debtors' prisons, or poorhouses. Even those born in America had little of what we currently conceive of as freedom: to choose their own work and education or to move at will. But as the threat of cross-racial servant uprisings became real in the late 1600s—particularly after the bloody Bacon's Rebellion, in which a black and white rebel army burned the capital of colonial Virginia to the ground—colonial governments began to separate the servant class based on skin color.

A look through the colonial laws of the 1680s and early 1700s reveals a deliberate effort to legislate a new hierarchy between poor whites and the "basically uncivil, unchristian, and above all, unwhite Native and African laborers." Many of the laws oppressing workers of color did so to the direct benefit of poor whites, creating a zero-sum relationship between these two parts of the colonial underclass. In 1705, a new Virginia law granted title and protection to the little property that any white servant may have accumulated—and simultaneously confiscated the personal property of all the enslaved people in the colony. The zero sum was made quite literal when, by the same law, the church in each parish sold the slaves' confiscated property and gave the "profits to the poor of the parish," by which they meant, of course, the white poor.

Just how unfree were the enslaved Africans in early America? The lack of freedom extended to every aspect of life: body, mind, and spirit; it invaded their family, faith, and home. The women could not refuse the sexual advances of their masters, and any children born from these rapes would be slaves the masters wouldn't have to purchase at market. Physical abuse was common, of course, and even murder was legal. A 1669 Virginia colony law deemed that killing one's slave could not amount to murder, because the law would assume no malice or intent to "destroy his own estate."

In a land marked by the yearning for religious freedom, enslaved people were forbidden from practicing their own religions. The Christianity they were allowed to practice was no spiritual safe haven; the Church condoned their subjugation and participated in their enslavement. (In colonial Virginia, the names of slaves suspected of aiding runaways were posted on church doors.) Black people in bondage were not allowed the freedom to marry legally and had no rights to keep their families intact. Tearing apart families by selling children from parents was so common that after Emancipation, classified ads of black people seeking relatives buoyed the newspaper industry. In sum, the life of a black American under slavery was the living antithesis of freedom, with black people subject to daily bodily and spiritual tyranny by man and by state. And alongside this exemplar of subjugation, the white American yearning for freedom was born.

Most Euro-Americans were not, and would likely never be, the wealthy aristocrat who had every social and economic privilege in Europe. Eternal slavery provided a new caste that even the poorest white-skinned person could hover above and define himself against. Just imagine the psychic benefit of being elevated from the bottom of a rigid class hierarchy to a higher place in a new "racial" hierarchy by dint of something as immutable as your skin color. You can imagine how, whether or not you owned slaves yourself, you might willingly buy into a zero-sum model to gain the sense of freedom that rises with the subordination of others.

Racial hierarchy offered white people a reprieve from the class hierarchy and gave white women an escape valve from gender oppression. White women in slaveholding communities considered their slaves "their freedom," liberating them from farming, housework, child rearing, nursing, and even the sexual demands of their husbands. Historian Stephanie E. Jones-Rogers's *They Were Her Property: White Women Slaveholders in the American South* reveals the economic stake that white women had in chattel slavery. In a society where the law traditionally considered married women unable to own property separate from their husbands', these women were often able to keep financial assets in human beings independent of their husbands' estates (and debts). In addition to relative financial freedom, slavery gave these women carte blanche to use and abuse other humans. *They Were Her Property* recounts stories of white women reveling in cruelties of the most intimate and perverse sort, belying the myth of the innocent belle and betraying any assumption that womanhood or motherhood would temper depravity, even toward children. An image that will never leave my mind is Professor Jones-Rogers's description of a white mother rocking her chair across the head of a little enslaved girl for about an hour, while her daughter whipped the child, until the black girl's face was so mangled that she would never again in life eat solid food.

**FROM THE ECONOMY** to the most personal of relationships to the revolution itself, early America relied on a zero-sum model of freedom built on slavery. The colonies would not have been able to afford their War of Independence were it not for the aid provided by the French, who did so in exchange for tobacco grown by enslaved people. Edmund S. Morgan, author of *American Slavery, American Freedom: The Ordeal of Colonial Virginia*, wrote "To a large degree it may be said that Americans bought their independence with slave labor." Its freedom purchased, the newborn nation found itself on the verge of creating something entirely novel in the world and not at all guaranteed to succeed: a new nation of many nations, made chiefly of people from European communities that had long been at war. To forge a common basis for citizenship in this conglomerate country, a new, superseding identity would need to emerge. This citizenship would guarantee freedom from exercises of state power against one's home or religion, free movement and assembly, speech, and most significantly, property. Citizenship, in other words, meant freedom.

And freedom meant whiteness. In the founding era, northerners' ambiguity about slavery in their own states didn't stop them from profiting from the slave economy—or from protecting its survival in the Constitution. Ten out of the eleven passages in the U.S. Constitution that referred to slavery were pro-slavery. The founders designed the new U.S. Congress so that slave states gained bonus political power commensurate with three-fifths of their enslaved population, without, of course, acknowledging the voice or even the humanity of those people. It was to this slavocratic body that the Constitution delegated the question of who could be an American citizen and under what terms. The First Congress's answer, in the 1790 Naturalization Act, was to confine citizenship to "free white persons," encoding its cultural understanding of whiteness as free—in opposition to blackness, which would be forever unfree. Though people of African descent were nearly one-fifth of the population at the first Census, most founders did not intend for them to be American. For the common white American, the presence of blackness—imagined as naturally enslaved, with no agency or reason, denied each and every one of the enumerated freedoms—gave daily shape to the confines of a new identity just cohering at the end of the eighteenth century: white, free, citizen. It was as if they couldn't imagine a world where nobody escaped the tyranny they had known in the Old World; if it could be blacks, it wouldn't have to be whites.

WITH EACH GENERATION, the specter of the founding zero sum has found its way back into the American story. It's hard for me to stand here as a descendant of enslaved people and say that the zero sum wasn't true, that the immiseration of people of color did not benefit white people. But I have to remind myself that it was true only in the sense that it is what happened—it didn't have to happen that way. It would have been better for the sum of us if we'd had a different model. Yes, the zero-sum story of racial hierarchy was born along with the country, but it is an invention of the worst elements of our society: people who gained power through ruthless exploitation and kept it by sowing constant division. It has always optimally benefited only the few while limiting the potential of the rest of us, and therefore the whole.

In decade after decade, threats of job competition—between men and women, immigrants and native born, black and white—have perennially revived the fear of loss at another's gain. The people setting up the competition and spreading these fears were never the needy job seekers, but the elite. (Consider the *New York Herald*'s publishing tycoon, James Gordon Bennett Sr., who warned the city's white working classes during the 1860 election that "if Lincoln is elected, you will have to compete with the labor of four million emancipated negroes.") The zero sum is a story sold by wealthy interests for their own profit, and its persistence requires people desperate enough to buy it.

THAT SAID, WHENEVER the interests of white people have been pitted against those of people of color, structural racism has called the winner. So, how is it that white people in 2011, when Norton and Sommers conducted their research, believed that whites were the victims? I tried to give their perspective the benefit of the doubt. Perhaps it was affirmative action. The idea of affirmative action looms large in the white imagination and has been a passion among conservative activists. Some white people even believe that black people get to go to college for free—when the reality is, black students on average wind up paying more for college through interest-bearing student loans over their lifetimes because they don't have the passed-down wealth that even poorer white students often have. And in selective college admissions, any given white person is far more likely to be competing with another white person than with one of the under-represented people of color in the applicant pool.

Is it welfare? The characters of the white taxpayer and the free-loading person of color are recurring tropes for people like Norton and Sommers's survey respondents. But the majority of people receiving government assistance, like the majority of people in poverty, are white; and people of color pay taxes, too. The zero-sum idea that white people are now suffering due to gains among people of color has taken on the features of myth: it lies, but it says so much.

The narrative that white people should see the well-being of people of color as a threat to their own is one of the most powerful subterranean stories in America. Until we destroy the idea, opponents of progress can always unearth it and use it to block any collective action that benefits us all. Today, the racial zero-sum story is resurgent because there is a political movement invested in ginning up white resentment toward lateral scapegoats (similarly or worse-situated people of color) to escape accountability for a massive redistribution of wealth from the many to the few. For four years, a tax-cutting and self-dealing millionaire trumpeted the zero-sum story from the White House, but the Trump presidency was in many ways brought to us by two decades of zero-sum propaganda on the ubiquitous cable news network owned by billionaire Rupert Murdoch. This divide-and-conquer strategy has been essential to the creation and maintenance of the Inequality Era's other most defining feature: the hollowing out of the goods we share.

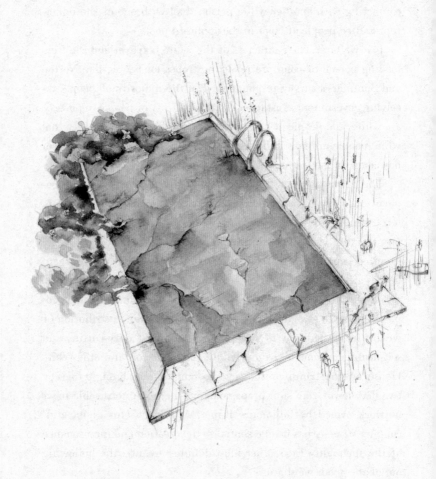

## Chapter 2

# RACISM
# DRAINED
# THE POOL

The United States of America has had the world's largest economy for most of our history, with enough money to feed and educate all our children, build world-leading infrastructure, and generally ensure a high standard of living for everyone. But we don't. When it comes to per capita government spending, the United States is near the bottom of the list of industrialized countries, below Latvia and Estonia. Our roads, bridges, and water systems get a D+ from the American Society of Civil Engineers. With the exception of about forty years from the New Deal to the 1970s, the United States has had a weaker commitment to public goods, and to the public good, than every country that possesses anywhere near our wealth.

Observers have tried to fit multiple theories onto why Americans are so singularly stingy toward ourselves: Is it a libertarian ideology? The ethos of the western frontier? Our founding rebellion against government? When I first started working at Demos in my early twenties, the organization had a project called Public Works that tried to understand antigovernment sentiment and find ways of communicating that would overcome it. Community-based advocates who were fighting for things like food stamps, public transit, and education funding sought the project's help as they faced resistance both in their legislatures and when knocking on doors. Public Works' research revealed that people have fuzzy ideas about government, not understanding, for example, that highways, libraries, and public schools are, in fact, government. The project encouraged advocates to talk about government as "public structures" that build economic opportunity, with a goal of activating a mindset of "citizens" as opposed to "consumers" of public services.

As I sat in Demos's staff meeting listening to the two people leading the project present their research, I took notes and nodded. I was just an entry-level staff person not involved in the project, but when the presentation wrapped, I raised my hand. The two presenters were white, liberal advocates from Texas who had spent their lives pushing for economic fairness and opportunity for children. I had no research experience in communications, but having grown up in the 1980s and '90s, I had the impression that every time anybody in politics complained about government programs, they invoked, explicitly or otherwise, lazy black people who were too reliant on government. So, I had to ask, "Did race ever come up in your research?" It turned out they hadn't even asked the question.

The organization eventually stopped working on the Public Works project. Years later, when I set out on my journey to find the roots of our country's dysfunction, I had a chance to come at the question again—but this time, informed by conversations with community organizers, social scientists, politicians, and historians who did ask the question, I was able to discover a more convincing rationale for why so many Americans had such a dim view of government.

IN 1857, A white southerner named Hinton Rowan Helper published a book called *The Impending Crisis of the South: How to Meet It.* Helper had taken it upon himself to count how many schools, libraries, and other public-serving institutions had been set up in free states compared to slave states. In New Hampshire, for instance, he counted 2,381 public schools; in Mississippi, just 782. Maine had 236 libraries; Georgia, 38. The disparity was similar everywhere he looked.

Helper was an avowed racist, and yet he railed against slavery because he saw what it was doing to his fellow white southerners. The slave economy was a system that created high concentrations of wealth, land, and political power. "Notwithstanding the fact that the white non-slaveholders of the South are in the majority, as five to one, they have never yet had any part or lot in framing the laws under which they live," Helper wrote. And without a voice in the policy making, common white southerners were unable to win much for themselves. In a way, the plantation class made an understandable calculation: a governing class will tax themselves to invest in amenities that serve the public (schools, libraries, roads and utilities, support for local businesses) because they need to. The wealthy need these assets in a community to make it livable for them, but also, more important, to attract and retain the people on whom their profits depend, be they workers or customers.

For the owners in the slave economy, however, neither was strictly necessary. The primary source of plantation wealth was a completely captive and unpaid labor force. Owners didn't need more than a handful of white workers per plantation. They didn't need an educated populace, whether black or white; such a thing was in fact counter to their financial interest. And their farms didn't depend on many local customers, whether individuals or businesses: the market for cotton was a global exchange, and the factories that bought their raw goods were in the North, staffed by wage laborers. Life on a plantation was self-contained; the welfare of the surrounding community mattered little outside the closed system.

With his book, Hinton Rowan Helper aimed to destroy that system. He even took on the most common objection to abolition at the time: the question of how to compensate slave owners for their losses (which President Lincoln managed for District of Columbia slave owners loyal to the Union during the Civil War, at three hundred dollars per enslaved person). But Helper argued that owners should actually have to compensate the rest of the white citizens of the South, because slavery had impoverished the region. The value of northern land was more than five times the value of southern land per acre, he calculated, despite the South's advantage in climate, minerals, and soil. Because the southern "oligarchs of the lash," as he called them, had done so little to support education, innovation, and small enterprise, slavery was making southern whites poorer.

Today, according to the U.S. Census Bureau, nine of the ten poorest states in the nation are in the South. So are seven of the ten states with the least educational attainment. In 2007, economist Nathan Nunn, a soft-spoken Harvard professor then in his mid-thirties, made waves with a piece of research showing the reach of slavery into the modern southern economy. Nunn found that the well-known story of deprivation in the American South was not uniform and, in fact, followed a historical logic: counties that relied more on slave labor in 1860 had lower per capita incomes in 2000.

He was building on global comparative research by Stanley Engerman and Kenneth Sokoloff, which found that "societies that began with relatively extreme inequality tended to generate institutions that were more restrictive in providing access to economic opportunities." Nunn's research showed that although of course slave counties had higher inequality during the era of slavery (particularly of land), it wasn't the degree of inequality that was correlated with poverty today; it was the fact of slavery itself, whether on large plantations or small farms. When I talked to Nathan Nunn, he couldn't say exactly how the hand of slavery was strangling opportunity generations later. He made it clear, however, that it wasn't just the black inhabitants who were faring worse today; it was the white families in the counties, too. When slavery was abolished, Confederate states found themselves far behind northern states in the creation of the public infrastructure that supports economic mobility, and they continue to lag behind today. These deficits limit economic mobility for all residents, not just the descendants of enslaved people.

A FUNCTIONING SOCIETY rests on a web of mutuality, a willingness among all involved to share enough with one another to accomplish what no one person can do alone. In a sense, that's what government is. I can't create my own electric grid, school system, internet, or healthcare system—and the most efficient way to ensure that those things are created and available to all on a fair and open basis is to fund and provide them publicly. If you want the quality and availability of those things to vary based on how much money an individual has, you may argue for privatization—but even privatization advocates still want the government, not corporations, to shoulder the investment cost for massive infrastructure needs. For most of the twentieth century, leaders of both parties agreed on the wisdom of those investments, from Democratic president Franklin D. Roosevelt's Depression-era jobs programs to Republican president Eisenhower's Interstate Highway System to Republican Richard Nixon's Supplemental Security Income for the elderly and people with disabilities.

Yet almost every clause of the American social contract had an asterisk. For most of our history, the beneficiaries of America's free public investments were whites only. The list of free stuff? It's long. The Homestead Act of 1862 offered 160 acres of expropriated Indigenous land west of the Mississippi to any citizen or person eligible for citizenship (which, after the 1790 Naturalization Act, was only white immigrants) if they could reach the land and build on it. A free grant of property! Fewer than six thousand black families were able to become part of the 1.6 million landowners who gained deeds through the Homestead Act and its 1866 southern counterpart. Today, an estimated 46 million people are propertied descendants of Homestead Act beneficiaries.

During the Great Depression, the American government told banks it would insure mortgages on real estate if they made them longer-term and more affordable (offering tax deductions on interest along the way)—but the government drew red "Do Not Lend" lines around almost all the black neighborhoods in the country with a never-substantiated assumption that they would be bad credit risks.

The New Deal transformed the lives of workers with minimum wage and overtime laws—but compromises with southern Democrats excluded the job categories most black people held, in domestic and agricultural work. Then the GI Bill of 1944 paid the college tuition of hundreds of thousands of veterans, catapulting a generation of men into professional careers—but few black veterans benefited, as local administrators funneled most black servicemen to segregated vocational schools. The mortgage benefit in the GI Bill pushed the postwar white homeownership rate to three out of four white families—but with federally sanctioned housing discrimination, the black and Latinx rates stayed at around two out of five, despite the attempts of veterans of color to participate.

The federal government created suburbs by investing in the federal highway system and subsidizing private housing developers—but demanded racial covenants ("whites only" clauses in housing contracts) to prevent black people from buying into them. Social Security gave income to millions of elderly Americans—but again, exclusions of job categories left most black workers out, and southern congressmembers opposed more generous cash aid for the elderly poor. You could even consider the New Deal labor laws that encouraged collective bargaining to be a no-cost government subsidy to create a white middle class, as many unions kept their doors closed to nonwhites until the 1960s.

Between the era of the New Deal and the civil rights movement, these and more government policies worked to ensure a large, secure, and white middle class. But once desegregation lowered barriers, people with power (politicians and executives, but also individual white homeowners, business owners, shop stewards, and community leaders) faced the possibility of sharing those benefits. The advantages white people had accumulated were free and usually invisible, and so conferred an elevated status that seemed natural and almost innate. White society had repeatedly denied people of color economic benefits on the premise that they were inferior; those unequal benefits then reified the hierarchy, making whites actually economically superior. What would it mean to white people, both materially and psychologically, if the supposedly inferior people received the same treatment from the government? The period since integration has tested many whites' commitment to the public, in ways big and small.

**THE AMERICAN LANDSCAPE** was once graced with resplendent public swimming pools, some big enough to hold thousands of swimmers at a time. In the 1920s, towns and cities tried to outdo one another by building the most elaborate pools; in the 1930s, the Works Progress Administration put people to work building hundreds more. By World War II, the country's two thousand pools were glittering symbols of a new commitment by local officials to the quality of life of their residents, allowing hundreds of thousands of people to socialize together for free. A particular social agenda undergirded these public investments. Officials envisioned the distinctly American phenomenon of the grand public resort pools as "social melting pots." Like free public grade schools, public pools were part of an "Americanizing" project intended to overcome ethnic divisions and cohere a common identity—and it worked. A Pennsylvania county recreation director said, "Let's build bigger, better and finer pools. That's real democracy. Take away the sham and hypocrisy of clothes, don a swimsuit, and we're all the same." Of course, that vision of classlessness wasn't expansive enough to include skin color that wasn't, in fact, "all the same." By the 1950s, the fight to integrate America's prized public swimming pools would demonstrate the limits of white commitment to public goods.

**IN 1953, A** thirteen-year-old black boy named Tommy Cummings drowned in Baltimore's Patapsco River while swimming with three friends, two white and one black. The friends had been forced to swim in the dangerous waterway because none of the city's seven public pools allowed interracial swimming. Tommy was one of three black children to die that summer in open water, and the NAACP sued the city. It won on appeal three years later, and on June 23, 1956, for the first time, all Baltimore children had the chance to swim with other children, regardless of skin color. Public recreation free from discrimination could, in the minds of the city's progressive community, foster more friendships like the one Tommy was trying to enjoy when he drowned. What ended up happening, however, was not the promised mingling of children of different races. In Baltimore, instead of sharing the pool, white children stopped going to the pools that black children could easily access, and white adults informally policed (through intimidation and violence) the public pools in white neighborhoods.

In America's smaller towns, where there was only one public pool, desegregation called into question what "public" really meant. Black community members pressed for access to the public resource that their tax dollars had helped to build. If assets were public, they argued, they must be furnished on an equal basis. Instead, white public officials took the public assets private, creating new private corporations to run the pools. The town of Warren, Ohio, dealt with its integration problem by creating the members-only Veterans' Swim Club, which selected members based on a secret vote. (The club promptly selected only white residents of the town.) The small coal town of Montgomery, West Virginia, built a new resort pool in 1942 but let it lay untouched for four years while black residents argued that the state's civil rights law required equal access. Unable to countenance the idea of sharing the pool with black people, city leaders eventually formed a private "Park Association" whose sole job was to administer the pool, and the city leased the public asset to the private association for one dollar. Only white residents were allowed admission. Warren and Montgomery were just two of countless towns—in every region in America, not just the South—where the fight over public pools revealed that for white Americans, the word *public* did not mean "of the people." It meant "of the white people." They re-placed the assets of a community with the privileges of a club.

Eventually, the exclusion boomeranged on white citizens. In Montgomery, Alabama, the Oak Park pool was the grandest one for miles, the crown jewel of a Parks Department that also included a zoo, a community center, and a dozen other public parks. Of course, the pool was for whites only; the entire public parks system was seg-regated. Dorothy Moore was a white teenage lifeguard when a fed-eral court deemed the town's segregated recreation unconstitutional. Suddenly, black children would be able to wade into the deep end with white children at the Oak Park pool; at the rec center, black el-ders would get chairs at the card tables. The reaction of the city council was swift—effective January 1, 1959, the Parks Department would be no more.

The council decided to drain the pool rather than share it with their black neighbors. Of course, the decision meant that white fam-ilies lost a public resource as well. "It was miserable," Mrs. Moore told a reporter five decades later. Uncomprehending white children cried as the city contractors poured dirt into the pool, paved it over, and seeded it with grass that was green by the time summer came along again. To defy desegregation, Montgomery would go on to close every single public park and padlock the doors of the commu-nity center. It even sold off the animals in the zoo. The entire public park system would stay closed for over a decade. Even after it re-opened, they never rebuilt the pool.

I went to see Oak Park for myself in 2019 and walked the grounds looking for signs of what used to be. I was able to spot the now-barren rock formation where the zoo's monkeys used to climb. I asked the friendly women in the parks office where the pool had been, but nobody was quite sure. Oak Park used to be the central gathering place in town for white Montgomery; on that hot afternoon, I was one of only four or five people there. Groundskeepers outnumbered visitors. I noticed an elderly white couple sitting in a car in the park-ing lot. They saw me approaching and stared without welcome. I stood for a beat, smiling at the car window, before the man reluctantly rolled it down.

"Hi, sir, ma'am," I ventured, getting nods in return. They appeared to be in their eighties. "Are you from around here?" More nods. "I am doing a project and was wondering if you remember when there used to be a big pool here?" The couple looked at each other, still wary.

"Yes, of course," the man replied curtly.

"Do you remember where it was?" They hesitated, and then the woman pointed straight ahead to where they'd been looking moments before. I took a sharp breath of excitement. Had I interrupted them reminiscing about the pool? Maybe they'd met there as teenagers? I leaned forward to ask more, but the man recoiled and rolled up his window.

I backed off. Where the woman had pointed was a wide, level expanse rimmed with remembering old oak trees. The only sounds were the trilling of birds and the far-off thrum of a lawn mower.

The loss of the Oak Park pool was replicated across the country. Instead of complying with a desegregation order, New Orleans closed what was known as the largest pool in the South, Audubon Pool, in 1962, for seven years. In Winona, Mississippi, if you know where to look, you can still see the metal railings of the old pool's diving board amid overgrown weeds; in nearby Stonewall, a real estate developer unearthed the carcass of the segregated pool in the mid-2000s. Even in towns that didn't immediately drain their public pools, integration ended the public pool's glory years, as white residents abandoned the pools en masse.

Built in 1919, the Fairground Park pool in St. Louis, Missouri, was the largest in the country and probably the world, with a sandy beach, an elaborate diving board, and a reported capacity of ten thousand swimmers. When a new city administration changed the parks policy in 1949 to allow black swimmers, the first integrated swim ended in bloodshed. On June 21, two hundred white residents surrounded the pool with "bats, clubs, bricks and knives" to menace the first thirty or so black swimmers. Over the course of the day, a white mob that grew to five thousand attacked every black person in sight around the Fairground Park. After the Fairground Park Riot, as it was known, the city returned to a segregation policy using public safety as a justification, but a successful NAACP lawsuit reopened the pool to all St. Louisans the following summer. On the first day of integrated swimming, July 19, 1950, only seven white swimmers attended, joining three brave black swimmers under the shouts of two hundred white protesters. That first integrated summer, Fairground logged just 10,000 swims—down from 313,000 the previous summer. The city closed the pool for good six years later. Racial hatred led to St. Louis draining one of the most prized public pools in the world.

Draining public swimming pools to avoid integration received the official blessing of the U.S. Supreme Court in 1971. The city council in Jackson, Mississippi, had responded to desegregation demands by closing four public pools and leasing the fifth to the YMCA, which operated it for whites only. Black citizens sued, but the Supreme Court, in *Palmer v. Thompson*, held that a city could choose not to provide a public facility rather than maintain an integrated one, because by robbing the entire public, the white leaders were spreading equal harm. "There was no evidence of state action affecting Negroes differently from white," wrote Justice Hugo Black. The Court went on to turn a blind eye to the obvious racial animus behind the decision, taking the race neutrality at face value. "Petitioners' contention that equal protection requirements were violated because the pool-closing decision was motivated by anti-integration considerations must also fail, since courts will not invalidate legislation based solely on asserted illicit motivation by the enacting legislative body." The decision showed the limits of the civil rights legal tool kit and forecast the politics of public services for decades to come: If the benefits can't be whites-only, you can't have them at all. And if you say it's racist? Well, prove it.

As Jeff Wiltse writes in his history of pool desegregation, *Contested Waters: A Social History of Swimming Pools in America*, "Beginning in the mid-1950s northern cities generally stopped building large resort pools and let the ones already constructed fall into disrepair." Over the next decade, millions of white Americans who once swam in public for free began to pay rather than swim for free with black people; desegregation in the mid-fifties coincided with a surge in backyard pools and members-only swim clubs. In Washington, D.C., for example, 125 new private swim clubs were opened in less than a decade following pool desegregation in 1953. The classless utopia faded, replaced by clubs with two-hundred-dollar membership fees and annual dues. A once-public resource became a luxury amenity, and entire communities lost out on the benefits of public life and civic engagement once understood to be the key to making American democracy real.

Today, we don't even notice the absence of the grand resort pools in our communities; where grass grows over former sites, there are no plaques to tell the story of how racism drained the pools. But the spirit that drained these public goods lives on. The impulse to exclude now manifests in a subtler fashion, more often reflected in a pool of resources than a literal one.

AS SOMEONE WHO'S spent a career in politics, where the specter of the typical white moderate has perennially trimmed the sails of policy ambition, I was surprised to learn that in the 1950s, the majority of white Americans believed in an activist government role in people's economic lives—a more activist role, even, than contemplated by today's average liberal. According to the authoritative American National Elections Studies (ANES) survey, 65 percent of white people in 1956 believed that the government ought to guarantee a job to anyone who wanted one and to provide a minimum standard of living in the country. White support cratered for these ideas between 1960 and 1964, however—from nearly 70 percent to 35 percent—and has stayed low ever since. (The overwhelming majority of black Americans have remained enthusiastic about this idea over fifty years of survey data.) What happened?

In August 1963, white Americans tuned in to the March on Washington (which was for "Jobs and Freedom."). They saw the nation's capital overtaken by a group of mostly black activists demanding not just an end to discrimination, but some of the same economic ideas that had been overwhelmingly popular with whites: a jobs guarantee for all workers and a higher minimum wage. When I saw that white support for these ideas crumbled in 1964, I guessed it might have been because black people were pushing to expand the circle of beneficiaries across the color line. But then again, perhaps it was just a coincidence, the beginning of a new antigovernment ideology among white people that had nothing to do with race?

After all, white support for these government commitments to economic security has stayed low for the rest of the years of ANES data, through a sea change in racial attitudes. As the civil rights movement successfully shifted cultural norms and beliefs, it became rarer and rarer to hear the argument that people of color were biologically inferior. That kind of "old-fashioned," biological racism waned relatively quickly over the decades (by 1972, 31 percent of white people subscribed to it; by 1986, just 14). Racism couldn't still be lowering support for government antipoverty efforts today.

It turns out that the dominant story most white Americans believe about race adapted to the civil rights movement's success, and a new form of racial disdain took over: racism based not on biology but on perceived culture and behavior. As professors Donald R. Kinder and Lynn M. Sanders put it in their 1996 deep dive into public opinion by race, *Divided by Color: Racial Politics and Democratic Ideals*, "today, we say, prejudice is preoccupied less with inborn ability and more with effort and initiative." Kinder and Sanders defined this more modern manifestation of anti-black hostility among whites as "racial resentment." They measured racial resentment using a combination of agree/disagree statements on the ANES that spoke to the black work ethic, how much discrimination black people had faced as compared to European immigrants, and whether the government was more generous to blacks than to whites. They found that "although whites' support for the principles of racial equality and integration have increased majestically over the last four decades, their backing for policies designed to bring equality and integration about has scarcely increased at all. Indeed in some cases white support has actually declined."

I wasn't surprised to read that Kinder and Sanders found that people with high racial resentment opposed racial public policies such as nondiscriminatory employment and college quotas. The researchers couldn't explain this correlation away using demographic characteristics or other beliefs, like abstract individualism or opposition to government intervention in private affairs; nor could they pin it to a genuine material threat. But my data analyst colleague Sean McElwee and I found that white people with high levels of resentment against black people have become far more likely to oppose government spending generically: as of the latest ANES data in 2016, there was a sixty-point difference in support for increased government spending based on whether you were a white person with high versus low racial resentment. Government, it turned out, had become a highly racialized character in the white story of our country.

When the people with power in a society see a portion of the populace as inferior and undeserving, their definition of "the public" becomes conditional. It's often unconscious, but their perception of the Other as undeserving is so important to their perception of themselves as deserving that they'll tear apart the web that supports everyone, including them. Public goods, in other words, are only for the public we perceive to be good.

I could understand how, raised in an explicitly white-supremacist society, a white New Dealer could turn against the Great Society after the civil rights movement turned government from enforcer of the racial hierarchy to upender of it. But how to explain the racial resentment and the correlated antigovernment sentiments by the 1980s? By then, white folks had seemed to acclimate themselves to a new reality of social equality under the law. The overt messages of racial inferiority had dissipated, and popular culture had advanced new norms of multiculturalism and tolerance. What stopped advancing, however, was the economic trajectory of most American families—and it was on this terrain that racial resentment dug in.

While racial barriers were coming down across society, new class hurdles were going up. It began immediately after the federal civil rights victories of the mid-1960s, when President Johnson accurately predicted that, by signing these bills into law, he had given away the South. Over the next decade, the New Deal–era social contract that existed between white power-brokers in government, business, and labor came to a painful end. It had never been a peaceful one, but over the 1940s, '50s, and '60s, its signatories had generally seen a mutual benefit in ensuring better and better standards of living for white men and their families as they moved up from the tenement and the factory to the suburb and the office. Economic growth and wage growth were high, as were taxes (which hit their peak as a percentage of the economy in 1965). The biggest industries were highly regulated, and antitrust protections worked to prevent monopolies. During these years, the leaders in government, big business, and organized labor were often white men only years or a generation away from the same circumstances as the guy on the shop floor; perhaps this accounted for the level of empathy reflected in decisions to, for example, pay low-skilled workers middle-class wages and benefits, or spend hundreds of billions to make homeownership possible to millions with no down payment. Perhaps managers still saw themselves in workers, people they considered their fellow Americans. I often picture it literally—three white men seated in a room, signing a contract: Walter Reuther of the United Automobile Workers; Charles Wilson, the General Motors chief executive; and President Dwight Eisenhower. Their handshakes seal the deal for a broad, white middle class. Then, in the mid-sixties, there's a commotion at the door. Women and people of color are demanding a seat at the table, ready to join the contract for shared prosperity. But no longer able to see themselves reflected in the other signatories, the leaders of government and big business walk out, leaving workers on their own—and the Inequality Era was born.

That era began in the 1970s, but the policies cohered into an agenda guided by antigovernment conservatism under the presidency of Ronald Reagan. Reagan, a Californian, was determined to take the Southern Strategy (launched by President Nixon) national. In southern politics, federally mandated school integration had revived for a new generation the Civil War idea of government as a boogeyman, threatening to upend the natural racial order at the cost of white status and property. The Reagan campaign's insight was that northern white people could be sold the same explicitly antigovernment, implicitly pro-white story, with the protagonists as white taxpayers seeking defense from a government that wanted to give their money to undeserving and lazy people of color in the ghettos. (The fact that government policy created the ghettos and stripped the wealth and job opportunities from their residents was not part of the story. Nor was the fact that people of color pay taxes, too, often a larger share of their incomes due to regressive sales, property, and payroll taxes.)

My law professor Ian Haney López helped me connect the dots in his 2014 book *Dog Whistle Politics: How Coded Racial Appeals Have Reinvented Racism and Wrecked the Middle Class*. Reagan's political advisers saw him as the perfect carrier to continue the fifty-state Southern Strategy that could focus on taxes and spending while still hitting the emotional notes of white resentment. "Plutocrats use dog-whistle politics to appeal to whites with a basic formula," Haney López told me. "First, fear people of color. Then, hate the government (which coddles people of color). Finally, trust the market and the 1 percent." This type of modern political racism could operate in polite society because of the way that racial resentment had evolved, from biological racism to cultural disapproval: it's not about who they are; it's about what some (okay, most) of them do. He went on, "Dog-whistle politics is gaslighting on a massive scale: stoking racism through insidious stereotyping while denying that racism has anything to do with it."

For a few moments in a tape-recorded interview in 1981, however, the right-wing strategist for Presidents George H. W. Bush and Ronald Reagan, Lee Atwater, admitted to the plan:

> You start out in 1954 by saying, "Nigger, nigger, nigger." By 1968 you can't say "nigger"—that hurts you, backfires. So you say stuff like, uh, forced busing, states' rights, and all that stuff, and you're getting so abstract. Now, you're talking about cutting taxes, and all these things you're talking about are totally economic things and a byproduct of them is, blacks get hurt worse than whites. . . . "We want to cut this," is much more abstract than even the busing thing, uh, and a hell of a lot more abstract than "Nigger, nigger."

In the 1980s, Republicans deployed this strategy by harping on the issue of welfare and tying it to the racialized image of "the inner city" and "the undeserving poor." (An emblematic line from President Reagan, "We're in danger of creating a permanent culture of poverty as inescapable as any chain or bond," deftly suggests that black people are no longer enslaved by white action, but by their own culture.) Even though welfare was a sliver of the federal budget and served at least as many white people as black, the rhetorical weight of the welfare stereotype—the idea of a black person getting for free what white people had to work for—helped sink white support for all government. The idea tapped into an old stereotype of black laziness that was first trafficked in the antebellum era to excuse and minimize slavery and was then carried forward in minstrel shows, cartoons, and comedy to the present day. The welfare trope also did the powerful blame-shifting work of projection: like telling white aristocrats that it was their slaves who were the lazy ones, the black welfare stereotype was a total inversion of the way the U.S. government had actually given "free stuff" to one race over all others. To this day, even though black and brown people are disproportionately poor, white Americans constitute the majority of low-income people who escape poverty because of government safety net programs. Nonetheless, the idea that black people are the "takers" in society while white people are the hardworking taxpayers—the "makers"—has become a core part of the zero-sum story preached by wealthy political elites. Whether it's the more subtle "47 percent" version from millionaire Mitt Romney or the more racially explicit Fox News version sponsored by billionaire Rupert Murdoch, it works. In 2016, the majority of white moderates (53 percent) and white conservatives (69 percent) said that black Americans take more than we give to society. *We take more than we give.*

Seeing this high a number among white moderates jogs a memory: I'm in the seventh grade, for the first time attending an almost all-white school. It's a government and politics lesson, and the girl next to me announces that she and her family are "fiscally conservative but socially liberal." The phrase is new to me, but all around me, white kids' heads bob in knowing approval, as if she's given the right answer to a quiz. There's something so morally sanitized about the idea of fiscal restraint, even when the upshot is that tens of millions of people, including one out of six children, struggle needlessly with poverty and hunger. The fact of their suffering is a shame, but not a reason to vote differently to allow government to do something about it. (We could eliminate all poverty in the United States by spending just 12 percent more than the cost of the 2017 Republican tax cuts.) The media's inaccurate portrayal of poverty as a black problem plays a role in this, because the black faces that predominate coverage trigger a distancing in the minds of many white people.

As Professor Haney López points out, priming white voters with racist dog whistles was the means; the end was an economic agenda that was harmful to working- and middle-class voters of all races, including white people. In railing against welfare and the war on poverty, conservatives like President Reagan told white voters that government was the enemy, because it favored black and brown people over them—but their real agenda was to blunt government's ability to challenge concentrated wealth and corporate power. The hurdle conservatives faced was that they needed the white majority to turn against society's two strongest vessels for collective action: the government and labor unions. Racism was the ever-ready tool for the job, undermining white Americans' faith in their fellow Americans. And it worked: Reagan cut taxes on the wealthy but raised them on the poor, waged war on the unions that were the backbone of the white middle class, and slashed domestic spending. And he did it with the overwhelming support of the white working and middle classes.

The majority of white voters have voted against the Democratic nominee for president ever since the party became the party of civil rights under Lyndon Johnson. The Republican Party has won those votes through sheer cultural marketing to a white customer base that's still awaiting delivery of the economic goods they say they want. Despite the dramatic change in white Americans' support for government antipoverty efforts, the typical white voter's economic preferences are still more progressive than those of the Republican politicians for whom they vote. I looked at the two economic issues that have been top priority for Republicans in Washington since 2008, healthcare and taxes. Republican politicians have thoroughly communicated their positions on these issues to their base through campaign ads, speeches, and the conservative media echo chamber, so one would think that their voters would get the message. That message is: cut taxes whenever possible and oppose government involvement in healthcare. But 46 percent of Republicans polled in the summer of 2020 actually supported a total government takeover of health insurance, Medicare for All—even after a Democratic primary where the idea was championed by a Democratic Socialist, Vermont senator Bernie Sanders. Zero Republican politicians support this policy, and almost all voted in 2017 to repeal the relatively modest government role in healthcare under the Affordable Care Act. On taxes, nearly half of Republican voters support raising taxes on millionaires by 4 percent to pay for schools and roads, but the Republican Congress of 2017 reduced taxes by more than a trillion dollars, mainly on corporations and the wealthy. In the Inequality Era brought to us by racist dog-whistle politics, white voters are less hostile to government policies that promote economic equality than the party they most often vote into power. But vote for them they do. Racial allegiance trumps.

Most white voters will deny that racism has anything to do with their feelings about government. And many political pollsters will believe them. For instance, in fall 2009 focus groups, conservative anti-Obama Republicans mentioned race only in order to complain that they couldn't express their opposition to Obama without being labeled racists. The influential Democratic pollsters Stan Greenberg and James Carville, who were conducting the focus groups, took them at their word, writing in their summary of the findings, "The press and elites [who] continue to look for a racial element that drives these voters' beliefs . . . need to get over it." But they were missing how political race-craft works. There is such a strong cultural prohibition on being racist (particularly during the color-blind triumphalism in the wake of Obama's election) that it's important to look at what voters feel and perceive, not just what they say. Race isn't a static state; it's better understood as an action, and one of its chief functions is to distance white people from people who are "raced" differently. When race is introduced in this fashion to white voters, it activates seemingly race-neutral reactions such as demonization, distrust, zero-sum thinking, resistance to change, and resource hoarding. Note how Greenberg and Carville followed the section in their memo advising commentators to "get over" the role of race in opposition to President Obama:

> They are actively rooting for Obama to fail as president because they believe he is not acting in good faith as the leader of our country. Only 6 percent of these conservative Republican base voters say that Obama is on their side, and our groups showed that they explicitly believe he is purposely and ruthlessly executing a hidden agenda to weaken and ultimately destroy the foundations of our country.

Experts on the way racialized thinking operates would read the same comments and see the fingerprints of racism all over them. In studying the same anti-Obama sentiment during the same period, psychologist Eric Knowles and his colleagues devised experiments to minimize the silencing impact of social desirability (that is, giving answers you know society wants you to give); to analyze based on implicit, not explicit, bias; and to control for other rationales such as ideology and partisanship. With all that stripped away, racial prejudice remained. They explained, "People may fail to report the influence of race on their judgments, not because such an influence is absent, but because they are unaware of it—and might not acknowledge it even if they were aware of it."

There are many white Americans who think of themselves as nonracist fiscal conservatives and who are sincerely "unaware" of the influence of race on their judgments, as Knowles describes. Then there are the increasing numbers of white Americans who are aware of the influence of racism and yet do not acknowledge it—further still, they claim that it's the liberals and the people of color who are the racists. This is the narrative they receive from millionaire right-wing media personalities, and hysteria over Obama's secret plan for racial vengeance was one of their mainstay narratives during his presidency. Here's Rush Limbaugh:

> Obama has a plan. Obama's plan is based on his inherent belief that this country was immorally and illegitimately founded by a very small minority of white Europeans who screwed everybody else since the founding to get all the money and all the goodies, and it's about time that the scales were made even. . . . It's always been the other way around. This is just payback. This is "how does it feel" time.

It sounds a lot like Greenberg and Carville's focus group respondents, but with the race part dialed all the way up. Here's Glenn Beck: "Have we suddenly transported into 1956 except it's the other

way around? . . . Does anybody else have a sense that there are some
that just want revenge? Doesn't it feel that way?" Or Bill O'Reilly: "I
think Mr. Obama allows historical grievances—things like slavery,
bad treatment for Native Americans, and U.S. exploitation of Third
World countries—to shape his economic thinking . . . leading to his
desire to redistribute wealth, thereby correcting historical grievance." Just what were the anti-white comeuppance policies Obama
was pushing to merit these reactions? Economic recovery from the
financial crisis and the radical idea that wealthy people and businesses depended on public investments such as roads and the internet.

Racism, then, works against non-wealthy white Americans in two
ways. First, it lowers their support for government actions that could
help them economically, out of a zero-sum fear that it could help the
racialized "undeserving" as well. Yet racism's work on class consciousness is not total—there are still some New Deal–type economic
policies that the majority of white Americans support, like increasing the federal minimum wage and raising taxes on the wealthy. But
the racial polarization of our two-party system has forced a choice
between class interest and perceived racial interest, and in every
presidential election since the Civil Rights Act, the majority of white
people chose the party of their race. That choice keeps a conservative
faction in power that blocks progress on the modest economic agenda
they could support.

Political scientists Woojin Lee and John Roemer studied the rise
of antigovernment politics in the late 1970s, '80s, and early '90s and
found that the Republican Party's adoption of policies that voters
perceived as anti-black (opposition to affirmative action and welfare,
harsh policing and sentencing) won them millions more white voters
than their unpopular economic agenda would have attracted. The
result was a revolution in American economic policy: from high marginal tax rates and generous public investments in the middle class
such as the GI Bill to a low-tax, low-investment regime that resulted
in less than 1 percent annual income growth for 90 percent of Amer-

ican families for thirty years. According to Roemer and Lee, the culprit was racism. "We compute that voter racism reduced the income tax rate by 11–18 percentage points." They conclude, "Absent race as an issue in American politics, the fiscal policy in the USA would look quite similar to fiscal policies in Northern Europe."

In the social democracies of Northern Europe, families are far more economically secure; middle-class workers there don't have American families' worries about their healthcare, retirement, childcare, or college for their kids. But if government tried to secure these essential public benefits for families in the United States, in the political culture of the last two generations, it would signal a threat to the majority of white voters. Government help is for people of color, the story goes. When you cut government services, as Reagan strategist Lee Atwater said, "blacks get hurt worse than whites." What's lost in that formulation is just how much white people get hurt, too.

# Chapter 3

# GOING WITHOUT

For generations, college-going white Americans could count on public money from their governments, whether federal or state, to pay most if not all of their costs of higher education. The novel idea of flourishing public colleges—at least one in every state—took shape in the 1860s, when the U.S. government offered the states over ten million acres of land taken from Indigenous people to build on or to sell for institutions of higher education for their citizens. More free federal money for higher education came with the GI Bill, which paid tuition plus living expenses for World War II veterans and swelled college coffers: in 1947, veterans made up 50 percent of U.S. college admissions. (Racist program administration and educational segregation left black veterans in the South largely excluded from these opportunities, however.) Public commitment to college for all was a crucial part of the white social contract for much of the twentieth century. In 1976, state governments provided six out of every ten dollars of the cost of students attending public colleges. The remainder translated into modest tuition bills—just $617 at a four-year college in 1976, and a student could receive a federal Pell Grant for as much as $1,400 against that and living expenses. Many of the country's biggest and most respected public colleges were tuition-free, from the City University of New York to the University of California system. This massive public investment wasn't considered charity; an individual state saw a return of three to four dollars back for every dollar it invested in public colleges. When the public meant "white," public colleges thrived.

That's no longer the case. Students of color comprised just one in six public college students in 1980, but they now make up over four in ten. Over this period of growth among students of color, ensuring college affordability fell out of favor with lawmakers. State legislatures began to drastically cut what they spent per student on their public colleges, even as the taxable income base in the state grew. More and more Americans enrolled nonetheless, because other policy decisions in the labor market made a college degree necessary to compete for a middle-class job. By 2017, the majority of state colleges were relying on student tuition dollars for the majority of their expenses. The average public college tuition has nearly tripled since 1991, helping bring its counterpart, skyrocketing student debt, to the level of $1.5 trillion in 2020. This represents an alarming stealth privatization of America's public colleges.

The rising cost of college feels to most Americans like so many aspects of our economy: unexplained and unavoidable. But at Demos, we researched the causes of rising tuition and linked them squarely to the withering government commitment to public funding. The federal government for its part slowly shifted its financial aid from grants that didn't have to be repaid (such as Pell Grants for low-income students, which used to cover four-fifths of college costs and now cover at most one-third) to federal loans, which I would argue are not financial aid at all. Yes, student loans enable Americans to pay their college bills during enrollment, but the compounding interest means they must pay at least 33 percent more on average than the amount borrowed. Millions of students are also paying double-digit interest on private loans.

The new "debt-for-diploma system," as my former Demos colleague Tamara Draut called it, has impacted black students most acutely, as generations of racist policies have left our families with less wealth to draw on to pay for college. Eight out of ten black graduates have to borrow, and at higher levels than any other group. In my high school, the seniors had a tradition of posting college admissions letters on the school counselor's wall: right side up for acceptance, sideways for waitlist, and upside down for rejection. So much bravado in that transparency, and yet nobody was putting their financial aid letters on the wall. I borrowed five figures for college and nearly six for law school, including a high-interest private loan that my grandmother had to cosign. At forty years old, I'm still paying it all off, and I don't know a single black peer who's not in the same boat, even those whose parents were doctors and lawyers. Because wealth is largely shaped by how much money your parents and grandparents had, black young adults' efforts at higher education and higher earnings aren't putting much of a dent in the racial wealth gap. This generation was born too late for the free ride, and student loan repayment is making it even harder for black graduates' savings and assets to catch up. In fact, white high school dropouts have higher average household wealth than black people who've graduated from college.

As with so many economic ills, student debt is most acute among black families, but it has now reached 63 percent of white public college graduates as well and is having ripple effects across our entire economy. In 2019, the Federal Reserve reported on what most of my generation knows: student debt payments are stopping us from buying our first home, the irreplaceable wealth-building asset. It's even contributing to delays in marriage and family formation. And by age thirty, young adults with debt have half the retirement savings of those who are debt-free.

Fundamentally, we have to ask ourselves, how is it fair and how is it smart to price a degree out of reach for the working class just as that degree became the price of entry into the middle class? And how is it fair or smart to create a new source of debt for a generation when that debt makes it harder for us to achieve the hallmarks of middle-class security: a house, marriage, and retirement savings? There is neither fairness nor wisdom in this system, only self-sabotage. Other countries learned from the midcentury American investment in higher education and have now raced ahead. A third of developed countries offer free tuition, and another third keep tuition lower than $2,600. In the United States, recent policy proposals to restore free college are generally popular, though race shapes public opinion. There's a 30-percentage-point gap in support for free college between white people on the one hand (53 percent) and black and Latinx Americans on the other (86 and 82 percent). The most fiercely opposed? Among the very people who benefited the most from the largely whites-only free college model and who now want to pull the ladder up behind them: older, college-educated (white) Republicans.

In the story of how America drained the pool of our public college system, racism is the uncredited actor. The country's first ambitious free college system, in California, was created in 1868 on a guarantee of no tuition and universal access; this public investment helped launch California's rise as an economic giant and global hub of technology and innovation. But the state's politics shifted radically in the 1970s, spurred by a backlash to the civil rights policy gains of the 1960s and, in an important harbinger of national trends, rising resentment of immigration and demographic change. The older, wealthier, and whiter political majority began voting for ballot initiatives opposing civil rights, fair housing, immigration, and taxes. In 1978, a ballot initiative known as Proposition 13 drastically limited property taxes by capping them at 1 percent of the property's value at purchase, limiting increases and assessments, and requiring a supermajority to pass new taxes. Property tax revenue from corporate landowners and homeowners in the state dropped 60 percent the following year. The impact was felt most acutely in public K–12 schools; California went from a national leader in school funding to forty-first in the country. But Prop 13 also swiftly destroyed the local revenue base for California's extensive system of community colleges and put them in direct competition for state funding with the more selective state schools and universities. The resulting squeeze accelerated the end of the free college era in California. Between 1979 and 2019, tuition and fees at the four-year public colleges increased eightfold.

Dog-whistling was ever-present in the campaign to win Proposition 13, from flyers claiming that lower property taxes would put an end to busing for integration purposes to messaging questioning why homeowners should pay for "other people's children." Conservative columnist William Safire put it most directly, however, when he endorsed the proposition in *The New York Times:* "An underlying reason is the surge in the number of illegales—aliens fleeing poverty in Mexico—who have been crossing the border by the hundreds of thousands. . . . As one might expect, property taxpayers see themselves giving much more than they are getting; they see wage-earners, both legal and illegal, getting more in services than they pay for in taxes." A decade later, voters in Colorado, another state with a growing Latinx immigrant population, passed a constitutional amendment severely limiting taxes. TABOR (Taxpayer's Bill of Rights) has forced Coloradans to go without a long list of public services, including for two years children's vaccines when the state couldn't afford to purchase them—and the state has dropped to forty-seventh place in higher education investments.

**THE RISE IN** student diversity shifted the politics of state education spending across the country. As part of the antigovernment fervor in the 1980s and '90s, spending on the welfare of youth fell out of favor, but meanwhile, legislatures were tripling their expenditures on incarceration and policing. By 2016, eighteen states were spending more on jails and prisons than they were on colleges and universities. The path to this system of mass incarceration is another story of racist policy making creating unsustainable costs for everyone.

The loss of good factory jobs in the mid-1970s hit the cities first, and with cities, their segregated black residents. Instead of responding to the economic problem with economic development, jobs programs, and stronger safety nets, the federal government cut back massively on urban social spending in the 1980s. In its place, it waged a drug war. Dehumanizing and unpitying stereotypes about the dangers of drug use in the inner cities fueled a new era of harsher sentencing and post-release penalties to create a system of mass incarceration. While the so-called crack epidemic is far behind us, the system rolls on, and today, more than 1.25 million people are arrested each year for drug possession. These are not kingpins or high-level dealers; more than four times as many people are arrested for possessing drugs as for selling drugs, often in amounts so tiny they can only be intended for personal use. In 2016, the number of arrests for marijuana possession exceeded the total number of arrests for all violent crimes put together.

The racist nature of our mass incarceration system has been well documented. White and black people are equally likely to use drugs, but the system is six times as likely to incarcerate black people for a drug crime. Sentences for possession of crack cocaine, which is more widely used by African Americans than whites, are about eighteen times harsher than penalties for the powder version of the drug, which is used more often by whites. For decades before policy changes in 2010, this sentencing disparity was about one hundred to one.

Over the last twenty years, however, a striking change has taken place. Getting locked up over drugs and related property crimes has become more and more common among white people and less so among black folks. A primary factor in this shift is, as *The New York Times* wrote, "Mostly white and politically conservative counties have continued to send more drug offenders to prison, reflecting the changing geography of addiction. While crack cocaine addiction was centered in cities, opioid and meth addiction are ravaging small communities" in largely white locales. The "pathology" long ascribed to urban communities as integral and immutable characteristics of black life (drug addiction, property crimes to support a habit, broken families) has now moved, with deindustrialization, into the suburbs and the countryside. By 2018, an estimated 130 people were dying every day from opioid overdoses, and over 10 million people were abusing prescription opioids.

The option to treat poverty and drug addiction as a public health and economic security issue rather than a criminal one has always been present. Will our nation choose that option now that white people, always the majority of drug users, make up a soaring population of people for whom addiction takes over? The woes that devastated communities of color are now visiting white America, and the costs of incarceration are coming due in suburban and rural areas, squeezing state budgets and competing with education. It's not a comeuppance but a bitter cost of the white majority's willingness to accept the suffering of others, a cost of racism itself.

**AS RACIALIZED AS** the politics of government spending has become, the victims of this new higher education austerity include the majority of white students. When Demos was working to build the research case for debt-free college, we partnered with a then-small online group organizing students and graduates with debt, called the Student Debt Crisis. Now more than one million members strong, the Student Debt Crisis—run by Natalia Abrams, a white Millennial grad of the University of California, Los Angeles—speaks for an indebted generation, lifting up the stories it collects in an online story bank. "We recently polled the activists on our list, and about seventy percent identify as white," Abrams told me.

Josh Frost is thirty-nine and works full time at a news station and part time at a gas station. He pays three-quarters of his salary toward his student debt while living with his parents. Though he did everything society told him to do, he's nearing forty but feels like adulthood is passing him by: "I'm watching everyone I know start families and buy homes," he said. Emilie Scott from St. Paul, Minnesota, needed to go to college to fulfill her goal of becoming a teacher. She worked four jobs while studying, to keep her borrowing low, but still graduated with $70,000 in private and public student loans. Four years after graduation, making payments of $600 a month, she has paid off $28,000, but because of interest rates close to 10 percent, her remaining balance is $65,000. "This is madness," she says. "How can I keep up with this? And for how long?" Unfortunately for Emilie, more than three million senior citizens who still owe $86 billion in student loans can attest that the "madness" doesn't really end. Seniors with student loans are more likely to report rationing medical care, and the government garnishes Social Security payments for seniors in default.

Robert Settle Jr. was sixty years old in 2016, and although he is completely disabled and lost all his savings in the financial crisis of 2008, he is still being sued for $60,000 in private student loans he obtained while working for a master's degree to advance his career. Robert points his ire at the government for allowing this system to flourish, and he is eager to tell his story. "I want the entire country to see how a disabled, elderly couple is treated by our federal government!"

The saddest, most common refrain in dozens of interviews and testimonials from borrowers is "I wish I had never gone to college." If growing cynicism about higher education is the result of this sudden and total shift from public to private, then our entire society will bear the cost.

THE SUDDEN DEMISE of our public college system and the growing scourge of student debt are recent phenomena, but there may be no question that has vexed Americans for longer than why our healthcare system isn't better: more affordable, less complex, more secure for everyone. We pay more individually and as a nation for healthcare and have worse health outcomes than our industrialized peers, all of whom have some version of publicly financed universal coverage. But the United States doesn't—even though the closest thing we have to European-style single-payer care, Medicare for the elderly, is successful economically and popular with its beneficiaries. (Even the theoretical opposition to universal healthcare is weaker than it seems; at the height of public opposition to the Affordable Care Act, eleven out of twelve of the bill's provisions polled with majority support.) In the modern era, more elections have been won, lost, and fought on healthcare than on any other single issue besides the overall economy. Why can't we fix this?

In some ways, the story of America's healthcare dysfunction comes back to the pool. Health insurers use that exact term when they refer to the number of people in the "risk pool" of a plan. A high number minimizes the risk posed by any individual's health costs. Whether we're talking about insurance or drug trials or vaccines or practice improvements, in health, the key is getting everybody in. Healthcare works best as a collective endeavor, and that's at the heart of why America's system performs so poorly. We've resisted universal solutions because when it comes to healthcare, from President Truman's first national proposal in 1943 to the present-day battles over Medicaid expansion, racism has stopped us from ever filling the pool in the first place.

UNITED STATES SENATOR Claude Pepper of Florida was a towering figure topped with bright red hair. He gained national prominence when he became President Harry Truman's most reliable southern Democratic champion for national health insurance. According to Jill Quadagno, who tells the story in her book *One Nation, Uninsured*, Claude Pepper was "a farm boy from the red clay country of eastern Alabama who never saw a paved road until he went to college [and] entered public life because he believed that government could be a force to enhance the greater good." That farm boy never would have anticipated he'd grow up to be public enemy number one of the American Medical Association. The AMA is a trade group of doctors known to most Americans now for its labeling on consumer products, but in the 1940s, it acted as a scorched-earth lobbying group whose leadership viewed any kind of insurance that mediated between the patient and the doctor with suspicion. Government insurance, with the potential for cost-rationing, portended a threat to the profitability of the entire medical profession. The AMA launched the first modern public relations and lobbying campaign to paint government insurance as a threat not to doctors' finances, however—but to the entire American way of life. They labeled the idea socialist.

Racism gave the accusation of socialism added power. Red-baiting tapped into many white Americans' fears about what it would mean in the United States to mandate equality: an end to white supremacy. Segregationists regularly tried to marginalize the issue of civil rights by calling groups like the NAACP "a front and tool by subversive elements . . . part and parcel of the Communist conspiracy." Claude Pepper's cause of universal healthcare would ultimately get him lumped in with "the communist-inspired doctrine of racial integration and amalgamation."

After Pepper came out as a champion of government-funded healthcare and other liberal programs, he became a prime target in the 1950 election. The effort to unseat him was a coordinated campaign led by a wealthy businessman who opposed Pepper's economic liberalism, including his support for higher wages and taxes. In an early example of plutocratic dog whistle politics (that is, using racism to further an economic agenda), a group of anti-Pepper businessmen "collected every photo of Pepper with African Americans . . . and charged that northern labor bosses were 'paying ten to twenty dollars to blacks to register' and vote for him." The physicians' lobby joined in, running newspaper ads with a photo of Senator Pepper with Paul Robeson, the black actor and Communist activist. The racist red-baiting campaign worked. Universal healthcare's biggest Senate champion lost his 1950 race by more than sixty thousand votes.

The bare-knuckle assault on universal health insurance signaled the beginning of the end of the New Deal Democrats' reign in national politics. Liberal southern Democrats who saw the transformative potential in government action, like Claude Pepper, were a dying breed, and Harry Truman could not get the segregationist caucus of southern "Dixiecrat" Democrats in his party behind his vision of national healthcare. Truman was the first president to champion civil rights since Reconstruction, desegregating the armed forces and forming a President's Committee on Civil Rights. The southern Democratic bloc saw the civil rights potential in his healthcare plan— which was designed to be universal, without racial discrimination—as too great a cost to bear for the benefit of bringing healthcare to their region. As Jill Quadagno writes, "If national health insurance succeeded, it would be without the support of the South." Needless to say, it would not succeed. Truman declined to run again in 1952, and national health insurance receded from the legislative agenda for the next decade.

To be clear, the beneficiaries of Truman's universal coverage would have been overwhelmingly white, as white people at the time made up 90 percent of the U.S. population. Few Americans, black or white, had private insurance plans, and the recent notion that employers would provide it had yet to solidify into a nationwide expectation. The pool of national health insurance would have been mainly for white Americans, but the threat of sharing it with even a small number of black and brown Americans helped to doom the entire plan from the start.

After the defeat of Truman's proposal, unions increasingly pressed employers for healthcare benefits for workers and retirees. By the 1960s, as part of his "war on poverty," President Johnson created a generous federal healthcare program for the elderly (an even whiter population than the overall population) in Medicare and a less generous patchwork for low-income people and children, Medicaid. Johnson's Congress conceded to leave whether and how to offer Medicaid to the individual states, in a compromise with racism that curtailed the program's reach for decades. Medicaid was intended to insure all Americans living in poverty by 1970, but by 1985, the Robert Wood Johnson Foundation estimated that less than half of low-income families were covered. Then corporations began cutting back on offering health benefits to their employees in the 1980s, and the number of uninsured skyrocketed. As of 2020, we still have no universal health insurance.

The closest the United States has come to a universal plan is the Affordable Care Act, created by a black president carried into office with record turnout among black voters and passed with no congressional votes from the Republican Party. The Affordable Care Act created state-based markets for consumers to comparison-shop healthcare plans, with federal subsidies for moderate- to middle-income purchasers. It also stopped private insurance companies from some of their most unpopular practices, such as denying insurance to people with preexisting conditions, dropping customers when they were sick, and requiring young adults to leave their parents' insurance before age twenty-six. But Congress rejected the reform ideas that would have relied the most on Americans swimming in one national pool: a federal "public option" plan and collective bargaining to lower prescription drug costs. The idea of a Truman-style national health insurer never made it to a vote. As comparatively modest as it was, Obamacare has been deeply unpopular with the majority of white voters. White support remained under 40 percent until after the law's namesake left office, and as of this writing, it has yet to surpass the 50 percent mark.

Blame President Obama—not for strategic missteps; blame him for being black. Numerous social science studies have shown that racial resentment among white people spiked with the election of Barack Obama. When the figurehead of American government became a black man in 2009, the correlation between views on race and views on government and policy went into overdrive. Professor Michael Tesler, a political scientist at Brown University, conducted research on the way that race and racial attitudes impacted Americans' views of the Affordable Care Act in 2010. He concluded that whites with higher levels of racial resentment and more anti-black stereotypes grew more opposed to healthcare reform after it became associated with President Obama. "Racial attitudes . . . had a considerably larger impact on our panel respondents' health care opinions in November 2009 than they did before Barack Obama became the Democratic nominee for president," Tesler explained in a Brown University interview. He also ran an experiment to try to disassociate health reform proposals from Obama. "The experiments . . . revealed that health care policies were significantly more racialized when they were framed as part of President Obama's plan than they were for respondents told that these exact same proposals were part of President Clinton's 1993 reform efforts."

Three researchers out of Stanford looked at anti-black prejudice and people's willingness to support Barack Obama and his healthcare policies. What Eric Knowles, Brian Lowery, and Rebecca Schaumberg found was that respondents who held strong implicit biases were less likely to support Obama and more opposed to his healthcare plan, usually citing policy concerns. Like Tesler, they also tried attributing the same plan details to Bill Clinton and found that the link between healthcare opinion and prejudice dissolved. "In sum," they wrote, "our data support the notion that racial prejudice is one factor driving opposition to Obama and his policies." Of course, you don't have to look far upstream to find the racialized rhetoric that filled this story in white people's minds: in 2010, Rush Limbaugh's line on the ACA was "This is a civil rights bill, this is reparations, whatever you want to call it." Rep. Joe Wilson was so certain that the ACA would benefit undocumented immigrants that he shouted "You lie!" in the middle of President Obama's State of the Union address.

**RURAL AMERICA IS** experiencing a quiet crisis. Rural hospitals account for one in seven jobs in their areas, but over the past ten years, 120 rural hospitals have closed, dealing a body blow to the economy and health of the country's mostly white, overwhelmingly conservative rural communities. A quarter of the remaining rural hospitals are at risk of closing. One thing that all of the states with the highest hospital closures have in common is that their legislatures have all refused to expand Medicaid under Obamacare.

Texas leads the country in rural hospital closures, with twenty-six hospitals permanently closing or whittling down services since 2010. The state has half the hospitals it had in the 1960s. In 2013, an eighteen-month-old died after choking on a grape because her parents couldn't reach the nearest hospital in time. The outrage from that story swept the state, but it was short-lived. What would reopen the hospitals, according to Don McBeath, an expert in rural medicine who now does government relations for a Texas network of rural hospitals called TORCH, is something that the powers that be in the state capital are dead set against, and that's Medicaid—both fully funding Texas's share and expanding eligibility for it, as Congress intended with the Affordable Care Act.

I caught up with McBeath by phone at the beginning of the coronavirus outbreak and asked him why Texas's hospital system was in crisis. "There's no question, [it's the] uninsured in Texas," he said, and then let his characteristic sarcasm slip in. "I mean, we're running about twenty-five, twenty-six percent before the Affordable Care Act. And now—oh gosh, yeah, we're down to a whopping sixteen percent. And so that is a huge problem. When you know that one out of every six, seven people walking in your hospital is not going to pay you . . ."

I asked him if, as my research had suggested, Medicaid expansion would help shore up the rural hospital system. "I'm sure you're aware, Texas has probably one of the narrowest Medicaid coverage programs in the country," he said. I was aware. I'd had to double-check the figure because I couldn't believe it was so low, but in fact, if you make as little as four thousand dollars a year, you're considered too rich to qualify for Medicaid in Texas, and even that has exclusions, as McBeath explained.

"I hear this all the time: even some of my friends will go, 'Oh, those lazy bums. They need to get off that Medicaid and go to work.' And I go, 'Excuse me? Who do you think's on Medicaid?' First of all, there's no men on Medicaid, period, in Texas. No adult men, unless they have a disability and they're poor. And there's no non-pregnant women, I don't care how poor they are."

Failing to insure so many people leaves a lot of unpaid medical bills in the state, and that drains the Texas hospital system. The conservative majority in the Texas legislature has been so opposed to the idea of Medicaid that they shortchange the state's hospitals in compensating for the few (mostly pregnant women) Medicaid patients they see. Then, by rejecting Obamacare's Medicaid expansion, they lose out on federal money that would insure about 1.5 million Texas citizens. As a result of this and some federal policies, including budget cuts in the government sequestration that the Tea Party forced during Obama's second term, rural healthcare is rapidly disappearing. Texas politicians' government-bashing is both ideological and strategic; they benefit politically by stopping government from having a beneficial presence in people's lives—as white constituents' needs mount, the claim that government is busy serving some racialized other instead of them becomes more convincing.

McBeath sighed. "The thing that we've seen in this state is, our politicians have so demonized the term 'Medicaid expansion,' that they'll never reverse course on that as long as they're in control. And we can prove to them all day long that [it] may be the way to go. But . . . we quit barking up that tree, because we're not gonna get anywhere."

What the mostly white and male conservatives in the Texas legislature are doing to sabotage the state's healthcare system doesn't hurt them personally—the state provides their health insurance—but it's costing their state millions. Before Medicaid expansion, working-class people had basically no option for health insurance; most low-wage employers don't offer coverage, and buying it on your own cost an average of $4,000 a year for families. If you were under sixty-five, this left only Medicaid, whose rules were mostly set by the states in another southern congressional compromise, leading to an average income eligibility cap of just $8,532 for a family of three, well below the minimum wage for one earner. If you lived in a southern state, the likelihood of your being eligible was even lower.

Alabama: $3,910; Florida: $6,733; Georgia: $7,602; Mississippi: $5,647; Texas: $3,692—these are the paltry annual amounts that a parent in a southern state must earn *less than* in order to qualify for Medicaid in 2020; adults without children are usually ineligible. When the Affordable Care Act passed in 2010, it expanded qualification for Medicaid to 138 percent of the poverty level for all adults (about $30,000 for a family of three in 2020) and equalized eligibility rules across all states. But in 2012, a Supreme Court majority invoked states' rights to strike down the Medicaid expansion and make it optional. Within the year, the lines were drawn in an all-too-familiar way: almost all the states of the former Confederacy refused to expand Medicaid, while most other states did. Without Medicaid expansion, people of color in those states struggle more—they are the ones most likely to be denied health benefits on the job—but white people are still the largest share of the 4.4 million working Americans who would have Medicaid if the law had been left intact. So, a states' rights legal theory most often touted to defend segregation struck at the heart of the first black president's healthcare protections for working-class people of all races.

Expanding Medicaid should be a no-brainer for states, cost-wise. The federal government paid 100 percent of the cost for the first few years and 90 percent into the future. The states that expanded saw hundreds of thousands of their working-class citizens go from being uninsured—where an accident can cause bankruptcy and preventable illnesses can become fatal—to being able to afford to see a doctor. The benefits don't stop with individual people, though. Stable Medicaid funding has allowed rural medical clinics in expansion states to thrive financially. In Arkansas, the first southern state to accept expanded Medicaid, a health clinic in one of the poorest towns in the country has constructed a new building, created jobs, and served more patients, creating measurable improvements in the community's health. Terrence Aikens, an outreach employee at the clinic, told a reporter in 2020, "What we've experienced in the last few years has been nothing short of amazing."

Why wouldn't a state's politicians take free money to have such amazing health and economic outcomes in their communities, including rural ones with disproportionate conservative representation and fewer options for economic activity? It's not that it's unpopular; expanding Medicaid has polled higher than Obamacare since the bill passed. The answer is all too familiar: racism. Colleen M. Grogan and Sunggeun (Ethan) Park of the University of Chicago found that racialization affects state Medicaid decision making. First, they found that just after the Supreme Court decision that made it optional, Medicaid expansion had robust support among black and Latino Americans at 82 and 65 percent respectively, but slightly below-majority support among white Americans, at 46 percent. Across the country, state-level support for Medicaid expansion ranged between about 45 and 55 percent, and interestingly, some of the highest support was found in the South (where the larger black populations drove up the average).

But that larger black population also prompted a sense of group threat and backlash from the white power structure; Grogan and Park found "as the percent of the black population increases, the likelihood of adoption decreases." The zero-sum story again. As with the public swimming pools, public healthcare is often a benefit that white people have little interest in sharing with their black neighbors. Grogan and Park's model found that it didn't matter whether a state's communities of color supported the expansion if the white community, with its greater political power and representation, did not. "State adoption decisions are positively related to white opinion and do not respond to nonwhite support levels," they concluded.

When I pointed out this study to Ginny Goldman, veteran community organizer in Texas, she threw her hands up. For ten years, Ginny built a nonprofit called the Texas Organizing Project (TOP), which aimed to improve Texas's democracy by engaging residents of color in issue activism and elections. Ginny gives one the impression of being battery-powered. She's a fast talker with eyes that size you up quickly—but she's just as quick to reveal her deep compassion for people who struggle. The idea that it wouldn't matter how much black and brown Texas supported better healthcare if white Texas did not—"it just flies in the face of everything that we spend our time doing," she told me. Ginny tells her members, "There's power in numbers. You're the majority. You have to organize. You've got to get out. You've got to vote. You've got to be loud!" But then, as the study I showed her suggested, "there's actually this tiny sliver of a minority of people who will outdo you."

The thing is, that "tiny sliver" is overrepresented in Texas government. Texas is considered a majority-people-of-color state (41 percent non-Hispanic white, 40 percent Latinx, 13 percent black, and 5 percent Asian in 2018), but the legislature is two-thirds white and three-quarters male. After the Supreme Court Obamacare decision, TOP joined a coalition advocating for Texas to expand Medicaid above its abysmally low income cap of $3,692, so that more working- and middle-class Texans could be insured. The upside for Texas was clear: one out of every five nonelderly Texans lacks health insurance, the highest percentage in the country. The problem is not just about poverty, either; the state has the highest uninsured rate for families earning less than $50,000 a year (who would be eligible for expanded Medicaid), but also the highest uninsured rate for those making over $100,000 (who may qualify for middle-income subsidies under Obamacare). The uninsured are disproportionately Latino, but there are over a million white non-Hispanic Texans without any health-care coverage. The benefits of Medicaid expansion would be widespread; the cost, minimal. But as soon as the Supreme Court made it optional for states, the state's governor, Rick Perry, "did his announcement, which was like, 'Hell, no, I'm not taking the money,'" Ginny recalled.

I asked her what arguments Texas's leaders made for turning away free money to help solve that state's worst-in-the-nation health coverage crisis. She recalled accompanying TOP members to state legislative hearings, "and Republican legislators would say, you know, 'These folks are gonna come out of the woodwork like bugs.' These freeloaders who are just gonna come out from everywhere. And comparing them to insects and bugs . . . rodents. Asking for stuff."

This particular racist trope, the language of infestation, is usually deployed against immigrants and, in the current immigration debates, those from Latin America. In Texas, Latinx people are the largest group of uninsured. But Ginny saw how some in the very community that would be most helped by Medicaid expansion were inclined to oppose it because of anti-black stereotypes about Medicaid. "When we first started to collect postcards and signatures and support around this, I remember Latino organizers coming back to the office and [saying], 'We're not doing very well.' Because a lot of the folks [in] Latino communities were like, 'We don't want a handout. We work for what we earn. We're not asking for anything for free.' "

That's a late-stage benefit of a forty-year campaign to defund and degrade public benefits; in the end, they're so stigmatized that people whose lives would be transformed by them don't even want them for fear of sharing the stigma.

"I think Republicans were pretty good at what they're always good at, right? Pitting communities against each other and using a lot of dog whistle politics around, like, 'Medicaid equates to black freeloading people,'" Ginny said with a sigh. "And unfortunately, that's resonating. Or hitting some of the underlying tension that already exists between African American and Latino communities. So, we had to fight a lot against that."

The Texas Organizing Project campaigned within the deserving-versus-undeserving narrative it was dealt. "Our talking points were overwhelmingly, like, 'We work. Why can't we have healthcare?' So, we always had to go out of our way to kind of counter this sense of, you know, just this idea that people are wanting 'free stuff' and not carrying their part."

If you're trying to understand Texas's healthcare crisis, Ginny believes you can't ignore conservative white Texans' resistance to the first black president. "Abbott, who's the governor now, was the attorney general then. And he would just say, 'I get up in the morning. I go to the office. I sue President Obama, and I come home.' It was just so apparent that it was like, 'We can't have Obama having any success, even if it makes perfect sense, economic sense and healthcare sense, for the state. There's just no way it's happening.'" (Interestingly, the strategy to deny President Obama victories did make some inroads, even with the president's base. Ginny recalls that "when people still weren't getting healthcare, especially first-time voters and communities of color that we were organizing, they blamed it on Obama at first. . . . Because the Republicans' megaphone's just always bigger than ours.")

The struggle for affordable healthcare for the working class continues in Texas and, as of summer 2020, twelve other states. Meanwhile, conservatives threaten Obamacare with court challenges, legislative repeals, and regulatory rollbacks. The healthcare advocates I spoke with could still remember people they knew who died because, without insurance, they couldn't afford to see a doctor. Toward the end of our conversation, Ginny began to cry while recalling "a funeral of a woman who was the daughter of one of the first people I ever organized with. This African American man whose daughter died because she had lupus," a highly treatable disease.

"She had to wait and wait and wait until it got really, really bad. Then she could go to the emergency room. Then they would give her something, then they would turn her out. And she can never get ongoing care. She can never get medication or any treatment. She worked all sorts of low-wage jobs, from one to another. She has kids. And she's dead, at my age. In her late forties." Ginny's voice shook with both grief and rage. "People are dying because they would choose . . . a political victory over an actual victory that serves millions of people."

**FOR RON POLLACK**, a fifty-year leader in the fight for healthcare, housing, and other antipoverty measures, the person he won't forget is John, a Texan he met over twenty years ago, during the Clinton administration's lost battle for universal healthcare. "John told us the story about his wife," Ron told me. "He worked for a radio station. Wasn't making a lot of money. He talked about his wife being a very strong person. And she started getting stomach pains, and John would say to his wife, you know, 'We've got to see a doctor.'

"And she said, 'Well, we don't have the money to see a doctor. I'm gonna be okay.' And this persisted for months, until one day, she collapsed in excruciating pain, and she was taken by ambulance to a hospital. And they found this huge tumor in her stomach. And it was a very advanced tumor. And it was clear that she was going to pass away from this. And while she was at her deathbed, we were gonna start the bus trip" across Texas to advocate for universal healthcare.

"And John was encouraged by his wife to get on the bus for three weeks to join us. And John said, 'Well, I don't feel comfortable leaving you like this.' She said, 'The last favor I have of you is that you join the bus trip. And tell my story, so that nobody experiences what we have experienced.'

"We were about halfway in the trip, and his wife died. And he flew back to bury her. And then he flew back to rejoin the bus. And he told his story at the White House. And of course, there wasn't a dry eye in the place," Ron said, his voice getting weak with the weight of the memory.

He cleared his throat. "So, yes, there have been quite a few people I have met—too numerous to count—who paid the ultimate price for their inability to get health coverage."

After a moment, I asked him about John's racial background.

"He was white."

**RON POLLACK WAS** born in 1944, during the golden era when the government erected the structures that created a white middle class comprised of the sons and daughters of millions of European immigrants, like his own parents. He became a young man during the brief part of that century when all three branches of the U.S. government took major leaps toward realizing the American Dream for all her children, regardless of race or status—and it forever shaped him.

"I grew up in the period when, in the 1960s, there was this tiny glimmer of hope that we were going to do something serious about poverty in America." Ron was the student body president at the (then tuition-free) City University of New York when his classmate Andrew Goodman was murdered on a trip to Mississippi during Freedom Summer, and from then on, he threw himself into what would become a lifelong fight to extend America's promise to all. He founded the country's premier anti-hunger organization, the Food Research and Action Center, whose litigation and advocacy helped create the Supplemental Nutrition Assistance Program for Women, Infants and Children, including the food stamp program that feeds nearly forty million Americans. His organization Families USA was at the forefront of both the Clinton and Obama healthcare reform battles that eventually won healthcare for twenty-five million people, and at seventy-six years old, he has lately turned his passions to preventing evictions and ensuring affordable housing.

Ron Pollack is not a household name by any means, but he has dedicated his life to extending the public web of protection around more Americans, and tens of millions of Americans are better off because he has. When I got the chance to talk with him, I wasn't so sure that he'd be willing to speak about the often-invisible headwinds of racism in his antipoverty efforts; I've known many a white liberal who was uncomfortable talking about racism's impact on politics. But he never shied away from naming racism, and when I asked him my final question, he shared with me the vision for America that has guided him through five decades of advocacy.

Ron said that, in his vision, "nobody in this country is deprived of the necessities of life—whether it's food, whether it's healthcare, whether it's housing—in a country that's as wealthy as ours."

To realize this vision, he said, "I wish there was a greater consciousness about how we're all in this together. For those people who are opposed to [government aid] out of an animus to people who look different than they are . . . that lack of social solidarity causes harm to their own communities.

"If we didn't have these sharp divisions based on race, we could make enormous progress in terms of making sure that people are not hurting as badly as they are, [or] deprived of what clearly are the necessities of life. And I would like to think it was possible if we had a sense of social solidarity."

Ron Pollack's diagnosis of the United States—that we suffer because our society was raised deficient in social solidarity—struck me as profoundly true, and, true to my optimistic nature, I suppose, I found the insight galvanizing. I began to think of all that a newfound solidarity could yield for our country, so young, so full of promise and power. Starting with healthcare and public college, I began to see the Solidarity Dividends waiting to be unlocked if more people would stop buying the old zero-sum story that elites use to keep us from investing in one another.

**THE STORIES OF** the declining public university and the shuttered public pools have parallels across the country, from the infrastructure we have (collapsing bridges and poisoned pipes) to the public goods we are desperately missing (universal childcare and healthcare). There's a way to tell these stories without race, as my early colleagues at Demos attempted to do. That story makes sense—up to a point. But when I became the organization's president and had the chance to lead a new research project over a decade later, the Race-Class Narrative Project, I made sure to add race to the investigation. Working with my old law professor Ian Haney López and the linguistics expert Anat Shenker-Osorio, I discovered that if you try to convince anyone but the most committed progressives (disproportionately people of color) about big public solutions without addressing race, most will agree . . . right up until they hear the counter-message that does talk, even implicitly, about race. Racial scapegoating about "illegals," drugs, gangs, and riots undermines public support for working together. Our research showed that color-blind approaches that ignored racism didn't beat the scapegoating zero-sum story; we had to be honest about racism's role in dividing us in order to call people to their higher ideals.

A coalition of grassroots organizations in Minnesota decided to use our research to develop messages during the 2018 election, an election they knew would be a referendum on demographic change in their historically white state. Once a northern Tea Party hotbed, Minnesota had more than its share of right-wing politicians who campaigned on fear about the state's growing Latinx and African Muslim population of refugees and immigrants. The coalition's organizers used insights from our Race-Class Narrative Project to develop a campaign they called "Greater Than Fear."

Minnesota organizer Doran Schrantz recalled, "We decided to emphasize the joy and benefit of things we do together, like sharing meals at a potluck and the feeling of shared accomplishment that every Minnesotan knows: digging each other out of the snow." But instead of an all-white cast for these campaign videos and posters, the Greater Than Fear storytelling included faces of all shades pushing a minivan out of the snow; and Muslim women in hijabs sharing dishes of homemade food with white women at a potluck. The narratives weren't communicating simply feel-good diversity; it was a familiar and values-based way for door-knocking canvassers and volunteers at phone banks to open up conversations about what all Minnesotans needed: healthcare, better infrastructure, more funding for education. And the campaign specifically called out the opposition strategy of dog-whistling by using humor, asking voters to send in pictures of their dogs to show real dogs standing up to racist dog-whistling. The Minnesota Democratic Farmer-Labor Party (the state Democratic Party) gubernatorial ticket adopted the Greater Than Fear messaging for its campaign in its final weeks, and won—the Farmer-Labor Party also took control of the statehouse, allowing the advocates in the Greater Than Fear coalition to have a bigger say in shaping the state's budget. The budget that emerged was a repudiation of the conservative policy of prioritizing "corporations, the wealthy, and insurance companies [while] underfunding our schools, transportation, health care," according to a statement by the majority leader when the budget was introduced. The House Speaker boasted that the budget would freeze college tuition and take steps toward enacting a public healthcare option, "honest investments" for families "no matter where in the state you live, or what you look like."

This kind of cross-racial public investment could be a new governing ethos for America, a country that has always linked what we give to who you are. As we become a nation with no racial majority, we will need more of this spirit to create a new basis for investing in ourselves, broadly and without prejudice.

# Chapter 4

# IGNORING
# THE CANARY

When Janice and Isaiah Tomlin married in 1977, they promised each other that by their first anniversary, they'd become the first people in their families to own their own home. Janice's mother had always dreamed of owning a house, but segregation limited the options for black people in Wilmington, North Carolina. On the salaries of an elementary school teacher and an auto mechanic, the Tomlins saved up about a thousand dollars for a down payment and bought a two-bedroom, bright blue house on Creecy Avenue for $11,500. They moved in right before their anniversary.

All the houses on Creecy have inviting front porches, and that's where Janice was sitting when I met her and Isaiah in the summer of 2020. A consumer attorney I've known for nearly two decades, Mike Calhoun, introduced me to them and connected us by a video call on their porch instead of the trip I'd planned to take to visit them, due to the pandemic. Janice told me about her introduction to the neighborhood: One night before they moved in, she was in the house painting over the dreadful lime green the previous owners had chosen for all the rooms, when she needed to make a call. The Tomlins' phone wasn't hooked up yet, but a nice white lady who lived next door offered to let her come in and use hers to call Isaiah. "And I thought, 'Gee, this is so nice. This is so kind,'" she recalled.

Her soon-to-be neighbor was out on the porch when Isaiah arrived later that night. Tall and deep mahogany–skinned, Isaiah was decidedly *not* what the white neighbor was expecting to see. Janice is fair-skinned and had just pressed her hair straight. "If you could have seen her face." Janice whistled as Isaiah laughed at the memory. "I will tell you that she was gone within months. Never spoke to us again, and was gone within months . . . and I thought, 'Oh, did we do that?'" She nodded to herself. "We did."

More black families moved in, and by the late 1990s, Janice said, it was a black neighborhood. Janice and Isaiah were raising two children and kept improving their dream house. As the equity grew and the neighborhood changed, the phone calls started coming in from people marketing refinance loans. It just so happened that Janice was determined to send her children to parochial school, and like many parents, she looked to their nest egg to help finance the tuition.

In the early spring of 1998, a company called Chase Mortgage Brokers had called the Tomlins multiple times, so Janice made an appointment to go in. "The very first meeting, the lady was so—I look back now—exceptionally kind. Just overbearing with kindness and patience," Janice recalled. "And I'm a question person. I ask a lot of questions. And she sat and she listened to me."

For all Janice's questions, however, there were some answers she wouldn't get from Chase—not until they showed up as evidence in a class-action predatory lending lawsuit. It turns out that Chase held itself out as a broker, someone a borrower hires to find them the best loan and who has a fiduciary duty to the borrower under North Carolina law. But Chase had a secret arrangement with just one lending company, Emergent. The exceptionally kind salesperson received kickbacks for every Emergent loan she sold, and no matter how low an interest rate a borrower might have qualified for, if the salesperson could sell them a higher-priced loan, she received even more of a kickback.

The salesperson at Chase also hid from Janice the extent of the high-cost fees that would be taken out of the Tomlins' home equity at signing. The included costs amounted to 12 percent of the loan on day one. Unbeknownst to them, the Tomlins had refinanced their dream home with a subprime mortgage with an annual interest rate in the double digits, unrelated to their credit scores.

This last point was important, because the official justification for the exorbitant cost of subprime mortgages was that higher costs were necessary for lenders to "price for the risk" of defaults by borrowers with poor credit. But lenders have no duty to sell you the best rate you qualify for—the limit is whatever they can get away with. I asked Janice, "Had you ever been late on your payments or missed a mortgage payment?"

Her warm voice turned firm. "Never."

"Never," I repeated. "That was very important to you?"

"Very important. Never late," she said, shaking her head emphatically.

*Subprime* would become a household word during the global financial crisis of 2008. I first came across the term when I started working at Demos in 2002 and when, as part of my outreach about our consumer debt research, I went to community meetings with dozens of borrowers just like the Tomlins, disproportionately black homeowners who were the first to be targeted by mortgage brokers and lenders. The loans are called *sub*prime because they're designed to be sold to borrowers who have lower-than-prime credit scores. That's the idea, but it wasn't the practice. An analysis conducted for the *Wall Street Journal* in 2007 showed that the majority of subprime loans were going to people *who could have qualified for less expensive prime loans.* So, if the loans weren't defined by the borrowers' credit scores, what did subprime loans all have in common? They had higher interest rates and fees, meaning they were more profitable for the lender, and because we're talking about five- and six-figure mortgage debt, those higher rates meant massively higher debt burdens for the borrower.

If you sell someone a prime-rate, 5 percent annual percentage rate (APR) thirty-year mortgage in the amount of $200,000, they'll pay you back an additional $186,512—93 percent of what they borrowed—for the privilege of spreading payments out over thirty years. If you can manage to sell that same person a subprime loan with a 9 percent interest rate, you can collect $379,328 on top of the $200,000 repayment, nearly twice over what they borrowed. The public policy justification for allowing subprime loans was that they made the American Dream of homeownership possible for people who did not meet the credit standards to get a cheaper prime mortgage. But the subprime loans we started to see in the early 2000s were primarily marketed to existing homeowners, not people looking to buy—and they usually left the borrower worse off than before the loan. Instead of getting striving people into homeownership, the loans often wound up pushing existing homeowners out. The refinance loans stripped homeowners of equity they had built up over years of mortgage payments. That's why these diseased loans were tested first on the segment of Americans least respected by the financial sector and least protected by lawmakers: black and brown families.

In the latter half of the 1990s, the share of mortgages that were subprime nearly doubled. By 2000, half of the refinance loans issued in majority-black neighborhoods were subprime. Between 2004 and 2008, black and Latinx homeowners with good credit scores were three times as likely as whites with similar credit scores to have higher-rate mortgages. A 2014 review of the pre-crash mortgage market in seven metropolitan areas found that when controlling for credit score, loan-to-value, debt-to-income ratios, and other risk factors, black and Latinx homeowners were 103 percent and 78 percent, respectively, more likely to receive high-cost mortgages.

**AT THE CLOSING**, Janice saw that her interest rate was high, but the sales rep reassured her. "She told me . . . that I could come back in and we could lower the interest rate once I had paid on it for a certain amount of time. [I]t was like a perk for me; the interest rate will be lower. So, I thought, 'Well, this is good. It sounds like she's doing everything on my behalf.'"

Then there was the God part. Janice's sweet voice grew an edge as she said, "She had figured me out." Janice had told the broker that they were looking to refinance in order to free up money to pay for their children's Christian schooling. "And so, she talked about her Christian faith, which resonated with me. I remember the crosses that she had in the office."

The sales rep had touched Janice's hand and told her, "I know that God must have sent you to us. We're here for you."

Janice shook her head at the memory of "this person who is talking about God . . . and is trying to show me that she's giving me probably the best deal that I can get . . .

"I wasn't taught to doubt people who presented themselves as God-fearing people. So, I didn't doubt." She and Isaiah signed the paperwork.

Soon after, the address the Tomlins sent their monthly payments to began to change, frequently—the loans were being repeatedly sold—but, Janice says, "we were just trucking along and making the payments." It wasn't until Isaiah had a chance encounter with a local attorney that the Tomlins learned just how predatory their refinance loan was. That lawyer, Mallard "Mal" Maynard, was helping Isaiah recover a stolen tractor when Isaiah mentioned his refinance loan. (Unlike his wife, Isaiah had never had a good feeling about the salesperson or Chase.) Maynard asked if they still had the paperwork, and Janice did. "Of course I do," she'd told her husband. "I'm a schoolteacher. I keep papers."

Mal Maynard had joined our conversation on the porch. "I got copies of his paperwork and it just blew me away," he told me.

"What blew you away about it, Mal?" I asked. "It wasn't the monthly payment, right, because it sounds like the monthly payment was reasonable."

"It was the equity stripping. It was the yield-spread premiums. It was the origination fee. It was the duplicative fees. They had lots of duplicative fees with words that really made no sense as to what they were for." Chase had even charged the Tomlins a discount fee, which is what a borrower might pay a broker to get a lower rate than they qualify for—which was absurd, given that the Tomlins' rate was *higher* than they qualified for.

"But Mal, they weren't the only ones, right?"

"Oh, no. That was just the tip of the iceberg when I ran into Janice and Isaiah. Started looking at the Registered Deeds Office and tracking down dozens and then hundreds of other similar loans," Maynard said. He pointed to Janice. "She's being modest. She was the lead plaintiff [for] thirteen hundred folks [whose homes] she helped save . . . who had gone through this same thing."

Overcoming their shame to be named plaintiffs in a class-action lawsuit wasn't easy for Janice and Isaiah. "In the courtroom . . . there would be someone to make a mockery of my ignorance. That was really hard to swallow," Janice admitted. "But I knew that, in the end, there would be others who would benefit from it."

As I listened to their story, my mind kept wandering back to what I'd seen early in my career, and to the millions of families who weren't so lucky. The way the Tomlins' story began—an American Dream deferred by segregation, white flight, a black neighborhood targeted by unscrupulous lenders, and the steering of responsible black homeowners into equity-stripping predatory mortgages— could have been cut and pasted from a report of hundreds of black middle-class neighborhoods across the country in that era. In the early 2000s, the economy had recovered quickly from the tech bubble and 9/11–related recession, housing prices seemed to know no limit, and financial sector profits were soaring. At Demos, when we did our first visit to Congress with copies of our research report on debt called *Borrowing to Make Ends Meet*, a Democratic senate staffer told us point-blank not to bother, that the banks "owned the place." We were laughed out of the offices of Republican members of Congress with our passé talk about regulation. The consensus to loosen the rules on Wall Street investment houses and consumer banks had become bipartisan during the Clinton administration, and the proof, it seemed, was in the profits. But through my job, I had a front-row seat to what was really driving it all, a tragedy playing out in black and brown communities that would later take center stage in the global economy.

I'll never forget a trip I took to the Mount Pleasant neighborhood in Cleveland, Ohio. On a leafy street, residents told me how, a few years back, house by house, each homeowner—over 90 percent of them black, with a few Latinx and South Asian immigrants—had opened an envelope, answered a knock on the door, or taken a call from someone with an offer to help consolidate their debt or lower their bills. In the ensuing years, with quiet shame and in loud public hearings—with supportive aldermen, pastors, and lawyers outmatched by the indifference of bankers and regulators with the power to help them—residents had fought to keep their homes. But by 2007, the block I was on had only two or three houses still in the hands of their rightful owners. I excused myself from the group and walked around the corner, barely getting out of their eyesight in time to fall to my knees, chest heaving. It was the weight of the history, the scale of the theft, and how powerless we had proven to change any of it. These were properties that meant everything to people whose ancestors—grandparents, in some cases—had been sold as property. To this day, it's hard for me to think about it without emotion.

That's why, as I looked at the Tomlins smiling at each other on their porch more than a decade later, it was like I'd slipped into the world as it could have been—as it *should* have been. With the relative rarity of a lightning strike—an available and dogged lawyer, a well-timed suit in a state with good consumer protections, and a particularly corrupt and inept defendant—the Tomlins had saved their home and protected more than a thousand other working- and middle-class homeowners in their state. Had more black families targeted by subprime lenders in those early years found the Tomlins' happy ending, history would have turned. The mortgage market would have learned its lesson about subprime mortgages earlier in the 2000s, and the worst excesses would have been checked before they spun out of control and toppled the entire economy, causing $19.2 trillion in lost household wealth and eight million lost jobs—and that was just in the United States. The earliest predatory mortgage lending victims, disproportionately black, were the canaries in the coal mine, but their warning went unheeded.

BEFORE THE CORONAVIRUS-DRIVEN downturn of 2020, the financial crisis of 2008 (and the ensuing Great Recession) was widely considered to be the single most traumatic event in the financial life of the nation since the Great Depression. Less commonly known is that we're beginning to understand how the tail effects may even eclipse those of the Depression in terms of lost wealth. In 2017, the country had four hundred thousand fewer homeowners than in 2006, although the population had grown by some eight million households since then. Homeownership rates reversed their historic pattern of steady increases, shrinking from 69 percent in 2004 to less than 64 percent in 2017. More than a decade after the crash, the typical family in their prime years has still not recovered the level of wealth held by people the same age in previous generations. Families headed by Millennials, who entered adulthood during the Great Recession, still have 34 percent less wealth than previous generations. They will likely never catch up.

The blast radius of foreclosures from the explosion on Wall Street was far-reaching and permanent. By means of comparison, in 2001, about 183,000 home foreclosures were reported across the nation. By 2008, a record 983,000. In 2010, a new record: more than 1,178,000. An accounting on the tenth anniversary of the crash showed 5.6 million foreclosed homes during the Great Recession. Although homeowners of color were represented out of proportion to their numbers in society, the majority of these foreclosed homes belonged to white people.

From lost homes, the losses cascaded out. Nearby houses lost value: some 95 million households near foreclosed homes lost an estimated $2.2 trillion in property value. Local communities brought in less tax revenue, which led to widely felt cuts in school funding, vital services, and public jobs. It was a contagion, and not just metaphorically. Even the dispossessed homes themselves spread sickness, as demolitions of vacant houses sent decades-dormant lead toxins as far as the wind would carry them; in Detroit, a surge in childhood lead poisoning would mark the decade after the recession. One study identified home foreclosures as the likely cause of a sharp rise in suicides during 2005–2010, while another found that the Great Recession triggered "declining fertility and self-rated health, and increasing morbidity, psychological distress, and suicide" in the United States. In 2017, an examination of all third through eighth graders in the United States revealed "significantly reduced student achievement in math and English language arts" linked to the Great Recession. Between December 2007 and early 2010, 8.7 million jobs were destroyed.

**AMY ROGERS IS** a white woman whose life has been forever changed because of the Great Recession. In 2001, she and her husband bought their first home, a three-bedroom house she describes as funky and long on character. She had her own savings and the money her late parents had left her ($50,000) to put into the purchase to keep their mortgage payments modest. By 2005, Amy had a great job for the first time in her life, one with a good salary and benefits, working for her county government. Then she discovered that without her knowledge, her husband had pulled all the equity out of the house and used it for his own purposes. Shocked, she began divorce proceedings. In 2007, the divorce became final, and Amy got the house refinanced in her own name. But she had to buy out her husband's debt to do so. "Having had the house for seven years," she said, "we owed more than we had paid. I took on $275,000 or so of debt."

As it turns out, the booming county Amy worked for was the

home of the city whose fortunes had risen with the rise of the financial sector in the 1990s and 2000s, nicknamed "Banktown." Charlotte, North Carolina, was the headquarters for large national banks that were growing by leaps and bounds in the lead-up to the crisis, including Bank of America and Wachovia. But the year after her divorce became final, all the construction of houses and office towers ground to a halt. The city began to cut back. By 2009, government employees like Amy were feeling it hard. "The first thing they did was reduce our benefits, and take away our holidays, and put us on furlough without pay. Then they gave us pay cuts. Then, after amputating us one limb at a time, I got fired."

She was able to get COBRA to extend her healthcare, but the monthly cost soared from a subsidized $80 to $779. Her mortgage payment, on a conventional thirty-year mortgage, stayed at $1,200 a month—manageable, but just barely, based on unemployment insurance, alimony, and the little bits of income she could pull together through freelance jobs.

As part of its belt-tightening, the local government reassessed properties and revalued Amy's $255,000 house at $414,000, which almost tripled her property taxes. Six months after she was laid off, Amy realized she wasn't going to be able to manage both her mortgage and her increased property taxes. Things were "starting to snowball," she said.

She called the owner of her mortgage, Wells Fargo, and told them that although she had not yet been late with a payment, her financial situation had changed and she wanted to sign up for one of the programs it offered to reduce borrowers' mortgage payments. "Then they start putting me through the wringer," Amy said.

Although she had no credit problems, Wells Fargo told her she needed to attend credit counseling. "Okay, fine, I go," Amy said. "I went to the 'Save Your Housing' fair. I went to the Housing Finance Agency. I went and did every single thing that was out there to do. Wells Fargo had me jumping through hoops for three years." The Obama administration had started a number of programs, she recalled, to enable people to extend the term of their mortgage or, in some cases, reduce the interest rate or even the principal. "I went for everything," Amy said. "And everywhere I went, they blocked me and said, 'You can't apply for this [program] if you're under consideration for that. You can't apply for that while you're under consideration for this. Oh, that program is over.' And it went around and around for months and months and months.

"The minute you go and you ask for help, even if you're not late [making your payments], your credit score drops one hundred points. So, what that meant was that my Exxon card that I'd had since 1984, [which] had six or seven hundred dollars on it for oil changes and tires—all of a sudden, they jack up the interest rate to thirty-five percent. I've never been late, but I'm now a 'high-risk borrower.'

"My unemployment's running out, and I'm selling jewelry to make the mortgage payments. And I realize they're going to take the house anyway." Amy put her home up for sale. "I owed altogether two hundred seventy-five thousand, and we brought them offers within ten thousand of that, and Wells Fargo turned every one of them down." The bank would not accept a sale price any less than the full amount owed, nor would they take possession of the house instead of foreclosing on it.

"I did everything I could to avoid foreclosure," said Amy, "knowing what that would do to my credit and my employability. So, [at this point,] I'm fifty-five years old. I'm doing piecemeal work everywhere and paying self-employment tax and COBRA and just going down in flames."

In 2013, Wells Fargo finally foreclosed on Amy Rogers. She was one of 679,923 Americans to experience foreclosure that year. But the shocks didn't end there. When her house went up for auction, Wells Fargo bought it—from itself—for $304,000. Why such a high price for a house that was selling for $275,000? "Because every time they sent me a letter from a lawyer or made a phone call, they billed me," Amy said. "They wanted to recoup all their costs to foreclose on me."

As the final step in the foreclosure process, "the sheriff in his big hat and his big car drives up to your house in broad, damn daylight, comes and knocks on your door and serves you with an eviction notice," said Amy. "That is a dark day."

She sold or gave away most of her belongings and moved into a small rental condo, where she lived until she had to move again in 2017. When Amy shared these details a year later, she said the rent on her new place was affordable, but the rundown neighborhood was gentrifying, so she feared the landlord would soon raise the rent. "I pay over ten thousand dollars a year in rent," she said. "I earn about twenty-four thousand."

"When they foreclosed on me for the house," said Amy, "they got [everything]. I got zero. They ruined my credit. And they ruined my employability, because any employer you go to work for now does a credit check on you. I couldn't get a job for ten dollars an hour in Costco. I tried.

"I paid into that house for thirteen years. I've worked every day of my life since I'm seventeen years old. And now, today, I'm sixty-three years old, I'm unemployable, I work three part-time jobs, and I'm praying I can last long enough to get Medicare so I'll have some health coverage."

Every part of Amy's story was one that I knew well from my research and advocacy at Demos, from the jacked-up credit card rate, to the insufficient foreclosure prevention programs (I lobbied staff at the U.S. Treasury Department to improve them), to the job discrimination against people with weak credit (we wrote a bill banning the practice). Not a single part of her story surprised me, but it moved me still. I was grateful that she'd been willing to share her story with me, knowing it would be made public. There's so much shame involved in being in debt. In my experience with the bankers on the other end, however, shame is hard to find, even over their discriminatory and deceptive practices. Amy sighed. "I've kept it under wraps for ten years," she said, "too afraid of the way the world would perceive me."

"If I could leave anybody who's gone through this with one message," she said, "it is this: Do not say, 'I lost my house.' You did not lose your house. It was taken away from you."

The people who took Amy's house could do so with impunity in 2013 only because they had been doing it to homeowners of color for over a decade already, and had built the practices, corporate cultures, and legal and regulatory loopholes to enable that plunder back when few people cared. Subprime mortgages and the attitude of lender irresponsibility they fomented would, we now know, later spread throughout the housing market. But to truly understand where the crisis began, we have to go back earlier than the 1990s, to the reason it was so easy for lenders to target homeowners of color in the first place.

**THE EXCLUSION OF** free people of color from the mainstream American economy began as soon as black people emerged from slavery after the Civil War. Black people were essentially prohibited from using white financial institutions, so Congress created a separate and thoroughly unequal Freedman's Bank, managed (and ultimately mismanaged into failure) by white trustees. In the century that followed, the pattern of legally enforced exclusion continued in every segment of society, from finance to education to employment to housing. In fact, the New Deal era of the early 1930s—a period of tremendous expansion of government action to help Americans achieve financial security—was also a period in which the federal government cemented residential segregation through both practice and regulation.

"We think of the New Deal and all the great things that came out of it—and there were many—but what we don't talk about nearly as often is the extent to which those great things were structured in ways that made sure people of color didn't have access to them," said Debby Goldberg, a vice president of the National Fair Housing Alliance. I worked closely with the advocates at NFHA back in the early 2000s. Debby is an advocate who spends her days fighting the latest attempts to roll back commitments to fair housing, and she has an encyclopedic knowledge of the history of American homeownership, and the housing policies that had paved the way for the subprime mortgage crisis.

In 1933, during the Great Depression, the U.S. government created the Home Owners' Loan Corporation. Debby explained, "Its role was to buy up mortgages that were in foreclosure and refinance them, and put people back on their feet. It did a huge amount of that activity—billions of dollars' [worth] within a short period of time in the thirties."

Perhaps this agency's most lasting contribution was the creation of residential security maps, which used different colors to designate the level of supposed investment risk in individual neighborhoods. A primary criterion for defining a neighborhood's risk was the race of its residents, with people of color considered the riskiest. These neighborhoods were identified by red shading to warn lenders not to invest there—the birth of redlining. (A typical assessment reads: "The neighborhood is graded 'D' because of its concentration of negroes, but the section may improve to a third class area as this element is forced out.")

The redlining maps were subsequently used by the Federal Housing Administration, created in 1934. In its early years, Goldberg explained, the FHA subsidized the purchase of housing "in a way that made it very easy for working-class white people, who had previously been renters and may never have had any expectation of becoming a homeowner, to move to the suburbs and become a homeowner because it was often cheaper than renting. Both the structure and the interest rate of the mortgage made it possible for people to do that with very little savings and relatively low income.

"But the FHA would not make or guarantee mortgages for borrowers of color," she said. "It would guarantee mortgages for developers who were building subdivisions, but only on the condition that they include deed restrictions preventing any of those homes from being sold to people of color. Here we have this structure that facilitated . . . white homeownership, and therefore the creation of white wealth at a heretofore unprecedented scale—and [that] explicitly prevented people of color from having those same benefits. To a very large degree, this was the genesis of the incredible racial wealth gap we have today." In 2016, the most recent available authoritative data, the typical white family in America had about $171,000 in wealth, mostly from homeownership—that's about ten times that of black families ($17,600) and eight times that of Latinx families ($20,700). That kind of wealth is self-perpetuating. I thought of Amy, who on a modest income had still been able to afford a house with a low monthly payment largely because of $50,000 from her parents.

Learning this history was crucial to me in my early days at Demos. In order to help craft new laws to change the world we inhabited, I needed to understand how government decisions had shaped it. I underwent a steady process of unlearning some of the myths about progressive victories like the New Deal and the GI Bill, achievements that I understood to have built the great American middle class. The government agencies most responsible for the vast increase in home ownership—from about 40 percent of Americans in 1920 to about 62 percent in 1960—were also responsible for the exclusion of people of color from this life-changing economic opportunity. Of all the African Americans in the United States during the decades between 1930 and 1960, fewer than 2 percent were able to get a home loan from the Veterans Administration or the Federal Housing Authority.

The civil rights movement brought changes to housing laws, but lending practices changed more slowly. For instance, although the Fair Housing Act of 1968 outlawed racially discriminatory practices by banks, it would take another twenty-four years for the Federal Reserve System, the central bank of the United States, to monitor and (spottily) enforce the law.

It is little wonder, then, that a fringe lending market flourished to offer credit and reap profits from people of color who were excluded from the mainstream financial system. These included rent-to-own contracts for household appliances and furniture and houses bought on contract. These contracts enabled black people to buy on the installment plan—and lose everything if they missed a single pay-ment. Unlike a conventional mortgage, land contracts did not allow buyers to build equity; indeed, they owned nothing until the final payment was made. And because the loans were unregulated, ped-dlers of these early forms of subprime mortgages could charge what-ever exorbitant rates they chose. My great-grandmother bought the apartment building where I was born on a predatory contract.

In the 1970s, residents of redlined neighborhoods—including, actually, some white working-class as well as African American and Latinx activists—banded together to demand access to credit and economic investment in their communities. These local groups were backed and coordinated by community organizing networks such as the Chicago-based National People's Action and by national organi-zations that ranged from the National Urban League to the Catholic Church.

As a result of this activism, Congress passed reforms to the dis-criminatory lending market in the 1970s, finally giving residents tools to combat redlining. One reform was the 1975 Home Mortgage Disclosure Act (HMDA), which required financial institutions to make public the number and size of mortgages and home loans they made in each zip code or census tract, so that patterns of discrimina-tion could be easily identified. Another was the 1977 Community Reinvestment Act (CRA), which required financial institutions to make investments in any community from which they received de-posits. (For example, a 1974 survey of federally insured Chicago-area banks revealed that in several communities of color, for each dollar residents deposited in local banks, the community received only one penny in loans.)

The CRA enabled community and civil rights groups to monitor whether banks were fulfilling their obligations—and to challenge the banks when they fell short. In 1978, two of the earliest formal complaints against banks that failed to meet their CRA obligations resulted in a total of more than $20 million in home loans for low-income residents of Brooklyn, as well as the St. Louis area, where financial institutions admitted they had been making loans in only one neighborhood—a neighborhood that was all white. But 1978 also saw an ominous sign of a coming wave of deregulation when a Supreme Court decision interpreted the National Bank Act to mean if a lender was in one of the few states without any limits on interest rates, it could lend without limits nationwide, effectively invalidating thirty-seven states' consumer protections—and Congress declined to amend the law. That's why, today, most of your credit card statements come from South Dakota and Delaware, states with lax lending laws.

By the mid-1990s, the financial sector had become the component of the economy that produced the most profits, supplanting manufacturing. The financial sector also became the biggest spender in politics, contributing more than one hundred million dollars per election cycle since 1990 to federal candidates and political parties, on both sides of the aisle. Translating unprecedented profits into unprecedented influence netted the industry carte blanche with legislators and regulators, who were often eyeing lucrative jobs as lobbyists or banking consultants after their tours of duty in government service. The deregulatory revolution in financial services was also spurred by antigovernment, pro-market libertarian and neoliberal economic thinking that gained a popular common sense, particularly among white people, with rising distrust of an activist government.

By the end of the 1990s, a bipartisan majority voted to repeal most of Glass-Steagall, the law that had protected consumer deposits from risky investing for decades since the Great Depression. Free of restraints, the financial sector grew wildly and with few rules.

This growth included an explosion of mortgage brokers and non-bank holding companies like those that pursued the Tomlins, many of which were not subject to the CRA and were unregulated and unaccountable to anything but the bottom line. Most important, there was no single regulator whose primary responsibility was to protect consumers; the four federal banking regulators' primary purpose was to ensure that banks were doing well—which put the profit machine of subprime directly at odds with the regulators' secondary consumer protection responsibilities.

The upshot for the lending market was the unchecked growth of loans and financial products that were predatory in nature, meaning they benefited the lender even when they often created a net negative financial situation for the borrower, imposed harsh credit terms out of proportion to the risk the lender took on, and used deception to hide the reality of the credit terms from the borrower. And this formula was tried and tested on black homeowners.

Doris Dancy became a witness in a federal fair lending lawsuit based on what she saw as a credit manager for Wells Fargo in Memphis during the boom. "My job was to find as many potential borrowers for Wells Fargo as possible. We were put under a lot of pressure to call these individuals repeatedly and encourage them to come into the office to apply for a loan. Most—eighty percent or more—of the leads on the lists I was given were African American." The leads came from lists of Wells Fargo customers who had credit cards, car loans, or home equity loans with the company.

"We were supposed to try and refinance these individuals into new, expensive subprime loans with high interest rates and lots of fees and costs," Dancy explained. "The way we were told to sell these loans was to explain that we were eliminating the customer's old debts by consolidating their existing debts into one new one. This was not really true—we were not getting rid of the customer's existing debts; we were actually just giving them a new, more expensive loan that put their house at risk.

"Our district manager pressured the credit managers in my office to convince our leads to apply for a loan, even if we knew they could not afford the loan or did not qualify for the loan. . . . I know that Wells Fargo violated its own underwriting guidelines in order to make loans to these customers.

"Many of the mostly African American customers who came into the offices were not experienced in applying for loans. . . . Our district manager told us to conceal the details of the loan. He thought that these customers could be 'talked into anything.' The way he pressured us to do all of these unethical things was as aggressive as a wolf. There was no compassion for these individuals who came to us trusting our advice."

Mario Taylor, another Wells Fargo credit manager in Memphis, explained how the bank applied pressure to its almost entirely African American prospects. "We were instructed to make as many as thirty-five calls an hour and to call the same borrower multiple times each day," he said. "Some branch managers told us how to mislead borrowers. For example, we were told to make 'teaser rate' loans without informing the borrower that the loan was adjustable. . . . Some managers . . . changed pay stubs and used Wite-Out on documents to alter the borrower's income so it would look like the customer qualified for the loan. Borrowers were not told about prepayment penalties [or] . . . about astronomical fees that were added to the loan and that Wells Fargo profited from."

A common misperception then and now is that subprime loans were being sought out by financially irresponsible borrowers with bad credit, so the lenders were simply appropriately pricing the loans higher to offset the risk of default. And in fact, subprime loans were more likely to end up in default. If a black homeowner finally answered Mario Taylor's dozenth call and ended it possessing a mortgage that would turn out to be twice as expensive as the prime one he started with, is it any wonder that it would quickly become unaffordable? This is where the age-old stereotypes equating black people with risk—an association explicitly drawn in red ink around America's black neighborhoods for most of the twentieth century—obscured the plain and simple truth: what was risky wasn't the borrower; it was the *loan*.

Camille Thomas, a loan processor, testified that "many of these customers could have qualified for less expensive or prime loans, but because Wells Fargo Financial only made subprime loans, managers had a financial incentive to put borrowers into subprime loans with high interest rates and fees even when they qualified for better-priced loans."

The bank's incentives to cheat its customers were rich. Elizabeth

Jacobson, a loan officer from 1998 to 2007, explained the incentive system. "My pay was based on commissions and fees I got from making [subprime] loans. . . . In 2004, I grossed more than seven hundred thousand in sales commissions," nearly one million in 2020 dollars. "The commission and referral system at Wells Fargo was set up in a way that made it more profitable for a loan officer to refer a prime customer for a subprime loan than make the prime loan directly to the customer." Underwriters also made more money from a subprime than a prime loan.

Looking at these numbers, one could be tempted to minimize the role of racism and chalk it up to greed instead. I'm sure that most of the people involved in the industry would claim not to have a racist bone in their body—in fact, I heard those exact words from representatives of lending companies in the aftermath of the crash. But history might counter: What is racism without greed? It operates on multiple levels. Individual racism, whether conscious or unconscious, gives greedy people the moral permission to exploit others in ways they never would with people with whom they empathized. Institutional racism of the kind that kept the management ranks of lenders and regulators mostly white furthered this social distance. And then structural racism both made it easy to prey on people of color due to segregation and eliminated the accountability when disparate impacts went unheeded. Lenders, brokers, and investors targeted people of color because they thought they could get away with it. Because of racism, they could.

Loan officer Tony Paschal was one of the few African American employees in his section at Wells Fargo in Virginia. "Wells Fargo's managers were almost entirely white, and there was little to no opportunity for advancement for minorities," he testified. "Wells Fargo also discriminated against minority loan applicants by advising them that the interest rate on their loan was 'locked,' when in fact, Wells Fargo had the ability to lower the interest rate for the applicant if the market rates dropped prior to the loan closing," and, he said, the bank often made this adjustment for white applicants.

"I also heard employees [of the Mortgage Resource division] on several occasions mimic and make fun of their minority customers by using racial slurs. They referred to subprime loans made in minority communities as 'ghetto loans' and minority customers as . . . 'mud people.' " In addition, he said, his branch manager used the N-word in the office—not in 1955, but in 2005.

Testimonies of Wells Fargo's corruption abound, but that bank was far from alone in its exploitation of black and brown people through the aggressive marketing of subprime mortgage loans. As one of many examples, Countrywide Financial Corporation agreed in 2011 to pay $335 million to settle claims that it overcharged more than two hundred thousand black and Latinx borrowers for their loans, and steered some ten thousand borrowers of color into risky subprime loans instead of the safer and cheaper conventional loans for which they qualified. According to an analysis conducted by the U.S. Department of Justice of 2.5 million mortgage loans made from 2004 to 2008 by Countrywide, black customers were at least twice as likely as similarly qualified whites to be steered into subprime loans; in some markets, they were eight times more likely to get a subprime loan than white borrowers with similar financial histories.

So much profit and so little accountability. The country's most ubiquitous bank, Bank of America, bought the infamous Countrywide in June 2008. AmeriQuest, BancorpSouth, Citigroup, Washington Mutual, and many other banks and financial companies contributed to a wave of foreclosures that shrank the wealth of the median African American family by more than half between 2005 and 2009 and of the median Latino family by more than two-thirds.

THERE WAS A TIME—years, in fact—when the epidemic of home foreclosures could have been stopped. Bank regulators and federal policy makers were well aware of what was happening in communities of color, but despite pleas from local officials and community groups, they did nothing to stop the new lenders and their new tactics that left so many families without a home. Between 1992 and 2008, state officials took more than nine thousand legal, regulatory, and policy

actions to try to stop the predatory mortgage lenders that were devastating their communities and their tax bases. But Washington
wouldn't listen. The Federal Reserve—"the one entity with the authority to regulate risky lending practices by all mortgage lenders"—
took no action at all, and the Office of the Comptroller of the
Currency, the regulator in charge of national bank practices, took
one action: preemption, to make sure that no state's consumer protections applied to its national banks.

In the virtually all-white realm of federal bank regulators and
legislators, there was a blindness in those early years. Lisa Donner is
a slight woman whose speech is peppered with almost involuntary
little laughs, which I decided, after years of working in the consumer
protection trenches with her, was a defense mechanism, a release
valve for the pressure of having seen all the injustice she's seen. She
got her start organizing working-class New Yorkers of color around
affordable housing and foreclosure prevention with the Association
of Community Organizations for Reform Now (ACORN) thirty years
ago. She's now the executive director of Americans for Financial Reform, the David founded in the wake of the crash to take on Wall
Street's lobbying Goliath and create a new regulatory structure to
prevent a crash from happening again. Lisa has sat across the table
from more financial regulators and bankers than probably anyone
else in the country. I got in touch with her to reminisce about what it
was like in the early days of the subprime phenomenon, when families like the Tomlins were being targeted by the block.

The regulators were "just refusing to see that there was a problem at all," Lisa said with one of her little laughs. "Because it wasn't
their neighbors or their neighborhood or people who looked like
them, or people they knew, in the elite decision-making circles."

I have many such memories, but I'll never forget a meeting with
a young blond Senate banking committee staffer in 2003. After hearing our research presentation, she said with a sad little shake of her
head, "the problem was we put these people into houses when we
shouldn't have."

I marveled at the inversion of agency in her phrasing. Who was the "we"? Not the hardworking strivers who had finally gotten their fingers around the American Dream despite every barrier and obstacle. No, the "we" was well-intentioned people in government—undoubtedly white, in her mental map. Never mind that most of the predatory loans we were talking about weren't intended to help people purchase homes, but rather, were draining equity from existing homeowners. From 1998 to 2006, the majority of subprime mortgages created were for refinancing, and less than 10 percent were for first-time homebuyers. It was still a typical refrain, redolent of long-standing stereotypes about people of color being unable to handle money—a tidy justification for denying them ways to obtain it.

Lisa Donner understood the work that race was doing in shifting blame for irresponsible lending and deception onto the borrower. "Race was a part of weaponizing the 'It's the borrower's fault' language," she said to me.

Conservative pundit Ann Coulter asserted it clearly, in capital letters, in the headline of one of her nationally syndicated columns: THEY GAVE YOUR MORTGAGE TO A LESS QUALIFIED MINORITY. Another conservative columnist, Jeff Jacoby, wrote, "What does it mean when Boston banks start making many more loans to minorities? Most likely, that they are knowingly approving risky loans in order to get the feds and the activists off their backs." By 2008, Jacoby was declaring the financial crisis "a no-win situation entirely of the government's making." When asked during the market panic on September 17 about the root causes of the crisis, billionaire and then New York City mayor Michael Bloomberg told a Georgetown University audience that the end of redlining was to blame. "It probably all started back when there was a lot of pressure on banks to make loans to *everyone*. . . . Redlining, if you remember, was the term where banks took whole neighborhoods and said, 'People in these neighborhoods are poor; they're not going to be able to pay off their mortgages. Tell your salesmen don't go into those areas,'" Bloomberg said.

"And then Congress got involved—local elected officials, as

well—and said, 'Oh that's not fair; these people should be able to get credit.' And once you started pushing in that direction, banks started making more and more loans where the credit of the person buying the house wasn't as good as you would like." A man who'd made his fortune in financial information did not know that the mortgages at the root of the crisis were usually refinances, not home purchases, and that creditworthiness was often beside the point. But he knew enough of the elite conventional wisdom to blame the victims of redlining.

The public conversation and the media coverage of the subprime mortgage crisis started out racialized and stayed that way. We've had so much practice justifying racial inequality with well-worn stereotypes that the narrative about this entirely new kind of financial havoc immediately slipped into that groove. Even when the extent of the industry's recklessness and lack of government oversight was clear, the racialized story was there, offering to turn the predators themselves into victims. After the crash, conservatives were quick to blame the meltdown on people of color and on the government for being too solicitous of them. Ronald Utt of the Heritage Foundation claimed that "some portion of the problem—perhaps a significant portion—may stem from 'predatory borrowing,' defined as a transaction in which the borrower convinces the lender to lend too much." With this banker-as-victim tale, the casting was familiar: undeserving and criminal people of color aided and abetted by an untrustworthy government. A conservative member of the U.S. Financial Crisis Inquiry Commission (FCIC), Peter Wallison, wrote a vitriolic dissent of the commission's conclusion that the crisis was the result of insufficient regulation of the financial system. Calling that conclusion a "fallacious idea," he claimed that "the crisis was caused by the government's housing policies," specifically a set of policies called "Affordable Housing Goals." Banks, he said, "became the scapegoat." And so many pundits blamed the Community Reinvestment Act for the financial crisis that the FCIC had to devote pages of its report to refuting the CRA's role conclusively.

Jim Rokakis was the treasurer of Cuyahoga County, Ohio, from

1997 to 2011 and saw all the devastation. In 2006, he went to his U.S. Attorney's office having amassed boxes of evidence he hoped would lead to a RICO conspiracy case about widespread mortgage industry fraud in the mostly black and immigrant neighborhoods in and around Cleveland. In a room of men in suits from the FBI and other government agencies, Rokakis was sure that his impressive display of charts and graphs, foreclosure data maps, and transcripts was spelling out a slam-dunk case for prosecuting a man named Roland Arnall. Arnall was one of President George W. Bush's top donors (whom Bush had nominated as ambassador to the Netherlands in 2006)—and the CEO of the country's biggest subprime lender at the time, AmeriQuest, and its subsidiary Argent Mortgage. But the racialized story was blinding to the government agents; they just couldn't see that the wealthy and well-connected white man was the criminal.

"At one point, one of the U.S. attorneys . . . turned and said, 'Well, who's the victim?' And I lost it. I said, 'You're the victim! We're all the victims! Don't you get it? I'm here because Argent did this! I'm here because Roland Arnall and his minions have gutted Cleveland!'" Unable to see those with power as sufficiently blameworthy, the federal prosecutors declined to pursue Rokakis's case. He told me that county prosecutors did end up using his data to prosecute lower-level people. "But it was too late. Had they gotten to this early, and gotten to the foundation of this tree, Arnall and his executives, that tree would have withered and died."

Lisa Donner saw how blame-shifting to borrowers of color was so effective after the crash that it stopped the Obama administration from mounting a full-throated campaign to save black wealth. "People who knew better let that language"—*it was the borrowers' fault; they took out loans they couldn't afford*—"control the politics of the response," she recalled. "A whole bunch of Obama administration folks let that incredibly racialized story and their fear of the story—even if they didn't believe the story themselves—give us the recovery that we got. Which was one that increased inequality and economic vulnerability."

The Obama administration staff wasn't wrong about the perils of white public opinion and its political implications. In a study conducted in President Obama's final year in office, researchers simply switching the race of a man posing in front of a home with a Foreclosure sign from white to black made Trump-supporting whites angrier about government mortgage assistance programs and more likely to blame individuals for their situation.

But back in the early 2000s, when I was digging through the data and immersing myself in the stories of loss, at first I didn't understand how the lenders were getting away with it, mostly escaping unharmed while making loans that were designed to fail. Why was the system not self-correcting, when the loans so quickly became unaffordable for people and ended up in foreclosure? Then I discovered that the secret was mortgage *securitization*: lenders were selling mortgages to investment banks who bundled them and sold shares in them to investors, creating mortgage-backed securities. Instead of mortgage originations being driven by how much cash from deposits banks had to lend, now the driver was the virtually limitless demand from Wall Street for new investments. Unscrupulous financial companies could sell predatory mortgages they knew would sink the homeowner, package up those mortgages, and sell them to banks or Wall Street firms, which would then sell them to investors who could then resell them to still other investors—each of the sellers collecting fees and interest and then passing on the risk to the next buyer. Wall Street brokers even came up with a lighthearted acronym to describe this kind of hot-potato investment scheme: IBGYBG, for "I'll be gone, you'll be gone." If someone gets burned, it won't be us.

Securitization cut the tie of mutual interest between the lender and the borrower. Before securitization, however reluctant lenders had been to offer mortgages to people of color, once the loan was made, both parties had a vested interest in making sure it was properly serviced and repaid. Now that connection had been severed. The homeowner's loss could be the investor's gain.

Such financial malfeasance was allowed to flourish because the people who were its first victims didn't matter nearly as much as the profits their pain generated. But the systems set up to exploit one part of our society rarely stay contained. Once the financial industry and regulators were able to let racist stereotypes and indifference justify massive profits from demonstrably unfair and risky practices, the brakes were off for good. The rest of the mortgage market, with its far more numerous white borrowers, was there for the taking. Having learned how profitable variable rates and payments could be by testing them out on borrowers of color in the 1990s, lenders created a new version for the broader market. These were adjustable-rate mortgages called "option ARMs."

Jim Vitarello, formerly of the U.S. Government Accountability Office, described option ARMs as "the rich man's subprime loans." A significant proportion of these, he said, went to white middle-class people. The average FICO credit score of borrowers who got option ARM mortgages was 700, which made them eligible for prime loans. (More than half of the $2.5 trillion in subprime loans made between 2000 and 2007 also went to buyers who qualified for safer, cheaper prime loans.)

What made option ARMs so appealing to this clientele was the choice. Debby Goldberg explained: "With an option ARM, you could pick what you wanted your monthly payment to be based on. Was it going to be enough to pay off your whole mortgage? Or was it going to be only the interest? Or was it going to be not even the interest? In that case, you had a loan that was negatively amortizing—you were building up more and more debt, because you weren't even paying the full interest on the loan that you had on your home." These whiter, higher-wealth option ARM borrowers were coming in at the peak of a housing boom and could see only the upside. But borrowers could choose their payments for only so long, a couple of months to a couple of years, before the lender reset the terms so that borrowers had to pay off the full amount of the loan during the remaining years of the mortgage. "And you'd have a huge increase in your monthly payment," Goldberg explained, "because you'd go from not even paying the full amount of interest that you owed to paying a higher principal balance . . . plus all the interest." That gamble worked only if the housing prices kept climbing.

By 2006, up to 80 percent of option ARM borrowers chose to make only the minimum monthly payments. Housing values began to stall and slide in some areas, and immediately, more than 20 percent of these borrowers owed more than their house was worth. The option ARMs were ticking time bombs now nestled alongside other kinds of trap-laden mortgages buried in securities owned by pension funds and mutual funds across the globe. And it wasn't just homeowners who were dangerously leveraged; the Federal Reserve had loosened the requirements on the five biggest investment banks, so they had been investing in securities based on debt with borrowed money thirty and forty times what they could pay back. In late 2007, when interest rates rose and housing prices started falling, the mortgage market at the center of the economy began to crumble. Wall Street firms that had bet heavily on the IBGYBG formula knew better than to trust the other investment houses that had done the same, and suddenly the market froze. By the time the housing market reached bottom, housing prices would fall by over 30 percent and all five of the major investment houses would either go bankrupt or be absorbed in a fire sale.

With the banks and the houses went the jobs. In the recession that followed, "people were losing their jobs or having their hours cut back," Goldberg recalled. "In that situation, you had mortgages that were perfectly safe and [that,] in ordinary circumstances, should have been sustainable, but people just couldn't afford them anymore because they had lost income. And they couldn't sell their home because home values were going down all across the country." It was a vicious circle. This third wave of the financial disaster crested in 2008–2009, the period generally designated as the Great Recession, but the devastation that wave created continues even now.

———

**THE WAVE SWEPT** over Susan Parrish, a white woman living in Vancouver, Washington, and changed her life in ways she couldn't have imagined. In 2011, Susan was fifty-one years old, recently divorced, and living in the three-story house where she and her ex-husband had raised their three children. She worked as the communications manager of a nonprofit organization. "My ex-husband was a teacher, so between us we were making close to one hundred thousand dollars a year," Susan said. "We were both working full time. We were doing okay."

Then she got laid off from her job. The recession had already eaten away at her organization; several staff members had been laid off in 2009 and a few more shortly before Susan was let go.

"I started looking for other work right away," Susan recalled. To tide her over, she applied for unemployment insurance. "I had never filed for unemployment in my life. It was an all-new thing for me. . . . I had to go in and sit in these classes with people from all walks of life. It was just sobering to see how many people were out of work at that time."

The classes were about how to write a résumé and conduct a job interview—things Susan had thought she was good at. "But in the years since, that's proven to be untrue," she said. "I haven't been able to secure a job that pays anywhere near what I made."

Immediately after she got laid off, Susan realized she wouldn't have the money to make the next house payment. She knew she had to sell the house—and she also knew how difficult that would be, given that she and her ex-husband had tried to sell it both before and after their divorce.

"Thankfully," she said, "I was able to sell it, but I only made seventeen hundred dollars, which was just enough to pay first month's rent and a deposit on a six-hundred-square-foot, one-bedroom apartment in a not-great part of town. It was all I could afford." And she couldn't afford it for long.

"I was unemployed for three and a half months. [Finally,] I was hired as a news clerk, and it was about twenty thousand less than I

had been making. I took it because I didn't see any other prospects."
Six months later, she was promoted to the role of education reporter.
"It was good, but it was still not a living wage, and I couldn't afford
to rent an apartment now, because housing was so expensive."

"I moved five times in five years," Susan said, "three times in
three months. I spent three months living in a backyard shed/artist
studio with no heat or running water or toilet or kitchen, because I
had to save money to get my car fixed. That was hard, but I was glad
I had the chance to live cheap so I could afford to get my car fixed."

Susan was by all measures middle class—a college degree, a
white-collar journalism job—but the Great Recession had pushed
her to the brink of homelessness. "I've tried not to be bitter," she
said. She could not find a place to live that she could afford. "After I
lived in that backyard shed, my retired minister and his wife offered
me their mother-in-law suite at below-market prices," she said. She
lived there for four years, becoming part of their family.

At almost sixty, Susan had a life very different from the one she
imagined before the recession. She lived with her partner in an RV—
323 square feet in size—on a ranch he owned. Ten years after the
recession, she was still freelancing and looking for full-time work.

SUSAN'S STORY OF cascading loss and downward mobility has been
replicated millions of times across the American landscape due to the
financial industry's actions in the 2000s. While the country's GDP
and employment numbers rebounded before the pandemic struck
another blow, the damage at the household level has been permanent. Of families who lost their houses through dire events such as
job loss or foreclosure, over two-thirds will probably never own a
home again. Because of our globally interconnected economy, the
Great Recession altered lives in every country in the world.

And all of it was preventable, if only we had paid attention earlier
to the financial fires burning through black and brown communities
across the nation. Instead, the predatory practices were allowed to

continue until the disaster had engulfed white communities, too—and only then, far too late, was it recognized as an emergency. There is no question that the financial crisis hurt people of color first and worst. And yet the majority of the people it damaged were white. This is the dynamic we've seen over and over again throughout our country's history, from the drained public pools, to the shuttered public schools, to the overgrown yards of vacant homes.

Being among the outmatched and unheeded few who tried to prevent the catastrophe that would become the Great Recession was an experience that would forever shape my understanding of the world. I saw how money can obscure even the most obvious of truths. I learned that in order to exploit others for your own gain, you have to first sever the tie between yourself and them in your mind—and racist stereotypes are an ever-ready tool for such a task. But when I watched the CNN ticker tape announce the fall of Lehman Brothers on September 15, 2008, I was struck by an even deeper truth: ultimately, it's impossible to sever the tie completely. Wall Street had recruited the brightest technological minds—those who a generation ago would have been putting a man on the moon or inventing vaccines—to engineer a way to completely insulate wealthy people and institutions from the pain inflicted by their profits. Ultimately, they failed, and so did one of the oldest and most successful financial firms in U.S. history, setting off a financial contagion we still feel today.

It wasn't until years later that my research would reveal just how literally the country's original economic sin was connected to the financial crisis of 2008. The first mortgages and collateralized debt instruments in the United States weren't on houses, but on enslaved people, including the debt instruments that led to the speculative bubble in the slave trade of the 1820s. And the biggest bankruptcy in American history, in 2008, was the final chapter of a story that began in 1845 with the brothers Lehman, slave owners who opened a store to supply slave plantations near Montgomery, Alabama. The brothers were Confederate Army volunteers who grew their wealth profiteering during the Civil War, subverting the cotton blockade, buying cotton at a depressed price in the Confederacy and selling it overseas at a premium. They first appeared on what would become Wall Street by commodifying the slave crop, cofounding the New York Cotton Exchange. Although the company would later diversify its business beyond the exploited labor of African Americans, like so much of American wealth, Lehman Brothers would not have existed without it.

One hundred fifty years later, a product created out of a synthesis of racism and greed yet again promised Lehman Brothers unprecedented profits, and delivered, for a short while: heavy investments in securitized toxic loans brought it the highest returns in its history from 2005 to 2007. Even as defaults on mortgages began to skyrocket across the country, the company's leadership held on to the idea that it could endlessly gain from others' loss. Lehman's CFO asserted boldly on a March 2007 investor conference call that rising mortgage defaults wouldn't spread beyond the subprime customers, and the market believed him. So many wealthy—and yes, white—people assumed that the pain could be contained on one side of the imaginary human divide and transmuted into ever-higher profits on their side. During the same summer that I stood in the middle of the street with a foreclosure map that exposed the devastation behind almost every black-owned door, Lehman would go on to underwrite more mortgage-backed securities than any other firm in America.

By the end of the next summer the illusion had been broken. In a free fall that began on a weekend in mid-September, Lehman Brothers would go on to lose 93 percent of its stock value. A company born out of a system that treated black people as property died from self-inflicted wounds in the course of destroying the property of black people. Lehman's fate provides no justice for the enslaved people whose misery the company enabled in the nineteenth century, nor for the dispossessed homeowners ruined by Lehman-owned mortgages in the twenty-first century, but it is a reminder that a society can be run as a zero-sum game for only so long.

———

**BACK ON CREECY** Avenue with the Tomlins, I felt like I was glimpsing not only an alternate past in which more borrowers had their just resolution, but maybe an alternate society in which more people had their values.

I was asking Janice and Isaiah about the court case when the lawyer Mal Maynard jumped in. "I gotta throw in my two cents here. Of course, Janice is one of my all-time heroes. One of the greatest days I've ever had in court was in Winston-Salem in . . . the North Carolina Business Court, which is always a bad [place] for consumer cases. There was a judge who was really famous for being very, very hard on the class actions, especially when they were filed by consumers."

After Janice took the stand, the skeptical judge asked her, basically, why she was there—why she was willing to swear an oath to represent the interests of over a thousand people she didn't know.

Janice continued in her own words: "I just remember telling [the judge] that every morning when I walked into my classroom before we started our day, I taught my second-graders to place their hands on their hearts and quietly say the Pledge of Allegiance.

"And I had taught them that when you give allegiance to something, you say that 'I honor this' and that 'I have faith in it.' And I knew that if I taught that to my children, that I best be living by it myself."

Maynard continued: "And from that moment forward, she transformed Judge Tennille. She really did. He believed in us, and he believed in our case from that point forward. There was still a lot of hard-fought litigation, but he knew, and Janice convinced him, that this was really legitimate, heartfelt work that was being done by her and by the lawyers in the case."

A far-off look in Janice's eyes made me wonder what else had been guiding her that day. Finally she said, "My daddy used to say, 'Drop a little good in the hole before you go.' That sticks with me. I was just trying to be a good citizen. And I was just letting that judge know that I had no other reason to come here. . . . Because some-body's name had to be there. Did I want it to be our names? No, I did not."

Maynard and the Tomlins' suit for deceptive, unfair, and excessive fees and breach of fiduciary duty to the borrower prevailed in 2000, with a settlement of about $10 million. "So, borrowers all over North Carolina got checks, thanks to Janice and Isaiah," Maynard said with pride.

Janice allowed a small smile. "That's a lot of people being served. You know? It was more than worth our names being in the newspaper. We should have been so very embarrassed at the end of that, but I wasn't, because I felt like I had put a little good in the hole."

## Chapter 5

# NO ONE
# FIGHTS
# ALONE

On August 4, 2017, a group of workers at a Nissan auto factory in Canton, Mississippi, held a historic vote about whether they should join the United Auto Workers (UAW), a move that would bring their wages, job security, and benefits closer to those of the unionized factories in the Midwest. Pro-union activists had spent ten years organizing and campaigning, but in the end, their side failed by a margin of five hundred votes.

When I first read about this—autoworkers voting against unionizing—it struck me as a "man bites dog" story. I grew up in the Midwest, where driving a foreign car was seen as low treason, where the people who built American cars had the best jobs around, and where everybody knew that this was because the Big Three (GM, Chrysler, and Ford) had to negotiate with workers through the United Auto Workers. News coverage about the Nissan "no" vote referenced racial divisions in the plant, and I felt I had to learn more about what had happened. I flew into Medgar Evers Airport in Jackson, Mississippi, and drove up I-55 until I saw the bright white Nissan water tower come up on the horizon. The plant itself soon came into view. Not many windows, set back from the highway, it extended for four miles of road.

After circling the plant, I continued driving a few miles more to the worker center, where I was to meet Sanchioni Butler, the UAW organizer. The worker center was in a storefront in a strip mall that held vacant stores and a health clinic. When I walked in, I told a man sitting at the front desk that I had an appointment with Sanchioni, and he asked me to have a seat. In the lobby was a coffee machine, a small fridge, and a dozen chairs around the walls, half-full with workers from the plant: four black men, two black women, and one white man, standard-issue Styrofoam coffee cups in most hands. They were all post-shift, leaning back heavily in their folding chairs—though, as we talked, their voices regained the energy their bodies had given up for the day. Most were wearing black T-shirts with REMEMBER on the front and a list on the back: INJURED COWORK-ERS, FROZEN PENSIONS, INEQUALITY FOR PATHWAYS WORKERS, REDUCED HEALTHCARE, WORKERS FIRED WITHOUT CAUSE, along with a name, DERRICK WHITING—a man who had collapsed on the plant floor and later died. Some wore a similar shirt with a positive message: WE DESERVE: A NEGOTIATED PENSION, FAIRNESS FOR PATHWAYS, A SAFER PLANT, BETTER HEALTHCARE PLANS, UNION REPRESENTATION. One woman's shirt had a pair of clasped hands and the words NO ONE FIGHTS ALONE emblazoned across the back.

I introduced myself. Melvin, a black man with a quick smile, an obvious charmer, rose to shake my hand first and adjusted the chairs so that I could sit in the middle of everyone. Earl was the oldest of the bunch, with gray in his mustache and a sharp crease in his pants that set his attire apart from the work pants and jeans around the room. Rhonda was the youngest-looking person in the room, wearing a gray-and-black camouflage hat with an American flag on it. The daughter of a union worker, she had kind eyes and a dimple that ap-peared with her tight-lipped smile. Johnny was a tall white man in a cutoff shirt with a sleeve of tattoos and a contrary attitude. (When I asked him what he did at the plant, he said wryly, "It's the same job. I've been doing the same job for fourteen years.")

Over the course of the first morning I spent in the worker center, half a dozen more people would come through and join the conversation. Almost all were black men and women, a few white guys, and, I noticed, no white women. The name "Chip" came up a couple of times, and I jotted it down: a white guy who had caved to pressure in the final weeks and, they said, switched sides. Talking to the group about what problems they hoped a union would solve, I heard about their having to pay thousands of dollars in deductibles before their health coverage kicked in. I heard about the frozen pensions for those who had been with Nissan in the beginning, when benefits were more generous, and the insecure 401(k) for everybody else. I heard stories of women eight months pregnant being denied light duty and forced to lift fifty-pound parts. I heard, in a level of detail I wish I could forget, about the way an assembly line part can tear off a finger, yanking it away and taking the tendon with it, up and out, all the way up to the elbow.

**IT WAS JARRING** to hear auto plant jobs described this way, as everybody knows that manufacturing jobs are the iconic "good jobs" of the American middle class. But the truth is factory jobs used to be terrible jobs, with low pay and dangerous conditions, until the people who needed those jobs to survive banded together, often overcoming violent oppression, to demand wholesale change to entire industries: textiles, meatpacking, steel, automobiles. The early-twentieth-century fights to make good jobs out of dangerous ones—the fights, in fact, to create the American middle class—could never have been waged alone. Desperate for work and easily exploited, workers had power only in numbers. One worker could ask for a raise and be shown the door, behind which dozens of people were lined up to take his place. But what remade American work in the industrial era was the fact that companies didn't face individual pleas for improvement; they faced mass work stoppages, slowdowns, armed protests, and strikes that forced employers to the bargaining table. The result was jobs with better pay, benefits, and safety practices and upward mobility for generations of Americans to come. These victories were possible only when people recognized their common struggles and linked arms.

And linking arms for those workers usually meant forming a union. The first time I heard the word *union*, it was from my father's best friend, Jim Dyson, a man I called "Uncle Jimmy." Uncle Jimmy was a union man in my neighborhood on the South Side of Chicago, and he wore the power of that backing like a wool coat in winter. He exuded pride in his work. His family had things that I knew, even as a child, were prized—vacations to the dunes in Wisconsin every year, braces for his daughter when the dentist said she needed them, a good-sized house that we all gathered in to watch football on Sundays. I remember once being in the back seat of my dad's car and watching Uncle Jimmy through the open window, in a neighborhood not our own. He was standing on the street, joking and backslapping with a group of Polish- and Italian-accented men. I'd never seen that before. Later, I would put it together: Uncle Jimmy was in a union, the only place where men like that would know and trust one another in segregated Chicago.

**AT THE CANTON** worker center, the men and women had that same ease as they told me a shared story of the way the company kept workers apart and vying for positions at the plant. They spoke of a very clear, though informal, ranking of jobs at Nissan. First, there was a hierarchy of job status. On the top tier were the so-called "Legacy" workers, who started at Nissan when the company first came to Canton, making front-page news by offering a pay and benefits package that was generous by Mississippi standards. A few years later, the company contracted out those exact same jobs to subcontractors like Kelly Services, at about half the pay, a practice I still can't believe is legal. Kelly is a temporary employment agency, and Nissan classifies the jobs as such—but I spoke to workers who had been full-time "temps" for more than five years. These workers, earning about $12 an hour with no benefits, were on the bottom tier. In between the top and bottom tiers were workers on a program Nissan called "Pathway," where temp workers were put on a path to full-time status, though never at the Legacy level of pay and benefits. The result was that thousands of workers did the same job with the same skill, side by side on the line, but management kept the power to assign workers to different categories—meaning different pay, different benefits, different work rules.

Labor experts call this kind of stratification a tactic: create a sense of hierarchy and you motivate workers to compete with one another to please the bosses and get to the next category up, instead of fighting together to get rid of the categories and create a common, improved work environment for everyone. Though the company has been reluctant to publicly release exact numbers about its staffing, estimates put the number of non-employee "Pathway" and temporary workers at the plant as high as 40 percent. The non-employee workers were not allowed to cast a ballot in the union drive, which silenced the voice of the lowest-paid and most precarious workers. As Sanchioni Butler would later tell me, "I think that it's fair to say that if I'm working side by side with you, we're doing the same work. I think I should be paid the same for sure. . . . That's the cry of the two-tier Pathway person."

The workers also spoke of an invisible ladder of difficulty that stretched from the assembly line, where workers maneuvered parts at the relentless pace of machines, to the "offline" jobs—for instance, as pre-delivery inspectors (PDI) who walk around a finished car checking off items on a list. Earl wanted me to understand the difference between being on the line or offline: "Those PDI jobs are so cush, those folks can leave work and go straight to the happy hour—they don't even have to go home and shower. That's how you can tell how cush the job is." Everyone I spoke to—white, black, management, and production—admitted that the positions got whiter as the jobs got easier and better paid.

In the face of a possible cross-racial organizing drive, it seemed to be a company strategy to make white workers feel different from, better than, the black majority in the plant. Rhonda had been working in the physically demanding "trim" section for years. When I asked her about conversations with white workers in her section, she shrugged. "I don't have any white workers in my section."

After hearing the descriptions of the racial ranking when it came to the most physically taxing jobs, I had a hard time squaring that reality with one of the other things I heard repeated in my conversations with workers, particularly the antiunion white workers: that management said the black workers were lazy, and that's why they wanted a union. If they were so lazy, why were they doing all the hardest, most relentless and dangerous jobs, the ones that also happened to be the lowest-paying?

When I finally got in to see her, I asked Sanchioni Butler, the UAW organizer, about this contradiction. A black woman with a determined expression, Sanchioni was once a "regular hourly worker" in parts distribution at a unionized Ford plant in Memphis, Tennessee, but she signed up one day for a UAW class on organizing and got hooked. "I'm second-generation union," she told me with some pride. Knowing the difference that her father's good union job had made in her family, she moved deeper south to help factory workers organize in Georgia and then Canton, where she'd been for the whole Nissan campaign. She said the claim that the black workers were lazy was something she came up against all the time, and to deal with it, she would ask the person to compare that stereotype with what they saw at the plant: "I'll say, 'Okay, let's be real. You're working on the assembly line. You have to keep up with the line; it's constant, repetitive movement. How can you be lazy in a job like that?' And then they'll say, 'You know what, you're right.' But [I have to get] them to think about the seed that the company is dropping to divide these people."

**IN THE TWO-HUNDRED-YEAR** history of American industrial work, there's been no greater tool against collective bargaining than employers' ability to divide workers by gender, race, or origin, stoking suspicion and competition across groups. It's simple: if your boss can hire someone else for cheaper, or threaten to, you have less leverage for bargaining. In the nineteenth century, employers' ability to pay black workers a fraction of white wages made whites see free black people as threats to their livelihood. In the early twentieth century, new immigrants were added to this competitive dynamic, and the result was a zero sum: the boss made more profit; one group had new, worse work, and the other had none. In the war years, men would protest the employment of women. Competition across demographic groups was the defining characteristic of the American labor market, but the stratification only helped the employer. The solution for workers was to bargain collectively: to band together across divisions and demand improvements that lifted the floor for everyone.

America's first union that had the ambition to organize workers across the economy into collective bargaining—the only exclusions were the morally questionable categories of "bankers, land speculators, lawyers, liquor dealers and gamblers"—was the Knights of Labor. Their motto was "That is the most perfect government in which an injury to one is a concern of all." When the Knights began organizing in the volatile years of Reconstruction, they recruited across color lines, believing that to exclude any racial or ethnic group would be playing into the employers' hands. "Why should working men keep anyone out of the organization who could be used by the employer as a tool in grinding down wages?" wrote the official Knights newspaper in 1880. With black workers in the union, white workers gained by robbing the bosses of a population they might exploit to undercut wages or break strikes; at the same time, black workers gained by working for and benefiting from whatever gains the union won. The Knights also included women in their ranks. A journalist in 1886 Charleston, South Carolina, reported on the Knights' success in organizing members in that city: "When everything else had failed, the bond of poverty united the white and colored mechanics and laborers."

This cross-racial win-win was the elusive holy grail of worker organizing: everybody in, nobody undercutting the cause, all fighting for a prize that would be shared by all. It wasn't easy. When the Knights of Labor held its 1886 national convention in Richmond, Virginia, a New York branch agitated to integrate the facilities in town. The conflict grew so public that it cleaved opinion along racial lines, both within the order and among the watching public. In covering the convention, *The New York Times* concluded, "It is generally considered that the Order will never contain any considerable strength among the white population in the South." But the Knights stuck together. The union spread throughout the country during the 1880s, boasting seven hundred thousand members at its peak, including many southern chapters where an estimated one-third to one-half of its members were black. But its reign lasted only a decade as the 1890s saw the birth of Jim Crow, the end of black-white fusion politics under Reconstruction, and the promotion of white supremacy as a cultural and political force to unite whites across class. Meanwhile, employers held the line on worker demands and essentially militarized, funding standing militias and building local armories for National Guard troops increasingly deployed as strike breakers. An 1886 explosion in Chicago's Haymarket Square during a demonstration for shorter working hours created a public backlash against the violence increasingly accompanying labor unrest. By the late 1880s, the less radical and more discriminatory American Federation of Labor had replaced the Knights as the primary labor organization in the country.

The AFL allowed affiliates to exclude black workers, ensuring that the version of organized labor that grew in the early twentieth century had self-defeating prejudices in its DNA. In the 1920s, the leaders of the AFL endorsed eugenicist beliefs about southern and eastern European immigrants and supported racist anti-immigration policies. Exclusion of black workers was so prevalent in many AFL unions that whites in early unions saw black people as synonymous with strike breakers; because unions rejected black workers, employers routinely brought them in as substitute workers to cross picket lines.

Only when external pressures forced racial and gender integration on unions—labor shortages during World War II and the Great Migration of African Americans into the industrial Midwest put more women and people of color in factories—did the barriers begin to fall. A more radical faction of unions split off from the AFL to form the Congress of Industrial Organizations (CIO) in 1935, with an explicit commitment to interracial unity and to organizing entire industries regardless of "craft" or job title. As the great black historian W.E.B. Du Bois wrote in 1948,

> Probably the greatest and most effective effort toward interracial understanding among the working masses has come about through the trade unions. . . . As a result [of the organization of the CIO in 1935,] numbers of men like those in the steel and automotive industries have been thrown together, fellow workers striving for the same objects. There has been on this account an astonishing spread of racial tolerance and understanding. Probably no movement in the last 30 years has been so successful in softening race prejudice among the masses.

**IT WAS IN** these years of cross-racial organizing that unions experienced a Solidarity Dividend, with membership climbing to levels that let unions set wages across large sectors of the economy. More and more of the country's workforce joined a union on the job, with membership reaching a high-water mark of one out of every three workers in the 1950s. The victories these unions won reshaped work for us all. The forty-hour workweek, overtime pay, employer health insurance and retirement benefits, worker compensation—all these components of a "good job" came from collective bargaining and union advocacy with governments in the late 1930s and '40s. And the power to win these benefits came from solidarity—black, white, and brown, men and women, immigrant and native-born.

OF COURSE, THAT was then. It's hard to find a good union job today, and it's not because nonunion labor is so rich with benefits. Almost half of adult workers are classified as "low-wage," earning about $10 an hour, or $18,000 a year, on average. Less than half of private employers offer health insurance. Only 12 percent of private-sector workers have the guaranteed retirement income of a traditional pension. After the 1950s peak, the share of workers covered by a collectively bargained work contract has fallen every decade. Today, it's just one out of every sixteen private-sector workers. I was born at a time when the loss of union factory jobs on the South Side of Chicago was changing everything: families split up and moved, stores closed and schools cut programs, folks turned to illegal work, and neighbors stopped sitting on their porches after the streetlights came on. As factory unions weakened, it felt like everything else did, too.

So, as I sat and listened to the men and women at the Nissan worker center describe the future they had glimpsed, fought for, and lost, I knew that what they'd been struggling for could have made a difference in their lives and in the trajectory of inequality in America. The share of workers in a union has directly tracked the share of the country's income that goes to the middle class, and as union density has declined, the portion going to the richest Americans has increased in step. A worker under a union contract earns over 13 percent higher wages than a nonunionized worker with the same education, job, and experience. And it's not just the factory jobs. Even today's typically lower-paying service jobs can be made into good jobs by bargaining: In Houston in 2006, thousands of striking janitors won a union contract, a near-50 percent pay raise, health insurance, and an increase in guaranteed hours. In Las Vegas, hotel kitchen and hospitality workers joined a union and earned four dollars more per hour than the national median, and more benefits. In 2020, during the COVID-19 epidemic, thirty-six thousand casino and resort employees in Las Vegas, including those who had been furloughed, maintained their health benefits until March 2021, thanks to union bargaining. Interestingly, the benefit of unionization spreads beyond just the workers fortunate enough to be in the contract; having a higher standard in any industry forces employers to compete upward for labor. Economists have calculated that if unions were as common today as they were in 1979, weekly wages for men *not* in a union would be 5 percent higher; for noncollege-educated men, 8 percent higher. If that bump sounds small, compare that to the fact that, since 1979, wages for the typical hourly worker have increased only 0.3 percent a year. Meanwhile, pay for the richest 1 percent has risen by 190 percent.

This is not to say that unions are perfect. Like any human institution, a union can suffer from infighting, bureaucratic waste, pettiness, discrimination, and corruption. (And, in fact, leaders at the UAW and Fiat-Chrysler were accused of misusing corporate and union funds in the last few years.) Unions have been accused of being outdated, and the democratic rules do make it easy for them to prioritize the needs of current members (in most cases, older, whiter, more male members) over changing strategies to organize new workers. But forty years of declining union membership and rising inequality have proven that we still haven't figured out a better way to ensure that the people who spend all day baking the pie end up with a decent slice of it.

And so, the questions loom: If joining a union is such a demonstrable good, why are unions on the decline? Why would any worker hoping to better her lot in life oppose a union in a vote? People close to the issue usually offer two answers that have nothing to do with race: bare-knuckle antiunion tactics by corporations and job insecurity. Both have merit. Business did begin to organize in the early 1970s to influence politics and set a common strategy in a way it never had before. Business lobbies like the Chamber of Commerce, the National Association of Manufacturers, and the Financial Services Roundtable expanded and created political action committees to give targeted donations to candidates willing to press their antiunion agenda.

What broke labor? Many people will point to the PATCO air traffic controllers' strike of 1981, when Ronald Reagan shocked the country by firing more than eleven thousand striking controllers rather than negotiate. PATCO signaled to the private sector that it was "open season" on unions. It also came after Federal Reserve chairman Paul Volcker's aggressive efforts to combat high inflation had tightened credit and weakened the job market; years of high unemployment had diminished the bargaining power of unions to the point where the PATCO defeat was even possible.

But labor's breaking point came less suddenly than that single blow: over the course of the late 1970s, businesses had begun to freely flout the laws protecting workers' rights to organize, accepting fines and fees as a tolerable cost of doing business. Today, one in five unionizing drives results in charges that employers illegally fired workers for union activity, despite federal protections. It's illegal to threaten to close the workplace rather than be forced to bargain with your employees, but the majority of businesses facing union drives do it anyway. The Nissan employees attested that they heard those threats on constant repeat from the plant's TV screens and loudspeakers, and the National Labor Relations Board issued a complaint against Nissan about illegal tactics.

A backdrop of economic insecurity makes these tactics more powerful. A job—no matter what the pay or conditions—can seem better than the ever-present threat of no job at all. And it's true that labor's enemies were aided and abetted by new rules of global competition and technological change that made American jobs less secure. As large American companies began to automate and look to nations in the Global South for labor in the 1970s and '80s, the threat and reality of job losses proved powerful in forcing unions to make concessions and slow the pace of new organizing. The North American Free Trade Agreement (NAFTA) in 1994, the normalization of trade with China in 2000, and other trade policies supported by multinational corporations accelerated the decline of the most union-dense industries in the private sector, manufacturing. After 2001, the country lost 42,400 factories in just eight years. The United States doesn't build much anymore; in 2017, the total value of our exports was one of the lowest in the world.

**BUT OTHER COUNTRIES** have also faced globalization and automation and still maintained high rates of unionization. So, why did Americans allow their government and corporations to collude on attacking unions and depleting union membership? As it turns out, it wasn't all Americans. Somewhere along the line, white people stopped defending the institutions that, more than almost any other, had enabled their prosperity for generations. According to Gallup, public approval of unions was the highest in 1936, the year the question was first asked, and in 1959, but it began to trend downward in the mid-1960s. The era of declining support was one in which one of the country's most visible unions, the United Auto Workers, was staking its reputation on backing civil rights, supporting the March on Washington for Jobs and Freedom of 1963 and using its political clout to press the Democratic Party for civil rights. The unionized capital of American manufacturing, Detroit, had also become an epicenter of black cultural and economic power, and white people were abandoning the city for federally subsidized and racially exclusive suburbs.

White men began to leave the unionized working class as well. More and more white men moved into the professional and managerial ranks of big nonunion industries like financial services and technology, and the recession of the 1970s put the white working class on the ropes with years-long lockouts and high unemployment. Over time, a slightly higher share of black workers remained in unions than did white workers—today, membership is at 12.7 percent for black workers versus 11.5 for white, with Asian American and Latinx workers at around 10 percent. (That's because the public sector moved earlier and more successfully to integrate its workforce than the private sector, leading to a higher share of black workers in public service, where government neutrality in union drives has kept the antiunion attacks more at bay. Today, the public sector has a unionization rate more than five times higher than that in the private sector.)

Detroit reappeared in between the lines of the Gallup data I was studying when I noticed that the all-time-lowest approval of unions happened in August 2010. The country was still reeling from the financial crisis, and the Obama administration had just saved the domestic auto industry by extending federal loans (popularly seen as bailouts) to GM, Chrysler, and Ford. Resentment about the auto rescue drove support for unions down in 2010, but interestingly, white people—already slightly less favorable toward unions than people of color but, up to this point, still showing majority approval—had the most negative response to Obama's Detroit rescue. White approval of unions fell from 60 percent to just 45 percent in 2010.

Where was this new antiunion narrative among white people coming from? The right-wing media echo chamber made the auto rescue an explicit racial zero-sum story: to them, it was a racially redistributive socialist takeover. Rush Limbaugh would explain, "[Obama] doesn't see himself as a capitalist reformer saving a stupid automobile company. He sees this as his opportunity to take it away from the people who founded it and give it to the people he thinks have a moral right to it because somehow they have been taken advantage of, used, exploited, paid unfairly, what have you. Yeah, it's socialist." But more broadly, starting with Ronald Reagan and accelerating under Newt Gingrich's conservative takeover in 1996, the political party to which most white voters belong began to consider unions the enemy. When Wisconsin governor Scott Walker attacked the collective bargaining rights of public employees in 2011, the rhetoric about taxpayers paying for teachers' bloated benefits was redolent of the "welfare queen" charges.

When I was growing up in the Midwest, the union was a symbol of strength: the union could make or break politicians; the union had the backs of men like Uncle Jimmy; and the "union guys" in the city were the tough guys. The international union fight song, "Solidarity Forever," has "The union makes us strong" as its refrain. At Nissan in Canton, the antiunion forces won in part by turning the union into a sign of weakness, a refuge for the "lazy." Messages linked the union with degrading stereotypes about black people, so that white workers wouldn't want any part of it. Even black workers might think they were too good to "need" a union.

At the worker center, I asked Melvin about how unions are perceived where he lives. "The people that we see, as soon as they see UAW, and even if you bring up union, they just think color. They just see color. They think that unions, period—not just UAW—they just think unions, period, are for lazy black people. . . . And a lot of 'em, even though they want the union, their racism, that hatred is keeping them from joining."

Johnny agreed with Melvin's assessment of his fellow white workers. "They get their southern mentality. . . . 'I ain't votin' [yes] because the blacks are votin' for it. If the blacks are for it, I'm against it.'"

I looked around the office, which included posters from various UAW Nissan rallies invoking the civil rights movement and the March on Washington. I wondered how the explicit embrace of civil rights imagery and language had played with the white co-workers they were trying to organize. It seemed like a catch-22: the majority of the plant was black, and the base of the worker organizing needed to be, too—so, invoking black struggle made sense. But particularly in the South, white workers might not see anything for themselves in a campaign redolent of the civil rights movement; at worst, the association could trigger the zero-sum reaction.

The word *union* itself seemed to be a dog whistle in the South, code for undeserving people of color who needed a union to compensate for some flaw in their character. As the workers spoke, I realized that it couldn't be a coincidence that, to this day, the region that is the least unionized, with the lowest state minimum wages and the weakest labor protections overall, was the one that had been built on slave labor—on a system that compensated the labor of black people at exactly zero.

The leadership of the labor movement has long known that the South was its Achilles' heel. After World War II, the CIO launched an ambitious campaign to organize the South. It believed that the region's low wages and hostility to unions threatened labor's gains in the North and West and that the antilabor politics of the southern congressional delegation would continue to cripple national legislation for workers' rights. But the campaign unofficially known as Operation Dixie failed spectacularly, and racism did it in.

Given the reign of white supremacy in the South, the CIO faced a choice about which fights to take on: it could champion equal rights on the job in order to recruit black workers and change the consciousness of white workers, or it could accommodate Jim Crow and rely on white workers' class interest as a basis for organizing. A cadre of more progressive CIO organizers tried the former, organizing the union-enthusiastic black workers in integrated and majority-black industries like tobacco, lumber, and food processing. But the CIO leadership took a different tack: they bet on the segregated white textile industry and assiduously avoided any talk of social justice or equality. The CIO's southern organizing campaign director said that as far as he was concerned, "there was no Negro problem in the South." The white southern workers' hostility to what nonetheless felt like a northern incursion caught the CIO organizers by surprise. By the end, only about 4 percent of the region's textile workers had organized into a union, and the CIO unofficially admitted defeat.

The failure of Operation Dixie would shape American industry and society for generations, as the South's business owners would remain mostly unbothered by organizing among the region's multiracial working class, up until the present day. As a result, southern comfort with people working for nothing hasn't changed much in the past two hundred years. The five U.S. states that have no minimum-wage laws at all are in the South: Alabama, Louisiana, Mississippi, South Carolina, and Tennessee. Georgia has a minimum wage, but it is even lower than the federal one.

As unions succumbed to attacks in the 1980s, more employers felt free to relocate to places where workers didn't demand high wages—both overseas and in the U.S. South. After 2000, American factories began to shutter at a faster pace, but not all regions suffered equally.

The number of jobs in the industrial Midwest has never recovered, while at the same time, the number of jobs in the South grew by 13.5 percent. Japanese automakers Nissan and Toyota opened factories in the United States to step up competition with Detroit, but they planted them primarily in the nonunionized South. The foreign auto industry moved to the American South for the low wages, and once there, it drove worker pay down even further. From 2001 to 2013, the pay of workers at auto parts plants in Alabama dropped by 24 percent; in Mississippi, it was 13.6 percent. There just seemed to be no bottom, with wages for the same jobs in the same industry falling year after year. Southern states simply lacked any countervailing force, any way for workers to push back as a group against downward mobility. The later you were hired, the worse it got.

This low-wage southern labor model is no longer contained to the geographic South nor to manufacturing. (For the past two decades, the biggest driver of retail markets in the United States has been southern-based Walmart, the country's largest private employer by far. As Walmart expanded from Arkansas, it brought its fiercely low-wage and antiunion ethos with it—and local wages and benefits tumbled in its wake.) The wage difference between workers in the industrial Midwest and the South was nearly seven dollars an hour in 2008; three years later, wage cuts in the Midwest had slashed the regional difference in half. As journalist Harold Meyerson puts it, "the South today shares more features with its antebellum ancestor than it has in a very long time. Now as then[,] white Southern elites and their powerful allies among non-Southern business interests seek to expand to the rest of the nation the South's subjugation of workers." To a large degree, the story of the hollowing out of the American working class is a story of the southern economy, with its deep legacy of exploitative labor and divide-and-conquer tactics, going national.

**WHEN I WENT** back to my hotel after the first day of conversations with Nissan workers, I was dismayed and perplexed. I had assumed that white solidarity with black workers would be in the white workers' self-interest, but after listening to a day of stories about the ways that white workers were given special advantages at the plant, I wasn't so sure. Maybe the status quo—where being white actually did make it easier for you to get ahead, where a mostly white management could arbitrarily act to the benefit of those with whom they felt a kinship—was actually better for the average white worker than a union and its rules. I thought about Trent, a verbose pro-union white guy still working on the line, because, as he said proudly, he was too mouthy for white management to have promoted him to an easier job. But when describing his fellow white workers, he had said: "The unions are for putting people on equal ground. Some people see that as a threat to their society." As Earl had said, "Even the white guys on the line, they felt they would lose some power if we had a union. The view is, white people are in charge, I'm in charge."

I realized that I had been naive to think that the benefits of the union would be obvious to white workers. Having grown up in the Midwest, I knew that the Nissan plant workers were getting a bad deal compared to unionized autoworkers—lower pay, uncertain retirement, no job security, no way to bargain for better conditions at all. But the white workers in Canton were still getting, or had the promise of getting, a better deal than *someone*. The company was able to redraw the lines of allegiance—not worker to worker, but white to white—for the relatively low cost of a few perks. A white worker starting a job on the line would quickly learn the unwritten racial rules. He'd see that he could get promoted to a "cushier" job if he played his cards right, and that included not signing a union card. No matter that nobody on the plant floor, no matter how cushy their job, had a real pension or the right to bargain for improvements at the plant. They could be satisfied with a slightly better job that set them just above the black guys on the line, more satisfied by a taste of status than they were hungry for a real pension, better healthcare, or better wages for everyone.

I had traveled to Mississippi with a few books in my suitcase, and one of them was W.E.B. Du Bois's seminal 1935 work, *Black Reconstruction in America: 1860–1880*. I pulled it out and read again its most famous passage, which had never felt truer to me than it did that evening. Du Bois was describing the black and white southern workforce of the late nineteenth century:

> There probably are not today in the world two groups of workers with practically identical interests who hate and fear each other so deeply and persistently and who are kept so far apart that neither sees anything of common interest.
>
> It must be remembered that the white group of laborers, while they received a low wage, were compensated in part by a sort of public and psychological wage. They were given public deference and titles of courtesy because they were white. They were admitted freely with all classes of white people to public functions, public parks, and the best schools. The police were drawn from their ranks, and the courts, dependent on their votes, treated them with such leniency as to encourage lawlessness. Their vote selected public officials, and while this had small effect upon the economic situation, it had great effect upon their personal treatment and the deference shown them. White schoolhouses were the best in the community, and conspicuously placed, and they cost anywhere from twice to ten times as much per capita as the colored schools. The newspapers specialized on news that flattered the poor whites and almost utterly ignored the Negro except in crime and ridicule.
>
> On the other hand, in the same way, the Negro was subject to public insult; was afraid of mobs; was liable to the jibes of children and the unreasoning fears of white women; and was compelled almost continuously to submit to various badges of inferiority. The result of this was that the wages of both classes could be kept low, the whites fearing to be supplanted by Negro labor, the Negroes always being threatened by the substitution of white labor.

———

**THE WAGES OF** whiteness seemed to be good enough for a majority of the workers eligible to vote at the Nissan plant, a group that excluded the most precarious (and disproportionately black) temporary workers. As difficult as it was for me to put myself in the shoes of an anti-union white factory worker, in order to truly understand what had happened to the American working class, I had to try. Perhaps, when it comes down to it, I wrote in my notebook, the being matters more than the having. Often, what we have (a nice house, cash in the bank, a good car) is a simple way of telling ourselves and others who we are. Work and our rewards for it are the means; the end is, above a certain level of subsistence, our sense of self-esteem. So, perhaps to a white person facing this tradeoff, some tangible financial benefits are easy to give up if you already have what money buys in our society, which is belonging and status.

White people today, particularly outside the South, often distance themselves from slavery and Jim Crow by insisting that their immigrant ancestors had nothing to do with these atrocities and, in fact, themselves faced discrimination but were able to overcome it. (In fact, this popular belief is one of the core ideas contributing to white racial resentment against black people and newer immigrants of color.) But the Irish, Germans, Poles, Slavs, Russians, Italians, and other Europeans who came to the United States underwent a process of attaining whiteness, an identity created in contrast to the blackness of unfree and degraded labor. As immigrants, these groups had an opportunity to ally themselves with abolition and, later, equal rights and to fight for better social and economic conditions for all workers. They chose instead, with few exceptions, the wages of whiteness.

Irish immigrants present a clear example. Upon the first wave of immigration in the 1820s, the jobs and even neighborhoods the Irish had access to were full of black people, enslaved or just barely not. As ditch diggers in the expanding Deep South, domestic servants, dock workers, and livery drivers, the Irish were thrown into a labor pool where they worked shoulder to shoulder with black people. One of the most influential Irish nationalist leaders of the 1830s and '40s, Daniel O'Connell, was an abolitionist who railed against slavery and the exploitation of all workers; he saw that any society that treated some workers in that way would always abuse others.

But the zero-sum story proved too powerful. Every day, Irish immigrants heard from employers that they would hire either Irish or black workers for the most menial and labor-intensive jobs, whichever group they could pay the least. They heard the zero sum from Democratic Party leaders whose strategy was twofold: become the anti-black, pro-slavery foil to the Republicans and recruit Irish men as voters in large cities. Think about it: if you came to a country and saw the class of people in power abusing another group, and your place in relation to both groups was uncertain, wouldn't you want to align yourself with the powerful group, and wouldn't you be tempted to abuse the other to show your allegiance? As they fought to be considered more white than black, Irish people gained a reputation in black neighborhoods as brutal enforcers of the racial hierarchy, attacking those beneath them to ensure their place. "Irish attacks on blacks became so common in New York City that bricks were known as Irish confetti," wrote historian Michael Miller Topp. In the Civil War Draft Riots that took place in New York City over four days in July 1863, more than a thousand Irish immigrants in mobs attacked the black community, including children in an orphanage. They caused so much carnage and terror that the black population of New York decreased by 20 percent afterward. The logic of the massacre, as much as one can find logic in mass atrocity, was the zero sum: the Irish rioters didn't want to go fight in a war that might free millions of black workers to come north and compete for their jobs.

David Roediger, a history and African American studies professor at the University of Kansas, wrote the books *The Wages of Whiteness* and *Working Toward Whiteness: How America's Immigrants Became White*, which recount the process by which European immigrants were sold membership to the top category of the racial caste system. The price they paid was acquiescence to an economic caste system.

Immigrants who were able to attain whiteness got the voting rights (even before becoming citizens in many places, including New York City), jobs, and education that American citizenship offered. Even as they struggled with the exploitation of sweatshops and slums, becoming "white" afforded them a civic and social esteem that could constantly be compared against the black second-class citizens one rung below them.

Roediger uses the term "Herrenvolk republicanism" to describe American society as a representative democracy only for those considered, like Aryans under Nazism, to be part of the master race. In his words, "Herrenvolk republicanism had the advantage of reassuring whites in a society in which downward mobility was a constant fear—one might lose everything but not whiteness." In order to keep what Du Bois called a psychological wage, white workers needed not to contest too strongly for more material wages. To fight for a fairer system, the working class would have needed collective action, which has always been in tension with the pull of American racism.

**I WAS ON** the phone one afternoon with Robin DiAngelo, the white writer who coined the expression "white fragility," when she took a personal digression from the topic we were discussing. DiAngelo and her two sisters were raised in poverty by their single mom. "She was not able to feed, house, or clothe us," DiAngelo recalled. "I mean, we were flat out. We lived in our car. We were not bathed. My mother could not take care of us. And yet, anything I ever wanted to touch, like food someone left out—I was hungry, right?—I was reprimanded: 'Don't touch that. You don't know who touched it, it could have been a colored person.' 'Don't sit there. You don't know who sat there, it could have been a colored person.' That was the language—this was the sixties. The message was clear: If a colored person touched it, it would be dirty. But *I was dirty*. Yet in those moments, the shame of poverty was lifted. I wasn't poor anymore. I was white."

Robin's story called to mind a study coauthored by Michael Norton, one of the professors who identified the increasingly zero-sum mindset among white people. Norton and his colleagues would call the psychology behind DiAngelo's mother's warnings "last place aversion." In a hierarchical system like the American economy, people often show more concern about their relative position in the hierarchy than their absolute status. Norton and his colleagues used games where they gave participants the option to give money to either people who had more money than they had, or those who had less. In general, people gave money to those who had less—except for people who were in the second-to-last place in the money distribution to begin with. These players more often gave their money to the people above them in the distribution so that they wouldn't fall into last place themselves. The study authors also looked at real-world behaviors and found that lower-income people are less supportive of redistributive policies that would help them than logic would suggest. Even though raising the minimum wage is overwhelmingly popular, people who make a dollar above the current minimum "and thus those most likely to 'drop' into last place" alongside the workers at the bottom expressed less support. "Last-place aversion suggests that low-income individuals might oppose redistribution because they fear it might differentially help a last-place group to whom they can currently feel superior," the study authors wrote. That superior feeling, however, doesn't fill your stomach, as DiAngelo learned as a child.

**THE STORIES I** heard on the ground in Mississippi painted a picture of an economic pessimism that sapped the aspirations of most workers, white and black. The Nissan job was one of the best in the state, and the company threatened that, with a union, the plant would disappear. Workers heard this messaging 24/7 on video screens inside the plant, on leaflets (paid for by the Koch brothers) left in mailboxes at their homes, and in every statewide politician's talking points on the radio and local news. One of the most successful threats was that with a "yes" union vote, Nissan would repossess the company cars that many workers had leased. No matter that a union would have given workers a say in this and all other benefits; "the threat of your wife or Momma's car going missing was scary enough for some," Melvin told me with a sigh. I thought about how, in addition to the legacy of centuries of racist programming, white antiunion workers were also dealing with at least forty years of economic programming that told them that the best days for unions and for the middle class were behind them and that everyone was on their own to grab what they could from a dwindling pie.

On my last morning in Canton, I had breakfast in my hotel's lobby with Chip Wells, the man who'd become a controversial figure at the plant in the final weeks before the election. He had been an outspoken white voice on the pro-union organizing committee—so much so that he became the target of intimidation from antiunion people at the plant. He showed me a snapshot on his phone of his employee ID photo printed out as a poster in the security guards' room—someone had drawn a teardrop tattoo onto his left cheek and some kind of cross or swastika on his forehead. One of the people he worked alongside in the generally antiunion maintenance depart-ment (one of the better-paid departments) began to joke about Chip "gettin' hurt or fallin'." Eventually, Chip said he thought, " 'Maybe he ain't joking,' you know? 'Cause he's from Natchez, and that's where they actually had [slave] auction blocks and stuff."

The pressure eventually got to him, and at a rally one Sunday, Chip donned an antiunion shirt, signaling to the cheers of white workers around him that he had switched sides. Chip told me that during the time he was "anti," as they called it, he was struck by the zero-sum mindset of the people on his team. "The idea's that if you uplift black people, you're downin' white people. It's like the world has a crab-in-a-barrel mentality. Every time somebody's gettin' on top, we gotta pull them down 'cause they might try to do us wrong or keep us down."

White workers who supported the union, like Trent and Johnny, told me that their view was different from that of most of their white peers because they saw their interests as the same as those of the black workers. In their telling, everybody would benefit from better healthcare, plant safety, pay raises, job security, retirement benefits, and a fair system for promotions to replace what they call the "buddy buddy" system, where who you hunt with matters more than your work ethic. With the yes/no, black/white divide so stark, I wanted to know how a black pro-union worker would approach a white worker on the opposite side. Melvin broke it down for me.

"You find out what you have in common—that common ground. And whenever you're tired, and they're tired, it's the same. We bleed the same. We get tired the same. We sweat the same. When it's hot, you hot. You just find out that common ground. And that's how we reach the white workers. Some, you may not ever reach. Some, they look at me and they just look at you like you a nigger. No matter what.

"And this union organizing stuff, we have to be some of the most insane people. Because you take even the most racist, the most hateful people, and you're willin' to put your job on the line to fight for them, you understand? We have to be losin' our minds. So, it doesn't matter. The ones that hate you the most are the ones that you fight for the most. And you care about 'em the most. You keep 'em close to you. You keep 'em close to you. But this is how you deal with your white co-workers. They are people, too. Hey, look, they got kids, you got kids. Y'all just find that common ground."

When Melvin finished speaking, there were plenty of nods around the room at the worker center, but Earl was less confident that white folks wanted to share any kind of ground with him. "If we all have better pay and better benefits, maybe now I can buy a house in Deerfield," a white enclave in their area, he said, eyebrows arched.

"Maybe I would move in next to an Ole Miss law grad, and Saturday morning, when he comes out to get his paper, I'd be there watering my lawn. Maybe I'll be able to demand better education for our kids." Earl knew the exact amount by which the governor had cut the education budget in the most recent session, mentioning it multiple times. "The governor just cut five-point-three million dollars from the education budget. The union could have fought that in the statehouse."

The guys at the worker center wanted me to know that the problems didn't stop at the factory door. They felt that nobody had a long-term commitment to the state—not the company, not the politicians. They thought a lot about what would happen to the workers after their bodies inevitably wore down. "Folks will need disability, but the governor moves to cut that, make it harder to get on disability. That drives the whole state down," said Trent. They told me about the favors Nissan got in the statehouse, including hundreds of millions in tax breaks at a time when the state's schools are chronically under-funded. In order to appease the community, Nissan made donations in lieu of taxes to local schools, but the worker group saw that as a sham as well. "The company gets to decide where those voluntary school payments get made—and they end up directed to the districts where the upper management's kids go." Earl connected the dots: "You don't need someone to be educated if you want them to work menial jobs and feel lucky for doing it. It goes hand in hand with the goals of Nissan."

At the end of a long week in Mississippi, I boarded a small regional plane out of the state. As I sat looking over my notes, a grief I'd held at bay during all my conversations with those extraordinary everyday people grabbed at me. What they wanted for themselves, their children, and their community—what they wanted even for the people in the plant who despised them—was a little more say over the decisions that shaped their lives. And they'd been defeated, by a powerful, profitable corporation and the very old zero-sum story.

BUT THERE'S ANOTHER story woven through the history of worker struggle in America, of people refusing to fight alone and winning the Solidarity Dividend of better jobs, despite the odds. Over the past decade, that story gained a new chapter, written by some of the least likely, lowest-paid workers in our economy. The movement began on

November 29, 2012, when about two hundred fast-food workers rallied just outside Times Square, in the heart of Manhattan. They were hourly workers at the bottom of the pay scale, almost all brown and black, mostly young adults, often with children. They worked at Burger King, McDonald's, Subway, and Sbarro, but they had either walked off the job or not gone in at all in order to attend an unprecedented one-day strike across the city. They chanted slogans like "One-two-three-four, time for you to pay more! Five-six-seven-eight, don't you dare retaliate!" Without a union's protection, they could have been fired upon their return to work, but they gained courage in numbers. Their demand? A raise from the minimum wage of $7.25 an hour to $15 an hour and a union. It was audacious.

I'll count myself among the gobsmacked. My Demos colleagues and I had been pressing the case to raise the minimum wage for years, using research and advocacy to argue that a poverty wage that hadn't kept up with rising costs was contributing to economic inequality, rising debt, and bankruptcies. But the consensus advocacy goal had been a raise to $10.10, and even that modest an increase had gone precisely nowhere—little press attention, no big rallies, unsigned bills languishing in statehouses and congressional committees. Then, seemingly out of nowhere, a new, game-changing goal appeared that said to some of the country's poorest workers: "This could change your life."

Within a year, what would become the Fight for $15 had spread across the country. Everyday workers gained the courage to demand more with the organizing support of local antipoverty community organizers and the Service Employees International Union (SEIU). Many workers credited the 2011 Occupy Wall Street movement for raising their consciousness about the unfairness of working in poverty for profitable corporations. In fact, fast food was the most unequal industry in the economy; Demos research calculated an over one-thousand-to-one average CEO-to-worker pay gap.

Then, in November 2013, the impossible happened: a $15-an-hour victory, won by airport baggage handlers, jet fuelers, food vendors, and wheelchair attendants. These were subcontractors at the Seattle-

area Sea-Tac Airport, making around $9.70 an hour, a poverty wage
for the Seattle area. The diversity was wide-ranging—black Americans, white Americans, immigrants from Greece, Uzbekistan, Haiti,
Vietnam, Somalia, the Philippines, and elsewhere. While the non-
citizen/citizen divide could have been an opening for a divide-and-
conquer strategy, the organizers focused on training immigrants in
their rights and teaching them the broader story of income inequality in America, a story that was reinforced by the native-born workers. Veteran employees could recall when their airport service jobs
had been decent ones, just a decade before; but with sudden deregulation and subcontracting, almost overnight the pay and conditions
for the exact same work had plummeted. This sudden change—and
its clear origin in management decisions—made it easier for workers
to place the blame on the companies that abruptly changed the rules
to squeeze more profit, not on the new, immigrant workers. The multi-
hued group of activists, supported by the local SEIU and Seattle-area
community groups, won a ballot initiative in the airport town, Sea-
Tac, to raise airport worker wages to $15. The margin of victory was
just 77 votes.

Sensing momentum, however, the coalition of supporters made a
wild bet that they could win in an even bigger fight, in Seattle itself.
By that time, in the spring of 2013, Seattle fast-food workers of every
color were walking out in one-day strikes and organizing across the
city. By August 29, on a national day of action that coincided with the
fiftieth anniversary of the March on Washington, the streets of sixty
cities teemed with fast-food workers demanding higher wages. But
they weren't alone: retail workers from department stores like Ma-
cy's and chains like Victoria's Secret also joined in. A year later, the
demonstrations would include adjunct professors with graduate degrees. By May 2014, the Seattle City Council voted to make theirs the
first American city to raise its minimum wage to $15 an hour.

**TERRENCE WISE NEVER** thought that this would be his life at age forty.
It's not that he was surprised to be working in fast food: his mother

raised him on a Hardee's paycheck, so he grew up knowing that big chain restaurants offered hard but honest and always available work. Too many family bills to juggle caused Terrence to drop out of high school to work full time, and in the twenty years since, he'd barely seen a raise. Even though he worked so many hours that he was always missing his three daughters, he hadn't been able to avoid a spell of homelessness. All that, though depressing, seemed pretty much the norm in America. What Terrence never expected, though, was that he'd find himself in the leadership of a global movement, speaking at the White House and testifying before the U.S. Congress. Though he'd been an honors-track student and won awards for public speaking in high school, all that promise was far from his mind on the Sunday in 2012 when three people—two black, one white—walked into his Burger King and asked him to imagine more.

"It was a Domino's worker, McDonald's worker, and a Subway worker," Terrence recalled to me with a smile in his voice. The three workers asked him: Do you think fast-food workers should earn a living wage, vacation, and health benefits? "Well, I hadn't seen a doctor—at that point, it'd been years, over a decade—so, yeah," he recalls telling the workers. "We deserve the opportunity for benefits, paid time off, sick days, things that we don't have." They told him that they were organizing their fellow fast-food workers across the city. Terrence told them to count him in, and by the end of the day, he had signed up the six co-workers on his shift to join Stand Up KC (Kansas City), a group that would eventually join in the national Fight for $15.

Terrence got his first taste of collective action's power when he and his co-workers wrote up a petition and confronted the supervisor to demand simple safety improvements: stock up the first-aid kit, fix the broken wheels on the grease trap, replace the hoses that were leaking hot grease ("just simple things that we know billion-dollar corporations like McDonald's, Burger King, can afford")—and it worked. The first time he went out on a one-day walkout protest from his job at Burger King, he came back, and his boss gave him a dollar or so raise, when he had been refusing for years. "So, I've seen the power of coming together and organizing, and how it can make change. And I've definitely lived the life of when we were not organized . . . and how life just deteriorated over the years."

Part of what had kept the fast-food workers in Kansas City unorganized was a racial and cultural divide. Historically one of the country's most segregated cities along lines of black and white, Kansas City had also seen an increase in the Latino population in the late 1990s, after NAFTA. Workers of different cultures didn't communicate much; language was a barrier in some instances, and there were rumors that Latino managers were giving Latino workers higher pay and sick days. Getting workers out of the stores, into each other's homes, and sharing their stories helped dispel these myths. From the beginning, Stand Up KC named racism as a common enemy. Its first printed banner read: UNITED AGAINST RACISM—GOOD JOBS FOR ALL.

The message has resonated with Terrence. "We've got to build a multiracial movement, a different kind of social justice movement for the [twenty-first] century. And we've got to talk about it, multiracial organizing and how to build the movement, you know?

"We've got to have a new vision for America. We're building the Fight for $15 and a union movement, and we've got to have a new identity for the working class. What do we do every day in this country? All of us get up and go to work. We make this country run. And now, more than ever, workers are producing more wealth than we've received, you know? We're being exploited across the board," he told me over the phone, and I could just picture him bringing a crowd to its feet.

Many of the signs that workers carried in their Stand Up KC rallies and strikes made it clear that cross-racial solidarity was the point. RACIAL UNITY NOW: WE WON'T FIGHT EACH OTHER, read one sign. BLACK, WHITE, BROWN: WE FIGHT WAGE SLAVERY AND RACIAL DIVISION, read another. And another, BLACK, WHITE, BROWN: DEFEAT MCPOVERTY, DEFEAT HATE. I thought back to Canton; the UAW's message about race had invoked civil rights for black workers, but the fast-food message explicitly included white people in the coalition and named division, not just racial oppression, as a common enemy. That story helped transform the way Bridget Hughes saw the world.

Bridget is a white woman whose Irish ancestry shows up in her reddish hair and whose Missouri accent is slight but unmistakable to those who know how to listen for it. She has three children and has worked in fast food for over a decade. Like Terrence, she was an honors student with college potential, but she had to drop out to support her family when her mother got sick. When Bridget was first approached by a co-worker at Wendy's about joining Stand Up KC, she was skeptical, to say the least. "I didn't think that things in my life would ever change. They weren't going to give fifteen dollars to a fast-food worker—that was just insane to me." But she went to the first meeting anyway. When a Latinx woman rose and described her life—three children in a two-bedroom apartment with plumbing issues, the feeling of being "trapped in a life where she didn't have any opportunity to do anything better," Bridget was moved.

"I was really able to see myself in her. And at that point, I decided that the only way we was gonna fix it was if all of us came together. Whether we were white, brown, black. It didn't matter." For Bridget to see herself in a Latinx worker was a breakthrough. She admitted, "When I first joined the movement, I had been fed this whole line of 'These immigrant workers are coming over here and stealing our jobs . . . not paying taxes, committing crimes, and causing problems.' [It was] other white people in my family who believe these kind of racist ideas. You know, us against them." But she said she saw her bosses at Wendy's target Latinx workers, falsely promising them a raise if they didn't join the strikes. "They knew that if our Latino workers joined with our black and white workers, that we'd have our strength in numbers, and that we was gonna win."

Since joining Stand Up KC, Bridget's worldview has changed. "In order for all of us to come up, it's not a matter of me coming up and them staying down. It's the matter of, in order for me to come up, they have to come up, too—because we have to come up together. Because honestly, as long as we're divided, we're conquered. The only way that we're going to succeed is together." And they did succeed: Stand Up KC lobbied the city council to raise the local minimum wage to $13 an hour. (Almost immediately, the Republican state legislature passed a law forbidding any municipality from requiring a wage higher than the state's $7.70, a move that would be replicated by Republican legislatures across the country.)

As I got to know more of the workers and leaders in the Fight for $15, it became clear to me that they had thought through their racial analysis. In their protest signs, speeches, and demands, they weren't just talking about class issues while tacking on comments about racial pay disparities, they were explicitly saying that overcoming racism was crucial to their class-based goal. They understood that black workers would likely be their most dedicated base of organizers. Indeed, the Fight for $15's first two national days of action were set to commemorate anniversaries of the civil rights movement. And in the early days, many chapters cross-organized with Black Lives Matter activists, recognizing that the people who were active against police brutality were often working in fast food and retail by day.

The stakes of raising pay were explicitly racial in Birmingham, Alabama, in 2016. The mostly black city government dared to raise the minimum wage for work within the city limits to $10.10 to escape what city officials and activists called "the Jim Crow economy." In response, the mostly white state legislature quickly voted to block the pay raise from going into effect. The advocates sued, and a federal court sided with the city, finding that the white state legislature had acted with racial animus against the black city government. Birmingham wasn't wrong to say that making people work for so little that they can't meet their needs is redolent of the Jim Crow economic order: the twenty-one states that have kept their minimum wages at the lowest possible level ($7.25) have some of the largest African American populations in the country. Most people of color are operating in a poverty-wage economy; nationwide, the majority of African Americans and Latinos earn less than $15 an hour. But white people are still suffering from that same economy, and in great numbers. While only a third of white workers earn less than $15 an hour, they are still the majority of under-$15 workers, and thus will be the largest group to benefit from the organizing spearheaded by workers of color. This fight for decent pay has, like many labor struggles before it, exposed the fact that workers of color suffer the most acute economic injustices, but most of the people harmed in a wage structure built on racism are white. And like every truly successful labor movement, it has found its reach and its strength because of cross-racial solidarity.

What distinguished the autoworkers' organizing drive from the fast-food campaign? Both were explicit about the racial dynamics at play, both invoked the civil rights struggle, and both had black workers in leadership. But management's divide-and-conquer strategy did not work against the Fight for $15. When the movement first emerged, there were press reports and social media stories about usually white workers earning around $15 feeling that their work would be degraded if "burger flippers" earned just as much. Fast-food work, after all, is one of the lowest-status jobs in the economy. With the face of the fast-food worker in early press coverage being black, I remember worrying that age-old stereotypes about the low value of black work (and black life) would doom the audacious campaign. But this time would be different. The multiracial American working class had shouldered deindustrialization, deunionization, the financial crisis, and the squeeze of unaffordable housing and healthcare. At a time of record corporate profits, these service workers had become the driving force of the American economy, working underpaid jobs that couldn't be outsourced and that required human touch, voice, and judgment. Those fighting for $15 undoubtedly had less to lose—the Legacy Nissan workers who could vote made more than twice what fast-food workers were paid and, in a way, could "free-ride" on a wage floor lifted by decades of labor organizing in Detroit. But the campaign's strategies were also different. By inviting white workers to see how the powerful profited from selling them a racist story that cost everybody ("whether brown, black or white," as workers so often said), the Fight for $15 had managed to win the support of whites as well.

By almost every financial measure, the Fight for $15 has been a success, creating a Solidarity Dividend that reversed a trend of two generations of stagnant and declining wages for the lowest-paid workers. Many of the workers who rallied on that first day in 2012 near Times Square went on to testify at the New York State Capitol in 2016, when they won a statewide $15 minimum wage. So, too, did workers in states including California, Connecticut, Illinois, Maryland, Massachusetts, New Jersey, and Washington, D.C., as well as cities that include Flagstaff, Arizona; the Twin Cities; and Seattle, all of which have raised, or committed to raising, wages to $15 an hour. In addition to these policy wins, workers won private wage increases at giant employers including Walmart, Bank of America, McDonald's (which also announced it would stop lobbying against minimum wage increases), and Amazon. All this progress was won against the prevailing business and conservative argument that raising the minimum wage would hurt exactly the workers who went on strike across the country—and that raising it to something approaching a living wage would be catastrophic. Instead, the result has been $68 billion more in the pockets of 22 million low-paid workers. It turns out that more money in people's pockets is not just good for rich people when it comes to tax cuts—and that employers could have afforded it all along. There was no drop in employment in places with wage increases, and in fact, many places have found the opposite.

The more elusive goal for the Fight for $15 and a union has been the last part: the union. With high turnover and hundreds of shops per city, organizing workers restaurant by restaurant might take decades. The key to unionization of the thousands of franchises is for the law to recognize that umbrella corporations like McDonald's are joint employers with the franchise owners, as they set virtually all the terms of business. The SEIU made this case before the courts, the National Labor Relations Board agreed with them in 2015, and it looked like American fast-food workers were going to join their counterparts in many European countries in having a way to bargain for higher wages and benefits. But one of the first moves from the Trump administration was to reverse the Obama NLRB decision on franchise joint employment.

The majority of workers in American fast food come from the same white, working-class pool of voters who went overwhelmingly for Trump, a man whose campaign was dominated by promises to fight for the (white) working class and punish immigrants. When I spoke with her after the 2016 election, Bridget connected Trump's election to the urgency of Stand Up KC's cross-racial organizing: "Kind of the whole point of this movement is for white workers to understand that racism affects white workers as well. Because it keeps us divided from our black and our brown brothers and sisters. So, we need to understand that as white workers, we, too, need to stand up and fight against racism."

**AS I WAS** wrapping up my last visit to the worker center in Canton, Mississippi, I took the time to walk around the space. An unadorned storefront had been transformed with posters, printed and hand-drawn; photos from rallies; and pictures of workers' kids. People came in for coffee and company after their overnight shifts ended at dawn, and they'd come in before work to gear up for the long shift ahead. I recalled something Chip had said that morning as I got ready to leave our breakfast. First, he wanted me to know that despite his visible defection in the last weeks, he'd stayed true when the time came: "I got in that booth, and it was very liberating to vote yes." Second, even though he was afraid he wouldn't be welcome anymore at the worker center, he needed me to know about the solidarity he felt there. "I felt a sense of belonging, of love, of togetherness, friendship," he said, with emotion in his voice. "We went through a lot together, and did a lot together, and accomplished a lot. . . . I loved it. I loved goin' over there. . . . It was, I guess, utopia without havin' utopia."

## Chapter 6

# NEVER
# A REAL
# DEMOCRACY

I got into public policy out of concern for what was happening in American economic life, but I learned to look further upstream to what was wrong with our democracy when I joined Demos, an organization whose name means "the people of a nation." It's the root word of *democracy*. Working alongside voting rights lawyers and experts on campaign finance rules, I learned how our democracy is even less equal than our economy—and the two inequalities are mutually reinforcing. When I think about the nice things we just can't seem to have in America, a functioning, representative democracy is probably the most consequential.

**"I BELIEVE IF** you can't have your fundamental right of voting, what do you have? You don't have nothin'." These words could have been spoken by a black person during the march from Selma to Montgomery for voting rights in 1965, but they were spoken in 2017 by Larry Harmon, a middle-aged white Ohioan. A Navy veteran and software engineer, Larry has a round face, a salt-and-pepper beard, and eyebrows that are quick to flight when he's incredulous about something—which he was often as Demos and the ACLU represented him in a case that went all the way to the U.S. Supreme Court. It was a case that aimed to strike down a process that had imperiled Larry's right to vote, a right he'd be the first to admit that he, unlike his black fellow citizens, never thought he'd have to fight for.

Democracy is a secular religion in America; faith in it unites us. Even when we are critical of our politics, we wouldn't trade our form of government for any other, and we have even gone to war to defend it from competition with rival systems. Yet our sacred system allows a Larry Harmon to lose his opportunity for self-governance as easily as one lets a postcard fall in with the grocery circulars and wind up in the trash.

The truth is, we have never had a real democracy in America. The framers of the Constitution broke with a European tradition of monarchy and aspired to a revolutionary vision of self-governance, yet they compromised their own ideals from the start. Since then, in the interest of racial subjugation, America has repeatedly attacked its own foundations. From voter suppression to the return of a virtual property requirement in a big donor-dominated campaign finance system, a segment of our society has fought against democracy in order to keep power in the hands of a narrow white elite, often with the support of most white Americans.

A recent study by political scientist Larry M. Bartels found that Republicans who score high in what he calls "ethnic antagonism"—who are worried about a perceived loss of political and cultural power for white people in the United States—are much more likely to espouse antidemocratic, authoritarian ideas such as "The traditional American way of life is disappearing so fast that we may have to use force to save it," and "Strong leaders sometimes have to bend the rules to get things done." Three out of four Republicans agreed that "it is hard to trust the results of elections when so many people will vote for anyone who offers a handout," a stunning opinion reflecting the way that decades of anti-immigrant, anti-poor, anti-black, and antigovernment political messaging can tip over into an antipathy toward democracy itself at a time of demographic change.

Then again, the antidemocratic concept of minority rule—and rule by only the wealthiest of white men, in fact—was the original design of American government, despite any stated "self-evident truths" about equality to suggest the contrary. When the Constitution was ratified, the majority of white men were excluded from participating in this vaunted new system of representation, given that every one of the original thirteen states limited the franchise to men wealthy enough to own property. I've found it's easier to understand the sorry state of today's elections if one starts by unlearning the grade school narrative of the framers' commitment to equality and democracy and recognize that the framers left holes in the bedrock of our democracy from the outset, in order to leave room for slavery.

The South won the Three-fifths Compromise in the Constitution, giving southern states added power in Congress based on a fraction of the nonvoting population of black people and diminishing the legislative power of white people in free states. Possibly the most consequential of the founding racist distortions in our democracy was the creation of the Electoral College in lieu of direct election of the president. James Madison believed that direct election would be the most democratic, but to secure slave states' ratification of the Constitution, he devised the Electoral College as a compromise to give those states an advantage. As a result, the U.S. apportions presidential electoral votes to states based on their number of House and Senate members. With the South's House delegations stacked by the three-fifths bonus, the region had thirteen extra electors in the country's first elections and Virginia was able to boost its sons to win eight of the first nine presidential contests. The three-fifths clause became moot after Emancipation and black male suffrage at the end of the Civil War, but the Electoral College's distortions remain. An Electoral College built to protect slavery has sent two recent candidates to the White House, George W. Bush and Donald J. Trump, who both lost the popular vote. The Electoral College still overrepresents white people, but in an interesting parallel to the free/slave tilt from the original Constitution, not all white people benefit. The advantage accrues to white people who live in whiter, less-populated states;

white people who live in larger states that look more like America are the ones underrepresented today.

**AS THE FREE** population of the new country skyrocketed—tripling that of the Revolutionary era in just four decades—states began to reconsider the property limitations on the franchise. In the South, the growing threat of both slave revolts and cross-racial uprisings by Africans and landless white men helped convince the plantation aristocracy that it might be better if all free white men, not just the richest, had a stake in defending a white-supremacist government. But in state after state in the North, the push for universal suffrage among men regardless of class came in the form of a zero sum, at the expense of the few black men who had heretofore been allowed to vote. Property requirements were eliminated in the 1820s, '30s, and '40s in the same stroke that removed the tenuous voting rights of free black citizens, so that only 6 percent of the free black population lived in states that allowed them to vote by the early 1860s. This move to make real the republic's promise of self-government, but only for those with white skin, sent a powerful zero-sum message that white equality would be purchased with white supremacy. Universal white male suffrage redefined the meaning of human worth in a society with whipsawing economic vicissitudes: wage-earning white men no longer needed to be wealthy to find esteem in the eyes of their society. They just needed to be white. In many states and territories in the nineteenth century, white-skinned immigrants didn't even need to become citizens to be granted the prized right of citizenship, the vote.

Anti-blackness gave citizenship its weight and its worth. Perhaps that helps explain why so many whites reacted to the post–Civil War possibility of black citizenship not with debate but with murderous violence. John Wilkes Booth made up his mind to assassinate President Abraham Lincoln after he heard him advocate for voting rights for black men. "That means nigger citizenship. That is the last speech he will ever make. . . . By God, I'll put him through," Booth declared. He assassinated Lincoln three days later.

In the years that followed, federal troops traveled across the South registering seven hundred thousand recently freed black men. The white backlash to black suffrage was immediate, and not just by elites who saw their political privilege threatened. In Colfax, Louisiana, for example, when a pro-Reconstruction candidate supported by black voters won a fiercely contested gubernatorial race in 1872, the following spring, a mob of armed white men attacked the courthouse where the certification of the election had been held, killing about one hundred black people who were trying to defend the building, and setting the courthouse on fire. The white citizens murdered their neighbors and burned the edifice of their own government rather than submit to a multiracial democracy.

THE NEXT ONE hundred years in American history were shaped by relentless assaults on the right of black and Indigenous Americans to vote and by elite efforts to prevent class-based interracial resistance. Because the Fifteenth Amendment barred states from denying the right to vote based on color, class served as a proxy. The Reconstruction era saw movements of impoverished white farmers making common cause with black freedmen in political parties and populist alliances sometimes known as "Fusion." Their aim was to break the grip the plantation oligarchy had on government and the economy, provide interest rate relief to debtors, raise taxes for public works, and resist railroad land grabs. The ruling class fought against the cross-racial populists with a campaign for "white supremacy," promising material and other advantages to whites who broke with blacks— and violent intimidation to those who didn't.

When they won, the white supremacists attacked the franchise first. In 1890, unsure that one barrier to the ballot would suffice to control growing Reconstruction-era black political power, Mississippi implemented literacy tests, new registration rules, standards for "good character," poll taxes, and more. Other states soon created similar laws, and poor white voters were caught up in the dragnet. For instance, poll taxes, usually in the range of one to two dollars (two dollars in 1890 being almost fifty-seven dollars in today's money), required cash of poor white, black, and Indigenous people who were often sharecroppers with little cash to their names. In some places, grandfather clauses exempted whites whose grandfathers could vote before the war; in others, candidates or party officials would pay white voters' taxes for them in exchange for their loyalty. But in many places, the poll tax continued to work almost as effectively to disenfranchise poor white people as it did black people, and the result was a slow death of civic life. After several southern states adopted the menu of voter suppression tactics, turnout of eligible white voters throughout the region plummeted. In the presidential election of 1944, when national turnout averaged 69 percent, the poll tax states managed a scant 18 percent.

Some of the voter manipulation tactics of the post–Civil War era remain in full force today. The requirement that we register to vote at all before Election Day did not become common until after the Civil War, when black people had their first chance at the franchise. Throughout its history, writes legal scholar Daniel P. Tokaji, "voter registration has thus been a means not only of promoting election integrity, but also of impeding eligible citizens' access to the ballot." Today, the burdensome and confusing registration process is particularly onerous on people who move frequently (young people, people of color, and low-income people) or who may not know about lower-profile, off-cycle election dates before the registration deadlines, which are as much as thirty days before the election in some states. One of the top barriers to voting, the registration requirement kept nearly 20 percent of eligible voters from the polls in 2016.

Over six million Americans are prohibited from voting as a by-product of the racist system of mass incarceration. (The only states that allow people with felony convictions to vote even while they're in prison are Maine and Vermont, the two whitest states in the nation.) Many felony disenfranchisement laws were enacted after the Civil War alongside new Black Codes to criminalize freedmen and women. "Some crimes were specifically defined as felonies with the goal of eliminating blacks from the electorate," as legal scholar Michelle Alexander wrote. These included petty theft in Virginia and, in Florida, vagrancy, which was a notorious catchall used to send into prison labor any black person in a public space without a white person to vouch for him. In 1890, Mississippi designated crimes such as bigamy and forgery as worthy of disenfranchisement, but not robbery or murder. The disenfranchisement laws, combined with discriminatory policing and sentencing, hit their target and today ensnare one in thirteen African American voters. But their reach is wider than their aim: one in fifty-six non-black voters is impacted as well. In Florida, voters in 2018 overturned the state's lifetime disenfranchisement of people with felony convictions by ballot measure, enabling more than a million people to regain their voting rights—the majority of whom are white.

Desmond Meade is the visionary founder of the Florida Rights Restoration Coalition. I got to know him during the multiyear ballot initiative campaign because of Demos's partnership with FRRC. We had frank conversations about the headwinds of racism and the challenges of creating a multiracial coalition on an issue as charged as criminal justice in such a conservative state. But like so many black leaders I've known, Desmond had a vision with an irresistible breadth, and it attracted the grassroots energy of people from all walks of life. I asked him to put me in touch with one of FRRC's white activists, and a week later, I was on the phone with a woman named Coral Nichols.

Coral is a white woman in her early forties from Largo, Florida, and is among the hundreds of thousands of white Floridians denied the right to vote under the state's Reconstruction-era felony disenfranchisement law. While she was still under probation, Coral started volunteering with FRRC —"because we've served our time, and we should be given the opportunity to belong," she explained to me.

Coral went door-to-door in her county encouraging local citizens to do what she could not—vote on a ballot initiative to restore voting rights to people like her. Coral could tell that a lot of people she spoke to had a preconceived notion about people with felony convictions: "They think that most felons are monsters. They don't see the depth of a personal story, which is why I think that stories are so important." Race played a role, too—and that's why Coral always chose to canvass alongside an African American "brother or sister," as she put it. "It was important that we were united together. When we encountered any type of stereotype, what could break the stereotype was what was standing in front of them." Amendment 4 passed with 65 percent of the vote on November 6, 2018, and on April 19, 2019, Coral finally got released from the ten years of probation that followed her incarceration and was free to register to vote.

In reaction to Amendment 4, Florida's Republican governor and legislature passed a state law that required people with a felony history to pay all outstanding fines and fees before voting. This move—redolent of the poll tax—is particularly troubling in Florida, where it is nearly impossible for returning citizens to find out what the state thinks they owe and where "there is no database . . . to be able to check all the different court costs that might be outstanding," as one county supervisor of elections testified. The restrictive new law was challenged in court but upheld by a federal appeals court in September 2020. Coral is among approximately eighty-five thousand returning citizens who registered to vote before the new restrictive law went into effect and who must prove they have paid up before they can vote.

**THINK ABOUT IT:** today, no politician worries that their position in a representative government is illegitimate even if only a minority of citizens votes in their election. They should. What does it mean when the officials who set policy in our name are elected by so few of us? We shouldn't take these low standards for granted. Our election system is full of unnecessary hurdles and traps—some set by malice and some by negligence—but I would argue that all are a product of the same basic tolerance for a compromised republic that was established at our founding, in the interest of racial slavery. Countries less boastful of their democracies do much better. In Australia, voting is mandatory, and nearly 97 percent of Australians are registered, compared to about 70 percent registration and 61 percent voting in the United States. Canada and Germany don't make voting compulsory, but their registration rates are about 93 and 91 percent, respectively.

America's fifty states, and even counties within them, confuse and discourage voters with an archaic patchwork of varying laws, rules, and practices. In some states, you can go to the polls on Election Day and sign up as you vote. In others, you have to register thirty days before an election, a deadline you're likely to know only if you've missed it. In some states—a growing number since the COVID-19 epidemic—you can vote at home and mail in your ballot, while in others, you have to provide an excuse for why you could not go in person. Not surprisingly, Americans at all educational levels are deeply uncertain about their own states' election laws. In states that prohibit early voting, only 15 percent of residents are aware of this restriction. In states that allow same-day registration, only a quarter of its residents know it. Around half of Americans are unsure whether their state permits them to vote if they have unpaid utility bills or traffic tickets—prohibitions that no states have adopted (yet).

To see what U.S. democracy would be like without the distorting factor of racism, we can look to the states that make it easiest to vote, which are some of the whitest. Oregon, for example, was judged the easiest state in which to vote by a comprehensive study. In Oregon, everyone votes by mailing in a ballot, and Oregon was the first state in the nation to adopt automatic voter registration (AVR), which means rather than making voters figure out how, when, and where to register, Oregon uses information the state already has, for instance from the DMV, to add eligible voters to the rolls. North Dakota, another largely white state, boasts of being the only state without any requirement of voter registration. Until a 2018 voter ID law aimed at Indigenous North Dakotans, you could simply have a poll worker vouch for you at the polling place. Mississippi, the state with the highest percentage of black citizens, is dead last of the fifty states in terms of ease of voting.

FOR MOST OF America's history, voter suppression was strongest in the Jim Crow states where the black population threatened white political control. But after the election of the first African American president, every state became a potential threat to white control. A new wave of voter suppression, funded by a coterie of right-wing billionaires, crashed into states like Florida, North Carolina, Ohio, and Wisconsin—swing states that could turn a presidential election.

These same billionaires funded a lawsuit, *Shelby County v. Holder*, to bring a challenge to the Voting Rights Act's most powerful provision. Decided by a 5–4 majority at the beginning of President Obama's second term, *Shelby County v. Holder* lifted the federal government's protection from citizens in states and counties with long records of discriminatory voting procedures. Immediately across the country, Republican legislatures felt free to restrict voting rights. North Carolina legislators imposed a photo ID law that "target[ed] African Americans with almost surgical precision," because it was based on research that pinpointed the kinds of identification to which white people had greater access and then allowed only those forms of ID. Texas introduced a voter ID law that essentially let the state design its own electorate, requiring photo IDs that over half a million eligible voters lacked and specifying what kinds of IDs would be permitted (gun permits, 80 percent of which are owned by white Texans) and denied (college IDs, in a state where more than 50 percent of students are people of color). Alabama demanded photo IDs from voters, such as a driver's license, and within a year, it closed thirty-one driver's license offices, including in eight out of ten of the most populous black counties. Between the 2013 *Shelby* decision and the

2018 election, twenty-three states raised new barriers to voting. Although about 11 percent of the U.S. population (disproportionately low-income people, seniors, and people of color) do not have access to photo IDs, by 2020, six states still demanded them in order for people to vote, and an additional twenty-six states made voting much easier if you had an ID.

These policies were targeted primarily to disadvantage people of color, but such broad brooms have swept large numbers of white people into the democratic margins as well. In general, about 5 percent of white people in the United States lack a photo ID. Within certain portions of the white population, however, the numbers increase: 19 percent of white people with household incomes below $25,000 have neither a driver's license nor a passport. The same is true of 20 percent of white people ages 17–20. Of the fifty thousand already-registered Alabama voters estimated to lack proper photo ID to vote in 2016, more than half were white.

Anti-voting lawmakers perhaps weren't intending to make it harder for married white women to vote, but that's exactly what they did by requiring an exact name match across all forms of identification in many states in recent years. Birth certificates list people's original surnames, but if they change their names upon marriage, their more recent forms of ID usually show their married names. Sandra Watts is a married white judge in the state of Texas who was forced to use a provisional ballot in 2013 under the state's voter ID law. She was outraged at the imposition: "Why would I want to vote provisional ballot when I've been voting regular ballot for the last forty-nine years?" Like many women, she included her maiden name as her middle name when she took her husband's last name—and that's what her driver's license showed. But on the voter rolls, her middle name was the one her parents gave her at birth, which she no longer used. And like that, she lost her vote—all because of a law intended to suppress people like Judge Watts's fellow Texan Anthony Settles, a black septuagenarian and retired engineer.

Anthony Settles was in possession of his Social Security card, an

expired Texas identification card, and his old University of Houston
student ID, but he couldn't get a new photo ID to vote in 2016 because his mother had changed his name when she remarried in 1964.
Several lawyers tried to help him track down the name-change certificate in courthouses, to no avail; his only recourse was to go to court
for a new one, at a cost of $250. Elderly, rural, and low-income voters
are more likely not to have birth certificates or to have documents
containing clerical errors. Hargie Randell, a legally blind black
Texan who couldn't drive but who had a current voter registration
card used before the new Texas law, had to arrange for people to drive
him to the Department of Public Safety office three times, and once
to the county clerk's office an hour away, only to end up with a birth
certificate that spelled his name wrong by one letter.

Possibly the most insidious anti-voting innovation to appear after
the Obama election was the purge of unwitting voters already registered to vote. In 2015, Larry Harmon's elected secretary of state, Jon
Husted, used a purge process to eliminate two hundred thousand registered Ohio voters from the rolls in the state's twenty most populous
counties, all in the name of list maintenance to prevent voter fraud.
As in most states, these high-population counties were also the ones
whose residents were most likely to be people of color and to vote
Democratic.

Here's how the purge process worked. If an Ohio voter failed to
vote during a two-year period—say, he voted in the presidential election but sat out the midterms—the state mailed the voter a postcard
to verify his address. If the voter didn't return the postcard, the state
launched a process that, unless the person cast a ballot within the
next four years, would result in his name being purged from the rolls:
no longer considered a valid voter in the state. There are a number of
problems with this approach, starting with the fact that in the United
States, voting is not a use-it-or-lose-it right. What's more, as Secretary Husted knew perfectly well, the vast majority of people who
receive these address-verification postcards in the mail do not return
them. In 2012, Ohio went to the trouble and expense to send out

1.5 million address-verification notices to people who hadn't voted in 2011—out of a total of only 7.7 million registered voters. Presuming a change in registration for almost one out of every five registered voters is a remarkably wasteful effort, given that only about three out of every one hundred people move out of a registrar's jurisdiction in any given year.

Of the 1.5 million postcard recipients, 1.2 million never responded. This should have been a clue that something was wrong with the state's notification process, not with the voters. Or perhaps the process was working precisely as intended: people of color, renters, and young people are significantly less likely to respond to official mail than are white people, homeowners, and older people, as the Census Bureau had discovered.

"I've lived in Ohio my entire life," explained Larry Harmon, "except for when I served in the Navy, and even then, I paid Ohio taxes." Yet, in 2015, Larry felt like he'd been disappeared in the eyes of the state. "When I went to vote, I went into the hall and I looked up my name, and I looked and I looked, but I didn't see my name.

"While I was at work on my lunch hour, I tried to google to see, did I do something wrong? . . . I didn't quite understand why I wouldn't be on the list; I'd voted there before." Then he ran across information on Ohio's purge of inactive voters. "I didn't think I was required to vote in every election!" Larry said, incredulity in his voice.

He had been voting since 1976, mostly in presidential elections. His reasons for skipping the 2012 election were, like those of so many Americans, both personal and political: a combination of a lack of inspiration and the pressures of real life. "I think I went through a period after my mother's death that I wasn't interested in voting, and I didn't think it did a whole lot of good, so I didn't vote for one presidential election and, they told me, one midterm election."

But in 2015, Larry was closely following an issue that he knew would be on the ballot—a proposal to legalize marijuana but to concentrate the industry in a few corporate hands. He was opposed to the idea and was eager to have his say. And the more Larry thought about being denied the opportunity to vote, the more upset he became.

"I thought, 'Well, jeez. You know, I pay my taxes every year, and I pay my property taxes, and I register my car.' So, the state had to know I'm still a voter. Why should we fight for the country if they're gonna be taking away my rights? I mean, I'm a veteran, my father's a veteran, my grandfather's a veteran. Now they aren't giving me my right to vote, the most fundamental right I have?"

Lawyers at my organization learned of Ohio's singularly aggressive purging practice—no other state initiated a purge process after just one missed federal election—and concluded that it violated federal law, the National Voter Registration Act of 1993. Most commonly known as the "motor voter" law because it made registration more available at DMVs and other government offices, the law also bars states from a number of burdensome voter registration practices, including purging registered voters for not voting. In early 2016, we took Ohio to court and, over the next two years, battled the case all the way up to the Supreme Court.

On January 10, 2018, I was in Washington, D.C., to watch the oral arguments before the Supreme Court for the case, which was now called *Husted v. A. Philip Randolph Institute* (APRI). A membership group of black trade unionists whose volunteer activities include voter registration were plaintiffs, along with Larry Harmon and the Ohio Coalition for the Homeless. The early morning was chilly as I walked to the Court building with my colleague Stuart Naifeh, who had argued the case successfully in the lower court. As we climbed the wide stone steps, I looked up at the words inscribed in marble above the Court's columns: EQUAL JUSTICE UNDER THE LAW. I couldn't help contrasting those stirring words with the mess Ohio had made of its voting system.

As another Demos colleague, Chiraag Bains, later wrote in a *Washington Post* op-ed, "In the United States, if you don't buy a gun for several years, you do not lose your Second Amendment right to bear arms. If you never write a letter to the editor or participate in a street demonstration, you retain your full First Amendment rights to free speech. If you skip church for years on end, the government cannot stop you from finally attending a service." But despite our contemporary reverence for the idea of equality under the law, the truth is the Constitution wasn't written with an affirmative right to vote for all citizens. It's always been a power struggle to create a representative electorate, and currently, the forces against equality have the upper hand. Purges and other kinds of voter suppression are forms of racial oppression that vitiate the goal of democracy, and white voters like Larry Harmon end up being collateral damage in a trap not set for them. Across the country, states purged almost 16 million voters between 2014 and 2016. Some 7 percent of Americans report that they or a member of their household went to their polling place only to be told that their name was not on the voter roll, even though they knew they were registered. In the courtroom, we didn't hear much about race—Demos was arguing that Ohio's purge process violated federal election law, not civil rights law or the Equal Protection Clause—until Justice Sonia Sotomayor, the country's first Latinx Supreme Court justice, spoke to what she called the "essence of this case."

She said, "It appears as if what you're reading is that the failure to vote is enough evidence to suggest that someone has moved. . . . [I]s that a reasonable effort to draw that conclusion, when [what] you do results in disenfranchising disproportionately certain cities where large groups of minorities live?" she asked. "There's a strong argument . . . that at least in impact, this is discriminatory." In the end, a conservative majority of the Supreme Court ruled against Harmon and allowed Ohio's secretary of state to continue deregistering voters for elections to come.

**WHERE DID JON** Husted get the idea to purge up to a million of his own state's voters? There is a playbook of anti-voting tactics drawn up by a connected set of benign-sounding organizations such as the legislation-drafting network of conservative lawmakers, the American Legislative Exchange Council, and the legal organizations Project on Fair Representation and the Public Interest Legal Foundation, all of which are funded in turn by a group of radical right-wing millionaires and billionaires, chief among them fossil fuel baron Charles Koch. (Until his death in 2019, Charles's brother David was his partner in these efforts, and the two men, among the richest in the world, were widely known as "the Koch brothers.") Over the past fifty years, the Kochs organized vast sums of money to advance a vision for America that includes limited democracy, a rollback of civil rights, and unfettered capitalism.

We wouldn't know much about the radical aims of the Koch brothers, whose political spending was often as secretive as their charitable giving was public (the dance hall at New York's Lincoln Center, for example, is the David H. Koch Theater), if it weren't for journalists like Jane Mayer and a little-known history professor named Nancy MacLean. In 2013, Duke University professor Nancy MacLean found a neglected storehouse of papers in the archives of James Buchanan, an influential economist who had recently died. The Buchanan papers became the basis for her award-winning book *Democracy in Chains: The Deep History of the Radical Right's Stealth Plan for America.*

MacLean has thick brown hair that she often pushes impatiently out of her eyes as she speaks, which she does at a breakneck pace. Her words chase one another out of her mouth, accelerating to a crescendo at the end of every packed sentence. Considering the astonishing revelations that are flying at you that quickly, the whole experience of a MacLean conversation can leave you feeling like you've just been picked up by a twister and dropped in an entirely different universe.

Sadly, though, the universe she describes is ours. Her work has exposed an influential movement of radical right-wing libertarians opposed to the very idea of democracy. Through five decades of money and organizing, this movement has permeated conservative media and the Republican Party with its fringe, self-serving vision of an undemocratic society. Its goal is a country with concentrated wealth and little citizen power to levy taxes, regulate corporate behavior, fund public goods, or protect civil rights. The obstacle to this goal is representative democracy.

That's why the hundreds of millionaires in the Koch network have taken aim at the rules of democracy, funding think tanks, legal organizations, public intellectuals, and advocacy groups to promote a smaller and less powerful electorate and weaker campaign finance laws. Since 2010, the groups they fund have spurred more than one hundred pieces of state legislation to make it harder to vote, almost half of which have passed; launched dozens of lawsuits attacking both voter protections and controls on big money in politics (including both *Shelby County v. Holder* and the case resulting in the notorious "corporations are people" decision, *Citizens United*); and invested in technology to allow extreme partisan gerrymandering. The scale of their organization is as large as a political party, but they use front groups and shell companies to keep their funding mostly secret. The core philosophy that unites their economic aims with their attacks on a multiracial democracy is that a robust democracy will lead to the masses banding together to oppose property owners' concentration of wealth and power.

On its face, the aim of this movement is not white supremacy. Professor MacLean says they're about "property supremacy." But racism has long been useful to the movement. James Buchanan was awarded a Nobel Prize for his ideas about taxes, the size of government, and the deficit, but he first made his name in 1959 by offering a way for Virginia to resist desegregating public schools after *Brown v. Board of Education*. Buchanan co-wrote a memo to Virginia legislators and advocated in support of using public funds for private (and therefore segregable) schools, which could be economically efficient if the state used the revenue from public assets like school buildings. Buchanan and his co-author wrote, "We believe every individual should be free to associate with persons of his own choosing. We therefore disapprove of both involuntary (or coercive) segregation and involuntary integration."

Many of today's right-wing political actors take their libertarian economic philosophy from people like Buchanan and their funding from the Koch brothers network. The success of their policy agenda hinges on an unrepresentative electorate, because their vision can't garner majority support. Their unpopular ideas include lowering taxes on the wealthy (64 percent of Americans want higher wealth taxes), slashing government spending and eliminating public transit (70 percent want a big infrastructure plan paid for by a wealth tax), and drastically minimizing the government's role in health insurance (56 percent support a fully public single-payer system).

This is where racism becomes strategically useful. Whatever the Koch movement operatives (which now include many Republican politicians) believe in their hearts about race, they are comfortable with deploying strategic racism because popular stereotypes can help move unpopular ideas, including limiting democracy. Take for example the widespread unconscious association between people of color and criminals; anti-voting advocates and politicians exploited this connection to win white support for voter suppression measures. They used images of brown and black people voting in ads decrying "voter fraud," which has been proven repeatedly to be virtually nonexistent and nonsensical: it's hard enough to get a majority of people to overcome the bureaucratic hurdles to vote in every election; do we really think that people are risking jail time to cast an extra ballot? Nonetheless, the combination of the first black president and inculcation through repetition led to a new common sense, particularly among white Republicans, that brown and black people could be committing a crime by voting. With this idea firmly implanted, the less popular idea—that politicians should change the rules to make it harder for eligible citizens to vote—becomes more tolerable.

And this opens the door to a complete undermining of American democracy. As one of the architects of today's right-wing infrastructure, Paul Weyrich, said in a 1980 speech, "I don't want everybody to vote. Elections are not won by a majority of people; they never have been from the beginning of our country and they are not now. As a matter of fact, our leverage in the elections quite candidly goes up as the voting populace goes down." Adherents to this belief system "see democracy as essentially infringing on economic liberty, and particularly the economic liberty of the most wealthy and corporations," MacLean told me.

Voter suppression, an age-old racist tactic, has been reanimated in recent years by subtly anti-black and anti-brown propaganda, but is now useful against a broad base of white people who could be in a multiracial coalition with people of color. MacLean recalled, "The voter suppression legislation in many cases, certainly in [my state of] North Carolina, didn't only aim at African Americans. It also aimed in particular at young people. And this older generation of white conservatives . . . understand[s] that young people are not liking these ideas. . . . That young people are . . . raising questions about the inequities in the way that capitalism is operating.

"So, for example, in my state, they took pains to eliminate a program that led to the automatic registration of high school students. . . . They took aim at early voting, which tends to be something that many young people also use. And frankly, many white people prefer, too.

"They also moved polling sites away from campuses," said MacLean. "A really egregious example of that was in Boone, North Carolina, which is a predominantly white community in the western mountains. . . . The Republicans in charge moved the polling place from the campus, which is right in the city and very convenient to lots and lots of people. . . . [T]hey moved it halfway down the mountain to a place where there was no parking, no public transportation, and it was dangerous to walk along the road to get to this place."

**IN 1956, TWENTY-FOUR-YEAR-OLD** Air Force captain Henry Frye went to register to vote in Richmond County, North Carolina. The state had enacted a literacy test in 1899 as part of the White Supremacy Democrats' defeat of the Fusion Party populists, but Frye, an honors college graduate, was more than literate. Nonetheless, he was turned away. The test as administered by the white clerk? Name all the signers of the Declaration of Independence. Nearly a decade later, North Carolina's voter suppression law and hundreds of similar restrictions across the country finally fell under the Voting Rights Act of 1965, Dr. Martin Luther King Jr.'s crowning achievement and the cause for which marchers were beaten on Bloody Sunday in Selma, Alabama. It's hard to overstate the difference that the Voting Rights Act made in the country's journey toward true democracy. The year before its passage, less than 10 percent of eligible African Americans in Mississippi were registered; five years later, that figure was almost 60 percent. In 1962, only 36 percent of black North Carolinians were registered; one year after the Voting Rights Act, it had grown to 50 percent. Throughout the South, about one million new African American voters registered within a few years of the Voting Rights Act's taking hold. Back in Richmond County, North Carolina, the law freed Henry Frye to become a voter, then to run and win a campaign for the state legislature. He would go on to become the chief justice of the North Carolina Supreme Court.

The fear that drives the violence and mendacity of American voter suppression is rooted in a zero-sum vision of democracy: either I have the power and the spoils, or you do. But the civil rights–era liberation of the African American vote in the South offered a Solidarity Dividend for white people as well. The elimination of the poll tax in particular freed up the political participation of lower-income white voters. Indeed, white voters in Georgia and Virginia had challenged the poll tax requirement, but the courts upheld it in 1937 and 1951. After the civil rights movement knocked down voting barriers, white as well as black registration and turnout rates rose in former Jim Crow states. And a fuller democracy meant more than just a larger number of ballots; it meant a more responsive government for the people who hadn't been wealthy enough to have influence before.

It meant a break, finally, from what the southern political scientist V. O. Key described in 1949 as the stranglehold of white supremacy, single-party politics, and the dominance of the Bible Belt planter class.

"When you talk about the effects of the Voting Rights Act and political participation, just going to the ballot and casting your vote is only one step," economist Gavin Wright told me. He's the author of *Sharing the Prize*, which details the economic benefits the civil rights movement brought to the entire South, whites included. "What the black political leadership got, and economic leadership, was a seat at the table." With that seat, they won investments in public infrastructure, including hospitals, roads, schools, and libraries that had been starved when one-party rule allowed only the southern aristocracy to set the rules. More voters of all races meant more competitive elections; for the first time since the end of Reconstruction, a white supremacy campaign wasn't enough. Candidates had to promise to deliver something of value to southern families, white and black. In *Sharing the Prize*, Wright writes that "after the Voting Rights Act . . . southern . . . gubernatorial campaigns increasingly featured nonracial themes of economic development and education."

Pre–civil rights Alabama was a quintessential example of racist inequality starving the public. Nearly half the state's citizens over age twenty-five had no more than an elementary school education in 1960. This was the case for two out of three black Alabamians, but also for two in five white Alabamians. After the Voting Rights Act swelled the electorate, Gov. Albert Brewer faced arch-segregationist George Wallace and hoped to appeal to a modern-day Fusion coalition of the white middle class, newly enfranchised black Alabamians, and working-class whites outside the retrograde former plantation counties in the Black Belt. So, he called a 1969 Special Session on Education that passed twenty-nine bills and appropriated an unprecedented one hundred million dollars toward education in the state. Brewer narrowly lost in a runoff, but the impact of the educational investments he spearheaded continued.

---

IN ORDER TO prevent a thriving multiracial democracy, the same movement that puts up barriers to voting has hacked away at the safeguards against money flooding into elections. It's not very often thought of this way, but the current big-money campaign finance system is a linchpin of structural racism, and the stealth movement to create it has been driven by people who often also work against government action to advance civil rights and equality. (Fifty years after libertarian economists laid out the case for school privatization instead of integration, a Koch brothers–founded libertarian group helped dismantle one of the country's first and few remaining voluntary school integration systems, in Wake County, North Carolina.)

Most people who wonder why our politics are so corrupt can't draw the line from racist theories of limited democracy to today's system, but the small group of white men who are funding the effort to turn back the clock on political equality can lay claim to a long ideological pedigree: from the original property requirement to people like John C. Calhoun, who advocated states' rights and limited government in defense of slavery, to the Supreme Court justices who decided *Shelby County* and *Citizens United*. Over the past few decades, a series of money-in-politics lawsuits, including *Citizens United*, have overturned anticorruption protections, making it possible for a wealthy individual to give more than $3.5 million to a party and its candidates in an election cycle, for corporations and unions to spend unlimited sums to get candidates elected or defeated, and for secret money to sway elections.

The result is a racially skewed system of influence and electoral gatekeeping that invalidates the voices of most Americans. When you consider the impact that the flow of money and lobbying has on policy making, it's no exaggeration to say that the white male property requirement for having a say in government is still the default mode of business. One pair of political scientists stated, "Economic elites and organized groups representing business interests have substantial independent impacts on U.S. government policy, while average citizens and mass-based interest groups have little or no independent influence." They conclude that "in the United States . . . the majority does not rule—at least in the causal sense of actually determining policy outcomes." Another political scientist found that "senators' [policy] preferences diverge dramatically from the preference of the average voter in their state . . . unless these constituents are those who write checks and attend fundraisers." Still another wrote that the preferences of people "in the bottom one-third of the income distribution have no discernable impact on the behavior of their elected representatives."

Since the early 1970s—not coincidentally, shortly after the 1965 Voting Rights Act began to dramatically increase the voting participation of African Americans—the donor class in America has grown more powerful and more secretive, but the number of donors who give contributions large enough to require tracking (above $200) is minuscule, less than 1.2 percent of the entire adult population. Their outsize donations totaled more than 71 percent of all campaign contributions during the 2018 election cycle.

This tiny coterie of elite donors who hold such sway over our political process do not look or live like most Americans. Obviously, they are wealthier than the rest of us; of donors who gave more than five thousand dollars to congressional candidates in 2012–2016, 45 percent are millionaires, while millionaires comprise only 3 percent of the U.S. population. As a team of *New York Times* reporters described in an exposé of the 158 families who dominated funding for the 2016 presidential election, "They are overwhelmingly white, rich, older and male, in a nation that is being remade by the young, by women, and by black and brown voters." The big-money campaign finance system is like so much of modern-day structural racism: it harms people of color disproportionately but doesn't spare non-wealthy white people; it may be hard to assign racist intent, but it's easy to find the racist impacts.

Two-thirds of Americans consider it a major problem that "wealthy individuals and corporations" have "disproportionate influence" in our elections. Though the impact is most acutely felt among people of color whose voices are the least represented, the reach is widespread enough that there's a powerful Solidarity Dividend waiting to be unlocked for all of us. After a history of high-profile corruption cases earned the state the nickname "Corrupticut" and led to the imprisonment of a sitting governor in 2004, Connecticut passed a sweeping campaign finance reform measure. The Connecticut Citizens' Election Program offered candidates the chance to qualify for public grants to fund their campaigns if they could collect enough grassroots donations from people in their district, in increments of five to one hundred dollars. In the first years after the reform, the change was dramatic. Candidates spent most of their campaigning time hearing the concerns of their constituents instead of those of wealthy people and check-writing lobbyists. James Albis, representative of East Haven, recalled, "I announced my reelection bid in February, and by April, I was done fundraising. So, from April to November, I could focus only on talking to constituents. Without public financing, I would have been fundraising through that entire period." Corporate lobbyists had less sway over legislators' agendas. Reform lifted the wealth requirement from running for office, too. "Public financing definitely made the legislature more diverse. There are more people of color, more young people, more women, and more young women," noted the secretary of state, Denise Merrill.

One of those people was state senator Gary Holder-Winfield, an African American activist and former electrical construction manager for a power plant, who describes himself as "the candidate who wasn't supposed to win." He was in the first class of legislators who ran under the Citizens' Elections system. He explains, "I didn't come from money. I am a candidate of color, and I wasn't a candidate for the political party or machine apparatus. I didn't have the nomination, and I was actually able to defeat the person that had the nomination by talking about issues that he wasn't.

"I'm beholden to the people who have been saying for a long period of time that we don't have a voice," he said. As I listened to Senator Holder-Winfield talk about his neighborhood constituents telling him they wanted him to focus on unfairness in the juvenile justice system, I realized I was hearing about something rare: a functioning representative democracy. "I don't know what the issue is going to be, but I know where it's going to come from," Holder-Winfield explained. "It's revolutionary in the way that it works." I couldn't help but think about the myth I'd learned as a child about the American Revolution creating that kind of bottom-up, egalitarian democracy—untrue then but within our grasp today.

Connecticut's Solidarity Dividend was almost immediate. In the first legislative cycles after public financing, the more diverse (by measures of race, gender, and class) legislature passed a raft of popular public-interest bills, including a guarantee of paid sick days for workers, a minimum wage increase, a state Earned Income Tax Credit, in-state tuition for undocumented students, and a change to an obscure law championed by beverage distributor lobbyists that resulted in $24 million returning to the state—money that could contribute to funding the public financing law. Despite regular efforts to curtail it, Connecticut's Citizens' Election Program has endured for over a decade, highly popular with both Connecticut residents and candidates, 73 percent of whom opted into the system in 2014. This kind of reform has national popular support as well; among the most potent opposition messages is that it's taxpayer money for politicians. Senator Winfield has a response to that: "Yeah, we are using the public's money, but it's the public's government, and if you want it to remain the public's government, you might have to use the public's money. Otherwise, you're going to have government by the few who have been paying for government."

OUR POLITICAL SYSTEM has been rigged, from the drafting of the Constitution onward, chiefly to diminish black political participation. This flawed system has also limited the choices and voices of poorer white Americans and thwarted working-class coalitions that could have made economic and social life richer for all. A genuine, truly representative democracy is still an aspiration in America, but the vision of it has propelled waves of communities to claim a right from which they were excluded in our founding slavocracy. Class-blind suffrage in 1855; black male enfranchisement in 1870; women's suffrage in 1920; the full enfranchisement of Native Americans in 1962; the Voting Rights Act of 1965; and the inclusion of young adults in 1971. Professor Nancy MacLean, who has studied how powerful the opposition to democracy is, continues to be optimistic. "I do think that something is happening now," she told me, "where not only is the audaciousness of the push to change the country from the right accelerating at a rapid pace that's waking a lot of people up, but also I think good people of all backgrounds and commitments are starting to . . . get into action to try to defend democracy. . . . And I'm heartened by the way that I see people, including so many white people, also recognizing that . . . we are all bound to one another. When one of us is hurting, that's going to come along and hurt everyone."

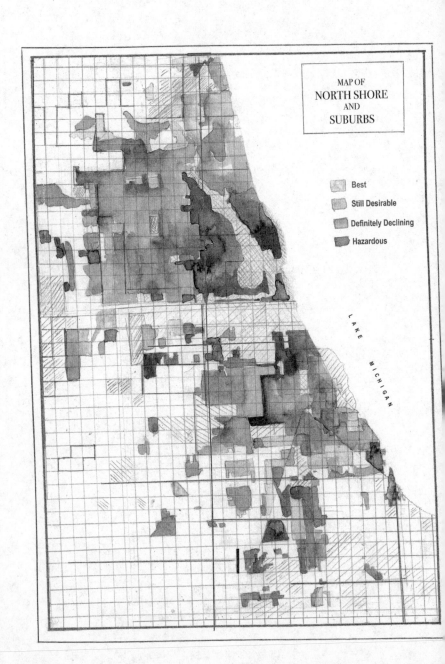

MAP OF
**NORTH SHORE**
AND
**SUBURBS**

Best

Still Desirable

Definitely Declining

Hazardous

LAKE MICHIGAN

## Chapter 7

# LIVING APART

A white boy with freckles telling me I was one of the good ones. Girls jumping double-dutch during recess, and the jelly sandals of Ayesha, who did her best to teach me how. In the cafeteria, knowing I should want the latest Lunchables but secretly preferring my hot lunch, served by Gracie, who reminded me of my aunt. The lonely walk up to the top floor to sit in reading class with the big kids in eighth grade, when I was just in third. The scratch of the phono-graph before "Lift Ev'ry Voice and Sing," which we sang after the Pledge of Allegiance instead of "The Star Spangled Banner." The white and Chinese boys rapping "Never date a girl with a weave, why? Because a girl with a weave has got a trick up her sleeve!" at me while they flicked my braids in homeroom. The lines I had to re-member, and the things I had to forget, to keep auditioning for plays with all-white characters. What it felt like to sit in class debating the Supreme Court cases that had treated my ancestors' humanity as a subject for debate.

These are the memories that flashed when I forced myself to think of all the places where I've been on the spectrum of integra-tion, from an entirely black school to a virtually all-white one; from a suburb famous for its integration to a 98 percent black neighborhood; and at a law school where there were four times as many Asian American students as black ones. At the age of eleven, I ended up in an all-white rural town for boarding school, a sacrifice my parents made to give a restless child access to elite educational circles, despite the culture shock they knew would await her. I was lonely, and it was hard, but eventually, I found loving teachers and some other misfits— a Puerto Rican girl from Queens, a pair of sisters from Hong Kong, a gangly white girl who shared my love of female-driven fantasy books like *The Mists of Avalon*—who helped me find my footing.

As I moved through school, then college, law school, and work, I was never again in as overwhelmingly white an institution as that early country school, but (like many black people) I was often navigating largely white worlds. I learned to expect to be the "only" black person in white rooms, the one who would force a new racial awareness. I know that these experiences of racial proximity and distance profoundly influenced me, for good and for bad—that I had to subtly redefine myself with each move and, more important, often wildly reevaluate what I thought of others. This is one of those truths that we Americans know without a doubt and yet like to deny: Who your neighbors, your co-workers, and your classmates are is one of the most powerful determinants of your path in life. And most white Americans spend their lives on a path set out for them by a centuries-old lie: that in the zero-sum racial competition, white spaces are the best spaces.

White people are the most segregated people in America.

That's a different way to think about what has perennially been an issue cast with the opposite die: people of color are those who are segregated, because the white majority separates out the black minority, excludes the Chinese, forces Indigenous Americans onto reservations, expels the Latinos. Segregation is a problem for those on the outside because what is good is reserved for those within. While that has historically been materially true, as government subsidies nurtured wealth inside white spaces and suppressed and stripped wealth outside, I wanted to investigate the damage done to all of us, including white people, by the persistence of segregation. The typical white person lives in a neighborhood that is at least 75 percent white. In today's increasingly multiracial society, where white people value diversity but rarely live it, there are costs—financial, developmental, even physical—to continuing to segregate as we do. Marisa Novara, a Chicago housing official, put it this way: "I think as a field, we use the word *segregation* incorrectly. I think we tend to use it as if it's a synonym for places that are low-income, where black and brown people live. And we ignore all of the places that are majority white, that are exclusive enclaves, as if those are not segregated as well."

**FEW PEOPLE TODAY** understand the extent to which governments at every level forced Americans to live apart throughout our history. Our governments not only imposed color restrictions on where people could live and work, but also where we could shop and buy gas, watch movies, drink water, enter buildings, and walk on the sidewalk. The obsession with which America drew the color line was all-consuming and absurd. And contrary to our collective memory, segregation didn't originate in the South; nor was it confined to the Jim Crow states. Segregation was first developed in the northern states before the Civil War. Boston had a "Nigger Hill" and "New Guinea." Moving west: territories like Illinois and Oregon limited or barred free black people entirely in the first half of the 1800s. In the South, white dependence on black labor, and white need for physical control and access to black bodies, required proximity, the opposite of segregation. The economic imperative set the terms of the racial understanding; in the South, blacks were seen as inferior and servile but needed to be close. In the North, black people were job competition, therefore seen as dangerous, stricken with a poverty that could be infectious.

The Reconstruction reforms after the Civil War should have ended segregation. Congress passed a broad Civil Rights Act in 1875, banning discrimination in public accommodations. During Reconstruction, many southern cities had "salt-and-pepper" integration, in which black and white people lived in the same neighborhoods and even dined in the same restaurants. Multiracial working-class political alliances formed in North Carolina, Alabama, and Virginia. As it did after Bacon's Rebellion, though, the wealthy white power structure reacted to the threat of class solidarity by creating new rules to promote white supremacy. This time, they reasoned that everyday physical separation would be the most powerful way to ensure the allegiance of the white masses to race over class.

In 1883, the U.S. Supreme Court struck down America's first Civil Rights Act, and the Black Codes of Jim Crow took hold, with mirrors in the North. In the words of the preeminent southern historian C. Vann Woodward, "Jim Crow laws put the authority of the state or city in the voice of the street-car conductor, the railway brakeman, the bus driver, the theater usher, and also into the voice of the hoodlum of the public parks and playgrounds. They gave free rein and the majesty of the law to mass aggressions that might otherwise have been curbed, blunted or deflected." Any white person was now deputized to enforce the exclusion of black people from white space, a terrible power that led to decades of sadistic violence against black men, women, and children.

For the next eighty years, segregation dispossessed Native Americans, Latinos, Asian Americans, and black Americans of land and often life. No governments in modern history save Apartheid South Africa and Nazi Germany have segregated as well as the United States has, with precision and under the color of law. (And even then, both the Third Reich and the Afrikaner government looked to America's laws to create their systems.) U.S. government financing required home developers and landlords to put racially restrictive covenants (agreements to sell only to white people) in their housing contracts. And as we've already seen, the federal government supported housing segregation through redlining and other banking practices, the result of which was that the two investments that created the housing market that has been a cornerstone of building wealth in American families, the thirty-year mortgage and the federal government's willingness to guarantee banks' issuance of those loans, were made on a whites-only basis and under conditions of segregation.

Even after the Supreme Court ruled in 1948 that governments could no longer enforce racial covenants in housing, the government continued to discriminate under the pretext of credit risk. Planners for the Interstate Highway System designated black and brown areas as undesirable and either destroyed them to make way for highways or located highways in ways that separated the neighborhoods from job-rich areas. The effects of these policy decisions are no more behind us than the houses we live in. Recent Federal Reserve Bank of Chicago research has found, with a granular level of detail down to the city block, that the refusal to lend to black families under the original 1930s redlining maps is responsible for as much as half of the current disparities between black and white homeownership and for the gaps between the housing values of black and white homes in those communities. Richard Rothstein, author of the seminal book on segregation, *Color of Law: How the Government Segregated America*, reminds us that there is no such thing as "de facto" segregation that is different from de jure (or legal) segregation. All segregation is the result of public policy, past and present.

Instead of whites-only clauses in rental advertisements and color-coded maps, today's segregation is driven by less obviously racially targeted policies. I've often wondered how our suburbs became so homogenous, with such similar house sizes and types. It turns out that, like so much of how we live, it was no accident: after the Supreme Court invalidated city ordinances banning black people from buying property in white neighborhoods in 1917, over a thousand communities rushed to adopt "exclusionary zoning" laws to restrict the types of housing that most black people could afford to buy, especially without access to subsidized mortgages (such as units in apartment buildings or two-family homes). These rules remain today, an invisible layer of exclusion laid across 75 percent of the residential map in most American cities, effectively banning working-class and many middle-income people from renting or buying there. Exclusionary zoning rules limit the number of units constructed per acre; they can outright ban apartment buildings; they can even deem that a single-family house has to be big enough to preserve a neighborhood's "aesthetic uniformity." The effect is that they keep land supply short, house prices high, and multifamily apartment buildings out. In 1977, the Supreme Court failed to recognize that these rules were racial bans recast in class terms, and the impact on integration—not to mention housing affordability for millions of struggling white families—has been devastating. Today, the crisis surrounding housing affordability in the United States is reaching a fever pitch: the majority of people in the one hundred largest U.S. cities are now renters, and the majority of those renters spend more than half their income on rent. Homeownership rates are falling for many Americans as costs continue to increase, construction productivity continues to decline, and incomes don't keep pace. Nationwide, the typical home costs more than 4.2 times the typical household income; in 1970, the same ratio was 1.7. One solution many cities are investigating or implementing is an increase in the housing supply by limiting or eradicating single-family zoning. While the net effect of increasing housing supply doesn't always lead automatically to greater affordability without additional policy changes, the lasting legacy of the racism designed into American property markets did increase costs for all Americans.

I WAS BORN on the South Side of Chicago, in a neighborhood that is still a working middle-class community, full of teachers and other public servants who found doors open in government that were closed in the private sector. There were also lots of owners of small businesses with an ethos that they'd rather make their own way than be "last hired, first fired," as the saying goes, in a white person's shop.

The apartment where I was born is located in a four-story brick building that my great-grandmother Flossie McGhee bought on a "land sale contract," one of the notorious high-interest contracts whites sold to black homebuyers lacking access to mortgages due to redlining and bank discrimination. (In the 1960s, 85 percent of black homeowners bought on contract.) As I discuss earlier, when you bought on contract, you built no equity until the end and could be evicted and lose everything if you missed a single payment. Against all odds, Grandma Flossie kept the payments coming with money she made by combining jobs as a nanny to white families with a lucky streak with the numbers. In our neighborhood of Chatham/Avalon, as far as I can recall and Census data can confirm, there were no white people within a fifteen-block radius of us. Chicago is one of the most segregated cities in America, by design. Before the 1948 racial covenant Supreme Court decision, 80 percent of the city of Chicago carried racial covenants banning black people from living in most neighborhoods, a percentage that was similar in other large cities around the country, including Los Angeles.

A few times a week after school, I would visit my paternal grandparents, Earl and Marcia McGhee, a Chicago police officer and Chicago public schools social worker. They lived on the other side of the "L," in a neighborhood known as "Pill Hill" because of all the single-family houses belonging to doctors from the neighboring hospital. Over there, it was the picture of success in brick and concrete: houses with manicured lawns, single-car garages, and monogrammed awnings over the doorsteps. But it was almost all-black, too; a few Jewish families hung on into the 1970s, but there were none on my grandparents' block when I was a kid. It was our own American Dream, hard-won and, for many who remember its glory days, almost utopian.

I asked my grandma Marcia about what the segregated South Side was like in those days. "We had a common history, all of us: parents who came up from terror and sharecropping to . . ." She laughed. "To deeds and degrees. In just one generation. And nobody gave us a thing. They were always trying to take, in fact. So, you'd walk down the street and see the new car in the driveway, the kids in the yard, and everybody was happy for each other's success, and you knew everybody'd be there for each other when you were down."

I was in kneesocks when Earl and Marcia McGhee were hosting regular card games and Democratic Party meetings in their finished basement on Bennett Avenue in Pill Hill, but I remember it as she does. There was a feeling that although the energy of the civil rights movement had dissipated, it hadn't completely moved on, but had settled in the fibers that connected us. Folks like my parents and grandparents had their day jobs, but they all knew that no matter what you were doing, you were also doing it at least in part for the betterment of the community.

I never knew why the South Side where I grew up was so black, or that it hadn't always been. In the 1950s, Chatham's population was over 90 percent white. Ten years later, it was more than 60 percent black. By the time I was born there, in 1980, the population had been over 90 percent African American for a decade. But when I left home in middle school for an almost entirely all-white boarding school in rural Massachusetts, I learned two things about where I came from. The first was that the thickness of my black community—close-knit, represented in civic institutions, and economically dynamic—was rare. In Boston, black meant poor in a way I simply had never realized. The everyday sight of black doctors and managers (particularly native-born) was a rarity in that old-money city where black political power had never gained a hold and where negative stereotypes of blackness filled in the space. Second, I learned that although we knew about white people even if we didn't live with them—they were co-workers, school administrators, and of course, every image onscreen—segregation meant that white people didn't know much about us at all.

For all the ways that segregation is aimed at limiting the choices of people of color, it's white people who are ultimately isolated. In a survey taken during the uprisings in Ferguson, Missouri, after the police killing of Michael Brown, an unarmed black teenager, the majority of white Americans said they regularly came in contact with only "a few" African Americans, and a 2019 poll reported that 21 percent "seldom or never" interacted with any people of color at all. In 2016, three-quarters of white people reported that their social network was entirely white.

This white isolation continues amid rising racial and ethnic diversity in America, though few white people say they want it to—in fact, quite the opposite. Diversity has become a commonly accepted "good" despite its elusiveness; people seem to know that the more you interact with people who are different from you, the more commonalities you see and the less they seem like "the other." Research repeatedly bears this out. Take, for example, a meta-analysis that examined 515 studies conducted in 38 countries from the 1940s through 2000, which encompassed responses from 250,000 people. The social psychologist Linda Tropp explained the findings of this research in 2014, when she testified before the New York City Council in a hearing about the city's school system, the most segregated in the United States. "Approximately ninety-four percent of the cases in our analysis show a relationship such that greater contact is associated with lower prejudice." What's more, she said, "contact reduces our anxiety in relation to other groups and enhances our ability to empathize with other groups."

This is the strange paradox with white attitudes toward integration: in the course of two generations and one lifetime, white public opinion went from supporting segregation to recognizing integration as a positive good. Ask most white people in the housing market, and they will say they want to live in racially integrated communities. But they don't. Professor Maria Krysan and her colleagues from the University of Illinois looked into how people of all races think about diversity in their neighborhood housing choices. In their study, white people could even specify how much diversity they wanted: a neighborhood with about 47 percent white people. Black and Latinx people who participated in Krysan's study also knew what level of diversity they sought: areas that are 37 percent black and 32 percent Latinx, respectively. I find it fascinating that all three groups say that, ideally, they want to live in communities in which they do not constitute a majority. Yet researchers found that while black and Latinx people actually search for housing in neighborhoods that match their desired levels of diversity, white people search in neighborhoods that are 68 percent white, and they end up living in areas that are 74 percent white. They say they want to be outnumbered by people of color; instead, they end up choosing places where they outnumber others three to one. Somewhere in between their stated desires and their actions is where the story of white racial hierarchy slips in—sometimes couched in the neutral-sounding terms of "good schools" or "appealing neighborhoods" or other codes for a racialized preference for homogeneity—and turns them back from their vision of an integrated life, with all its attendant benefits. It's a story that the law wrote in the mind and on the land through generations of mandated segregation.

In another study, Professor Krysan and her colleagues showed white and black people videos of identical neighborhoods, with actors posing as black and white residents, and asked them to rate the neighborhoods. They found that "both the racially mixed and the all-black neighborhood were rated by whites as significantly less desirable than the all-white neighborhood. The presence of African Americans in a neighborhood resulted in a downgrading of its desirability." The white people's judgment wasn't about class—they didn't use the actors' race as a proxy for how nice the houses were or how well the streets were maintained or what people on the block were doing outside—because all those cues remained the same in the videos. It was simply the presence of black people that made them turn from the neighborhood. Krysan's experiment was a video simulation, but the real-world patterns of persistent white segregation bear it out. White people are surely losing something when they end up choosing a path closer to their grandparents' racially restricted lives than the lives they profess to want for their children.

———

**PUBLIC POLICY CREATED** this problem, and public policy should solve it. Because of our deliberately constructed racial wealth gap, most black and brown families can't afford to rent or buy in the places where white families are, and when white families bring their wealth into black and brown neighborhoods, it more often leads to gentrification and displacement than enduring integration. The solution is more housing in more places that people can afford on the average incomes of workers of color. What gets in the way is objections about the costs—to real estate developers, to public budgets, and to existing property owners.

But what about the costs we're already paying? Frustrated by the usual hand-wringing over the costs of reform in Chicago, Marisa Novara and her colleagues at Chicago's Metropolitan Planning Council and the Urban Institute decided to flip the ledger. They asked instead, what is the cost of segregation to Chicago? They analyzed quality-of-life indicators that were correlated with segregation in the one hundred biggest cities and compared them to Chicago's, which allowed them to see how their city would benefit from not even eliminating segregation—but just from bringing it down to the not-very-good American average.

The findings are stark. Higher black-white segregation is correlated with billions in "lost income, lost lives, and lost potential" in Chicago. The city's segregation costs workers $4.4 billion in income, and the area's gross domestic product $8 billion. As compared to a more integrated city, eighty-three thousand fewer Chicagoans are completing bachelor's degrees—the majority of whom (78 percent) are white. That means a loss of approximately $90 billion in total lifetime earnings in the city. Reducing segregation to the national median would have an impact on Chicago's notoriously high homicide rate—by an estimated 30 percent—increasing safety for everyone while lowering public costs for police, courts, and corrections facilities; raising real estate values; and preserving the income, tax revenue, and priceless human lives of the more than two hundred people each year who would be saved from a violent death. By reducing the segregation between white and Latino residents, the researchers found, Chicago could increase life expectancy for both.

Our local economies and public health statistics aren't the only realms in which to measure the costs of segregation; the costs are environmental as well. The environmental justice movement has long established that industry and government decision makers are more likely to direct pollutants, ranging from toxic waste dumps to heavy truck traffic, into neighborhoods where people of color, especially black people, live. This injustice has typically been understood as a life-and-death benefit of white privilege: white people can sidestep the poisoned runoff of our industrial economy. But less well known is the fact that segregation brings more pollution for white people, too. It turns out that integrated communities are less polluted than segregated ones. It's a classic racial divide-and-conquer, collective action problem: the separateness of the population leaves communities less able to band together to demand less pollution in the first place, for everyone. An environmental health scientist from the University of California, Berkeley, Rachel Morello-Frosch, conducted a major study examining pollutants that are known carcinogens and found that more segregated cities had more of them in the air. As she explained it to me, "In those segregated cities, white folks are much worse off than their white counterparts who live in less segregated cities, in terms of pollution burden."

I marveled at the force of the finding: segregated cities have higher cancer-causing pollutants—for white people, too—than more integrated ones. Professor Morello-Frosch was quick to add: "And it's not explained by poverty. . . . That effect remains even after you've taken into account the relative concentrations of poverty."

**"THE WAY WE** talk about 'good schools' and 'good neighborhoods' makes it clear that the absence of people of color is, in large part, what defines our schools and neighborhoods as good," writes Robin DiAngelo. This old belief—which few white families would consciously endorse today—remains undeniably persistent as long as all public schools aren't "good schools." So, why aren't they? This thorny but solvable problem is rooted in our country's centuries-old decisions to segregate communities as well as decisions we continue to make today about how we draw our school districts and how we fund public schools.

Although the federal government kicks in a small portion, schools are financed primarily by local and state taxes, so the wealth of the community you live in will determine how well resourced your local schools are. White communities tend to draw their district boundaries narrowly, in order to make ultra-local and racially and socioeconomically homogenous districts, enabling them to hoard the wealth that comes from local property taxes. Meanwhile, areas with lower property values serve greater numbers of children of color with fewer resources. Nationwide, overwhelmingly white public school districts have $23 billion more in funding than overwhelmingly of-color districts, resulting in an average of $2,226 more funding per student. If we recall how much of white wealth is owed to racist housing subsidies, the decision to keep allowing local property taxes to determine the fate of our children becomes even less defensible.

Of course, even these all-white, high-income public school districts are rare, as most white parents know. Increasingly, public education has been hollowed out by the way that racism drains the pool in America: public goods are seen as worthy of investment only so long as the public is seen as good. Today, the majority of public school students in the United States are children of color. Why? Because a disproportionate number of white students are enrolled in private schools, comprising 69 percent of K–12 private school enrollment. The boom in private schools, particularly in the South and West, occurred as a reaction to school integration in the 1950s and '60s. Unsurprisingly given so many private schools' advent as "segregation academies," today, almost half of private school kids attend schools that are essentially all white.

The pricing up and privatization of public goods has a cost for us all—most white families included. A house in a neighborhood unencumbered by the systemic racism found in public schools serving children of color will cost significantly more. In the suburbs of Cincinnati, a house near a highly rated school cost 58 percent more per square foot than a nearby house with the same one-story design and high ceilings, just in a different school district. The national picture is consistent, according to the real estate data firm ATTOM Data, which looked at 4,435 zip codes and found that homes in zip codes that had at least one elementary school with higher-than-average test scores were 77 percent more expensive than houses in areas without. Paying a 77 percent premium may be fine for white families with plenty of disposable income and job flexibility, but it's a tax levied by racism that not everyone can afford. That's why so many families feel like they're in an arms race, fleeing what racism has wrought on public education, with the average person being priced out of the competition. ATTOM Data calculated that someone with average wages could not afford to live in 65 percent of the zip codes with highly rated elementary schools. (CNN covered that study with a blunt headline that would be surprising to few people: YOU PROBABLY CAN'T AFFORD TO LIVE NEAR GOOD SCHOOLS.) Families who can afford a house near a "good" school, in turn, get set up for a windfall of unearned cash: a 2016 report found that homeowners in zip codes with "good" schools "have gained $51,000 more in home value since purchase than homeowners in zips without 'good' schools."

In order to chase these so-called good schools, white families must be able and willing to stretch their budgets to live in increasingly expensive, and segregated, communities. This is a tangible cost both of systemic racism and of often unconscious interpersonal racism: fear itself. These white parents are paying for their fear because they're assuming that white-dominant schools are worth the cost to their white children; essentially, that segregated schools are best.

———

**BUT WHAT IF** the entire logic is wrong? What if they're not only paying too high a cost for segregation, but they're also mistaken about the benefit? Here's where things get interesting. Compared to students at predominantly white schools, white students who attend diverse K–12 schools achieve better learning outcomes and even higher test scores, particularly in areas such as math and science. Why? Of course, white students at racially diverse schools develop more cultural competency—the ability to collaborate and feel at ease with people from different racial, ethnic, and economic backgrounds—than students who attend segregated schools. But their minds are also improved when it comes to critical thinking and problem solving. Exposure to multiple viewpoints leads to more flexible and creative thinking and greater ability to solve problems.

The dividends to diversity in education pay out over a lifetime. Cultural competency is a necessity in today's multicultural professional world, and U.S. corporations spend about eight billion dollars a year on diversity training to boost it among their workforce. In the long run, research reveals that racially diverse K–12 schools can produce better citizens—white students who feel a greater sense of civic engagement, who are more likely to consider friends and colleagues from different races as part of "us" rather than "them," who will be more at ease in the multicolor future of America in which white people will no longer be the majority. The benefits of diversity are not zero-sum gains for white people at the expense of their classmates of color, either. Amherst College psychology professor Dr. Deborah Son Holoien cites several studies of college students—the largest of which included more than seventy-seven thousand undergraduates—in which racially and ethnically diverse educational experiences resulted in improvements in critical thinking and learning outcomes, and in the acquisition of intellectual, scientific, and professional skills. The results were similar for black, white, Asian American, and Latinx students.

All this untapped potential. All these perverse incentives pulling us apart, two generations after segregation's supposed end. I felt compelled to look again at the 1954 Supreme Court decision that should have changed everything, *Brown v. Board of Education of Topeka.* *Brown* struck down state and local laws that racially segregated public schools and rejected the premise of "separate but equal," which had been the law of the land since the Court's 1896 decision in *Plessy v. Ferguson.* The NAACP (and, later, the NAACP Legal Defense and Educational Fund) had been litigating against segregation since the 1930s, focusing less on why segregation was wrong and more on the government's failure to guarantee "equal" or even sufficient facilities, resources, and salaries at black colleges and public schools. It was a strategy to ratchet up the public cost of state segregation.

But in the end, what led to a historic unanimous decision from the Supreme Court was disapproval not of inequality but of separateness itself. In *Brown,* the civil rights lawyers employed the expertise of social scientists to argue that it was segregation and the message it sent, which reinforced the notion of human hierarchy, that hurt children more than mere out-of-date books and unheated classrooms ever could. Thirty-two experts submitted an appendix to the appellants' briefs detailing the damage of segregation to the development of "minority" children. The facts in this appendix were the indelible details—most memorably the black children learning to prefer white dolls—that formed the moral basis for the Court's decision in *Brown.* And *Brown* gave rise to a progeny of cases over the following decades, cases protecting brown and black children from the sting of inferiority, an inferiority signaled by being excluded from white schools.

But there was another path from *Brown,* one not taken, with profound consequences for our understanding of segregation's harms. The nine white male justices ignored a part of the social scientists' appendix that also described in prescient detail the harm segregation inflicts on "majority" children. White children "who learn the prejudices of our society," wrote the social scientists, were "being taught to gain personal status in an unrealistic and non-adaptive way." They were "not required to evaluate themselves in terms of the more basic standards of actual personal ability and achievement." What's more, they "often develop patterns of guilt feelings, rationalizations and other mechanisms which they must use in an attempt to protect themselves from recognizing the essential injustice of their unrealistic fears and hatreds of minority groups." The best research of the day concluded that "confusion, conflict, moral cynicism, and disrespect for authority may arise in [white] children as a consequence of being taught the moral, religious and democratic principles of justice and fair play by the same persons and institutions who seem to be acting in a prejudiced and discriminatory manner."

As Sherrilyn Ifill, president and director-counsel of the NAACP Legal Defense Fund, reminded us on the sixty-second anniversary of the decision, this profound insight—that segregation sends distorting messages not just to black and brown but also to white children—was lost in the triumphalism of *Brown*. She wrote, "I believe that we must have a public reckoning with the history of the full record presented to the Court in *Brown*, which predicted with devastating clarity the mind-warping harm of segregation on white children." The now-lost rationale for why segregation must fall—the rationale that included the costs to us all—might have actually uprooted segregation in America. After all, arguing that black and brown children suffered from not being with white children affirmed the reality of unequal conditions, but once the argument was divorced from the context of legal segregation, it also subtly reaffirmed the logic of white supremacy. Today, it's that logic that endures—that white segregated schools are better and that everyone, even white children, should endeavor to be in them.

It's a bit of a platitude that children don't see race, that they must learn to hate. It's in fact the subject of one of the most popular tweets of all time, from Barack Obama, who captioned a photo of himself looking into a window at the faces of four children: two white, one Asian, and one black: "No one is born hating a person because of the color of their skin or his background or his religion." But I think about my own childhood, which was filled with judgments, conflicts, and alliances around race, memories from as early as nursery school. The truth is, children do learn to categorize, and rank, people by race while they are still toddlers. By age three or four, white children and children of color have absorbed the message that white is better, and both are likely to select white playmates if given a choice. While still in elementary school, white children begin to learn the unspoken rules of our segregated society, and they will no longer say aloud to a researcher who asks them to distribute new toys that "these kids should get them because they're white." Instead, they'll come up with an explanation: "These [white] kids should get the new toys because they work harder."

For all my efforts to enumerate the costs of segregation, the loss is incalculable. "The most profound message of racial segregation for whites may be that there is no real loss in the absence of people of color from our lives," wrote Robin DiAngelo. "Not one person who loved me, guided me, or taught me ever conveyed that there was loss to me in segregation; that I would lose anything by not having people of color in my life."

MY JOURNEY INTRODUCED me to families who are discovering the Solidarity Dividend in integration. Because the dominant narrative about school quality is color blind—the conversation is about numerical test scores and teacher-student ratios, not race or culture, of course—it's easy to walk right into a trap set for us by racism. It's an easy walk for millions of white parents who don't consider themselves racist. It was even an easy walk for Ali Takata, a mother of two who doesn't even consider herself white.

"Full disclosure I'm fifty percent white," she wrote in an introductory email. "I'm Hapa—Japanese and Italian. My husband is Sri Lankan, born in Singapore and raised in Singapore and England. Even though we are a mixed Asian family," she freely acknowledged,

"I've approached public school as a privileged [half-white] person. Depending on the situation, I am white-passing, although it's always hard to know how people perceive me."

Ali and her family moved from the San Francisco Bay Area to Austin, Texas, so her husband could begin a new job at the University of Texas. Ali researched the area, using school-rating resources such as GreatSchools.org to find what she then considered "a good neighborhood and a good school" for their two daughters, who were in preschool and first grade, respectively.

"Austin is divided east and west," Ali said. "And the farther west you go, the wealthier and the whiter the city becomes. The farther east you go, the more impoverished and browner and blacker the people are." This was no accident, she explained. "The 1928 Austin city plan segregated the city, forcing the black residents east. Then Interstate Thirty-five was built as a barrier to subjugate the black and brown residents even further. So . . . historically I-35 was the divide between east and west."

Ali's family could have paid less for a home in East Austin, where the school ratings were lower, but instead, they found a house in what she described as "a white, wealthy neighborhood" on the west side of Austin. Ali herself had grown up in a similar community, in a suburb of Hartford, Connecticut. As someone who is part white and part Asian, she had never felt totally comfortable there. But everything was nudging her to choose a similar world for her kids: the social conditioning, the data, even the signals that our market-based society sends about higher-priced things simply being better.

So, the Austin neighborhood Ali chose in order to find a "good" school ended up being very much like suburban Connecticut in the 1980s. "I recall specifically feeling like something was wrong with my eyes," said Ali. "Where were the Asian people? And where were the black people? They were virtually invisible here. . . . And it was just because I live on the west side."

She sent her kids to the local public school, whose student body reflected the neighborhood. "I will say that the first year was great,"

Ali said. "I found the people very welcoming. . . . It took me about a year to find a niche at that school, among the white wealthy people. But I did, you know. And I called them friends."

And yet, certain aspects of the school's culture began to disturb her. Parents were deeply involved in the school—not only fundraising and volunteering, but intruding into the school day in ways that seemed to Ali like "helicopter parenting." Parents tried to "micromanage the teachers and curriculum," Ali saw, to "insert themselves into the inner workings of the school, and to assume that 'I know just as much or more than the teacher or administrator.'"

It slowly dawned on her that many of the behaviors of both students and parents that she found off-putting were expressions of white privilege. "I feel like there's a way in which we upper-middle-class parents . . . want [our kids] to be unencumbered in their lives," including, she feels, by rules. "It's this entitlement. And it's this feeling of . . . is there a rule? I don't need to respect this rule. It doesn't pertain to me."

By her children's third year in the school, Ali realized, "'I just can't do this. This is not me.' It just—I felt kind of disgusted by the culture." It was everywhere, and yet she didn't have a name for it until she became involved in an affinity group for parents choosing integrated schools. "The competitiveness, complete with humble bragging. The insularity and superficiality, the focus on 'me and my kid only,'" Ali said. "By staying at [that] school, I was supporting a white supremacy institution. That felt so wrong." Yet virtually her entire social circle in Austin was composed of parents who were active in the school and immersed in its values.

She began to research alternatives, visiting eight public schools on Austin's East Side, where her daughters would not be "surrounded by all that privilege," Ali said. "I was going to make this decision to desegregate my kids. You know, if the city wasn't going to do it, there's no policy around it, then I was going to do it.

"It was a very lonely process. I didn't talk to anybody about it except for my husband." The next fall, Ali and her husband transferred their daughters, then in second and fourth grade, to a school that was 50 percent African American, 30 percent Latinx, 11 percent white, 3 percent Asian, and 5 percent students of two or more races. Eighty-seven percent of the students were economically disadvantaged.

Ali's daughters are mixed Asian, with features and skin tones that make it unlikely they will be perceived by others as white, the way Ali sometimes is. At their old school or the new one, she said, "My girls will always go to school with kids who look different from them." Still, "I did not want to raise my girls in such a homogenous, unrealistic community. . . . I wanted them to experience difference."

The new school, she said, is predominantly "black and brown, and that is what . . . permeates the school. There's music playing right when you walk in. Fun music, hip-hop music. And there's a step team." Ali values that her children will not grow up ignorant of the culture of their peers on the other side of town, but the advantages of the new school go much deeper than music and dance. "It's also more community-focused, which is antithetical to the white, privileged culture" of making sure my child gets the best of everything.

As for the parents in the West Austin neighborhood, "there has been a deafening silence around my decision." When she runs into some of her former friends, they may talk about how their children are doing, but they don't ask her anything at all about hers. "The white community I left felt stifling and oppressive," Ali said. "That part surprised me. My profound relief surprised me. I had no idea that living my values would feel so liberating."

Transferring to a new school in which they are surrounded by kids with different experiences and frames of reference has had its bumps, but it "has been an eye-opening experience for [my girls], I think," Ali said. "And it has brought up really healthy [family] discussions . . . about wealth and class and how it feels for them . . . to be called [out] for being the rich kids. . . . I think it's been an amazing experience."

Integrated Schools is a nationwide grassroots effort to empower, educate, and organize parents who are white and/or privileged like

Ali, parents who want to shift their priorities about their children's education away from centering metrics like test scores or assumptions about behavior and discipline and toward contributing to an antiracist public educational system. The movement acknowledges that "white parents have been the key barrier to the advancement of school integration and education equity." Through resources including reading lists and guides for awkward conversations along with traditional community organizing and coalition building tactics, the movement encourages parents not to view "diversity primarily as a commodity for the benefit of our own children" and not to view schools that serve primarily students of color as "broken and in need of white parents to fix them." Rather, the goal of leveraging parents' choices about schools should be to disrupt segregation because of the ways it distorts our democracy and corrodes the prospects of all our children. The group offers tools and tips to enable parents to live their values and to raise antiracist children who can help build an antiracist future.

As for Ali Takata, she lost a circle of friends but gained something far more valuable. "Through my experience at the new school, I've been able to see how steeped in white upper-middle-class culture I had been," she said. And now, "Oh my goodness, I cannot believe the peace I feel with my decision and my life."

**SENDING HER TWO** children to the local public schools twenty-something years ago wasn't so much a decision for Tracy Wright-Mauer, a white woman who moved to Poughkeepsie, New York, when her husband got a job at IBM. It was more of a decision not to act, not to pull her children away from the urban neighborhood she fell in love with, with its beautiful old homes. "My husband and I, we didn't consciously say, 'Okay. We're going to . . . be, you know, be the integrators,' or anything. We just didn't think not to buy a house in the district, and we didn't think, 'Oh, well, I'll send my kids to private school [because] the school doesn't look like my kids.' " The most thought she ever gave to it was when other white parents would ask her questions such as "Well, when you get to middle school, are you going to send them to private school?" or "What about high school? You're going to send them to Lourdes, right?" referring the nearly 90 percent white Catholic school.

Many of these white parents had purchased their houses in Spackenkill, a wealthy part of Poughkeepsie that fought for school district independence in the 1960s and '70s. Spackenkill successfully sued to keep its district separate from the larger city, walling off its richer tax base (including the revenues from the IBM headquarters). One can find similar stories all across the country, with predominantly white school districts drawing narrower boundaries to serve far fewer children (typically just fifteen hundred) than majority of-color low-income districts that serve an average of over ten thousand. It's a hoarding of resources by white families who wouldn't have such a wealth advantage if it weren't for generations of explicit racial exclusion and predation in the housing market.

A few years ago, Tracy was cleaning her house and came across her daughter's second-grade class photo: fifteen smiling prepubescent boys and girls in their Photo Day best. She snapped a picture and posted it on Facebook, and one of her black friends pointed out to her that "other than the teachers, [Fiona] was the only white kid in the class." Her daughter, Fiona, is now in college; her son, Aidan, is wrapping up high school. They're both the products of what parents in the Integrated Schools Facebook group Tracy now belongs to call "Global Majority" public schools, and "both have learned to discuss race," she offered. "They talk about it all the time. They discuss class. They discuss racism and equity, and they just are really, really engaged with their friends about these subjects. And, you know, I think it's pretty awesome."

I had to ask Tracy the million-dollar question: Were they good schools? What about the standardized test scores, the yardstick by which all quality is measured? Tracy didn't pause: "Maybe I'm an anomaly. I think other parents look to the test scores . . . to judge a school. Just because the test scores are not, you know, the highest in the state, or in the top ten, it doesn't mean to me that the kids aren't getting really great teachers and being challenged and doing interesting things in their classes." Her son, Aidan, who was graduating the year we spoke, is the only white guy in his friend group, and all his friends were going on to college. "His friends are smart kids who work hard, and they do well on their SATs, and they're very motivated."

I was able to reach Fiona, a freshman on a rowing scholarship at Drexel University in Philadelphia, in her dorm room. I asked her what it had been like going to a high school where just 10 percent of the student body was white. Fiona recalled it making for some uncomfortable conversations with white kids in other school districts. They'd go something like this: "I'd say, oh, I'm from Poughkeepsie [High],' and they'd be like, 'Oh, I'm so sorry.' Which someone actually said to me." I cringed. "It's really just disappointing. Because I love Poughkeepsie [High], and I loved my time there, and the friends I made."

Fiona said her direction in life had been influenced by how she learned to see the world at Poughkeepsie High; she credited the experience with giving her the skills to be an advocate. "It helped me empathetically. I don't know if I want to be a politician, or if I want to work with some environmental justice organization, but empathy has a lot to do with that: looking at both sides of the story and not trying to put a Band-Aid over something, but getting to the root of the problem. I think that's where my skills lie. And . . . a lot of that comes from where I grew up and where I went to school."

Fiona's now at a college where more than half of the students are white, and just 8 and 6 percent are African American and Latinx, respectively. It's a big shift. Many of her white peers are just not as comfortable around people of color. "If there's a roomful of black people and [we walk in and] we're the only white people? I think they sort of say—like, 'Oh, like, let's leave.' Or they say, like, if we're out at night, 'Oh, this is, like, a little sketchy.' Things like that, I notice." But she also doesn't want to suggest that white kids who grew up in segregated schools are hopeless when it comes to race. "I think one of the downfalls of growing up in a homogeneous setting is that the process of understanding . . . racial inequalities and recognizing one's own privilege can be very uncomfortable and might take longer, but it doesn't mean they don't get there."

In that way, Fiona feels lucky. "I got to spend my time with people who didn't look like me, and that didn't really matter. And I hope to strive to feel that way throughout my whole life. To not be surprised when I'm in a diverse group of people, and just be like, 'This is normal. This is how it's supposed to be.'"

## Chapter 8

# THE
# SAME
# SKY

**N**ew mothers know the upside-down hours, between roughly midnight and dawn, when the physical needs of your newborn push you upright, pry open your eyes, and set your mind into motion at a pace unmatched by the dormant world around you. I was three weeks into the life of my son and had developed a routine. He'd wake up every four hours like clockwork, get a diaper change, nurse, and then return to sleep on the breast some forty minutes later. Once the initial challenge of breastfeeding was behind me, this routine gave me time for my mind to wander. On one such night, with one arm cradling my son's tiny body, I held my phone in the other and idly thumbed through news headlines. The *Guardian*'s feed was topped by a headline that read, WE HAVE 12 YEARS TO LIMIT CLIMATE CHANGE CATASTROPHE, WARNS UN. My arm tensed reflexively around my son, and he startled, opening his eyes. "It's okay, baby, it's okay," I murmured to him. But it's not.

I read the article—about the latest UN Intergovernmental Panel on Climate Change report—with rising dread, and then clicked and scrolled my way into a wormhole of terrifying environmental news. The story is simple and devastating. Climate change caused by manmade pollution is changing our world in ways that are making it less habitable for human and animal life as we know it. Cold spells have decreased, and record heat waves have increased; droughts and wildfires have become more frequent. Sheets of ice are rapidly melting around the globe, pushing up sea levels that were already rising because heat makes ocean water molecules expand. The impact on human life is already happening, with increases in casualties from climate-exacerbated weather events, malnutrition, and infectious diseases as well as declines in mental health. Those who say we can't sacrifice economic growth for environmental protection are failing to account for the economic costs of climate change that are already upon us: an estimated $240 billion a year in the United States currently, due to increased extreme weather. That figure represents nearly half the average annual growth of the U.S. economy from 2009 to 2019. Some scientists also say that we are in a new era of mass extinction, having lost half the animal population over the past forty years due to "habitat destruction, overhunting, toxic pollution, invasion by alien species and climate change." The news gets worse the more you read.

But the same spiral down into despair is the one you can take out of it: humans are creating these catastrophic problems for ourselves, and humans can turn things around. Solutions are at the ready that would slow global warming and avoid the worst impacts that scientists are portending. Business and government could help make the ways we travel, live, and work more energy efficient, while switching our reliance from polluting fossil fuels to cleaner renewable energy sources like solar and wind power. Twenty years ago, these new technologies were prohibitively expensive; now they're often cheaper than higher-pollution fuels, even without adding the true externalized costs of fossil fuels to their sticker price, as we could and should. It's possible for our food and farming systems to use fewer toxic chemicals, exploit fewer animals, and consume less water and land. In the transformation of whole industries, we could create millions more higher-paying jobs and target economic opportunities to the communities and people who have suffered the most under our unequal, polluting economic status quo. And the United States, the country that invented the solar cell, could lead the way.

But we are not. When I finally put my phone down hours later, my son in the deepest, most peaceful part of his sleep and me wondering if I could even close my eyes again before dawn, I thought, "When the entire weight of science the world over is sending us an alarm, why is my country refusing to rise?"

**THE UNITED STATES** is, in many ways, the problem. We are the biggest carbon polluter in history, but we have one of the strongest and most politically powerful factions opposed to taking action to prevent catastrophic climate change. In our peer countries, the conservative political parties draw contrast with the center and left by advocating for corporate climate solutions over government programs and regulations. Only in the United States does our conservative party, with very few exceptions, flat-out deny that there's a problem. The opposition of the American conservative political movement is the primary reason the United States has not taken stronger legislative action to reduce greenhouse gases; our inaction is one of the main reasons the world has continued to warm. In short, the loss of human and animal life and habitats that we are already experiencing is in no small part due to the American conservative political faction. And that political faction is almost entirely white.

On a cloudy Thursday morning in June 2019, Oregon State Senate president Peter Courtney walked into the Capitol Building intending to call the day's session to order. Courtney is a tall, white-haired Democrat, a somber public servant who's served the longest of any of the state's legislators. On the agenda that day was a long-negotiated bill to institute a statewide cap-and-trade emissions program to combat climate change. But when Senator Courtney looked around the two-story chamber, many of the Art Deco wooden desks that had been there since 1938 were empty. Only his Demo-

cratic colleagues were present. The entire Republican delegation had
refused to come to work in order to deny the Democratic majority a
voting quorum to even consider the climate change bill. As the governor and remaining legislators scrambled to find out what had happened, it became clear that the Republican senators had gone into
hiding to avoid the Oregon government for which they worked. In a
speech Senator Courtney delivered to a mostly empty chamber, his
voice faltered multiple times. He called it "the saddest day of my
legislative life."

Courtney asked Oregon's governor, Kate Brown, to send the state's
sheriffs to find the runaway lawmakers and bring them back to their
duties. Then a Republican state senator, Brian Boquist, suggested
that if that happened, he would kill the police. "Send bachelors and
come heavily armed," he said on camera. "I'm not going to be a political prisoner in the state of Oregon." (I tried to imagine a black
lawmaker making this statement and still walking free or holding
his job, as Boquist has, but my mind just couldn't compute it.) Right-
wing militias threatened the Capitol building in support of the runaway legislators. The Democrats tabled the bill.

The next year, Democrats offered major concessions to the rural
industries represented by the Republican lawmakers, even though
logging is the state's biggest source of greenhouse gas emissions.
Then the Oregon Republicans walked out again. It's hard to understand this brinkmanship if you assume that their goal is a bill that
better reflects their rural constituents' interests. But it's not: Senate
Republican leader Herman Baertschiger Jr. simply disbelieves the
scientific consensus that humans are responsible for climate change.
The cost to the people of Oregon of his defending this unfounded
and minority opinion was immense. Of the 258 bills introduced in
the legislative session, only three were passed due to the Republican
walkout.

The willingness to have their state make basically no improvements in policies for their citizens for an entire year reminded me,
yet again, of the drained public pool. The only-if-it-suits-us commit-

ment to government and democracy—from people who are paid to govern, no less—reminded me of the people (always all white) on the other side of Demos's voting rights lawsuits. I'd come to understand voter suppression and gutted public goods as contests for power that had everything to do with race, but the Oregon GOP's act of political warfare didn't seem to be about race; it was about stopping the majority from following scientific recommendations to save the planet for everyone. I couldn't easily connect the dots.

The biggest national environmental organizations (nicknamed the Big Greens) don't readily make the connection, either. Their narrative about their opposition has been about corruption and greed. They point to the millions of dollars spent by fossil fuel companies to turn skeptical scientists into sources for "both sides" reporting. They name-check the well-funded conservative think tanks able to produce a purported expert to sow doubt in every congressional hearing on the climate. They catalogue the campaign contributions and post-career lobbyist jobs that convince politicians to fall in line. And their story of how corruption has pushed us backward in environmental protection over the past generation, even as the stakes have gotten higher, is undeniably true.

Yet there's more to the story. I began to take notice of something that nobody in the Big Greens seemed to be talking about: the key players waging war against environmental protection were reliably white men, from the industry executives to the politicians to the media commentators. I also grew curious about why white Americans are more prone to following the political leadership of these antiscience crusaders in the Republican party, regardless of the catastrophic risks of their being wrong. That's where there's very little conventional wisdom in the green movement. I asked my friend May Boeve, a cofounder of one of the newer big climate groups, 350.org, whether she saw climate change denial as an identity issue. "Honestly, I don't know that anybody in the Big Greens does. We see that it's become a partisan issue, for sure—and we are very aware that communities of color are being hit first and worst by climate impacts. But generally speaking, our field sees race impacting climate as a disparities issue, not a racial politics issue."

May's organization was cofounded by a white climate expert named Bill McKibben and a group of white Middlebury College students from Vermont in 2009, with the aim of mobilizing hundreds of countries into mass action for climate solutions. It operates in 180 countries, training mostly young people for demonstrations that have included anti–Keystone Pipeline rallies, the People's Climate March in 2014, and the Global Climate Strike in 2019. The global, multicultural scope of 350.org's work, combined with its years of partnership with Indigenous climate activists, has spurred its leadership to deepen their racial justice analysis. So, as I set out to determine what was going on with the connection between racism and opposition to climate action, I promised to share with May what I was learning.

It turns out that white people in America are much less likely than people of color to rank environmental problems as a pressing concern. Public opinion surveys show that black and Latinx people are more supportive of national and international climate change solutions than white people are. In fact, if it were up to only white people, we might not act at all. According to the Yale Project on Climate Change Communication, fewer than 25 percent of white people said they were willing to join a campaign to convince government to act on climate change. The majority of white Americans fell into the categories the researchers called "Cautious," "Disengaged," "Doubtful," or "Dismissive," meaning they don't know enough, don't care, or are outright opposed to taking action. By contrast, 70 percent of Latinx and 57 percent of black people are either "Alarmed" or "Concerned." Like so many issues in public life, race appears to significantly shape your worldview about climate change.

When I shared this and other research about race and climate viewpoints with May on a phone call, she was reflective. "Maybe it's because, despite the prominence of so many leaders of color, white environmentalists play such an outsize role in the Big Green leader-

ship. This"—how resistant white Americans are to taking action—
"remains a blind spot for the mainstream environmental movement,"
she told me.

"In some ways, it makes sense," I replied. "The same power structures that advantage white people in the world are advantaging white
people in the advocacy field, and the cost of that is that the field is
not seeing where the biggest untapped base is for organizing."

"It's interesting," May said, "because 350 is a global organization,
so I do spend a lot of time thinking about how culture shapes different people's worldviews and what will move them to action . . . It's
different in Bangladesh versus Hong Kong versus Egypt versus the
U.S., or the many communities within each of those places. But, of
course, the most powerful worldview we need to contend with is
white supremacy. Of course it is," she said, then added with a little
laugh, "and the patriarchy." Indeed, the Yale Project on Climate
Change Communication found that of the six categories of American
opinion about climate change, the "Dismissive" were more likely to
be white, male, and have higher incomes.

But why? My first instinct is always to follow the money and
power: Are powerful interests using race to sell climate denialism to
white people? Polling shows that the racial divide on support for climate change action sharpened as Barack Obama made it a priority
during his administration, negotiating the international Paris Climate Accord, instituting higher fuel economy standards on automobiles, and launching a Clean Power Plan for states to switch to
renewable energy. Looking at the decline in white support for climate action under Obama, political science professor Salil D. Benegal
hypothesized that part of it was due to racial priming from conservative political elites, who "made explicit associations to Obama with
frequent use of frames and imagery highlighting a black president
harming jobs in predominantly white areas." Indeed, the fossil fuel
billionaire Koch brothers and their network covertly supported the
spread of the Tea Party movement, which actively opposed measures
to address climate change. By the 2016 election, the coal miner had

become a symbol of white masculinity under attack from big government.

Professor Benegal then analyzed the opinion data and found that, even when one controlled for partisanship, racial resentment ("a general orientation toward blacks characterized by a feeling that blacks do not try hard enough and receive too many favors") was highly correlated with climate change denialism. "Asking respondents if they agree that climate change is largely due to human activity, we see . . . a 57% probability that a white Republican disagrees that climate change is anthropogenic [caused by humans] at the lowest level of racial resentment, increasing to 84% at the highest level of racial resentment." So, it's not just a symptom of increased partisan polarization; even within the Republican Party, racism increases the likelihood of opposing climate action.

In an influential 2011 study cheekily named "Cool Dudes," the researchers Aaron M. McCright and Riley E. Dunlap examined public opinion data from the period of 2000 to 2010 and found that conservative white men were much more likely to be climate change deniers. The researchers attributed it not to any biological difference, of course, but rather, to the story that white men receive from elite white males in the political media with whom they identify, and the story they tend to believe about themselves, which they described as "identity-protection cognition" and a "system-justification" worldview that is resistant to change. McCright and Dunlap wrote, "Conservative white males are likely to favor protection of the current industrial capitalist order which has historically served them well."

I thought about the many, many moments in my career when politically moderate or conservative white men, whether in Congress or in the editorial pages, had weighed in against action on some social good—environmental protection, raising revenue for public investment, consumer financial regulation—by claiming that it would be "bad for the economy." Our side always had to then jump through hoops to make elaborate statistical models proving that it wouldn't be costly or that it would create jobs and stimulate overall economic growth. But what dawned on me, when I read the research showing that conservative white men tended to justify a system that had served them well, was that "the economy" being defended was not the textbook definition I'd learned: the sum total of our population's consumption, goods, and services. That definition of the economy is one that could go on quite well and even flourish without white men being such lopsided beneficiaries. "The economy" that they were referring to was *their* economy, the economic condition of people like them, seen through the lens of a zero-sum system of hierarchy that taught them to fear any hint of redistribution. Value-neutral admonitions about protecting "the economy" allowed them to protect their own status while resting easy knowing that they were not at all racist, because it wasn't about race—it was about, well, "the economy."

In 2016, a Finnish sociologist named Kirsti M. Jylhä published findings that built on McCright and Dunlap's "Cool Dudes" study, adding to their "system justification" worldview her finding that a "social dominance orientation" was predictive of climate change denial. After reading her work, I went to visit her at New York University, where she was visiting on a year-long fellowship. She is a tall woman with pale skin and almost white-blonde hair, originally from Finland and now living in Sweden. I joined her in her dimly lit and sparsely decorated cube of an office, and we delved right into her methodology. She was quick to clarify that social dominance orientation isn't about people who have a dominant personality; rather, it's people who express beliefs about the way things ought to be that are "learned in society through socialization.

"It's more about accepting that there are differences between groups," she said. "That some groups are better and some groups are worse. So, people who score high in social dominance orientation . . . tend to see the world as a competitive triangle, where it's natural and inevitable that hierarchies exist. And so, society shouldn't do anything to reduce [those hierarchies], because there's probably something in these groups who have a lower position that has caused their lower position."

I responded, "I think most liberals in the United States think that the reason Republicans deny the existence of climate change or are opposed to acting is because they are financially invested in the status quo. Either they're politicians who are paid by fossil fuel lobbies, or they work in resource-extractive industries. . . . Or they are opposed to government intervention, and they don't trust the government. So how," I asked, "is social dominance correlated to climate change?"

Jylhä responded: "There is some sort of unconscious risk calculation going on there, kind of like . . . Should we really do all these changes? Are the risks so high? . . . Social dominance orientation comes into play here. Based on this risk allocation, they think that, 'Hmm, it sounds quite horrible, but I don't think that I will be the one who would suffer if it's true.' . . . Future generations will suffer. Animals will suffer. And people in, for example, developing countries and in islands and so on, are already suffering because of climate change." But if white American men who buy the zero-sum story don't see themselves as suffering, their bias will be toward retaining a status quo that rewards them, even if it leads to suffering for others.

Jylhä told me about unpublished findings she and her U.S. colleagues were beginning to see, findings yielding an even further fine-tuned articulation of the dominance worldview, something they were calling "exclusionary preferences." (I wasn't sold on the euphemistic name.) She explained: "It's also about wanting to [resist] change [in] the society and wanting to maintain societal structures where, for example, discrimination is accepted and where the [native-born] . . . groups and men have the power positions that they [are] used to hav[ing]."

In the middle of our interview, the fire alarm went off, and the entire building was evacuated. We couldn't help but note the irony. Thrust from the stillness of her office, to a chaotic Manhattan sidewalk full of people, our conversation took a more personal turn. "When I came here, immediately from the first day," Professor Jylhä admitted thinking, " 'Wow. I am white.' "

I smiled. She continued, faltering as we so often do when getting personal about race, "People [were] not treating me in weird ways.

It's not like, how people respond[ed] to me. . . . Maybe it even comes from . . . the diversity."

"Yeah," I offered, "you're not used to seeing this many people who are not white in one place all the time . . . ?"

"Yeah. And also, the class differences are more. Because we don't have these types of class—I mean, we do also have class inequality in Sweden. But people who are poor, they are guaranteed to have their own apartments. They have food. And they have treatment if they have mental health issues, physical health issues. It's not like people are left, just thrown out from the system."

Hearing her describe Sweden's more humane society helped me connect the dots on how living in a society like ours could shape your perception of your own climate change risks. "That comes back to your social dominance orientation, right?" I asked. "If you're in a society where you've already let someone go without shelter, then what does it matter if they drown? If it's okay for people to suffer, then it's okay for people to suffer. And if your wealth has protected you from that suffering, then your wealth can probably protect you from another kind of suffering."

Our conversation moved to the other climate-relevant worldviews that other researchers had identified, including racial resentment and system justification. When she mentioned the Benegal racial resentment study, I said, "That is very American."

She said, "Yeah, yeah," but I wasn't sure that someone who grew up with a functioning social democracy in a pretty racially homogenous country would necessarily understand the nuances of American racism and its relationship to government action. So, I explained.

"Racial resentment goes through government for us. For most of our history, the government was the racist. But many white people now believe, consciously or unconsciously, that the government has taken the other side and is now changing the 'proper' racial order through social spending, civil rights laws, and affirmative action. This makes the government untrustworthy. And so, racial resentment by whites and distrust of government are very highly correlated. And then distrust of government and not wanting government to do anything about climate change . . ." I made a hand gesture to show that one could naturally follow the other. She took her notepad out of the purse she'd grabbed as we evacuated her office and took notes. We talked for a little while longer and then wished each other well.

On my rush-hour subway ride home, I was packed in tight with a cross-section of New York City: faces in every human hue; multiple languages within earshot; a kid I'd seen hop the turnstile for lack of the $2.75 fare holding the same pole as a woman in $800 shoes. Was Kirsti Jylhä on a train like this for the first time when she thought, "Wow, I'm white?" Or was she on a subway platform watching everyone give a wide berth to an unhoused man asleep on a bench?

"When I came here, [it became] not theoretical," she had told me that afternoon. "You know, there is a difference of knowing and understand[ing]. So, I think I have come to understanding."

It was sad for me to hear that a short time in my country had brought this idealistic Nordic academic a deeper understanding of the social dominance theory she'd been writing about: what it looks like when a group of people demonstrate little empathy for the suffering of others. But of course, it did. The Nordic countries' social-democratic policies—generous subsidies for housing, education, and retirement and, newly relevant to me, 480 days of parental leave in Sweden—are almost unimaginable in today's America, because the dominant American political culture would say that people lacking those privileges are responsible for their situations. You can't find a starker contrast between two versions of society that are both wealthy democracies. But the Nordic model of democracy rests on a mostly homogenous "demos"; unlike the United States, Finland didn't have mass slavery and genocide to cut their empathic cord at the country's birth. President Franklin D. Roosevelt had intended to get the United States closer to the Nordic model in his third term, announcing an "Economic Bill of Rights" proposal, with the right to a job, housing, and medical care "regardless of station, race or creed," in his second-to-last State of the Union address. But just as southern Democrats in Congress had weakened the New Deal in 1938 and would go on to kill national healthcare in 1948, they would have sabotaged FDR's Second Bill of Rights as well. Racism has a cost for everyone. And with the environment and climate change, many white people's skeptical worldview, combined with their outsize political power, has life-or-death consequences for us all.

Perhaps it makes sense, if you've spent a lifetime seeing yourself as the winner of a zero-sum competition for status, that you would have learned along the way to accept inequality as normal; that you'd come to attribute society's wins and losses solely to the players' skill and merit. You might also learn that if there are problems, you and yours are likely to be spared the costs. The thing is, that's just not the case with the environment and climate change. We live under the same sky. Scorching triple-digit days, devastating wildfires, and drought restrictions on drinking water have become the new normal for California's working-class barrios and gated communities alike. Wall Street was flooded by Superstorm Sandy; most of the 13 million people with imperiled seafront housing on the coasts belong to the upper classes. The cash crops at the base of the American agribusiness economy are threatened by more frequent droughts. The majority of white Americans are skeptical or opposed to tackling climate change, but the majority of white Americans will suffer nonetheless from an increasingly inhospitable planet.

It all seemed to come back to the zero-sum story: climate change opposition is sold by an organized, self-interested white elite to a broader base of white constituents already racially primed to distrust government action. The claims are racially innocent—we won't risk the economy for this dubious idea—but those using them are willing to take immense risks that might fall on precisely the historically exploited: people of color and the land, air, animals, and water. Like the zero-sum story, it's all an illusion—white men aren't truly safe from climate risk, and we can have a different but sustainable economy with a better quality of life for more people. But how powerful the zero-sum paradigm must be to knock out science and even a healthy sense of self-preservation. And how dangerous for us all.

**TO ACCEPT THAT** we live under the same sky is to reject the dominant U.S. approach to environmental risk, which has been to shunt off the pollution by-products of industry to what's known as "sacrifice zones." For nearly fifty years, grassroots activists living in these sacrifice zones—Richmond, California; Ocala, Florida; South Bronx, New York; Youngstown, Ohio, and many more—have been proving how racism shapes environmental policy. Collecting soil samples and keeping diaries of hospital visits, mapping the distance between incinerators and neighborhoods of color, they have built a damning record of environmental racism—and a movement for environmental justice.

Dr. Robert Bullard is a sociologist considered by many to be the father of that movement. It happened almost by accident: in 1978, a pioneering lawyer named Linda McKeever Bullard was preparing to file what would be the first lawsuit to use civil rights law to challenge the placement of pollutants in the black communities of Houston. She turned to Dr. Bullard, her husband, to conduct the research. "There was no environmental justice movement . . . no studies that dealt with race and environment, or environmental racism," he told me. "And so, we designed a study and collected the data, laid out the research protocol. And what we found was one hundred percent of all the city-owned landfills were located in black neighborhoods. . . . Six out of eight of the city-owned incinerators were in black neighborhoods. And three out of four of the private-owned landfills were in black neighborhoods. From the thirties up 'til 1978, eighty-two percent of all the garbage, waste, was dumped in predominantly black neighborhoods, even though blacks only made up twenty-five percent of the population." During the same period, he pointed out, "all of the city council members were white."

The theory behind the lawsuit, he said, was "that the city of

Houston was practicing a form of discrimination in placing landfills in . . . black communities. Even though everybody in Houston produced garbage, everybody didn't have to live near the garbage, the landfills, incinerators, and the waste facilities." While the lawsuit failed to stop the incinerator from being built in a black community, the damning data and the effective research protocols helped build a foundation for the environmental justice movement.

The birth of the "EJ" movement in the public consciousness was in 1982, when the state of North Carolina's decision to dump contaminated soil in the small black town of Warren was met with civil disobedience that resulted in five hundred arrests. One of those arrested was a leader of the United Church of Christ's Commission for Racial Justice, Dr. Benjamin Chavis Jr., who would go on to publish the first nationwide study on environmental racism five years later. The church's groundbreaking "Toxic Wastes and Race in the United States" report found that race was the most important predictor of proximity to hazardous waste facilities in America and that three out of five black and Latinx Americans lived in communities with toxic sites. Forty years later, government data still show that black people are 1.5 times more likely to breathe polluted air and drink unsafe water than the overall population.

I DECIDED TO travel to the San Francisco Bay Area city of Richmond, California, where a thriving cross-racial environmental justice movement has been taking on the city's rampant industrial pollution. Richmond is a sacrifice zone in the shadow of one of the country's largest oil refineries, with thirteen times as many air quality violations as the Bay Area's average over a decade. Miya Yoshitani, head of the Asian Pacific Environmental Network (APEN), reminded me that any story about sacrifice zones must start with an explanation of the decisions that created clusters of people of color to target in the first place. "These places are government creations to begin with, that are created by racist policy. . . . And people always want to say,

'People of color, they're poor, and so therefore they live in the less desirable places.' Well, you know . . . those less desirable places were the only places that they could legally own homes. . . . They're not accidental. . . . Those are intentional."

As Richard Rothstein documents in his book *The Color of Law*, Richmond is one of the quintessential stories of government-created American segregation. It was an epicenter of American manufacturing during World War II, and so, the government quickly created twenty-four thousand units of low-rent public housing—some exclusively for white workers and some for everybody else. Once the rental units reached capacity, the government contracted with a private developer to create a nearby suburban development, called Rollingwood, of higher-quality, permanent housing that white workers could lease or purchase. The Federal Housing Authority guaranteed the developer's financing on the condition that none of the seven hundred new homes be sold to anyone "not wholly of the Caucasian race." Barred by law from living in most of the rapidly developing county, black workers and their families were forced into an area known as North Richmond. North Richmond was an unincorporated area—meaning, not an official town at all, with no government services whatsoever: no roads, streetlights, water, or sewage. The African American wartime workers had to fend entirely for themselves while their white co-workers had all their housing needs met by government subsidy, policy, and planning.

The lines of opportunity and place that a racist government policy drew in the mid-1940s remain in Richmond to this day. In a county rimmed with suburbs that excluded black families, the city became predominantly black during the war. The manufacturing and chemical processing plants that created jobs and opportunity in the war era have either closed or become far less labor-intensive, so that Richmond is left with the worst of both worlds: few middle-class jobs and lots of toxic pollution, including abandoned waste. Richmond residents "live within a ring of five major oil refineries, three chemical companies, eight Superfund sites, dozens of other

toxic waste sites, highways, two rail yards, ports and marine termi-
nals where tankers dock"—some 350 toxic sites in all. The polluter
that's most synonymous with Richmond, however, is the one-
hundred-plus-year-old Chevron refinery, also the dominant player in
Richmond politics.

Today, North Richmond is 97 percent black, Latino, or Asian and,
amazingly, still unincorporated. Displacement and poverty have often
created tensions across these communities, but activists have helped
their neighbors see a common threat to unite them: the polluters in
everyone's backyard. Since forging a multiracial coalition to take
control of their city council and take on Chevron, Richmond community groups have won for their residents probably the most important Solidarity Dividend there is: the chance for better health.

To learn more about Richmond, Miya suggested I go for a drive
with Torm Nompraseurt, the longest-serving staff member of APEN
and one of the first Laotian refugees to the United States. (He arrived in 1975.) I met Torm on a Sunday afternoon at the local museum, where an exhibit about Richmond's Laotian community was
opening. Wearing a black traditional Laotian suit with red trim,
Torm greeted me in Lao-accented English, all soft consonants riding
on a melodic cadence. He generously introduced me to other community activists of every racial and ethnic background, and he had a
hard time making his exit from a gathering where everybody seemed
to know his name.

Torm finally said his last goodbyes and led me into his well-used
red car for a drive around his neighborhood on the "fence line" abut-
ting the massive Chevron refinery. As we drove, I saw few people out:
the day was bright but windy and cold, and besides, from what I
could see, there was little to attract them on the street. A chronically
disinvested city, Richmond has no full-service grocery store within
walking distance. I don't recall even seeing a corner deli during our
nearly hour-long drive around the fence-line neighborhood. What
you see most, however, is industry: salvage lots, tankers, freight cars,
a massive garbage dump, and factories . . . so many factories, making

pesticides and other chemicals, with none bigger than the nearly three-thousand-acre sprawling complex where Chevron refines about 250,000 barrels of crude oil a day.

We pulled up near an elementary school. In 1996, Richmond's African American community (spearheaded by Henry Clark, the veteran organizer of the West County Toxics Coalition), won a long battle to close a Chevron incinerator just behind the schoolyard. Even though Chevron has gotten rid of the unnerving sight of incinerator smokestacks jutting up behind a playground structure, the school is still just about a mile from the refinery. Its nearest neighbors are an oil distributor and a chemicals testing lab. Richmond children are hospitalized for asthma at almost twice the rate of those in neighboring areas. (The school is one of the worst-performing in the state, and research increasingly demonstrates a significant link between air quality and student performance.)

Richmond has disproportionately high rates of heart disease and cancer; the plant's closest neighbors are in the ninety-ninth percentile for asthma rates. The city has the double whammy of fixed and mobile pollution—it not only has an inordinate number of toxic industrial sites, but it's surrounded on all sides by highways. I asked Torm about his own health. "I am coughing all the time. You know, the Laotians, especially the young kids or the elders, have a lot of asthma and coughing and respiratory issues and so on and so forth. . . . [I]n the Laotian community, we have a member, someone who just passed this morning because she had cancer. . . . Most of the time when our members die, often eighty percent, ninety percent, the doctors say, 'Well, because of cancer.'"

Torm turned his car on to one of the freeways so that he could drive the length of the Chevron facility, which is awe-inspiring in its breadth and glittering detail. The fence surrounding Chevron is six miles long. The plant complex looks like a science-fiction city unto itself, with structures of every different shape interlaced with pipes and tubes, all accented with flickering lights and plumes of smoke. There are some thirty-odd massive round holding tanks that dot the hillside behind it, each painted a burnt umber in a beautification effort to blend them into the surroundings. (That paint job is an unfortunately apt metaphor for corporate social responsibility efforts that are only cosmetic; the darker color wound up making the tanks absorb more heat, leading to *more* toxic evaporation.) The Chevron plant spews over a thousand pounds of chemicals into the air on a good day. Then there are the bad days.

"On August sixth, 2012, when the siren came on . . . ," Torm told me, "I know that's not testing, because [they test on] Wednesday. And so, I know right away in my heart . . . this is real. And of course, I closed my door and the window and everything and do the shelter-in-place protocol. You put a towel on [the] bottom of the door, to make sure that the air doesn't come in your house, and close all the doors and windows.

"It's about a quarter mile from Chevron to my apartment at that time. And then I saw a couple [of] people who ran outside. They were Laotian, who live in the same apartment complex. They ran outside and kind of looked at the smoke. And I opened the door and yelled at them and said, "You cannot go out. Get in your house, and close the door and window and put a towel in your door right away, right now!" And then they said, "What?" I said, "It's a Chevron fire. It's chemical. Go in your house!"

The 2012 Chevron fire was caused by a leak from a degraded pipe that Chevron knew for years was at risk of corrosion. Internal recommendations to inspect and replace the pipes because of a common type of sulfur degradation went unheeded for nearly a decade. What began as a drip in the afternoon ended with a fire that sent plumes of chemical smoke into the community's air, in clouds visible for miles. The chemicals that Chevron cast to the wind that day reached not just Torm and his neighbors in the fence-line community, nearest to the refinery, but three neighboring towns. Medical providers and hospitals reported seeing fifteen thousand people sickened by the fumes in the coming days.

Torm exited the freeway and turned up a steep hill to get a better view of the refinery. As Torm's old car revved up the slope, it seemed the house values were climbing as well. "These houses seem like they're more expensive, maybe," I ventured as we passed a pink house with a Mercedes in the driveway.

"Yes. This is called Point Richmond. [This is] the rich community in Richmond."

POINT RICHMOND IS on the southwest edge of the city, a neighborhood up a hill that slopes down into a nature preserve along the harbor. With the median price of houses at $816,000 in 2020, the area is a segregated cluster of mostly white homeowners. Sitting in Torm's car, however, looking at the way the refinery towers could be seen over the million-dollar rooflines, I couldn't help but wonder: Aren't these white people breathing the same air? I asked him about it.

"Well, you know, it's a very interesting question you ask. Because the wind pattern—it always blows toward North Richmond," the unincorporated area that's almost all people of color. "And so, the people who live in Point Richmond—somehow they feel like the wind is doing them a favor, never flows down to their community," Torm said, and I chuckled at the image of a wind with favors to give.

"[But] one of the years that . . . a Chevron accident happened . . . somehow the wind happened to blow down to their side. And I remember, oh my God, they're screaming and yelling. And then we told them, 'See? Now you know what we mean.'"

Richmond has three community air quality monitors around the city, each one in a neighborhood occupying one rung of the city's stratification. One is in wealthy Point Richmond, another in the still-unincorporated area of North Richmond, and the third in Atchison Village, an affordable housing complex built during the war exclusively for white workers that's now a cooperative, home to mostly white seniors and Latinx families. I dug into the data, expecting to see that Point Richmond was largely spared the toxicity that permeated the other areas of the city, but that wasn't the case. In terms of the number of toxins recorded in the air and the number of days with toxins present, there wasn't much difference between the three neighborhoods. While the saturation levels may have varied as the wind blew—the data didn't show—the white part of Richmond was indeed still living under the same sky.

A 2012 study showed that this dynamic was borne out nationwide. Called "Is Environmental Justice Good for White Folks? Industrial Air Toxics and Exposure in Urban America," the study compared pollution levels by neighborhood in cities and found that the sacrifice zones had more spillover than one might expect. I reached out to one of the study's authors, Professor Michael Ash at the University of Massachusetts, to talk about what the researchers had discovered. "We wanted in particular to focus on places that had very unequal exposure," he explained to me. In places where it was "easier, for reasons of the power structure, to displace environmental bads onto vulnerable communities [we wanted to know] are those [the] places that tend to rack up a higher environmental bill across the board?"

He went on: "Not shockingly, places that are unequal are much worse for the socially vulnerable party, but they also turn out to be worse for at least some members of the socially less vulnerable classes."

Environmental racism, in other words, was bad for better-off white people, too. I asked Professor Ash how it worked. While the study proved correlation, not causation, he believed it was a question of power. He described the elite mindset: "Don't worry, this pollution can be displaced onto the Other, onto the wrong side of the environmental tracks. So . . . put on blinders, don't pay too much attention to the gross amount of pollution that is being produced."

It made sense. If a set of decision makers believes that an environmental burden can be shouldered by someone else to whom they don't feel connected or accountable, they won't think it's worthwhile to minimize the burden by, for example, forcing industry to put controls on pollution. But that results in a system that creates more pollution than would exist if decision makers cared about everyone equally—and we're talking about air, water, and soil, where it's pretty hard to cordon off toxins completely to the so-called sacrifice zone. It's elites' blindness to the costs they pay that keeps pollution higher for everyone. Professor Ash let exasperation creep into his voice when he said, "We have the idea that this environmental bad can be displaced on to a socially excluded community, that primes the pump for doing more of it. And then you end up with uncontrollable amounts that are bad absolutely for everyone."

What's most frustrating to Professor Ash is that the other side of the ledger—the cost of preventing pollution and saving lives—is usually so small. "The non-tradeoffs are what is shocking here. I mean, we are just—for chump change, we are exposing people to these terrible toxins. . . . It just wouldn't be that expensive to give everybody a clean and healthy environment."

IN THE EARLY 2000s, Richmond activists representing different causes and ethnic communities joined together to make a plan to take on Chevron—but they had a lot of mistrust and division to overcome. Chevron had polluted the politics of the city, both by controlling the city council and by cultivating relationships with local groups in ways that activists called cynical and racially divisive. Torm and Miya said that Chevron lobbyists had learned how to pit community groups against each other for small funding grants and scholarships, which Torm likened to Chevron's "throw[ing] candy on the floor to get a kid fighting."

He told me, "If you want to talk about this one, you have to look at the root of it. If you think about imperialism, capitalism, conquering and dividing people around the world . . . most of the white folks who control corporations still think those methods are still useful, and it still can work."

Through hard work and relationship building, the Richmond Progressive Alliance was born. "And that's when we launched a . . . strategy to recruit and support a [city council] candidate who would not take corporate money," Torm told me with triumph in his voice. "Chevron was dominant because they used a lot of money to buy the community leaders to work for their candidates. But then we launched the campaign to tell people that unless we change the city council decision making, we cannot fight. We can be screaming and yelling [in community meetings] until four in the morning, and the city council still votes the way Chevron wants them to."

The coalition proposed and vetted candidates, endorsed, knocked on doors, and convinced some of the most overlooked neighborhoods in Richmond to turn out for a progressive slate for the city council. "We were able to kick out the 'Chevron Five' and get a progressive majority into city council," Miya recalls. The coalition's most re- markable achievement was the election of Green Party mayor Gayle McLaughlin, a white woman, who became a thorn in Chevron's side. Permits and programs that for decades sailed through approval sud- denly met with more inquiry, investigations, hearings, and even law- suits. When the company sought to create a one-billion-plus-dollar plant expansion for processing the heavier, higher-sulfur crude oil that gas companies increasingly rely on, the coalition sued and won because Chevron hadn't provided enough information about the pollution impact. "It put the refinery into a major panic," recalled Miya. The pressure forced an environmental impact assessment and changes to the plan that would reduce emissions and guarantee cer- tain benefits to the community.

Torm drove me past a stunning sixty-acre field of solar panels outside the refinery gates. Called MCE Solar One, it's part of the community benefits agreement the coalition won and one of the more visible signs of the new day in Richmond. The public owns and generates the low-cost solar energy for residents, which lowers their utility bills and pollution. The solar array was built with 50 percent local labor in partnership with a training program that prepared hundreds of Richmond residents for clean-energy jobs.

"It's not just one solar project," Miya told me. "These local mod- els of Just Transition have started to really grow." Just Transition is a concept first formulated by unions to protect jobs in industries facing environmental regulations in the late 1990s, but environmental justice advocates have adopted it as a way to express the idea that the shift away from a fossil fuel economy doesn't have to mean massive job losses. In fact, a Just Transition must create good jobs and build community wealth for the low-income communities and people of color who have disproportionately suffered under the current polluting economy.

The Richmond coalition has started to create the green shoots of a Just Transition in a town that was built by racist policies and that has long been poisoned by corporate indifference. The coalition helped pass "a statewide policy that creates incentives for multifamily affordable housing to get solar on buildings that really help lower costs for low-income tenants," Miya said, excitement in her voice as she listed the ways that power had shifted in Richmond. "The local government even supported a fund that helped us start local-owned cooperatives." She described a community complex in development that would be a "climate resiliency hub," with solar power and a microgrid whose profits from electricity generation local youth would direct to investments in the community. "There's just so many exciting things and ideas that are emerging out of Richmond right now."

When Miya described the progress in Richmond and the community's vision for remaking their economy, it seemed like such a win-win to me. Save the planet, create new jobs, build community wealth—what's not to love? But that's not how the climate change opposition sees it. For them, it is a zero-sum competition between the environment and the economy as it is. Or perhaps, as the sociologists argue, it's deeper than that: a zero sum between the winners of the hierarchy today and those who are just fighting for air.


**THE GOOD NEWS** is the type of multiracial coalition that has begun to loosen Chevron's grip on Richmond is starting to assemble across the nation, putting within sight a Solidarity Dividend for people and the planet. Momentum has been growing at the grass roots. A historic assembly of people from an array of Indigenous communities, putting aside tribal differences and led by Native youth, camped at Standing Rock to protest the Dakota Access Pipeline and build power for Indigenous-led environmental protection. Environmental justice groups led by people of color forced conversations with the Big Greens and their funders about who gets the resources and sets the strategy for the movement. Young people staged record-breaking strikes and protests for climate action across the world. While cast into the wilderness of governing power during the Trump administration, the leaders who are the most committed to saving the planet finally got together to hash out their differences and discover places of mutual interest: labor unions and conservationists, Big Greens and grassroots environmental justice groups, and Native-led groups and youth activists.

This delicate emerging consensus received a jolt of energy when the Green New Deal framework was launched into the political stratosphere. The Green New Deal framework itself represents a multiracial alliance, coauthored by a young black woman policy wonk, Rhiana Gunn-Wright; sponsored in Congress by a septuagenarian white liberal named Ed Markey and a thirty-year-old Puerto Rican from the Bronx named Alexandria Ocasio-Cortez; and forced into the political conversation by a young Indian American woman named Varshini Prakash, whose Sunrise Movement staged a sit-in in soon-to-be House Speaker Nancy Pelosi's office. At the time of this writing, there is more energy and alignment in the climate field than there has been in decades, in large part because movement leaders have been forced to see to the damage posed by white supremacy, inside and outside their ranks.

Siloed and often at cross purposes, these groups weren't powerful enough to take on the strategic deployment of white identity politics backed by fossil fuel billions that slowed President Obama's progress and allowed Donald Trump to take power vowing to reverse it. Now they're linking arms around a shared vision of a sustainable, just transition from fossil fuels that guarantees economic security for all those who are suffering—whether they're asthmatic schoolkids of color or, yes, coal miners. That vision is popular with 59 percent of the population. Multiracial coalitions in cities and states have won versions of the Green New Deal in California, New Mexico, New York, and Washington.

May Boeve came to visit me at home in the fall of 2019, bringing a beautiful knit blanket for my son—and for me: good news about how the climate movement was changing from the inside. As we sat on my couch drinking tea, I felt that she was as optimistic as I'd ever seen her. "It was naive, looking back on it now," May said with her brow furrowed, "but we didn't realize how much racism was holding us back from building the kind of coalition we needed to win. We're trying to make sure that the whole field never makes that mistake again."

## Chapter 9

# THE HIDDEN WOUND

We were high in the balcony, so close to the projector that I could see the dust in the beam of light cutting across the auditorium. The grainy black-and-white images showed a veritable pantheon onscreen: Rosa Parks, the Rev. Dr. Martin Luther King Jr., and the unnamed heroes withstanding abuse at a lunch counter or leaning up against a wall, shielding their faces from the pounding spray of water hoses. Every February, for Black History Month, our school put on a display of the righteousness of black Americans. The organ struck up, and the white students looked to the lyrics in their programs.

> . . . *Stony the road we trod,*
> *Bitter the chastening rod,*
> *Felt in the days when hope unborn had died;*
> *Yet with a steady beat,*
> *Have not our weary feet*
> *Come to the place for which our fathers sighed?*
> *We have come over a way that with tears has*
> *been watered*

*We have come treading our path through the*
*blood of the slaughtered*
*Out from the gloomy past,*
*'Til now we stand at last*
*Where the white gleam of our bright star is cast.*

When we finished singing "Lift Ev'ry Voice and Sing," the black national anthem, Vanessa, a white girl in my sixth-grade class, turned to me and whispered, "I wish I was black."

**TO AN ELEVEN-YEAR-OLD**, this must have seemed like the inevitable conclusion to the morality play we'd just seen. Who would want to be one of the bad guys? Compared to freckle-faced Vanessa, my darker skin would afford me little privilege in life, except in one arena: the privilege of being born among the heroes in the American story of social progress, not among the villains. While watching *Eyes on the Prize*'s indelible footage, I never had to see people who looked like my parents with their faces contorted in fury, hurling abuse at a little girl walking to school. But Vanessa had—and the clear moral contrast made her want to switch sides. What's often forgotten, however, is that the bad guys on-screen believed that what they were doing was morally right.

It's just human nature: we all like to see ourselves as on the side of the heroes in a story. But for white Americans today who are awake to the reality of American racism, that's nearly impossible. That's a moral cost of racism that millions of white people bear and that those of us who've borne every other cost of racism simply don't. It can cause contradictions and justifications, feelings of guilt, shame, projection, resentment, and denial. Ultimately, though, we are all paying for the moral conflict of white Americans.

Over the years that I have sought answers to why a fairer economy is so elusive, it has become clearer to me that how white people understand what's right and wrong about our diverse nation, who belongs and who deserves, is determining our collective course. This is the crux of it: Can we swim together in the same pool or not? It's a political question, yes, and one with economic ramifications. But at its core, it's a moral question. Ultimately, an economy—the rules we abide by and set for what's fair and who merits what—is an expression of our moral understanding. So, if our country's moral compass is broken, is it any wonder that our economy is adrift?

**FOR WHITE PEOPLE** to free themselves from the debt of responsibility for racism past and present would be liberating. But there isn't an established route for redemption; America hasn't had a truth-and-reconciliation process like other wounded societies have. Instead, it's up to individuals to decide what they need to do in order to be good people in a white supremacist society—and it's not easy.

In the absence of moral leadership, there are just too many competing stories. For every call to become an activist for racial justice, there's a well-rehearsed message that says that activists are pushing too hard. For every chance to speak up against the casual racism white people so often hear from other white folks, there is a countervailing pressure not to rock the boat. If you want to believe that white people are the real victims in race relations, and that the stereotypes of people of color as criminal and lazy are common sense rather than white supremacist tropes, there is a glide path to take you there. And when your life trajectory has taught you that the system works pretty okay if you do the right things, then it's easy to wonder why whole groups of people can't seem to do better for themselves. Whichever story you choose to believe, nobody wants to be the villain, so there's an available set of justifications for why your view is morally right.

To understand how this dynamic works, I decided I needed to go all the way to one end of the spectrum, to talk to someone who had fully given herself over to white supremacy's alluring lies. I tracked down a woman named Angela King, who spent most of her life as a neo-Nazi.

Angela grew up in a rural all-white area of South Florida. She had learned pretty much every form of prejudice from her parents—"homophobia, racism, stereotypes, racial slurs," she told me. "I grew up thinking that was normal. And I grew up with an abnormal fear of people who weren't like me." I wondered about how she went from being afraid of people her parents had taught her were foreign to organizing her life around hating and terrorizing them.

Angela told me that she was bullied in school, and when she was twelve, it turned physical. "The school bully ripped my shirt open in front of the entire class, and here I was," Angela recalled, "this pudgy little girl in her training bra. And it did something to me. It provoked this rage that I really didn't know I had inside. So, I fought that bully back, and unfortunately that day, I became the bully." She told herself, "If I'm the one doing those kind of things, no one can ever humiliate me like that again."

In high school, Angela sought a place to fit in. She eventually chose a group that displayed swastikas and Confederate flags. "And honestly, I wasn't attracted to them because of the beliefs," she said. But "they were the one group I found that never questioned my anger or my aggression or my violence. They just accepted it. I never had to explain it or account for it. And that began my life in the violent far right." She was fifteen years old.

When I asked her how she justified her actions, she explained that she simply accepted the opportunity that the story of white supremacy has always offered: a way to shift the blame. Regarding slavery, for instance, she said, "I found a way to blame [it] on those who were enslaved . . . [saying] things like 'Africans sold their own people, so they deserve to be enslaved.'"

Angela discovered that Nazism gave her not only a justification for the race-based hierarchy of human value she believed in, but also a ready scapegoat for every disappointment in her life. At age twenty-three, she wound up in a federal detention center, sentenced for taking part in an armed robbery targeting a Jewish store owner. "And I not only didn't feel responsible," she recalled, "but [I] was at a place where . . . nothing was my responsibility. It was my parents' fault. It was black people taking my good jobs, even though I was a high school dropout, a drunk."

But inside prison, her all-white world was gone. "Oh, shit," she recalls saying aloud. "Now I'm the minority." One day, Angela was smoking by herself in the recreation yard when a black woman looked over at her. Angela, who was covered in racist tattoos, thought, "Oh, she's gonna start something." But instead, the woman invited her to play cards.

"And from that point on, we started a friendship," Angela said. "We didn't really talk about why we were there for a long time . . . about the fact that I came in there as a skinhead for a hate crime. . . . Even knowing that, this group of women treated me as a human being. I had no idea how to react to that. I couldn't find justification in the usual aggression and violence that I used.

"They didn't let me slide for long, though. Eventually, the very hard conversations started to happen." The woman who had first befriended her "would just out of the blue ask me questions like, 'So, if you met me before we came to prison, and I was with my daughter, what would you have done to us? Would you have called me the N-word? Would you have tried to kill my daughter? Would you have tried to hurt me?' And being in prison, and with the friendship I [had] forged with some of them, I couldn't get up and run away and not answer the questions. So, I was forced into not only being honest with them, but . . . with myself."

When she was released from prison at age twenty-six, Angela put her former life behind her and threw herself into education. She ended up earning three degrees. "I learned a great bit about history and systemic racism and oppression and got a clear understanding of the true history of our country. When I was growing up, I didn't get facts about how this country really began. I got the white version."

Angela became an activist, giving speeches around the country to share her story and cofounding an organization called Life After Hate, which helps people get out of violent white-supremacist groups. But the audience for her message is broader than neo-Nazis.

She doesn't want the existence of violent, racist gangs to let white people in the political mainstream off the hook. "[We are all] socialized into a society where racism is normal, and it's built into every aspect of our democracy, our government, and our social systems. . . . There are so many white people that have no clue," she told me.

"And when . . . you try to give them a clue, they become very defensive. Because no one wants to think that they are benefiting from a system that hurts other people. It's much easier just to pretend like you don't know."

White supremacy had given Angela something she desperately needed in order to feel better about herself: scapegoats. I thought about the function that immigrants, particularly from Latin America, are playing in today's racial theater, being blamed for the loss of jobs and even the more diffuse "way of life." Fox News host Laura Ingraham told her audience of millions, "In some parts of the country, it does seem like the America that we know and love doesn't exist anymore," and blamed it on immigration. Tucker Carlson raged, "Our leaders demand that you shut up and accept this. We have a moral obligation to admit the world's poor, they tell us, even if it makes our own country poorer, and dirtier, and more divided."

It's incumbent on all of us to understand how people with the privilege of being born citizens make moral sense of the deservingness of 11 million undocumented people in the United States, or the refugees seeking to become Americans every day—because fierce anti-immigrant sentiment has shifted our politics to the right on a whole host of issues. The baseline moral teaching about immigration is somewhere along the lines of the Bible's "Therefore love the stranger, for you were strangers in the land of Egypt," or the more secular version (emblazoned on the base of the Statue of Liberty), " 'Give me your tired, your poor, / Your huddled masses yearning to breathe free.' " So how do folks justify the opposite? Prominent white nationalists are clear they want to maintain a white America, but most people justify having animus toward immigrants in a "nation of immigrants" in moral terms: it's not the immigrant part; it's the "illegal" part. They broke the law; they're criminals.

As history shows us, once a group is criminalized, they're outside the circle of human concern. This moral story of law-abiding citizens and criminal immigrants hinges on people having, as Angela said, "no clue" about the racist structures that let the ancestors of many white Americans arrive with no restrictions or requirements save their whiteness, which extended them ladders of opportunity upon arrival that were the exact opposite of the walls and shadows today's immigrant workers face. This story blames some of the least powerful people on the planet for a problem created and sustained by the most powerful—corporations profiting from sweatshop labor and policy makers unwilling to update our immigration laws. Nonetheless, as it has for centuries, racism makes an immoral view of the world into a moral one. The elite adds in the urgency of the zero-sum story—they are taking what you have; they are a threat to you—and it's enough to keep a polity focused on scapegoats while no progress is made on the actual economic issues in most Americans' lives.

I thought about Melanie, a white woman I connected with on my journey via a mutual friend. Melanie is in her forties and grew up mostly in the rural Appalachian region of North Carolina amid her mother's large family, which she describes as "very conservative and very racist."

Melanie's family struggled financially and often lacked the money for heating oil or a telephone. "We knew the sick feeling of what a car breaking down felt like," she said. Melanie left her small town for college at age seventeen and never returned; her world, and her worldview, expanded. As an adult, she took it upon herself to help educate her mother out of the racist beliefs she had absorbed in her family and then cemented by listening to conservative talk radio.

"She used to tell me that it says in the Bible that there was a reason that black people were inferior," Melanie recalled. "And I basically got out the Bible and made her show me where it said that."

Melanie remembered a breakthrough moment when she was talking with her mother and stepfather. "They said something about 'the Mexicans,' and 'they all live in that house together,' you know, 'There are thirty-five people in that house.'

"And I sat down with them and had a conversation about what that looks like." They discussed the social and economic forces that might compel a large extended family, like their own, to live in one house. "And it's completely infuriating to me," Melanie said, "because we . . . didn't have any money. . . . We know economic pressures and the discrimination of being poor. And so, I just sort of laid it out for them like that, and they got it, you know? In a way that I don't think they had ever really thought about it before."

WHEN ANGELA KING was a skinhead, she saw race everywhere. But then again, so does everybody. The first thing you take in when you see someone is their skin color. Within a fraction of a second, that sight triggers your ingrained associations and prejudices. If those prejudices about a person's skin color are negative—as they overwhelmingly are among white people regarding darker skin—they alert your amygdala, the section of the brain responsible for anxiety and other emotions, to flood your body with adrenaline in a fight-or-flight response.

But when I was growing up in the 1980s, we were taught that the way to be a good person was to swear that race didn't matter, at least not anymore. We had all learned the lessons of the civil rights movement: everybody is equal, and according to the morals of the sitcoms we watched after school (*Diff'rent Strokes*, *Webster*, *Saved by the Bell*), what was racist was pretending that people were any different from one another. Furthermore, the most un-racist people didn't even see race at all; they were color blind. We now know that color blindness is a form of racial denial that took one of the aspirations of the civil rights movement—that individuals would one day "not be judged by the color of their skin but by the content of their character"—and stripped it from any consideration of power, hierarchy, or structure. The moral logic and social appeal of color blindness is clear, and many well-meaning people have embraced it. But when it is put into practice in a still-racist world, the result is more racism.

The sociologist Eduardo Bonilla-Silva, author of the ground-breaking book *Racism Without Racists: Color-Blind Racism and the Persistence of Racial Inequality in America*, describes how once we stop seeing racism as a factor and treat equality as a reality rather than an aspiration, our minds naturally seek other explanations for the disparities all around us. Color-blind racism is an ideology that "explains contemporary racial inequality as the outcome of non-racial dynamics . . . [W]hites rationalize minorities' contemporary status as the product of market dynamics, naturally occurring phenomena, and blacks' imputed cultural limitations." Such explanations "exculpate [white people] from any responsibility for the status of people of color."

In a way, color blindness makes the civil rights movement a victim of its own success: legal segregation is over, so now it must be up to people of color to finish the work themselves. As Bonilla-Silva puts it, if racism is no longer actively limiting the lives of people of color, then their failure to achieve parity with whites in wealth, education, employment, and other areas must mean there is something wrong with them, not with the social systems that somehow always benefit white people the most. Social scientists look to this question—whether you believe that racism is to blame for disparities or that black people just need to work harder—to help them determine what they call racial resentment. And racial resentment, in turn, is a predictor of opposition to policies that would improve the economic security of millions.

For two generations now, well-meaning white people have subscribed to color blindness in an optimistic attempt to wish away the existence of structural racism. But when they do, they unwittingly align themselves with, and give mainstream cover to, a powerful movement to turn back the clock on integration and equality. What my former University of California, Berkeley, law professor Ian Haney López calls "reactionary color blindness" has become the weapon of choice for conservatives in the courts and in politics. Racial conservatives on the Supreme Court have used the logic to rule that it's racist for communities to voluntarily integrate schools, because to do so, the government would have to "see" race to assign students. Well-funded political groups mount campaigns to forbid the government from collecting racial data because isn't that what a racist would do? Instead of being blind to race, color blindness makes people blind to racism, unwilling to acknowledge where its effects have shaped opportunity or to use race-conscious solutions to address it.

DENIAL THAT RACISM still exists; denial that, even if it does exist, it's to blame for the situation at hand; denial that the problem is as bad as people of color say it is—these denials are the easy outs that the dominant white narrative offers to people. Wellesley College professor Jennifer Chudy's research finds that only one in five white Americans consistently expresses high levels of sympathy about anti-black discrimination.

Color blindness has become a powerful weapon against progress for people of color, but as a denial mindset, it doesn't do white people any favors, either. A person who avoids the realities of racism doesn't build the crucial muscles for navigating cross-cultural tensions or recovering with grace from missteps. That person is less likely to listen deeply to unexpected ideas expressed by people from other cultures or to do the research on her own to learn about her blind spots. When that person then faces the inevitable uncomfortable racial reality—an offended co-worker, a presentation about racial disparity at a PTA meeting, her inadvertent use of a stereotype—she's caught flat-footed. Denial leaves people ill-prepared to function or thrive in a diverse society. It makes people less effective at collaborating with colleagues, coaching kids' sports teams, advocating for their neighborhoods, even chatting with acquaintances at social events.

Nor is denial easy to sustain. To uphold the illusion of effortless white advantage actually requires unrelenting psychological exertion. The sociologist Dr. Jennifer Mueller explains that color blindness is a key step in "a process of knowing designed to produce not knowing surrounding white privilege, culpability, and structural white supremacy."

But it was a white poet, novelist, and farmer named Wendell Berry whose words brought home to me most poignantly the moral consequences of denial. In August 2017, I traveled to Northern Kentucky to meet with a multiracial grassroots organization called Kentuckians for the Commonwealth. After a day of workshops, one of the members gave me a dog-eared copy of a book by Berry, a local hero who had grown up in rural Kentucky during the Jim Crow era. The book was called *The Hidden Wound*—Berry wrote it in 1968, in the midst of widespread protest and unrest—and that night in my hotel room, I read it from cover to cover.

By denying the reality of racism and their own role in it, Berry explained, white Americans have denied themselves critical self-knowledge and created a prettified and falsified version of American history for themselves to believe in, one built on the "wishful insinuation that we have done no harm." Of course, he understood the impulse of white people—himself included—to protect themselves from "the anguish implicit in their racism."

A few years before Berry published *The Hidden Wound*, James Baldwin, as keen an observer of human behavior as there's ever been, wrote his own account of what happens when white people open their eyes to racism. "What they see is a disastrous, continuing, present condition which menaces them, and for which they bear an inescapable responsibility. But since, in the main, they seem to lack the energy to change this condition, they would rather not be reminded of it." Baldwin went on to observe that white Americans "are dimly, or vividly, aware that the history they have fed themselves is mainly a lie, but they do not know how to release themselves from it, and they suffer enormously from the resulting personal incoherence."

Wendell Berry calls this suffering "the hidden wound." He counsels that when "you begin to awaken to the realities of what you know, you are subject to staggering recognitions of your complicity in history and in the events of your own life." Of this wound—this psychic and emotional damage that racism does to white people—he writes, "I have borne it all my life . . . always with the most delicate consideration for the pain I would feel if I were somehow forced to acknowledge it."

**AS I CLOSED** Berry's book in that Kentucky hotel room, I thought about what it must it be like to be part of the dominant group in an unfair "meritocracy" that denies its oppressions and pathologizes the oppressed. "I think white folks are terribly invested in our own innocence," says the scholar Catherine Orr. The belief that the United States is a meritocracy, in which anyone can succeed if only they try hard enough, also supports the notion that anyone who is financially successful is so because they've worked harder or are somehow more innately gifted than others. Both ideas operate as a justification for maintaining our profoundly unjust economic system. Recent research from social psychologists at Yale and Northwestern finds that "Americans, on average, systematically overestimate the extent to which society has progressed toward racial economic equality, driven largely by overestimates of current racial equality." Wealthy white Americans, they find, have the most unrealistic assessment of how much progress the United States has made in terms of economic equality (and thus how fair the competition has been that they seem to have won).

In a 2019 public opinion survey, majorities of both black and white people said that being black makes it more difficult to get ahead in America. Yet only 56 percent of white respondents believed the corollary: that being white helps you get ahead. And of those who recognized the obstacles black people face in terms of economic mobility, black respondents attributed this to systemic discrimination, such as having less access to good schools and high-paying jobs. White people, on the other hand, were more likely to blame problems such as the lack of good role models and family instability—group pathologies, in other words, that ultimately lay blame at the feet of black people themselves.

Morally defending your position in a racially unequal society requires the fierce protection of your self-image as a person who earns everything you receive. From the tradition that trade unions make a place for members' sons, to legacy admissions at colleges, to college students who can choose career-building but unpaid or low-paying internships because families can support them, to employers who seek "a good fit" by hiring younger versions of themselves, the deck is stacked on behalf of white people in ways that are so pervasive we rarely notice them. Within this context, many white people both resent affirmative action and imagine that it is vastly more widespread than it really is. The share of black and brown students at selective colleges has actually declined over thirty-five years despite stated affirmative action policies, and the overwhelmingly white categories of children of alumni, faculty, donors, or athletes made up 43 percent, for example, of students admitted to Harvard from 2010 to 2015. Meanwhile, according to a 2016 study by Harvard Business School professor Katherine DeCelles, black job applicants who removed any indications of their race from their résumés were significantly more likely to advance to an interview. Many other studies bear out similar findings, including an economic research paper that traced improved job prospects to whether applicants had names like "Greg" or "Emily" as opposed to "Lakisha" or "Jamal," and a sociological study in New York City that found that "Black applicants were half as likely as equally qualified whites to receive a callback or job offer."

Still, the idea that people of color are taking jobs from white people is another zero-sum belief that lumbers on from era to era. As Ronald, a middle-aged white man from Buffalo, New York, told the Whiteness Project, "I think affirmative action was nice. It had its time, but I think that time is over with. Are we going to keep this up another one hundred fifty years? 'Oh, we gotta have so many Asians in the fire department, we gotta have so many blacks in the fire de-

partment.' . . . The white guys will never have a chance to be a fire-
man or a cop anymore." Although using such numerical quotas to
achieve affirmative action in employment was outlawed in 1978 by
the Supreme Court, Ronald's grievance is evergreen, as is his cer-
tainty that white guys getting all the public service jobs was the natural order of things, not its own form of white affirmative action.

**NONE OF THESE** economic resentments and justifications has the life-
or-death consequences of the most powerful morally inverting force
in our society: white fear of people of color, particularly black people.
In the American moral logic—and, increasingly, with "Stand Your
Ground" laws, in the legal system—when you fear someone, no matter how objectively real the threat, you can be justified in doing them
harm. If you have a badge, that moral and legal license has been
seemingly without limit. In 2019, police officers nationwide shot and
killed more than one thousand people; there were only twenty-seven
days that year when no civilians died from police shootings. Black
people constituted 28 percent of those killed, more than twice our
presence in the population. Although 1.3 times more likely than
white people to be unarmed, black people were three times more
likely to be killed by police. Indigenous Americans are killed by police at shocking rates as high as or higher than those for African
Americans.

But we may actually have reached the moral limit. For eight minutes and forty-six seconds, people around the world watched a white
police officer kneel on the neck of George Floyd, a black man in
Minneapolis, until he died. In his dying moments, Floyd called out
for his "Mama," who had already died two years before. White Americans had seen and explained away videos of police killings before,
but this was too much. After months in isolation and fear from a cal-
lously mismanaged pandemic that disproportionately sickened and
killed people of color, it was too much. On the heels of the murder of
Ahmaud Arbery, chased by white men in a pickup truck while jog-

ging and then gunned down, it was too much. After the police killed Breonna Taylor, an emergency medical technician in Louisville, Kentucky, who had been asleep in her own bed before a botched raid, it was too much. An estimated 15 to 26 million people demonstrated to protest police brutality in the summer of 2020, a tidal wave of recognition about the reality of systemic anti-blackness that prompted dozens of laws reforming police practices.

Maureen Wanket is one of the many white people who has joined the Black Lives Matter movement. She's a middle-aged teacher who once worked at Sacramento High, the school where a young man named Stephon Clark used to play football and ace his first-period history tests. On March 18, 2018, two Sacramento police officers responding to a vandalism call shot at Stephon twenty times, killing him before identifying themselves. Many of those rounds were fired into Stephon's back. The twenty-two-year-old father of two was killed in his grandmother's backyard. The only "weapon" police found was a cellphone. Yet the officers faced no criminal charges because they could claim that they had been in fear for their lives.

In the days following the shooting, when Sacramento was roiled by protests and recriminations, one of Maureen's colleagues at the majority-white Catholic school where she now teaches approached her with sympathy. "You care more because you . . . taught there at Sac High, and so it's like when someone visits the zoo, they get really used to the animals."

The woman's words knocked Maureen breathless. Recalling that moment, she said, "This woman has been so kind to me since I first started working there. She thinks she's being cool." Yet she was likening black students to animals and suggesting that Maureen needed a reason to care about them.

This wasn't the first time Maureen encountered fellow white people who assumed she shared their racial fears. She recalls with overwhelming fondness her years teaching at Sacramento High, the public charter school whose students were all from working-class backgrounds and mostly African American, with a small percentage of Hmong and Latinx kids. "These were the best students of my career," she said. "If I gave the students something to read, they read it in three days. I would sometimes plan a lesson [unit] to go on for four or five weeks, and they were done in two weeks and wanted to write the paper because they were excited." Yet the most frequent question Maureen received from her white friends about the school and its students was "Are you scared?"

Her response: "Scared of what? Don't be scared of black kids. Be scared *for* them."

IN ONE YEAR, white people called the police on black people for engaging in such menacing behaviors as napping in a common room of their own dorm; standing in a doorway to wait out the rain; cashing a check in a bank; using a coupon in a store; waiting for a friend in a coffee shop; and (that most American of activities) going door to door to canvass voters. And in a taped encounter that went viral in 2020, Christian Cooper was bird-watching in Central Park when Amy Cooper (no relation) called the police on him for asking her to follow the law by leashing her dog.

When I was in Maine (the whitest state in the country), Peg, a white volunteer with the grassroots group Maine People's Alliance, told me how strong and automatic racialized fear could be. "I see people cross the street in front of my car," she said, "and I can feel my amygdala, which is that part of the brain, it's like, 'Oh. Foreign. Other.' And I, for a long time, have seen myself as a progressive person. But I . . . very quickly recognize it, and I identify it and call it into question, give myself some grace about it. And then puzzle about why, at my age and stage, is that so powerful still?"

Peg told me a story about leaving her friend's flower shop one day just as "three large black men" were entering. Sheer terror struck her, out on the sidewalk. "I thought, 'I need to go back, because Debbie's in there by herself.' And when I realized that [I was experiencing racial fear,] that's where I stayed. . . . I just felt so bad. And it would not go away." Her voice got soft. "It would not go away."

Peg paused for a moment, seemingly lost in wonder about the stubbornness of her fear. She looked up at me. "So, I'm sad about that. And I talked to her about that the next time I went in. And she said, 'They came in to buy the biggest bouquet you have ever seen for someone they love.' Duh. They were coming to buy something for someone they loved."

Where does this fear come from? Segregation breeds unfamiliarity; strategic disinvestment of many neighborhoods of color makes them economically depressed and appear to many white people like no-go zones. Then there's the news. Tuning in to your local news, you could easily reach the conclusion that far fewer white people than black people engage in criminal behavior, even though the opposite is true. Among those in the United States arrested for criminal activity, the vast majority, 69 percent, is white. Yet white people constitute only about 28 percent of the people who appear on crime reports on TV news, while black people are dramatically overrepresented. Yes, violent crime rates are higher in disinvested neighborhoods of color than in well-resourced white enclaves, but once you control for poverty, the difference disappears. Crime victimization is as prevalent in poor white communities as poor black communities; it's similar in rural poor areas and urban poor ones. In addition, less policing in middle-income and wealthy neighborhoods means that their violent crimes often go unreported.

White fear isn't just determinative of one-on-one interactions; it's a social force that can be manipulated through the media and politics to change voting and economic behavior. At the start of the summer of mass demonstrations against police violence in 2020, the moral contours of the struggle were crystal clear to the majority of Americans. A sea change in public opinion happened virtually overnight, and 95 percent of the counties where Black Lives Matter demonstrations were held were majority white. But as law enforcement escalated against some of the bigger protests, the media coverage was drawn to scenes of conflict. Right-wing social media began to proliferate images of chaos, and the White House Twitter account rhetoric about "law and order" increased. A new political narrative emerged:

the protestors are dangerous, in the wrong, and menacing. The specter of violence in the streets—even, as it was, between unarmed demonstrators and militarized police—managed to turn white public opinion as the summer wore on.

By early August, pollsters were showing a roughly even split between people who believed that the protests were mostly peaceful and those who believed they were mostly violent. As a result, support for the goals of the movement was down among conflicted, or swing, voters by 28 percent from June. "I am pretty moderate in my views, but I believe in law and order," said a typical white male focus group participant. The perception was that violence was as common as ordinary protest, but the most complete record of the summer 2020 racial justice protests shows that 93 percent of the events were peaceful, with no conflict, violence, or property destruction. As overblown as the fears might have been, the impact on solidarity with black people was real. The share of white Americans who said that racism was a big problem fell from 45 percent in June in the aftermath of George Floyd's death to just 33 percent in August, an abandonment of the 75 percent of black Americans whose concern about racism remained constant throughout.

Vanderbilt University professor of sociology and medicine, health, and society Jonathan Metzl has identified a way that white fear is also creating a death risk for the very people who feel it most. As he pointed out in his book *Dying of Whiteness*, white gun ownership skyrocketed during the Obama presidency and the early days of the Black Lives Matter movement. America's unhealthy obsession with guns—four in ten adults live in a household with a gun—has always been intertwined with our history of racial violence, but in recent years, right-wing media and an increasingly radical National Rifle Association have aggressively marketed to white fear: of terrorists, of home invaders, of criminal immigrants, and of "inner-city thugs." Shannon Watts, founder of Moms Demand Action for Gun Sense in America, told a *New Republic* reporter, "They have to make Americans afraid of one another. They're exploiting fear in America to sell

guns." All this fear has come in an era of record-low crime rates nationwide. The fantasy of marauding hordes is unlikely to material-
ize, but in the real world, white men have been increasingly and
disproportionately turning the guns on themselves in a tragic increase in gun suicides. As suicide experts now know, having a gun
handy during moments of frustration or despair can turn a passing
feeling into a death sentence. Suicide attempts with a gun have an 85
percent success rate, compared to a 3 percent rate for the most frequently used suicide method, drug overdose. White men are now
one-third of the population but three-quarters of the gun suicide
victims. And twice as many people die from gun suicides in America
each year as from the gun homicides people have been so conditioned
to fear.

MY MOTHER, WHO was born in 1950, grew up with a healthy fear of
white people. A white person would have been able to roll up beside
her in a truck and kidnap her, and probably nothing would have happened to him. A white person could have denied her a house—and
did—and nothing happened to them. For the life of her, she could
not understand why white people always professed to be so afraid of
people of color.

"It's so strange," my mother used to tell me, "because we're the
ones who live in terror of what white people can do with impunity."

It dawned on me as a teenager that many white people must fear,
at some deep level, that given half a chance, people of color would do
to them what they have long been doing to us. Later I would learn
that this dynamic of assigning others your own worst attributes has a
name: projection. The legal scholar Richard Thompson Ford writes,
"In order for the concept of a white race to exist, there must be a
black race which is everything the white race is not." It's not real, of
course. We are all complex individuals. But the total white power
over laws and culture has mapped these ideas onto our minds.

I grew up unwittingly devouring tales of racist projection. My dad would take me to watch the epic, sprawling Westerns I loved on the big screen whenever there was a revival: *The Searchers*; *The Good, the Bad and the Ugly*; *Stagecoach*. They were morality plays, all of them, and they taught generations of Americans not just about "how the West was won," but also about good guys and bad guys. There was just one problem: in a land where white Americans had committed one of history's greatest genocides, the white cowboys were the stoic heroes; the interchangeable, whooping Indians, the villains.

White fear can exist only in "a world turned upside down," writes Abraham Lateiner, a white man born into wealth who has become an activist for equality. "Because white people stole two continents and two hundred years of the backbreaking labor of millions, race reassures us that blackness is related to thievery," he wrote. "Because white men have raped Black and Brown women with impunity for centuries, race comforts us with the lie that it's black masculinity that is defined by hypersexual predation. Because white people penned black people in the 'ghetto' via redlining, race tells us that this 'ghetto' is an indictment of black pathology. People of color weren't the ones who created whiteness or violated my spirit with it. That was my own people. That is my peers. That is me, too."

One summer day in 2018, I was getting a ride from one interview stop to another with a white retiree I'll call Ken. The miles passed beneath the tires of his white SUV, and an oldies station played quietly beneath our chatter. The conversation turned to Colin Kaepernick, the professional football player who knelt during the playing of the national anthem to protest police brutality against black people. Ken had spent much of the car ride telling me how much he hated the racism and police brutality that seemed to be on the rise in the country and that he supported Black Lives Matter, so I expected him to agree with me when I praised Kaepernick's courage. Instead, he told me he felt attacked by this symbolic act.

"I don't understand," I said. "You agree that cops getting away with killing unarmed black people is wrong." To me, that put Ken on

Kaepernick's side. Why would he feel attacked by someone with whom he agreed?

"I do. I do," he said, nodding, thoughtful. Then he smacked his hand on the steering wheel. I swiveled in my seat to stare at him. "But it's like he's using a shotgun instead of a rifle," he said, "it's spraying too wide and hitting innocent bystanders."

I turned my gaze back to the road, unnerved by the way his analogy placed a gun in the hand of a kneeling, peaceful protestor. My thoughts were roiling. Who were the innocent bystanders? Not the black victims of police violence. Not the football players whose silent protest fell squarely in the democratic tradition. No, the innocents in Ken's mind were white people like him, people who may not approve of police officers killing the black citizens they were sworn to protect but who did not think it was fair to be reminded of those killings during a football game. The innocents were those who found more outrage in the act of protesting violence than in the violence itself. And why did Ken feel personally attacked—wounded, even? What part of Ken was so tightly woven into the flag that he perceived a protest against American injustice as a protest against him, even when he agreed with the message?

I found it hard to relate. I didn't share Ken's reverence for the pageantry, the performative love of country with no room for the truth about that country. But I do love America. I love its ideals: equality, freedom, liberty, justice. It's what Langston Hughes meant in 1936 when he wrote, "Let America be America again, for it has never been America to me." It is how Dr. King could say that his dream was rooted in the American Dream. It's why Kaepernick's protest says, "Not so fast. This America isn't living up to the bargain, so I won't shake hands until she does."

Wanting someone to stand for the national anthem rather than stand up for justice means loving the symbol more than what it symbolizes. Ken's attachment to American innocence made him take the side that opposed his own stated beliefs, just as our nation has done time and time again. It's the moral upside down of racism that si-

## 242      THE SUM OF US

multaneously extolls American virtues in principle and rejects them in practice.

America's symbols were not designed to represent people of color or to speak to us—nonetheless, the ideals they signify have been more than slogans; they have meant life or death for us. Equality, freedom, liberty, justice—who could possibly love those ideals more than those denied them? African Americans became a people here, and our people sacrificed every last imaginable thing to America's becoming. The promise of this country has been enough to rend millions of immigrants from their homes, and for today's mostly of-color immigrants, it's still enough, despite persecution, detention, and death, to keep them dreaming of finding freedom here. The profound love for America's ideals should unite all who call it home, of every color—and yet America has lied to her white children for centuries, offering them songs about freedom instead of the liberation of truth.

I THOUGHT ABOUT something that Robin DiAngelo said to me: "It's actually liberating and transformative to start from the premise that of course I'm thoroughly conditioned into [racism]. And then I can stop defending, denying, explaining, minimizing and get to work actually applying what I profess to believe with the practice of my life."

That's also what I heard from many of my white colleagues during the Racial Equity Transformation process I led at Demos. When I became the organization's president in 2014, I was the only person of color on my executive team, and the staff was about 75 percent white. We were all do-gooders who had made careers out of fighting inequality, but I knew that we were also all people conditioned by American culture and educated in our schools. So, somewhat naively, I decided that we could give every staff member—from the economists and lawyers to the accountants and office managers—what our country hadn't: the unvarnished truth about our collective inheritance and the skills to work together across race without papering things over.

To do this, we designed an original curriculum of books, articles, speeches, and videos and identified core competencies the staff should have to function well in a diverse environment (self-awareness, the ability to make authentic relationships across difference, direct communication skills, and a strong racial equity analysis). We overhauled our hiring process and employee handbook to minimize implicit bias in recruitment, retention, and promotions. We thought anew about all the work we did and asked critical questions about how racial equity intersected with our issues. People often talk about putting a new racial lens on your work, but I found it was more like taking off blinders to see what we'd been conditioned not to see. We expanded whom we partnered with and raised a stink about the racial power dynamics in lots of settings, from advocacy coalitions to philanthropy. At the end of my tenure, my three-quarters white organization had become a majority-people-of-color think tank.

When I started the Racial Equity Transformation process, it was important to me that we transform not by gaining a whole new staff—I actually liked my colleagues, a lot—but by growing, and proving that it was possible for white people to become moral and strategic partners in the fight for a racially just America. It wasn't perfect, and it certainly wasn't always easy, but the final report from our four-year process read, "One of the most common refrains from staff members about the Racial Equity Transformation at Demos was that it felt like a 'gift' to people who had, no matter their color, rarely received explicit investments in what may be the most important set of knowledge and skills a person can have to contribute and flourish today."

Everything we believe comes from stories we've been told. I've become acutely aware of the massive platform that the people who are selling the story of racial resentment have, from television to the internet to talk radio. Fox News is the most-watched cable news network and the most profitable; it's become the leading source of meaning-making for its overwhelmingly white audience. But Fox is not just news; it's a propaganda outlet owned by a right-wing billionaire, and it uses anti-immigrant and racist stereotypes to undermine white support not just for progressive policies but for basic societal norms, from democracy to social distancing during the pandemic. The right-wing message machine has also overtaken social media, particularly Facebook, where content from conservative meme factories predominates—so much so that, in June 2020, seven out of the ten most-shared Facebook posts about the biggest social movement in the country were anti-BLM, many of them containing disinformation.

Our classrooms don't do much better: a 2018 Southern Poverty Law Center report examined the curriculum standards in fifteen states and found that "none addresses how the ideology of white supremacy rose to justify the institution of slavery; most fail to lay out meaningful requirements for learning about slavery . . . or about how [enslaved people's] labor was essential to the American economy." What's more, the organization surveyed high school seniors from across the country and found that only 8 percent knew that slavery was a primary cause of the Civil War. I've got to admit, my jaw dropped when I read that statistic. Eight percent! Two-thirds of seniors didn't know that a constitutional amendment was required to outlaw slavery. Nor could the vast majority (78 percent) explain how slaveholders benefited from provisions in the Constitution.

Even with the racial consciousness-raising of the summer of 2020, there are massive gaps in knowledge about our racial past and present . . . and a massive gulf between how American people of color see racism impacting our lives and how much credence the majority of white people gives to that idea. Most people will never get the kind of process that my colleagues and I went through at Demos, and now there's a backlash telling white Americans it's unpatriotic even to try. Like so much in this country, resetting our moral compass is something we have to do on our own.

Julie Christine Johnson has taken it on herself. A white woman with light brown hair, blue eyes, and a thoughtful gaze, Julie lives in the town of Port Townsend, Washington, on the Olympic Peninsula, where she writes novels and works at the local School of the Arts.

The easy way she carries herself reveals her hours spent in the wild, hiking and biking, and in the yoga studio, where she is a master practitioner. She was born in 1969 and grew up in what she describes as a strict Christian family in a community in Washington State that was rural, white, and geographically isolated. The only black people she came in contact with were on television, like the Huxtables. As an adult, she was politically progressive and of course supported racial equality, although she had never thought much about it. But by 2015, two things had happened to change that. One was the rise of the Black Lives Matter movement, which reached her even in her largely white harbor town. The other thing was Michelle Alexander's book *The New Jim Crow: Mass Incarceration in the Age of Colorblindness.*

"That book just broke something open inside of me," Julie said. "It made me realize this entire paradigm that I had been raised in . . . I had somehow never questioned that mythology, and never questioned what we had done as a society to people of color, and to the young men of color that have been forced into this prison industrial complex that we'd all looked to [as] the savior. The rage that consumed me, and the sense of helplessness that consumed me, propelled me into looking for answers of what I can do."

She found a way to begin: a month-long online seminar designed to serve as an introduction to racism, particularly for white people. Led by a white southerner named Patti Digh, the program is named (and requires) Hard Conversations. Through the assigned readings and challenging discussions in the seminar, Julie realized "that I've never just stopped and shut up and listened. . . . I'd been seeking out ways to address [racism] before I'd really even looked at my own behavior.

"There was just a massive awakening," she recalled. She felt she was having a common experience with other white people, who were realizing, " 'Wait a second. This is our problem to solve. . . . We created this.' "

Julie and her cohort in the program discussed what she called "some really touchy issues." She thought some people approached the discussion with the sense that " 'I feel everything I say and ask is just loaded with ignorance, and I'm going to come out of this feeling attacked or feeling stupid. I just don't even know what's safe to talk about anymore.'

"That's a very vulnerable place to be," Julie observed. "But think about how it's felt for people of color, who [have] never felt and never will probably feel safe to have a voice and be visible. And that's a place to start."

As promised, the experience was not easy. "Uncovering some of my own biases and things that have been ingrained in me . . . [these] were really hard for me to examine, and for me to let go of. And that's an ongoing process."

She was exhilarated to participate in the Women's March in January 2017, then the largest one-day protest in U.S. history. "And within days of that came . . . articles from women of color, saying, 'Where have you all been?' And I just felt my heart so open to that," Julie said. "Instead of feeling defensive, I was like, 'Yeah, just stop and listen. Listen to these voices.' "

But some of her white women friends were not so open to women of color calling them out. "I got into a really uncomfortable conversation with a group of women whom I've known for a very long time and really treasure. . . . I got pounded into the ground for raising my voice and saying, 'I agree with them, that "Where have we been?"' That feminism has not given space to women of color, and we've turned away from these voices. . . . Where were the throngs for Black Lives Matter rallies? Where have people been? . . . And I thought, where have I been?

"The very people that I would think would be open and get this are still incredibly resistant." Julie does not exempt herself from this assessment. "It's every day," she said. "It's every single day that you have to be aware of your own behavior . . . and the choices that you make." Though she doesn't pat herself on the back for her newfound racial awareness and activism, Julie knows that now she's freer, and truer to her own values, and not afraid to venture into honest conversations about race. It's a liberating feeling.

——

**AS I TRIED** to figure out how the country's moral progress had stalled, I finally realized that I should ask people whose job—or, rather, calling—it is to guide us morally. But there was a quandary, and that is the role that the largest religion in America has played in perpetuating American racism—and the way racial hierarchy seeps into religious institutions of all faiths. When the Rev. Dr. Martin Luther King Jr. was leading the Birmingham antisegregation campaign in 1963, a group of white clergy signed on to a letter urging him to stop. The civil rights activists, the white clergy said, were breaking the law with their nonviolent demonstrations, and so were in the wrong. From jail, Dr. King famously wrote, "I am sorry that your statement did not express a similar concern for the conditions that brought the demonstrations into being. . . . We will have to repent in this generation not merely for the hateful words and actions of the bad people but for the appalling silence of the good people."

The African American Christian tradition is almost synonymous with social justice in America, from abolition to the civil rights movement to contemporary leaders like Rev. William Barber, who led the Moral Mondays Movement in North Carolina and now leads a revived Poor People's Campaign. But white Christian leadership is still grappling with its role in acknowledging and dismantling racism. To talk to one of those leaders, I visited an Evangelical church in Chicago called River City, founded by a pastor named Daniel Hill. I sat in the back of the large, unadorned room for services so as to observe and not intrude, but this inadvertently put me in the families and children section. I was surrounded by row after row of the largest group of interracial families I'd ever seen in one room. I asked Pastor Daniel about it after services. River City is a strict Evangelical church in that its congregants believe in the literal word of God as recorded in the Bible—and that Word, Pastor Daniel told me, compelled them to create a deliberately multicultural church.

"Well, Revelations 7:9 is a vision of heaven that is every tongue and every tribe that God's ever created." Furthermore, Pastor Daniel told me, "It's impossible to have a meaningful relationship with Jesus and not care about the evil in our day and age. The ideology of white supremacy is, if not the premier form of evil, it's at least one of the clearest forms of evil on a large scale in our day and age." So he uses his ministry to teach the antiracist lessons of the Bible, confront white privilege in Christianity, and create a multiracial church in the heart of segregated Chicago.

But Pastor Daniel and River City are the exceptions to the rule, and it took a conversation with someone I've known for years, Reverend Jim Wallis, to explain why. Jim is a white Evangelical minister in his seventies with the warm blue eyes and smiling face of a Little League coach (which he has been for more than twenty seasons). In a conspiratorial tone over a long phone call, Jim told me the story of ruffling feathers at a gathering of the small circle of primarily white men who head the major Christian denominations in America.

"Now," Rev. Wallis told the men, walking around the circle and making eye contact with each one, "you all have been told or taught or learned how slavery was common, and slavery was all over the world. But we uniquely did something. We Christians, in fact— British and American—were the ones who decided that we couldn't do to Indigenous people and kidnapped Africans what we were doing, if they were indeed people made in the image of God.

"So, we said they weren't. They weren't humans made in the image of God. What we did is we threw away *Imago Dei*. We threw it away to justify what we're doing. . . . white supremacy was America's original sin. . . . At the heart of the sin was a lie," he said.

It's this history of the American church's complicity with white supremacy that explains why, today, white Christians are about 30 percentage points more likely to hold racially resentful and otherwise racist views than religiously unaffiliated white people, according to a new analysis by Robert P. Jones, the founder of the Public Religion Research Institute. In his 2020 book *White Too Long: The Legacy of White Supremacy in American Christianity*, Jones writes, "The unsettling truth is that, for nearly all of American history, the Jesus conjured by most white congregations was not only indifferent to the status quo of racial inequality; he demanded its defense and preservation as part of the natural, divinely ordained order of things."

Jones goes on to explain that "perhaps the most powerful role white Christianity has played in the gruesome drama of slavery, lynchings, Jim Crow, and massive resistance to racial equality is to maintain an unassailable sense of religious purity that protects white racial innocence. Through every chapter, white Christianity has been at the ready to ensure that white Christians are alternatively—and sometimes simultaneously—the noble protagonists and the blameless victims."

On the phone with me, Jim Wallis's voice grew deeper and fuller as he leaned into his point. "As long as white people—even, you know, good-hearted, well-meaning, progressive white people—think that the issue of race is mostly about people of color and minorities and what has happened to them and what happens to them that we could help with—as long as that's the mindset, they're still stuck," he told me.

And they will remain stuck "until we understand as white people that the problem of racism is about us." Jim doesn't take this call lightly. He says that "to confront this and change this is necessary for our salvation. To confront racism is not a question of charity or virtue for white Christians," he declared. "This is to save our souls."

The same way that Pastor Daniel preaches about the many antiracist messages in the New Testament, Rabbi Felicia Sol, senior rabbi at the large New York City Jewish congregation B'nai Jeshurun, revealed how the spiritual imperative against racism is located deep in the foundational texts and stories of her faith. "For the leitmotif of the Jewish tradition, we have a redemption narrative at our core. The Exodus from Egypt is a Jewish story. And that story has been utilized for liberation movements throughout history." But, she said, many religious scholars consider that "redemption isn't a miracle. It's actually built into the structure of the world. . . . And therefore, racism is an impediment to the structure of the world, of a redeemed world.

"The story goes that God was trying to make the world, and the world wouldn't stand up until *teshuvah*—'repentance'—was created. . . . And I find that a deeply compelling narrative. The structure of the world understands . . . it would have to repair itself at its core. But that repair is on us, you know."

Rabbi Sol made the religious case that racism cuts both ways. "Racism actually has a dehumanizing aspect not only for those who experience racism, but [also for] those who perpetuate it. . . . Jewish tradition articulates . . . that everyone is stamped in the image of God." And in some Jewish traditions, she said, "there's a notion that God is not a hierarchical God, but that God is the oneness of all of us. . . . There's no difference between me and God. It's all the same. God is one. And so, racism is another way that divides that divine connection . . . because then we're not only inflicting pain on others, but we're maligning our purity."

Many of the leading lawyers, philanthropists, and student activists supporting the civil rights movement were Jewish, including a disproportionate share of the white youth who volunteered in the 1964 Freedom Summer. And while there have been powerful waves of solidarity between white American Jews, African Americans, and today's persecuted immigrants and refugees, the relationship between Judaism and American racism is complex. Yavilah McCoy has experienced how white supremacy stands not only between a person and God, but also between the Jewish people and their full, rich history. Based in Boston, McCoy is an Orthodox-raised, yeshiva-trained Jewish educator, activist, and spiritual leader who is also an African American woman, one of the approximately 12 to 15 percent of American Jews who are people of color. We talked on the phone for almost an hour in 2019, and Yavilah's Brooklyn-accented speech was comfortably familiar to me, even peppered as it sometimes was with Hebrew phrases.

"All of that stuff about whiteness came into the Jewish community pretty strategically as a result of the way white European Jews came to the U.S.," she said. "And the way in which white supremacy couldn't really grapple with what a Jew was, outside of trying to assimilate them into whiteness." This, she said, resulted in "the stripping away of the history. All the [early] rabbis . . . came from Iraq, Iran, Syria, Jerusalem. . . . These are brown people, right?" Atrocities such as the Inquisition in the fifteenth century and the Holocaust in the twentieth century took Jews of varied national, racial, and ethnic backgrounds and made of them one "race"—a race to be exterminated.

At the spiritual level, Yavilah believes, racism interrupts the human connection with the divine. When Yavilah was a child learning the prayer book, a phrase in Hebrew was posted high on the wall at the front of the classroom. In English, it translates to "Know before whom you stand." She recalled, "The teacher would say, 'Before you start to pray, you have to acknowledge that you're in the presence of something bigger than yourself.' . . . How could we act out white supremacy, or any other realm of oppression, if I feel like what I'm standing before is something that is essential, something that is sacred, something that is human?"

Islam also espouses a theology of equality and fraternity among all humankind, and certain interpretations of its teachings about self-reliance and equality have appealed to many generations of African Americans, including but by no means limited to civil rights icons like Malcolm X. Among non-black Muslim Americans with immigrant backgrounds, the shared experiences of suspicion and surveillance—especially after 9/11—have been a source of solidarity with antiracist struggles. When I spoke with Zaheer Ali, a Brooklyn-based oral historian, he pointed to the line in the Quran in which Allah proclaims to humankind that "we . . . made you into nations and tribes [so] that you may know each other, not that you may despise each other." Ali was born in Trinidad, the Caribbean island where the descendants of Indian laborers (Muslim, Hindu, and Sikh) and enslaved Africans commingled for over a century, and he has spent much of his career documenting the oral history of American Muslims. He painted a complicated picture for me of a religious doctrine that was profoundly anti-hierarchical and has attracted many black Americans away from the Christianity so entangled with white supremacy and slavery. But he also talked about the anti-blackness that many South Asian, Persian, and Arab Muslim immigrants adopt as part of their assimilation process in America.

Just hours after my conversation with Zaheer, Minneapolis police officers killed George Floyd. Zaheer wrote me an email the day after the city of Minneapolis and the country erupted. "That it was a Muslim/Arab-owned store that called the police on George Floyd throws some of what we discussed into sharper relief (and even greater urgency): the need to speak to anti-black racism within Muslim communities." I had taken note of that fact as well, but replied asking him if he'd seen the news story of a local Bangladeshi Muslim family whose business, a restaurant named Gandhi Mahal, a few doors down from the Third Precinct of the Minneapolis Police Department, had caught fire in the protests. After losing his family's business, the father, Ruhel Islam, reportedly said, "Let my building burn. Justice needs to be served." I had read Mr. Islam's next words with tears in my eyes: "We can rebuild a building, but we cannot rebuild a human." Racism taught generations of white Americans that we were no more than property. I didn't know how much I needed to hear someone say that even if it cost them everything, they knew better.

**FOR ALL THE** differences among the world's major religions, they all hold compassion and human interconnectedness as central values; they all subscribe to a sacred vision of a world without racism. As I traveled the country engaging with people about the costs of racism, I often began our conversations discussing laws and policies, wealth and income—but in the end, many of the talks settled into a quiet, personal place. People brown, black, and white revealed a moment of confession, of frustration, or of hope, and it all came from an emotional, even spiritual sense that this just isn't how we're supposed to be. It made me think more deeply about my own spiritual beliefs. I believe in a divine force to which we are all connected, and I admire the rituals and community building that organized religion offers, but I didn't grow up as a churchgoer. (My mother, a deeply spiritual woman and a feminist, could never really accept a religion that figured the divine creator as male.) Yet I realized that I pursue my professional calling not only to improve our economy, but also out of a belief in the unseen: a promised land of a caring, just society. Across my conversations for this book, I heard a unified yearning for a society like that.

Racism destroys every path to that promised land, for all of us. As Wendell Berry writes, "If white people have suffered less obviously from racism than black people, they have nevertheless suffered greatly; the cost has been greater perhaps than we can yet know."

# Chapter 10

# THE
# SOLIDARITY
# DIVIDEND

I parked in a vacant lot on the southernmost end of Lisbon Street, the main thoroughfare of Lewiston, Maine. The street dead-ends near the old canal, built to power the cotton mills that made Lewiston one of the more prosperous towns in America in the late-1800s. The mills, the prosperity, even much of the canal, are now gone. "Dying mill towns" like Lewiston have been ground zero for propagation of the zero-sum story: Lewiston was once great for its white residents and began to fall apart in the same era when civil rights were on the rise and the country grew more diverse. *Progress for people of color means a loss for white people.* But this equation adds up only if you leave out the decisions by corporate employers to seek cheaper labor, or the trade policies that were the final death knell in the 1990s and 2000s.

Maine is the state with the whitest and oldest population in the country, whose children are the least likely in the country to have a classmate of color. The state ranks among the top ten in opioid deaths. From 2011 to 2019, the state's governor, Paul LePage, campaigned and governed on rhetoric about illegal immigrants on welfare and drug-dealing people of color. ("These are guys by the name

D-Money, Smoothie, Shifty. These type of guys that come from Connecticut, New York. They come up here, they sell their heroin, then they go back home. Incidentally, half the time they impregnate a young, white girl before they leave, which is the real sad thing because then we have another issue we gotta deal with down the road.") Meanwhile, he vetoed Medicaid expansion for the working class five times and delivered large tax cuts for the wealthy. I traveled to the state's second-biggest city, Lewiston, because of the ways its residents are especially vulnerable to the zero-sum story, but also because of a promising phenomenon I saw signs of about ten minutes into my walk up the town's main street.

AT THE BEGINNING of my walk, many of the buildings I saw—richly constructed nineteenth-century brick with Italianate moldings—stood stately and vacant, with neatly boarded-up windows on the ground floor. Here and there, a storefront lawyer's office appeared with a couple of desks needing far less space than it had; a pawn shop complex occupied much of an entire block. But once I crossed Chestnut Street, Lisbon Street came alive. Windows were suddenly stacked high with goods, framed by posters for mobile wire transfers and prepaid cards. One store had an arresting display of caftans and hijabs in bright coordinated colors. Another, next to the shadow of a faded old grocery store sign, had a sign reading MOGADISHU BUSINESS CENTER. The shop offered groceries, a restaurant, money transfer, a seamstress, a tax preparer, cleaning services, halal meat—and sweet, strong coffee, as I learned when I stopped in to fuel up.

The door chimes marked my departure from the street into a warm, fragrant, and music-filled shop. In the aisle near a wall of bulk spices, I saw two men and a young boy speaking in a language I recognized as Somali. As I ordered my coffee from the young hijab-wearing woman behind the counter, we chatted about how long she'd been in Maine (seven years), the weather (what good comes from complaining?), and after my first sip, the spices in my coffee (a secret blend, but yes, cardamom). I exited the Somali shop and looked around at the white and black residents on the street with a smile. Maybe these somewhat accidental neighbors were destined to create another story, a different formula from the zero sum, one more fitting for our future as a nation of many.

I turned off Lisbon to enter the historic City Hall. Through the open doors, I saw a stately marble hallway flanked by large portraits of every mayor in Lewiston history. I understood the reason for the tribute, but I also recognized, from so many institutions I'd been in, how it feels to be a person who doesn't look like the images on the walls, which were almost all of white men. It's hard not to get the message that this place—no matter who occupies it at the moment— belongs to them, not you. Then, down the middle of that long hallway came bounding a man as animated as the portraits were still: Phil Nadeau, the deputy city administrator. He greeted me warmly and showed me into an office decked with maps and memorabilia. My eye immediately went to the famous photograph of Muhammad Ali in the boxing ring, lording over the knocked-down Sonny Liston. I was shocked when Nadeau told me that the heavyweight title fight had happened just around the corner in Lewiston, in a youth hockey rink in 1965.

Unlike the elected and largely symbolic mayors, Nadeau was an urban planner appointed to run the day-to-day nuts and bolts of the town. He explained Lewiston's decline in blunt terms: "It was a one-and-a-half-industry town. Come the sixties and seventies, when it's pretty clear [the jobs] are going, there's little that you can do to stop it. There were a variety of things that we tried to help those businesses remain viable. But it was a losing battle against a global economy." Soon, everything that was once manufactured in Lewiston would be made in the American South with cheaper labor, and eventually in China and Southeast Asia. By the 2000s, the loss of jobs had created a vicious circle: as young people left to find work, there was nobody to work the few service sector jobs that remained in the wake of shuttered factories. Then, with the town losing population year after year, it was impossible to attract new employers. Lisbon Street, once the second-biggest commercial district in the state, began to show as many vacant windows as store displays. When Nadeau moved to his position in Lewiston city government in the early 2000s, it became clear to him that only one thing would save the town: new people.

"Maine is the oldest state in the country. One of only two now in the country, Maine and West Virginia, where deaths now exceed births. None of this is good news."

I asked him why getting new people actually mattered to those who stayed; how did he counter the idea that newcomers were just competing for dwindling resources? He shook his head emphatically. "You can't convince businesses to either expand or move into your state or into your community if the bodies aren't there. These companies know this about Maine. But here's the city of Lewiston bucking that trend."

The secret to Lewiston's success was something of an accident: in the early 1990s, the U.S. government accepted thousands of refugees from the Somali Civil War and resettled many to the Atlanta suburbs of Georgia. Word of mouth got some to Portland, and then to Lewiston, where the quiet streets offered more peace and the low rents more security. Family by family, Lewiston's refugee population grew. Soon it wasn't just Somalis but many other African refugees, from the Congo, Chad, Djibouti, and Sudan.

"The refugee arrivals . . . are filling apartments that were vacant for a long time. They're filling storefronts on Lisbon Street that were vacant for a long time. They're contributing to the economy." Phil Nadeau is passionate about the value of the "new Mainers," as he calls them, to the revitalization of Lewiston. He boasts that while other Maine small towns had plummeting real estate values, fleeing young people, and shuttering schools, Lewiston is building new schools—and creating the jobs that come with that. Though Phil also credits good regional planning and maintenance of the historic assets—the infrastructure built nearly a century ago, the hundreds of thousands of square feet of factories that have not become blighted—he simply can't say enough about the benefit of migration to small towns like his. A bipartisan think tank calculated that Maine's African immigrant households contributed $194 million in state and local taxes in 2018.

When I met Nadeau, he was in his last weeks on a job that has taken him through multiple administrations of elected mayors who, to put it mildly, haven't shared his enthusiasm for the changing face of Lewiston. But Phil has seen the economic fortunes of the town reverse, and for a city planner, there's nothing controversial about that. He plans to spend his retirement crossing the country to share the good word about how immigration can be a win-win for locals. "I could talk about it all day long." Phil sat back in his chair and allowed a broad smile to finish his point.

Before I left, I asked Phil if I could take some pictures of his office for my recollection. I took a shot of his Ali portrait. Some in the town have adopted the story of Ali's knockdown punch as a symbol of Lewiston, where people knew how it felt to get knocked down: the old-timers who'd seen their fortunes fade when the jobs disappeared, but also of course the refugees who had lost everything before coming to America's shores. The Ali-Liston fight was historic for another reason that would be special to the new Mainers: it was the first time that Cassius Clay was introduced by his new Muslim name.

LEWISTON IS NOT alone in this new wave of new people; for the past twenty years, Latinx, African, and Asian immigrants have been re-populating small towns across America. Pick a state, and you'll find this story in one corner or another. Kennett Square, Pennsylvania, is now 50 percent Latinx, mostly from Mexico, and it's a community given new life by the families of migrant workers at the local mushroom farms. In Storm Lake, Iowa, the elementary school is 90 percent children of color. Towns across the Texas Panhandle have been drying up and losing population for years, but the potato farming

stronghold of Dalhart grew by 7 percent from 1990 to 2016 because
of Latinx families. Low-paid farm and food processing work is what
draws foreign-born people to these small towns at first, for sure. But
once there, immigrants have, as European immigrants did a century
ago, started businesses, gained education, and participated in civic
life (though the Europeans' transition to whiteness offered a glide
path to the middle class unavailable to immigrants of color today).
Even in the face of anti-immigrant policies and the absence of vehicles for mobility such as unions and housing subsidies, today's immigrants of color are revitalizing rural America. A study of more
than 2,600 rural communities found that over the three decades after
1990, two-thirds lost population. However, immigration helped
soften the blow in the majority of these places, and among the areas
that gained population, one in five owes the entirety of its growth to
immigration. In the decade after 2000, people of color made up
nearly 83 percent of the growth in rural population in America.

In many of these communities, longtime residents—who are
overwhelmingly white—have chosen not to feel threatened by these
new people of color. The temptation is there, and the encouragement
from anti-immigrant politicians is certainly there, but the growth
and prosperity the new people bring give the lie to the zero-sum
model. Locals know that the alternative to new people is compounding losses: factories, residents, then the hospitals and schools and the
attendant jobs. So, the residents are putting aside prejudices in order
to grow their hometowns, together. If they don't, wrote Art Cullen,
the local newspaper editor in Storm Lake, Iowa, "there will be nobody left to turn out the lights by 2050" in towns like his. "Asians and
Africans and Latinos are our lifeline," he declared flatly in 2018.

These small-town success stories are full of local gestures, both
big and small, to integrate the newcomers, ranging from free ESL
classes to community college partnerships to help new immigrants
get degrees. One of these gestures changed the life of Lewiston resi-
dent Cecile Thornton, but it wasn't she who offered the education to
her new neighbors; they gave it to her. A quarter of Maine citizens,
like Cecile, have Franco-American heritage—mostly descendants of

French-speaking Canadian immigrants who came to work the cotton mills and shoe factories a hundred years ago—but only 3 percent of the state speaks French regularly at home, and Cecile is among the many "Francos" who have lost their French. Cecile was born in 1955 to French-speaking parents and did her best to forget the French she'd learned at the dinner table, escaping to the living room once the family got a TV set and repeating the words of Walter Cronkite to learn how "real" Americans spoke. The "Francos" were the butt of schoolyard jokes, so by high school, Cecile made sure to suppress her accent altogether and held on to very few words of her native French.

When I met her, she'd also lost the closeness of her family. "All of my family is away, including my kids," she told me. "They're all out of state. And my aunts and uncles, my parents, all of those people are dead." The kind of isolation that Cecile faced when she retired to an empty home in Lewiston has become a growing epidemic among older people in rural and suburban America. The former U.S. surgeon general has linked it to the "diseases of despair" that are disproportionately haunting white Americans facing economic decline: alcoholism, drug abuse, and suicide. Social isolation has been found to lower life expectancy by a degree comparable to smoking almost a pack of cigarettes a day.

But a few years ago, Cecile made a decision that turned her story around. She got in her car to drive to the Franco Center downtown. She went looking for a connection—to other people, to her community, to the language that had filled her home as a child. What she found on the first day at the center, however, was a roomful of elderly people who had long ago traded away French for belonging—to become no longer "Francos," but simply, white. It was a cultural assimilation that happened in time to every group of white-skinned immigrants in the nineteenth and early twentieth centuries, from the Italians to the Poles. What America offered for the price of assimilation was inclusion in the pool of whites-only benefits that shaped the middle class, but we don't talk much about what they left behind.

The Franco Center had a rule: put a quarter in a jar every time you spoke English. The maximum penalty was one dollar, though, so when Cecile looked around, all the tables had jars full of dollars and conversations carrying on in English. She couldn't hide her disappointment: even here at the Franco Center, her community's language seemed lost. In her isolation, the idea of reclaiming her French had become a lifeline, so she wasn't giving up—she found the most talkative person in the room and complained. He told her, "You should go to the French Club at Hillview." Hillview is a subsidized housing project in Lewiston. When Cecile arrived at one o'clock on a weekday afternoon for the advertised French Club, she was shocked to see that she was the only white person there.

"I didn't even know at the time that we had Africans in the city who spoke French. I had no clue, none." The first man she spoke with, Edho, had just followed his wife and children to Lewiston from Congo. After a timid "Bonjour" from Cecile, she and Edho launched into the longest French conversation Cecile had had since her childhood, with Edho helping her recall long-gone words and phrases. By the end of the first session, she was exhausted but thrilled. "Just as an interested and curious person, when I was meeting these people, I just fell in love with them." She laughs, knowing what that sounds like. "Not that I really fell in love with them, but I felt like I belonged with them."

Over the next year, Cecile would make the Francophone African community of Lewiston the center of her life. When she noticed that it became hard for Hillview folks to attend French Club once they enrolled in community college downtown or got a job, she launched a new French Club, at the more convenient Franco Center downtown, but she heavily recruited her new African friends to come. With Cecile's encouragement, soon the two populations of French speakers were mixing: elderly white Mainers with halting vocabularies learning from new black Mainers who spoke fluently. Francophone Africans like Edho, once seen as strange folks from far away, were now teachers. Today, Cecile volunteers to help asylum seekers, doing winter coat drives and connecting new arrivals to services, but she'd be the first to say that what she gives pales in comparison with what she has received.

Bruce Noddin would say the same. A few years ago, Bruce was the father of two kids and the owner of a thriving sports equipment business—but he also had a drug and alcohol addiction that nearly killed him. He was on the verge of becoming a statistic, a white middle-aged man succumbing to the opioid epidemic stalking Maine and other white enclaves across America. But after he hit rock bottom, a chance encounter led him to becoming a community organizer. "My wife says my new addiction is being in the community," he told me with a chuckle.

In 2015, Bruce was participating in a jail ministry as part of his recovery. In the jail parking lot, he noticed a woman unloading from her car "the best-smelling food." She was bringing it to the handful of Muslim men in the jail who would break their fast after sundown. He'd of course noticed the rising numbers of African refugees in Lewiston over the years and generally found them a source of curiosity, but he'd never ventured a conversation. In the parking lot, he and the woman got to talking about what each of them was doing at the jail. She introduced herself as ZamZam, and then Bruce heard words coming out of his mouth that surprised even him: "God is God." They traded phone numbers on the spot.

After that, things happened quickly. ZamZam encouraged him to join the Maine People's Alliance, a 32,000-member-strong grassroots group advocating for policies like Medicaid expansion, a minimum wage increase, paid sick leave, and support for home care. His activism would take him into deeper engagement with the Muslim immigrant community in Lewiston. Somalis taught him how to handle a rude voter while canvassing on a mayoral campaign; as he shared his frustrations about corruption in the Catholic Church, men from Djibouti opened up about the hypocrisy of their religious leaders. Bruce has become a lead organizer of an annual cross-cultural festival, the Community Unity Barbecue, which brings out hundreds of Lewiston residents. Last summer, as he spent hours standing over a hot stove in the park learning to make Somali flatbreads, he couldn't help thinking of his own Franco ancestors who fled persecution and found refuge in Lewiston—and what they'd gone through to finally be accepted.

"The vision for me for this city," Bruce told me, "it's [that we will] embrace our past, embrace our ethnicity . . . and then embrace the people that are here now that are just like those people that came here one-hundred-plus years ago. They're exactly like that. But actually, they're even worse off. They didn't always have a job. They were escaping atrocities in their country. They were escaping possibly dying or seeing their children die. And they need[ed] to work. There should be this massive amount of empathy from that next two, three, four generations down from those people that went through the same stuff as these people are going through, and saying, 'We're going to embrace you. You're going to help us make this city great again.'"

MOMENTS LIKE BRUCE'S cross-cultural festival provide glimpses of the way Lewiston, and much of America, could be—but they're few and far between. The zero-sum tension is still prominent, even in Lewiston, with all its successes. Phil Nadeau's enthusiasm for the net economic gains of creating a more diverse Lewiston had me convinced that I'd found the antidote to the zero-sum narrative. But then I talked to Ben Chin, the Maine People's Alliance deputy director, who told me wryly, "Unless you are three relationships removed from Phil or closer, you haven't heard that and you don't believe it." After my conversation with Phil, I went back to Lisbon Street to the Mogadishu Business Center to talk with one of the owners, Said, a gregarious Somali man with soft brown eyes. Said told me that one of the first white Mainers to venture into the store was a woman named Brenda, who was drawn by the clothes hanging in the front. She asked so many questions that it became evident that she was a skilled seamstress who had been out of work for some time. She struck up a rapport with the store's other owner, Said's wife, known to all as

Mama Shukri. Mama Shukri offered Brenda a job repairing the hijabs and kaftans people would bring into the shop. Said explains, "And then she started making new clothes after that."

My eyes got wider. "So, Brenda started making African clothes?"

Said nodded matter-of-factly. "Yeah. She's very good."

He told me more stories about integration going well at the person-to-person level, including in the Lewiston Blue Devils soccer team, which African immigrant kids from six countries had led to three years of state championships. White Mainers and African Mainers doing business together was going well, too, he said. It's the government he worries about. In fact, Lewiston has been governed by mayors using harsh anti-immigrant rhetoric for all of the twenty years that Somalis have been present. After the first group of families arrived in Lewiston by word of mouth, then-Mayor Laurier Raymond Jr. wrote an open letter saying that the town was full, even though much of downtown lay vacant. "This large number of new arrivals cannot continue without negative results for all," Raymond wrote. The letter became a rallying cry for white supremacists, who descended on the town for a march soon after. An early Republican in the Trump mold, Governor Paul LePage won his elections campaigning against welfare, suggesting that immigrants were stealing resources from the local taxpayers. Said shook his head. "So, [the mayor] is going to a lectern and saying, 'Oh, because of the Somalis, we are going to cut the welfare. Because these people, they're coming here only for welfare.'"

His eyes got a little distant, as they did when he was talking about home. "In central and south[ern] Africa, there's a saying: 'When election day comes, keep your knife close.' That's when the problems happen, especially inter-clan problems. But once the election is gone, people are normal. Everyone is looking for his life. They are trading with each other, friends getting married together. But the one day election comes, the knives are out. The politicians will try to separate us."

*The politicians will try to separate us.* The people I met—Phil,

Bruce, Cecile, Said with his co-worker Brenda—belonged to a beach-head of solidarity amid a surge in xenophobia pushed relentlessly by politicians in Lewiston and across the country. The faith that the Lewiston people I met had in the idea of different cultures not only coexisting but thriving through their differences didn't come from theory or ideology; it came from lived experience. Each of them had had a reason to roll up their sleeves and put in the time to make some part of their community work better, and in so doing, they had bettered themselves. But the resistance of many white Mainers to new people isn't about just dollars and cents, if we're honest. It's also about the fear of a loss of community, of identity, of home. It was striking to me that what old Mainers were worried about losing is something that, by definition, the new Mainers have *actually* lost: home. And for people like Cecile and Bruce, cross-cultural friendships have given them a deeper sense of community than they ever had before.

Yet in Lewiston, with its thirty-five thousand residents, a 2015 mayoral campaign presaged the turn that national politics would take once Donald Trump launched his presidential campaign by calling Mexican immigrants "rapists." Incumbent Republican mayor Robert Macdonald, who was enthusiastically supported by the immigrant-bashing governor, ran a fear-mongering, zero-sum campaign against Democrat Ben Chin, of the Maine People's Alliance. A multiracial Millennial, Ben is a community organizer and Episcopalian lay minister who was explicitly trying to counter that division.

Ben looks even younger than his years, with the lean build of a triathlete. His grandfather was a Chinese immigrant who fought for the United States in World War II, built a successful business, and then was targeted in the McCarthy era. Ben grew up in Pittsburgh and Syracuse, New York, also declining manufacturing cities, but when he arrived at college in Lewiston, he found "the kind of issues that every big city has, but on a small enough scale where you can have some kind of impact and make a difference."

When Ben and his volunteers were out knocking on doors, he

heard firsthand the effect of the zero-sum narrative. Urban legends were repeated freely. "The big one was 'Somali people get a free car as soon as they come to America,'" he told me. "And that just stuck. Once LePage gets elected in 2010 and Mayor Macdonald gets elected in 2011, and you just have these two guys using the bully pulpit, just driving this relentless message that is anti-immigrant for all these strategic reasons that mostly end up hurting white people, like cutting Medicaid. . . . [W]hen I go out canvassing, sometimes you're in neighborhoods where, every other door, you're hearing something like that."

Ben's campaign for mayor focused on economic justice issues like increasing the minimum wage and access to affordable housing, and on integrating immigrants into the community. His campaign energized a cross-racial group of supporters and volunteers and relied on the community-organizing techniques of person-to-person outreach. His goal, he said publicly, was "to make sure Lewiston is a city where everyone has a shot at their dreams."

"When I ran the first time," he told me, "one of the slumlords that we [at the Maine People's Alliance] were holding accountable put up a bunch of signs around town calling me 'Ho Chi Chin,' with a racist caricature of my face and a hammer and a sickle." His story called to mind Senator Claude Pepper, whose support for a policy that would have benefited mostly white people led rich people to target him with a red-baiting racist campaign, as well. Ben countered these scorched-earth tactics with a base of young and passionate supporters, exceeding state fundraising records mostly with small donations and coming within 600 votes of unseating the incumbent mayor.

In 2017, Ben ran again, made it to a runoff, and then lost by just 145 votes after a leaked email thrust the issue of racism into the campaign weeks before the election. Ben had just finished a long day of door-knocking when he emailed notes to his campaign staff about his forty-seven conversations with voters that day: a woman who wanted to volunteer for him after losing her sister to an overdose; good talks with two African American families; swaying a former Macdonald supporter who was leaning his way; and "a bunch of racists, too . . ." he'd written. Somebody leaked the notes to the press, and Ben's frank appraisal caused a firestorm. The right-wing media seized on it and made it seem like he had accused the entire town: "Leaked Email: Ben Chin Says Lewiston Voters 'Bunch of Racists.' "

I asked Ben about it. It turns out "this particular street that I was referencing in this email was one of the wealthiest streets in town . . . so it hit a nerve, right? Because I actually think the racism in Lewiston—the center of gravity is not in the working-class parts. It's in these sort of swankier, more upscale parts of town." Through all the campaigning ups and downs, Ben held on to his conviction that white working-class voters would one day see through the racist narratives that his opponents were using to sell them an agenda that betrayed them. As someone who shared his conviction, I hoped he was right.

His opponents' agenda had already included three major tax cuts for the wealthy that squeezed public services and led to higher property taxes on the working and middle class. Ben's first opponent, Mayor Macdonald, proposed that all welfare recipients be publicly named on a website and that asylum seekers be banned from the state assistance program, even though the law also banned them from working for months while waiting for their legal status. And Governor LePage refused to expand Medicaid after passage of the Affordable Care Act, vetoing it five times during a period when almost 10 percent of the state's population was uninsured. These men invoked the age-old story of competition that is deployed to make people feel less generous and welcoming, and more supportive of austerity measures. But in Maine, white people constitute about 95 percent of the population, and 11.5 percent of them were in poverty in 2016—twice as many white people in poverty as there were people of color of all incomes in the whole state. The people who needed government services were overwhelmingly white.

Finally, starting in the fall of 2017, Ben and the thirty-two thousand members of the Maine People's Alliance were able to win a string of victories that began to refill the pool of public services in Maine—and justify Ben's faith. Maine became the first state in the nation to vote to expand Medicaid by ballot initiative over the governor's repeated refusal. The ballot campaign faced racist tactics but overcame them. "During the campaign there was certainly an attempt to racialize it . . . and the code word for that was *welfare*. And our canvassers would knock on doors and sometimes, unfortunately even people who would be eligible for Medicaid [said] they were against it, because they thought it could be going to immigrants and other people they thought would be undeserving. But we won it resoundingly."

I asked Ben how they were able to overcome the race-baiting, and he explained that the multiracial coalition was the key. "And by coalition, I really do mean this broader working-class set of folks that cross lines of race and all of that. We were hoping for a lot more support from bigwigs like folks in the hospital association . . . but it was this broader base of working-class people that actually got it across the finish line, not the muckety-mucks." The winning political coalition included, for the first time, immigrant-led political action committees, and the get-out-the-vote effort was anchored by a network of Somali taxi drivers who used their infrastructure of radios and vehicles to get elderly, homebound immigrant and poor Mainers to the polls safely.

Since then, Maine has experienced a Solidarity Dividend. Rejecting the scapegoating politics that enabled a right-wing government to deny healthcare and creating new political alliances between workers of all backgrounds resulted in sixty thousand Mainers winning access to healthcare. These same organizers and volunteers helped elect a wave of new politicians the following year, who passed reforms to address the opioid epidemic and guarantee a generous paid-time-off law for Maine workers. The next frontier of cross-racial coalition building, though, is for white people not just to stop voting against their own interests, but to vote for the interests of people of color, too, on issues of racial justice.

In the whitest state in the union, there are promising signs that this is happening: a slate of progressive school board candidates in Maine are running explicitly on racial equity. The slate includes a white suburban mom in Bangor; a Somali social worker; a South Sudanese graduate of Maine public schools; a twenty-five-year-old queer grocery clerk with Asperger's syndrome; and a white transgender man with twenty-four years' experience as a schoolteacher, who wears a T-shirt in his campaign video that reads: "I'm Not Black, But I Will Fight For You." The candidates have championed racial justice issues such as removing police in schools, equitably funding the increasingly diverse South Portland district, and creating antiracist curricula.

And back in Lewiston, the mayor who beat Ben Chin, Shane Bouchard, ended up resigning his seat over a racist text message. It turns out that the person who had leaked Ben's email had been having an affair with Bouchard; she eventually had a crisis of conscience and revealed the whole story, including Bouchard's texts with racist and sexist jokes. "All my jokes are quite racist lol," he wrote her. "What do you call 2 old black people sitting on your front lawn[?]" he had texted her. "Antique farm equipment." When I heard that, I was honestly shocked—and I don't shock easily. At first blush, it would seem implausible that a white Millennial from Maine—not Mississippi—would even have a frame of reference for making a casual, dehumanizing joke about slavery. But then I chided myself for buying the myth of northern innocence and forgetting how interconnected it all is. Maine once had the largest Ku Klux Klan membership outside of the South, and the textile mills that made the city of Lewiston were, of course, processing southern cotton.

## FIVE DISCOVERIES

My journey across the U.S. from California to Mississippi to Maine, tallying the costs of racism, has led me to five discoveries about how we can prosper together:

- The first is that we have reached the productive and moral limit of the zero-sum economic model that was crafted in the cradle of the United States. We have no choice but to start aiming for a **Solidarity Dividend**.

- The second is that the quickest way to get there is to **refill the pool of public goods**, for everyone. When our nation had generous public benefits, they were the springboard for a thriving middle class—but they were narrowly designed to serve white and soon-to-be-white Americans.

- Third, because of that, our people are not all standing at the same depths today, so we must resist the temptation to use universal instruments to attain universal ends. When it comes to designing solutions, **one size has never fit all**. Everywhere that I found white people paying the spillover costs of racism, I also found that, without exception, their co-workers and neighbors of color were paying even more, in lost wealth, health, and often lives. Getting white support to address those different levels of need, and to acknowledge the racism that caused those differences, is never easy—particularly when the zero-sum mental model turns every concession into a threat of loss.

- That's why uprooting the zero sum is so essential, as is embedding in its place the value that I found radiating out of the people who had the biggest impact on me and their communities: the knowledge that **we truly do need each other**.

- The fifth and final discovery is that we've got to get on the same page before we can turn it. We've tried a do-it-yourself approach to writing the racial narrative about America, but the forces selling denial, ignorance, and projection have succeeded in robbing us of our own shared history—both the pain and the resilience. It's time to tell the truth, with a nationwide process that enrolls all of us in setting the facts straight so that we can move forward with **a new story**, together.

**WHAT WE'VE GOT** now just isn't working. When the rules of the game allow a small minority of participants to capture most of the gains, at a certain point (for example, when the entire middle class owns less than the wealthiest 1 percent of Americans), fewer people can play at all. Extreme inequality robs too many people of the means to start businesses, invest in their families, and invent new ideas and solutions—and then it isn't a problem just for those families. Ultimately, having millions of people with potential on the sidelines because they have too much debt and not enough opportunity saps the vitality of the entire economy. There's a growing body of literature that shows that inequality itself impedes a country's economic growth—even more than the factors policy makers have emphasized in the past: liberalizing trade policies, controlling inflation, and reducing national debt. And America's racial inequality is not only the most extreme manifestation of our inequality, but also the template, setting up a scaffolding of hierarchy that increasingly few people, of any race, can climb.

The plutocrats have always known that solidarity is the answer, that the sum of us can accomplish far more than just some of us. That's why the forces seeking to keep the economic rules exactly as they are aim to cut off any sense of empathy white people who are struggling might develop for also-struggling people of color. Their "punching down" political attacks are how we know that empathy is a strength. Bridget from the Kansas City Fight for $15 discovered the power of solidarity in a basement organizing meeting, when she saw her own life reflected in that of a Latina fast-food worker. Until then, not only had Bridget bought into a dehumanizing narrative about people like the woman who spoke that night (and black people like Terrence), she'd also bought the idea that her own labor would never be worth $15 an hour. There's something about the mentality of degrading others in your same position that can make you unable to see a better life for yourself, either. When you believe the dominant story that you're on your own, responsible for all your own successes and failures, and yet you're still being paid $7.25 an hour, what does that say about your own worth? The problem with the easy out that the right wing offers—scapegoating immigrants and people of color instead—is that the scapegoats aren't actually the ones paying you poverty wages. As my friend George Goehl, head of People's Action, a grassroots network that organizes in rural America, says, "We've found the enemy, and it's not each other." Bridget and Terrence found that redirecting the blame toward the people actually setting the rules was liberating; finding a sea of potential allies in the people who worked alongside them was empowering. That's the Solidarity Dividend.

**THE MOUNTING CHALLENGES** we face in society are going to require strength and scale that none of us can achieve on her own. The crises of climate change, inequality, pandemics, and mass involuntary movements of people are already here, and in the United States, each has exposed the poverty of our public capacity to prevent and react. Save for the ultra-wealthy, we're all living at the bottom of the drained pool now. The refusal to share across race has created a society with nothing left for itself. With falling support for government over the past fifty years has come falling support for taxes, a brain drain from the public sector, and a failure to add to (or even steward) the infrastructure investments of the early twentieth century.

We have to refill the pool. Some restoration of public goods will be relatively straightforward, like rebuilding the fifty-year-old dams that are failing just in time for climate change to send heavier rains, or laying new pipes to replace the ones leaching toxins into our drinking water. We know how to do that; we've just lost the will. I'll acknowledge a bigger problem with the progressive vision for more robust government: we've let slip our capacity to deliver services with efficiency and skill. The old adage goes that poor people get poor services, and as we've ratcheted down the income level for government benefits over the past fifty years and squeezed public payrolls, the experience of dealing with the government has become increasingly frustrating and negative. Just ask the millions of people who applied for pandemic-related unemployment insurance from state agencies stripped by years of Republican budget cuts and who were still waiting months later; the graduates who were unable to get the public service loan forgiveness they'd organized their careers around due to technicalities; or the voters who navigated a maze of requirements to get a ballot and vote. Refilling the pool will require us to believe in government so much that we hold it to the highest standard of excellence and commit our generation's best and brightest to careers designing public goods instead of photo-sharing apps.

When we do, the potential is boundless. The crisis of youth un- and underemployment offers the opportunity to create millions of public-service jobs across the country to do the work that desperately needs doing. Every community in America could use the kind of renewable energy project that has engaged the youth in Richmond, from weatherizing buildings to installing solar arrays. The country needs new parks and community centers; childcare and camps to support working parents; literacy programs and home visits to the elderly. We need more internet service in rural and inner-city areas, oral histories of gentrifying urban communities and depopulating rural towns, and yes, even new public pools. Public pools were part of the "melting pot" project that fostered cross-cultural cohesion among white ethnic immigrants and their children in the early twentieth century, and it's absurd to think that something as shallow as skin color is an insurmountable obstacle to doing it again. The big and small public works our country needs now should be designed explicitly to foster contact across cultural divides, sending urban youth to rural areas and vice versa, and explicitly building teams that reflect the youth generation's astonishing diversity. An analysis Demos did in the middle of the Great Recession found that one hundred billion dollars spent directly hiring people could create 2.6 million public service jobs; spending the same amount on tax cuts trickles down to just one hundred thousand jobs.

———

**AS OUR COUNTRY** becomes more diverse, there's a way to design our policy making to get the best out of all our communities and create from the bottom of the social hierarchy an upward spiral of mutual benefit. There is a vanishingly small number of changes tailored for those struggling the most that wouldn't ultimately benefit us all. Policy advocate Angela Glover Blackwell calls this "the curb-cut effect," after a fix created by people using wheelchairs that now also helps non-disabled people carrying large loads or pushing strollers. The post–World War II GI Bill is a good example of a well-intentioned policy meant to benefit all veterans that in fact did almost nothing for black veterans for two generations, because the policy ignored the disparate conditions they faced, such as being excluded from most of the educational and home-owning opportunities the GI Bill was supposed to support. There's a better way. It's called "targeted universalism," a concept developed by law professor and critical race scholar john a. powell—he doesn't capitalize his name—who currently directs the Haas Othering and Belonging Institute at the University of California, Berkeley. With targeted universalism, you set a universal policy goal and then develop strategies to achieve the goal that take into account the varied situations of the groups involved.

Let's take homeownership, the center of financial security and wealth-building for most families—and for the American economy. The building, buying, selling, financing, and consumption of homes contributes to about 15 percent of the GDP. As we've seen, people of color and black people in particular have been disproportionately and intentionally excluded from this linchpin of economic freedom, so any program designed to boost homeownership that does not specifically address the barriers facing African Americans can only succeed in increasing the racial homeownership and wealth gap. A public policy that does manage to increase black homeownership to the same level as white homeownership would shrink the pernicious racial wealth gap by more than 30 percent. Today, however, our major federal commitment to homeownership comes through the color-blind home mortgage interest deduction, which allows people to deduct from their tax bill interest paid to lenders on all real estate properties they own. The problem is, this massive subsidy is upside down, bestowing the largest benefits on the richest people and effectively rewarding people with wealth for having it, as opposed to helping people without it find a toehold, as the whites-only housing programs did in the 1930s, '40s, and '50s. The ability of white families to count on inheritances from previous generations is the biggest contributor to today's massive racial wealth gap.

We can do better. The maps have already been drawn, through racist redlining, so instead of ignoring them and the damage they wrought, we can target down payment assistance to longtime redlined residents, as Kamala Harris and Elizabeth Warren proposed in the 2020 presidential primary. It's not difficult to imagine the knock-on benefits of increased home ownership among black people, which range from the financial security and mobility it would provide families to the spillover effects of higher property taxes and, therefore, education funding. If the United States adopted policy interventions to close the racial disparities in health, education, incarceration, and jobs, the economy would be eight trillion dollars larger in 2050, the year at which people of color are projected to be the majority. Generic, color-blind plans and policies can never achieve this.

A race-conscious housing effort to close the black-white gap in homeownership could be the centerpiece of a national effort for reparations for the economic harms of slavery, systematic discrimination, wealth suppression, and theft. Given the potential benefits to all of us from racial equity, the imperative for racial reparations becomes more urgent. In their 2020 book *From Here to Equality: Reparations for Black Americans in the Twenty-first Century,* professors William A. Darity Jr. and A. Kirsten Mullen make the case that it's the U.S. government that perpetuated the harms, and therefore must pay. The book proposes a straightforward process for identifying descendants of African slaves based on Census records and genealogy, and models possible payments based on various methods for determining the debt, from the worth of the elusive "forty acres and a mule" to their preferred route, closing the current racial wealth gap.

Wealth is where history shows up in your wallet, where your financial freedom is determined by compounding interest on decisions made long before you were born. That is why the black-white wealth gap is growing despite gains in black education and earnings, and why the typical black household owns only $17,600 in assets. Still, having little to no intergenerational wealth and facing massive systemic barriers, descendants of a stolen people have given America the touch-tone telephone, the carbon filament in the lightbulb, the gas mask, the modern traffic light, blood banks, the gas furnace, open-heart surgery, and the mathematics to enable the moon landing. Just imagine the possibilities if—in addition to rebuilding the pathways for all aspirants to the American Dream—we gave millions more black Americans the life-changing freedom that a modest amount of wealth affords. A 2020 Citigroup report calculated that "if racial gaps for blacks had been closed 20 years ago, U.S. GDP could have benefitted by an estimated $16 trillion."

Every day seems to bring more examples of the inverse: what happens when we do not address racial inequality. The 2020 COVID-19 crisis provides a tragically clear example of how failing to design policy with those most impacted in mind will create racist outcomes, ultimately endangering us all. The pandemic saw a color-blind virus attack people with disproportionate ferocity and fatality based on the way that racist and exploitative structures had unequally exposed us to the harm. At the beginning of the pandemic, there was a spirit of unprecedented interconnectedness in the country, when we first understood that in a contagious epidemic, we are all only as safe as our neighbors. The spirit of solidarity and self-sacrifice that blossomed instantaneously from the vast majority of Americans—sewing masks, volunteering to deliver groceries, upending their lives to stop the consumer-driven American way of life and work in order to keep

their community safe—was inspiring. But that should not have allowed the people in charge of the pandemic response to neglect the
fact that, even though we were facing the same storm, we weren't all
riding it out in the same boat. In the first months of the pandemic,
black, Latinx, and Indigenous people were multiple times more
likely than white people to get sick and to die. The factors were numerous and interlacing: more likely to have to keep leaving home for
work but less likely to have health insurance if they got sick; more
likely to be deemed "essential" but less likely to be treated so, as employers left low-wage workers in warehouses, care facilities, meatpacking plants, and retail stores without adequate protection; more
likely to live in formerly redlined, still-segregated areas where pollution degraded their lung quality, in crowded housing, detention centers, or jails without social distancing or on reservations where clean
water was hard to come by. A study modeling COVID-19 transmission routes in a representative U.S. city found that the majority of
the city's infections came from situations where racism was driving
higher exposure. "Any serious effort to fight this disease has to treat
inequity as a driver of infection and death for everyone, rather than
an unfortunate consequence for other people," the study co-authors
at the Center for Policing Equity wrote. "Covid-19 is telling us, in the
starkest possible terms, that the burdens of the most vulnerable—
and racism specifically—pose a collective threat."

The country was caught without public health capacity largely
because of the drained pool—antigovernment sentiment that has
hobbled the public health infrastructure, and decades of cuts to public hospitals in low-income and of-color communities that left half of
low-income areas without a single ICU bed when the pandemic hit.
In my hometown of Chicago, according to a ProPublica investigation, leaders cost lives by issuing one-size-fits-all guidance without
being attuned to the facts on the ground for black people—from
lower-quality, under-resourced hospitals; to transportation inequity;
to well-warranted suspicion of the medical system that, combined
with the generic message to stay at home, meant that far too many

black people stayed at home until they were already dying. It was people of color who could see the dreadful pandemic's effect in every single one of its manifestations—a clarity born of being maximally vulnerable.

This is why it's essential that we listen closely to the experiences and insights of people most exposed to all our society's ills, viral and human-made. It's become fashionable to say "trust black women" and to root for the leadership of women of color. And maybe it's because I am a woman of color and wasn't comfortable with how self-serving this advice seemed, or because it seemed to suggest a biological basis for some traits, I rejected this shorthand. But the truth isn't that there's some innate magic within us; it's that the social and economic and cultural conditions that have been imposed on people at the base of the social hierarchy have given us the clearest view of the whole system. We can see how it's broken and all those who are broken by it. That's why it's essential that women of color are at least as represented in government as we are in society. (As opposed to today, when over two-thirds of officials are white men, even though they're only a third of the population.) For nearly two decades in public policy, I saw how the fear of what white people would think held back the ambitions of some of the best policy thinkers in the business. Our politics have operated in the shadow of white disapproval my whole life. We need leaders who see color, who recognize the profound impact social hierarchies have had and continue to have on our national well-being, and who create new visions for how we can recognize our American diversity as the asset that it is.

**FOX NEWS HOST** Tucker Carlson, who has in recent years chosen to promote a sort of commonsense white nationalism to gain viewers, recently asked on air, "How precisely is diversity our strength? . . . Do you get along better with your neighbors or your co-workers if you can't understand each other or share no common values?"

What Carlson did there was a quick elision, from not sharing an ethnicity to not sharing values. In fact, it's just the opposite, I discovered. When people have a chance to create a bond that's not based on skin color or culture, what they actually connect on are the things they value in common: The joking friendship between Nissan workers Melvin and Johnny, built across a racial divide as deep and old as they come in this country, out of the raw material of their commitment to improving life at the plant. How Torm was able to make common cause with black ministers because he knew the refugee community needed to learn from the victories that black activists had won against Chevron in the past. The way that ZamZam and Bruce connected over their faith in redemption for people in jails and prisons.

This is not to say that it was always easy to bridge these divides. Nonetheless, the discomfort of cross-racial connections is actually the source of their power, according to the late Dr. Katherine W. Phillips of Columbia Business School, who was the first black woman to receive tenure there and who became the vice dean. After decades of research, Dr. Phillips made the conclusion that it's the mental friction that creates diversity's productive energy. "Members of a homogeneous group rest somewhat assured that they will agree with one another; that they will understand one another's perspectives and beliefs; that they will be able to easily come to a consensus. But when members of a group notice that they are socially different from one another, they change their expectations. They anticipate differences of opinion and perspective. They assume they will need to work harder to come to a consensus. This logic helps to explain both the upside and the downside of social diversity: people work harder in diverse environments both cognitively and socially. They might not like it, but the hard work can lead to better outcomes."

As one example, Phillips described an experiment she conducted to study the impact of racial diversity on small decision-making groups. She and her researchers created three-person teams, half of which were all white and half of which contained one person of color, and tasked the groups with solving a murder mystery. Each participant was given one important clue known only to them, but otherwise, the groups all had the same information. "The groups with racial diversity significantly outperformed the groups with no racial diversity," Phillips reported. "Being with similar others leads us to think we all hold the same information and share the same perspective. This perspective, which stopped the all-white groups from effectively processing the information, is what hinders creativity and innovation."

The power of diversity can help real-life juries find their way to justice as well. One of the professors I visited at Harvard Business School, Samuel Sommers, borrowed real jurors from a Michigan court and asked them to reach a verdict in mock trials he conducted. Of the six-person juries Sommers organized, some were composed of four white and two black jurors, and some had exclusively white people. The diverse juries deliberated longer and performed better, in part because the white people upped their game in mixed company. White people in the diverse teams "cited more case facts, made fewer errors, and were more amenable to discussion of racism when in diverse versus all-White groups."

So it turns out that the diversity that is causing an often-unconscious racial panic in so many white Americans is actually our biggest strategic asset. The research has borne this out in education, jurisprudence, business, and the economy. Put simply, we need each other. Our differences have the potential to make us stronger, smarter, more creative, and fairer. Once we abandon the false idea of zero-sum competition, the benefits of diversity become evident, from the classroom to the courtroom to the boardroom. Of course, it should be stated that it's quite possible to have a diverse society that still has a strict racial hierarchy. The assumption behind the research on diversity's benefits is that people of different backgrounds are meeting on a plane that is equal enough that they can all contribute—and that they share the will to work together. If that can happen, the benefits multiply. What we'll have to overcome, however, is the gulf that exists between our people's basic factual and moral understandings of who we are as a society. It's a gulf that has been profitable for power-ful people, in the media and politics, and we can't bridge it if we don't acknowledge the truth of how we got here.

**THE HUNDREDS OF** conversations I had on my journey convinced me that we can't each do it on our own. We can all buy books and go through trainings in an individualized, shopping-cart version of ra-cial truth-telling and truth-learning, but that is wholly insufficient to the scale of America's racial story. We need a national effort, rooted in community, one that brings us together and has the full backing of the body that has kept us apart: the U.S. government.

A model for such a process began locally, in 2017, when fourteen communities across the country launched efforts known as Truth, Racial Healing and Transformation (TRHT). The next year, the As-sociation of American Colleges and Universities did the same, and by 2018, twenty-four college campuses had TRHT centers. On June 4, 2020, after a week of nationwide protests sparked by the brutal police killing of George Floyd, members of the U.S. House of Representa-tives led by Rep. Barbara Lee (D-CA) introduced a resolution urging the establishment of a U.S. TRHT Commission. The TRHT frame-work was developed in 2016 with the input of a group of over 175 experts convened by the W. K. Kellogg Foundation. The experts learned from the forty truth-and-reconciliation processes across the globe that had helped societies process traumas—from South Africa to Chile to Sri Lanka—but they explicitly left the word *reconciliation* out of the name for the U.S. effort. "To reconcile," notes the TRHT materials, "connotes restoration of friendly relations—'reuniting' or 'bringing together again after conflict,' [whereas] the U.S. needs transformation. The nation was conceived . . . on this belief in racial hierarchy."

To launch a Truth, Racial Healing and Transformation effort, community leaders must gather a representative group of people, both demographically and in terms of the sectors in the community.

The framework involves a process of relationship-building and healing by sharing personal stories about race and racism, but it doesn't just help people "talk about race"—TRHT groups also identify community decisions that have created hierarchy in three areas: law, separation, and the economy. Bridging between the individual stories and the desired policy change is narrative change, accomplished by identifying manifestations of the belief in human hierarchy in our stories, be they school curricula or media portrayals or monuments, and replacing them with "complete and accurate stories that honor the full complexity of our humanity as the country forges a more equitable future." The TRHT guidebook lays out instructions for communities, making an idea that can seem lofty and abstract appear manageable but powerful.

That's what compelled Jerry Hawkins to give it a shot. Hawkins is a forty-something black man who made a career for himself in Dallas, Texas, as an early-childhood educator who cared deeply about the families of the children he taught, "immigrant parents primarily from Mexico and Central America," he explained to me. But when the TRHT came into his life, he had quit his job in frustration and was about to leave the city. It was the 2016 election summer, and the parents "were facing multiple issues of harassment and fear of deportation and reprisal. And so, we started to focus on racial equity in that work. I immediately felt a lot of pushback from folks who were just months ago supporting me doing early-childhood work. . . . They didn't want me doing racial equity work, period. They gave me an ultimatum." So, he left. But that summer was also the summer when a black veteran killed five Dallas police officers and two civilians, and civic leaders were calling for racial healing. Community leaders encouraged Jerry to apply for the job of leading the TRHT in Dallas.

"I had hesitations around racial healing," Jerry admitted, because in the aftermath of the Dallas tragedy, it could have pathologized black people. "I was really hesitant, until I read the guidebook." Three things in the document changed his mind.

"One was—and it was so random, because I just opened up the

page. It was, 'Do we need to rewrite the Constitution of the United States?' " He laughed a little. "Right? So, just saying that, period—I was like, 'Wow. This is not what I thought it was.'

"And then I looked at two things that I knew I had to do first, if I were ever to get this job. And they stuck out to me. A lot of the things in there are really suggestions, because they're inviting communities to do the work. But there are two things that are very clear, almost mandatory, that you need to do.

"One was a community racial history . . . this historical analysis of policy and place, of race, and the people from Indigenous times to present. And second was this community visioning process . . . this way of convening [a] multiracial, multifaceted group of people together, to come up with a shared community vision of how do we end this hierarchy of human value?"

Jerry was hired and is now the executive director of the Dallas TRHT. The multiyear process has solicited the input of hundreds of Dallas residents: civic leaders, businesspeople, police officers, and grassroots organizers, but also high school students and the general public, in community visioning sessions at public libraries across the city. The group published an illustrated report that, when I read it for the first time in 2019, made me gasp more than once. In the opening pages, bold orange words bleed to the edges of a two-page spread: DALLAS IS ON STOLEN LAND. A few pages later, again: DALLAS WAS BUILT WITH STOLEN LABOR. For all that I know and have written about these truths, I had never seen them stated so vividly in print, in a document that spoke for a city. In our conversation, Jerry called stolen land and stolen labor the first two public policies in Dallas.

A few pages later, I came upon a black-and-white photograph of a smiling group of white high school girls in poodle skirts talking to a cowboy hat–wearing Texas Ranger leaning nonchalantly against a tree. I almost turned the page before I noticed something in the background: at the top of the school building hung a life-size stuffed doll, an effigy of a black man, as a warning against families who had tried to enroll in 1956. A few pages later, a photo of a smiling twelve-year-old Mexican American boy, Santos Rodriguez, whom a police officer "shot and killed Russian roulette style in the back of a police car with [Rodriguez's] thirteen-year-old brother next to him" in 1973. Toward the end of the book is a present-day photo of a black woman standing in front of what appears to be a mountain, but the caption reads, "Marsha Jackson and the Shingle Mountain"—as in, a hill created when a plant illegally dumped seventy thousand tons of toxic roof shingle material in the backyard of Jackson's neighborhood.

The report, "A New Community Vision for Dallas," reads like a graphic novel of the racial history of the city in fewer than fifty pages. It has been an eye-opener for most people, Jerry said, white, black, and brown lifelong Dallas residents. "Ninety-nine percent of people who I talk to don't know what happened."

There have been some surprises from the Dallas TRHT process. The organization's director of strategy and operations, Errika Y. Flood-Moultrie, wanted me to know about a breakthrough moment in one of the community meetings after a presentation by longtime black activist turned city councilwoman, Diane Ragsdale. Errika told me how "a white suburban school superintendent raised her hand and said, 'I want to apologize to you, Miss Ragsdale. Because all this time, I thought that you were this horrible mean person who wasn't—' "

Jerry interrupted with the exact word she'd used: "Troublemaker!"

" 'Troublemaker,' " Erika continued, " 'that wasn't looking out for the interest of Dallas. I only saw you on TV. And when I saw you on TV, you were agitating. You were—you know, screaming. You were protesting. The media . . . showed you as this bad person. I always, even as a young person, thought of you as a bad person. And I want to apologize to you. Because having this conversation, I understand why it was required for you to [protest]. And what value you bring to Dallas. And that I'm changed because of it.' "

Breakthroughs in the hearts and minds of decision makers in

Dallas—and the cross-racial relationships that the TRHT process has engendered—are great to hear about, but I wanted to know what had changed in the city. Jerry arched his brow. "I think the mere presence of TRHT in the city of Dallas—I do want to say . . . this is so different from the coast. We are the only organization in the city focused on racial equity, period. So, that's number one. Where if you go to Oakland, there's like, you know, dozens. Right?"

But then Jerry proceeded to list off multiple points of impact. The Dallas school district now has an Office of Racial Equity. The city does, too. "That's something that the city of Dallas has never had, right? But it has it now," he said with some pride. A conservative city councilwoman—"one of the few council people who voted after Charlottesville to not remove Confederate monuments in Dallas. So that's the kind of person I'm talking about"—attended a TRHT National Day of Racial Healing event and decided to issue a city proclamation to recognize it officially, "which had never happened before." Jerry has joined the Dallas County Historical Commission, so he will have influence over the historical markers in the city. He and colleagues have trained most of the top city administrators. Jerry taught the students at Southern Methodist University Engineering School about redlining, blockbusting, and why there are such racial divides in the city's built environment—in the hope that they'll know how to plan for infrastructure equity over their careers.

After a white policewoman mistakenly walked into Botham Jean's apartment and killed him, the local media began to fall into the trap of denigrating the black victim—but this time, twenty groups organized through the TRHT process sent a letter to the local papers "saying that the narratives that are coming out of the Dallas Police Department and the *Dallas Morning News* were racist." Jerry attributes this swift coordinated response—which resulted in a meeting with the publisher of the paper about how the paper could atone for racist narratives and do better in the future—to the emphasis on narrative in the TRHT framework.

The demand for what TRHT is doing is outstripping its capacity, from all corners of Dallas society, Jerry said with a sigh. "There are now folks who are like . . . 'I'm a former accountant, and I want to do racial equity work. How do I join you all?' "

TRUTH, RACIAL HEALING and Transformation was the vision of a woman named Dr. Gail Christopher. She's an expert in public health and social policy, and she's my mother. At the very end of my three-year journey, I found myself in her home in Prince George's County, Maryland, outside Washington, D.C. We sat in a sunroom in the back of the house that she has transformed over the years into a social justice retreat center. She is a small woman with expressive hands and skin that looks like poured honey, even at seventy. Most people who meet her talk about her smile; when she bestows its light on you, you don't soon forget it. She and I were sitting on a cream-colored couch on the day that Congress introduced the resolution calling for a national TRHT, and I asked her why she felt the country needed a Truth, Racial Healing and Transformation effort on top of all the other policies I was advocating for to address inequality.

"It's a powerful, liberating frame to realize that the fallacy of racial hierarchy is a belief system that we don't have to have. We can replace it with another way of looking at each other as human beings. Then, once you get that opening, you invite people to see a new way forward. You ask questions like 'What kind of narrative will your great grandchildren learn about this country?' 'What is it that will have happened?' Truthfully, we've never done that as a country. We've been dealing with the old model, patching it over here, sticking bubble gum over there." She laughed.

"But we are young. What makes America America is the creative power of our people. It is our responsibility to take this privilege that has come from the exploitation of so many people and the land—to use that freedom to create and actualize the aspirations of tomorrow. We need to envision an America that is no longer bound by that belief in racial hierarchy—we owe it back to the universe. That's bend-ing that moral arc toward justice," she said, and though I'd heard that phrase countless times before, it meant something different to me at the end of my journey.

Dr. King said that the arc of the moral universe is long, but it bends toward justice. But we know that progress is not guaranteed. When the arc in America bends from slavery in the 1860s and returns to convict leasing in the 1880s; when it bends from Jim Crow in the 1960s and returns to mass incarceration in the 1970s; when it bends from Indigenous genocide to an epidemic of Indigenous suicides; when it bends, but as a tree does in the wind, only to sway back, we have to admit that we have not touched the root.

We have not touched the root because the laws we make are expressions of a root belief, and it is time to face our most deep-seated one: the great lie at the root of our nation's founding was a belief in the hierarchy of human value. And we are still there.

This moment is challenging us finally to settle this question: Who is an American, and what are we to one another? We have to admit that this question is harder for us than in most other countries, because we are the world's most radical experiment in democracy, a nation of ancestral strangers that has to work to find connection even as we grow more diverse every day.

But everything depends on the answer to this question. Who is an American, and what are we to one another? Politics offers two visions of why all the peoples of the world have met here: one in which we are nothing more than competitors and another in which perhaps the proximity of so much difference forces us to admit our common humanity.

The choice between these two visions has never been starker. To a nation riven with anxiety about who belongs, many in power have made it their overarching goal to sow distrust about the goodness of the Other. They are holding on, white-knuckled, to a tiny idea of We the People, denying the beauty of what we are becoming. They're warning that demographic changes are the unmaking of America. What I've seen on my journey is that they're the *fulfillment* of America. What they say is a threat is in fact our country's salvation—for when a nation founded on a belief in racial hierarchy truly rejects that belief, then and only then will we have discovered a New World.

That is our destiny. To make it manifest, we must challenge ourselves to live our lives in solidarity across color, origin, and class; we must demand changes to the rules in order to disrupt the very notion that those who have more money are worth more in our democracy and our economy. Since this country's founding, we have not allowed our diversity to be our superpower, and the result is that the United States is not more than the sum of its disparate parts. But it could be. And if it were, all of us would prosper. In short, we must emerge from this crisis in our republic with a new birth of freedom, rooted in the knowledge that we are so much more when the "We" in "We the People" is not some of us, but all of us. We are greater than, and greater for, the sum of us.

# Afterword for the Paperback Edition

The summer after the publication of *The Sum of Us,* volunteers with Maine People's Alliance, the grassroots organization I wrote about in chapter 10, were out knocking on doors in Lewiston again. But this door-knocking campaign was different from the ones they'd waged year after year throughout the Inequality Era. This time, they weren't asking people to sign a petition in the hopes that some relief would trickle their way. They were knocking on doors to tell people what they'd already won: "Have you heard of the new Child Tax Credit?"

The newly expanded Child Tax Credit offered families with children up to three hundred dollars monthly in refunded tax savings per child, no strings attached, out of the simple recognition that it's expensive to raise children and supporting families is a public good. Decades of Drained Pool Politics in the United States desiccated our welfare system, and the result was one of the highest child poverty rates of any advanced economy. But the tax credit reverses that trend, cutting child poverty in half. That's five million children with enough food to eat, with the heating bill paid in winter, with some of the stress of *never enough* abating from their parents' voices.

It's also a Solidarity Dividend. It exists only because a multiracial coalition of voters rejected the politics of divide-and-conquer in the presidential election of November 2020 and did it again in January for a special senatorial election in Georgia, giving Democrats control of the legislative agenda. The Child Tax Credit was part of the Democrats' first major bill, the American Rescue Plan, which also advanced an unprecedented public health effort to tackle the pandemic, including the no-cost vaccination of nearly 200 million Americans. The American Rescue Plan was popular with nearly 80 percent of voters, including 59 percent of Republicans, and the Biden administration laid it out along with another popular infrastructure agenda that would be paid for by taxing corporations and the wealthy. In fact, when voters learned that the infrastructure plan would be paid for by taxing the rich, an already popular plan got *even more popular*.

So, what is the right wing to do in the face of a popular agenda to meet the needs of most Americans, at a cost to many of their wealthiest financial backers?

Deploy the zero-sum lie.

As the pandemic has shifted the center of politics to embrace a robust role for government, the right has embraced even more nihilistic and extreme tactics from the zero-sum playbook. When I was writing chapter 6, back in 2020, I took pains not to overstate the case about the GOP's willingness to surrender democracy to preserve a white-supremacist power structure. But then on January 6 of the next year, a mob sporting Confederate flags and Nazi symbols breached the U.S. Capitol, beating police officers and threatening to hang elected officials, including the Republican vice president. Five people, including a police officer, died, and four officers who were in the battle that day have since committed suicide. The mob was trying to "stop the steal," as their slogan put it, of an election they were convinced beyond evidence had been taken from them by illegitimate voters in cities like Detroit, Phoenix, and Philadelphia. And despite universal condemnation in Washington during the violent siege, on the next day, the majority of the House Republican caucus

voted to do what the mob wanted: refuse to certify the election results. Within weeks, the guilt-minimizing logic of white supremacy
had allowed the right-wing narrative to completely absorb a *murderous insurrection attempt.* The siege was akin to a "normal tourist
visit," said one congressman, and multiple congress members have
criticized law enforcement for making "political prisoners" out of
"peaceful patriots." Soon, Republican officials nationwide were cynically amplifying the Big Lie that Democratic voters had stolen the
election, using it as a pretext to introduce nearly four hundred state
laws making it harder to vote.

The lie of the stolen election is not just a wild fantasy—it is anchored in our long history of zero-sum racial hierarchy. That's where
you'll find the Big Lie's racial common sense: of course the winner of
the white vote is the legitimate president, and votes cast by people of
color are by definition taking something from rightful white voters.
The elaborate conspiracy theory—what's needed to say this without
actually saying it—seems plausible to 50 million people only because
of the long-standing stereotype that people of color are inveterate
criminals. To believe the Big Lie, you have to think that it's just as
safe to assume that black and brown people are criminals committing
fraud as it is to assume that they're eligible citizens exercising their
civic duty.

*The Sum of Us* went to print months before the failed insurrection, but it did include the eerily similar story of the massacre in
Colfax, Louisiana, in 1873, when a white mob attacked the courthouse to overthrow an interracial government. It was the most violent of the many Reconstruction-era clashes between white people
defending the interests of the plantation class and black people defending democracy. "The white citizens murdered their neighbors
and burned the edifice of their own government," I wrote about a
history we were apparently willing to repeat, "rather than submit to
a multiracial democracy."

The iconic photo from January 6 of a white man proudly march-
ing the Confederate flag through the Capitol building is a reminder

of the many fronts on which we are still fighting the long war against the plantation class. We're fighting over laws to restrict the vote and, most insidiously, partisan takeovers of election administration to make it easier to overturn election results. The federal legislation that would save our democracy is stalled in Congress because of the filibuster, a Jim Crow–era relic that allows the Senate minority to block legislation. Although created in 1806 because of a drafting error, the filibuster was honed by white supremacists in the twentieth century to thwart civil rights bills, and now it's being used for just that purpose again. The tools and strategies of zero-sum racism are still wreaking havoc in our democracy, at a cost to the entire project of self-governance.

Once the insurrection cleared and Biden was inaugurated, we saw the first signs how the zero-sum strategy would be deployed against refilling the pool. The Republican minority unanimously refused to support the overwhelmingly popular American Rescue Plan as it advanced to the floor. But rather than mounting a defense of that decision on its merits, the right wing turned their wrath on . . . children's books. The lead story of the week on conservative networks was the Democrats' supposed war on Dr. Seuss, whose estate had decided to stop publishing some of his children's books because they depicted racist stereotypes. I happened to be a guest on MSNBC's *All In with Chris Hayes* that week, when the progressive host expressed some delight that conservatives were "playing into Biden's hands" with culture war distractions while the Democrats were running up the score with popular legislation. But writing this book had taught me not to discount the power of the zero-sum strategy.

"That's the only play they've got left," I said on the air. "And so it seems silly, but what they're doing is saying *they're coming for you. They're coming for your culture . . . and your way of life.* And what they know is that reflexively makes white voters more conservative and more conservative on fiscal issues."

Little did I know that the faux controversy over Dr. Seuss would soon look like child's play compared to the all-out assault on honest education that would sweep local school districts later that year. Conservatives brazenly opened a new front in the Lost Cause, the multi-generation campaign by white southerners to win the narrative over the Civil War, rewriting history through textbooks, public commemorations, and monuments to minimize the role of slavery and glorify antebellum culture.

As a matter of fact, the book you're holding may already be banned.

In the first half of 2021, twelve states passed laws limiting what can be taught in schools about racism and sexism. The Texas law bans teaching about unconscious bias. In Oklahoma, a community college class that taught about white privilege was derailed because of a new law that forbids lessons that make students feel "guilt or anguish" about actions committed by members of their race in the past. An activist with the conservative group Moms for Liberty used a similar Tennessee law to object to a lesson about Ruby Bridges integrating Louisiana schools when she was six years old, because it "made white students in the class feel uncomfortable." That's right: a six-year-old can be brave enough to walk through a violent mob of adults, but some white parents think their elementary school students are too delicate to even read about it.

This attack on honest education has been framed as a defense against teaching kids the academic discipline of "critical race theory," but the aim is to discredit all antiracist ideas. The campaign has been funded and coordinated by wealthy partisan elites, as always seems to be the case with zero-sum lies. A central figure in the plot is a fellow at the Heritage Foundation, a right-wing think tank. "The goal is to have the public read something crazy in the newspaper and immediately think 'critical race theory,'" he wrote. "We have decodified the term and will recodify it to annex the entire range of cultural constructions that are unpopular with Americans." The same secret-money groups that funded conservative judicial nominees and Trump election challenges are pouring millions into a network of groups to spread the bans, funding television ads and lawsuits, amplifying local stories on cable news, and bankrolling local school board campaigns.

The strategy is operating on multiple levels. It is first and foremost an electoral strategy among conservatives to energize their Evangelical Christian base while also making a broader play for white suburban parents. The suburbs would seem to be difficult ground for this conservative attack; they were crucial to President Biden's victory, with more educated suburban residents resoundingly rejecting Trumpist politics. But the GOP is banking on the fact that—as the history of school resegregation shows—parents violate their own political values all the time, and succumb to zero-sum thinking they would otherwise reject, in the name of what's supposedly best for their children.

Second, the attacks on honest education operate at the level of media narrative, creating a drumbeat of zero-sum culture war stories about "real Americans" versus the "woke mob." The right wing would rather the media cover these conflicts than expose their more covert battle against policies like paid family leave and universal child care—Solidarity Dividends that actually unite working parents across race. The right wing wants white parents to feel like they must choose between their history and some other hostile group's history. Of course, that's a zero-sum lie: it's our collective history. In fact, honest education about racism is the history of white people as much as it is that of Americans of color, and it's mostly white children who will be rendered ignorant if its teaching is banned. But that's the larger goal: a people who have been robbed of their history can be manipulated by the same forces, generation after generation.

A white suburban mother named Rachel told me about her "outrage" at this theft: even though her entire education had been in Oklahoma public schools, she had learned about the 1921 Tulsa massacre only recently. She recalled seeing a black Tulsa neighborhood as a child and having no answer for why it seemed so poor. In the absence of history, negative stereotypes filled the void. "What if people had been taught about *why* black communities were so marginalized?" she asked, her anger still audible. "A chance to fully understand something was taken away from me because I didn't learn about this moment. There was this flourishing black community and we were never aware of it, because that history was robbed from me."

Finally, these miseducation laws are classic Drained Pool Politics, aiming to weaken another integrated public good. Schools and teachers were already at the breaking point because of the pandemic, and conservative elites saw this attack on "critical race theory" as a way to turn white parents against their own schools, to spread chaos on local school boards and further drain the pool. In Tennessee, for example, a district with repeated violations of the new history ban can lose up to 10 percent of its state funding. In Rhode Island, a woman sent in more than two hundred public records requests about the teaching of race and gender issues, and a man with no children in the district demanded to see the entire school curriculum and any correspondence with the words "Black Lives Matter" or "equity." Timothy Ryan, executive director of the Rhode Island School Superintendents' Association, saw the larger plot for what it is, telling an NBC News reporter, "I believe their intent is really to have the public lose confidence in public education." A record number of school board recall petitions were filed in 2021. Activists have taken aim at public libraries as well, aiming to slash budgets and challenge what librarians are reading and teaching.

The zero-sum racism in our politics and policy making is costing us so much. And yet the Solidarity Dividends are getting bigger. As of this writing, the poverty rate in the United States is the lowest it has been since we started keeping track. Generous public benefits passed during the pandemic alleviated economic suffering across the board, and even more precipitously among children, rural Americans, and black folks.

After fifty years of draining the pool, we are finally, if tentatively and precariously, beginning to refill it. America's new, multiracial governing majority has demanded an ambitious agenda to use the power of the government to address the country's urgent needs. Upon taking office, the new administration announced a set of plans that read like a list of the "nice things" we've so long gone without: a massive infrastructure upgrade, aggressive action to stop climate change, tuition-free community college, universal elder care and childcare, paid family leave, a $15 national living wage, more generous public healthcare benefits, and extra federal dollars to coax states to expand Medicaid. I've lost track of the times commentators have likened this moment to the New Deal—when the ethos of public goods first helped build a strong middle class.

Not every promise and intention has yet made it into law—and I was just as surprised as anyone at the scope and scale of the ambition—but I have to admit that the Build Back Better Agenda (the American Rescue Plan and the Jobs and Families plans) represents a new era in American policy making, and a turn away from the austerity of the Inequality Era. This new center-left consensus is here because of cross-racial movement building by people like Terrence Wise and Bridget Hughes in the Fight for $15, and because of a climate action movement that takes environmental justice lessons from places like Richmond. What's more, the new era's Solidarity Dividends don't only include universal programs that white people should support out of self-interest; they also include an overdue recognition that racism held the pen as so many of our laws were written. The USDA admitted its long-standing racial discrimination and issued a program of debt relief intended for minority farmers (though conservative judges have blocked its application). After the initial 2020 Paycheck Protection Program for employers failed to deliver relief to most minority and women-owned businesses, the Small Business Administration prioritized grants for these underserved business owners in the 2021 American Rescue Plan. For the first time, the U.S. Transportation Department has officially acknowledged that highway projects systematically used eminent domain to destroy thriving communities of color, and it has proposed an initiative to remove the highways and repair the harm done.

These Solidarity Dividends are not guaranteed. They could still be defeated by the one-two punch of political racism and greed, with Republicans using culture war racism to cloak their opposition, and lobbyist-beholden Democrats claiming fiscal conservatism despite the enormous economic costs of inaction.

Insider politics and parliamentary procedure may yet doom the agenda. But the battle of ideas has shifted to a higher moral ground. Our nation is beginning to tell a different story about who we are to one another. The well-funded, cynical backlash is only a desperate attempt to hold back the tide. I was cooking dinner in my kitchen last January when a friend sent me a YouTube link of the newly inaugurated president's first speech on race. I nearly dropped the glass I was holding when President Biden started talking about the racial zero-sum strategy and made the argument that racial equity will make the nation more prosperous for everyone.

> For too long, we've allowed a narrow, cramped view of the promise of this nation to fester. You know, we've—we've bought the view that America is a zero-sum game in many cases: "If you succeed, I fail." "If you get ahead, I fall behind." "If you get the job, I lose mine." Maybe worst of all, "If I hold you down, I lift myself up."
>
> . . . I believe this nation and this government need to change their whole approach to the issue of racial equal—equity. Yes, we need criminal justice reform, but that isn't nearly enough. We need to open the promise of America to every American. And that means we need to make the issue of racial equity not just an issue for any one department of government; it has to be the business of the whole of government.
>
> . . . [Systemic racism] is corrosive, it's destructive, and it's costly. It costs every American, not just who have felt the sting of racial injustice. . . . [W]e are not just . . . morally deprived because of systemic racism; we're also less prosperous, we're less successful, we're less secure.

The events of 2021 have proven that this truth is the central lesson of our time. A multiracial antiracist majority is awakening to it. And as more and more of us come together, across lines of race and origin, to demand and work toward the dividends of solidarity, our newfound power will shape our common future.

# Acknowledgments

Compared to running an organization, folks warned me, a writer's life would be a lonely one. To the contrary, this book has been a collaboration from start to finish. I have so many people to thank.

First, the doulas and midwives who supported me most in bringing my book to life—chief among them Lynn Kanter, who provided invaluable research and writing support from proposal to final copyedit—as well as my agents Henry Reisch, Tina Bennett, and Dorian Karchmar; my fact-checker, Kelsey Kudak; and my primary research assistants, Aaron Carico and Erin Purdie, and transcribers Megan Weaver and Joanna Parson. Another team has done an amazing job of helping me get the word out: Racquel Royer and Michael Frisby, the Lavin Agency, Greg Kubie and the tireless team of publicists, marketers, and assistants at Penguin Random House. I hoped that art could help tell the book's story and was lucky to find a talented set of designers and illustrators in Rachel Ake, David McConochie, and Frances Tulk-Hart. Finally, I have been blessed to have the smartest editor and most supportive publisher I could have hoped for, Christopher Jackson and One World. Thank you for believing in this book from day one.

I am deeply grateful to every person who shared their America with me. That includes the interviewees named in this book and the dozens more whose insights and experiences shaped my journey— including Garry, my most unlikely friend. Thanks to the organizers who generously made connections for me, including Alex Amend, Asya Pikovsky, Michael Enriquez, the late Hector Figueroa, Mary Kay Henry, Desmond Meade, Anastasia Semien Douglas and the Florida Rights Restoration, Rafael Navar, Mike Calhoun and the Center for Responsible Lending, May Boeve, Dennis Williams, Mark and Sandra Haasis, Barb Fisher and the United Auto Workers, Maine People's Alliance, Kentuckians for the Commonwealth, Integrated Schools, Faith in Action, People's Action, Stosh Cotler, Linda Sarsour, and Rev. Julian DeShazier.

I leaned on the expertise of many who dug into key ideas with me and reviewed parts of the book: Ian Haney López (who has influenced my thinking in so many ways), Donovan X. Ramsey, Tammy Draut, Robert Master, Cathy Cohen, Angela Park, Ayanna Elizabeth Johnson, Lindsey Allen, Sean McElwee, Mark Huelsman, Anat Shenker-Osorio, Jonathan Voss, Zeinab Hussen, Sarah Merchant, Ellora Derenoncourt, Nathan Nunn, Corey Hajim, and Cassim's urbanist reading group. I will be forever grateful to Gina Welch for reading every single world of the first full draft with the precision of a great writer and the enthusiasm of a great friend.

Thank you to all of my former Demos colleagues, especially the Executive Team members who helped me grow the organization and supported my need to write this book; the trustees, including Amelia Tyagi, Josh Fryday, Miles Rapoport, Stephen Heintz, and my successor K. Sabeel Rahman; and Alissa Vladimir and Gwyn Ellsworth. My faith comes from having friends in the movement who are showing that a multiracial democracy is possible, especially Rashad Robinson, Alicia Garza, Tammy Draut, Lucy Mayo, Ai-jen Poo, George Goehl, Anna Galland, Maurice Mitchell, Waleed Shahid, Will Pittz, Robert Gass, Danny Cantor, and Auntie Elizabeth.

The book is the result of a multiyear writing process that found generous and generative support from Demos, the University of Chicago Institute of Politics, the Open Society Foundations, the Brooklyn Community Foundation, the Park Foundation, the Panta Rhea Foundation, and Oona Coy. I spent days writing in some memorable spaces, including Crossfields, the Mesa Refuge, the Hayes-Shaw studio, the Hogue-Neffinger home, Selina Medellín, Work Heights Clinton Hill, the Ntianu Center Library, and the corner seat of the bar at Peaches Shrimp and Crab.

I would be nowhere without my family: Mom, Dad and Mary, Hassan, Shannon and Ronny, Sadia and Andreas, Taiye, Annie and the Milton Girls, Jackie and the McGhees, and the Minors, Thayers, Boivins, Shepards, and Quraeshis. Riaz Shah Hassan Shepard-McGhee, this book is dedicated to your Nana, but it is for you, and all the children you'll link arms with as you remake the world. Finally, thank you to my best friend, best editor, and best partner in anything worth doing, Cassim. Your love makes all things possible.

# Notes

## Introduction

xi     **largest group of the uninsured** Forty-one percent of the uninsured as of 2018 are white; the next-largest share is "Hispanic" (of any race), at 37 percent. There are 18 million white Americans living under the poverty line; the next-largest demographic group is "Hispanic" (of any race), at 11 million. Jennifer Tolbert et al., "Key Facts about the Uninsured Population," Uninsured, KFF, December 13, 2019, https://www.kff.org/uninsured/issue-brief/key-facts-about-the-uninsured-population; "Poverty Rate by Race/Ethnicity (2018)," State Health Facts, KFF, https://www.kff.org/other/state-indicator/poverty-rate-by-raceethnicity.

xii     **more likely to be in debt** Tamara Draut and Javier Silva, "Borrowing to Make Ends Meet: The Growth of Credit Card Debt in the '90s," Demos, September 1, 2013, https://www.demos.org/sites/default/files/publications/borrowing_exec2.pdf.

xiii     **legislation to limit credit card rates and fees** Credit Card Accountability Responsibility and Disclosure Act of 2009, 15 U.S.C , § 1601 (2009).

xiii     **Legislators passed a bankruptcy reform bill** Bankruptcy Abuse Prevention and Consumer Protection Act of 2005, 109th U.S. Cong., § 256 (2005).

xiii     **ever to escape their debts** The bankruptcy reform bill raised the cost of filing for bankruptcy, implemented a means test, and made the path to a total "fresh start" Chapter Seven bankruptcy narrower. A 2010 study of the impact of the law noted, "Since BAPCPA's enactment, median family incomes have declined, basic expenses have risen, debt loads have multiplied, and the number of foreclosures and loan defaults has increased. Yet, fewer families have taken advantage of the bankruptcy debt relief system." Lois R. Lupica, "The Costs of BAPCPA: Report of the Pilot Study of Consumer Bankruptcy Cases," *American Bankruptcy Institute Law Review* 18 (2010): 51, https://digitalcommons.mainelaw.maine.edu/faculty-publications/39. It also made private student loans as difficult (nearly impossible) to discharge under bankruptcy as federally guaranteed student loans. See "No Recourse: Putting an End to Bankruptcy's Student Loan Exception," Demos, 2015, https://www.demos.org/research/no-recourse-putting-end-bankruptcys-student-loan-exception.

xiv   **About how quick so many white people** In a 2010 survey, 70 percent of white people agreed that "Irish, Italians, Jewish, and many other minorities overcame prejudice and worked their way up. Blacks should do the same without special favors," and 56 percent agreed that "it's really a matter of some people not trying hard enough; if blacks would only try harder they could be just as well off as whites." Christopher Parker, "2010 Multi-state Survey on Race and Politics," University of Washington Institute for the Study of Race, Ethnicity, and Sexuality, http://depts.washington.edu/uwiser/mssrp_table.pdf.

xvi   **cultural organizing of white grievance** Various studies found that racial grievance was important to organizing the Tea Party. Kristin Haltinner, "Individual Responsibility, Culture, or State Organized Enslavement? How Tea Party Activists Frame Racial Inequality," *Sociological Perspectives* 59, no. 2 (2016): 395–418.

xvii  **The majority of white Americans** Fifty-four percent of white voters voted for Donald Trump in 2016, and preliminary exit polls from November 3, 2020, show that 57 percent of white voters voted for him in 2020. While Trump's vote share appears to have grown by about 3 percentage points among black, Latinx, and Asian American voters, white voters remained the only racial group to give majority support to Trump. "An Examination of the 2016 Electorate, Based on Validated Voters," U.S. Politics and Policy, Pew Research Center, August 9, 2018, https://www.pewresearch.org/politics/2018/08/09/an-examination-of-the-2016-electorate-based-on-validated-voters; Edison Research November 2020 Exit Polls for National Election Pool, November 3, 2020, https://www.nytimes.com/interactive/2020/11/03/us/elections/exit-polls-president.html.

xviii **Psychologists Maureen Craig and Jennifer Richeson** Maureen A.

Craig and Jennifer A. Richeson, "On the Precipice of a 'Majority-Minority' America: Perceived Status Threat from the Racial Demographic Shift Affects White Americans' Political Ideology," *Psychological Science* 25, no. 6 (2014): 1191, 1189, https://doi.org/10.1177/0956797614527113; Maureen A. Craig and Jennifer A. Richeson, "Information About the US Racial Demographic Shift Triggers Concerns About Anti-White Discrimination Among the Prospective White 'Minority,'" *PLoS ONE* 12, no. 9 (2017), https://doi.org/10.1371/journal.pone.0185389. See also Brenda Major, Alison Blodorn, and Gregory Major Blascovich, "The Threat of Increasing Diversity: Why Many White Americans Support Trump in the 2016 Presidential Election," *Group Processes & Intergroup Relations* 21, no. 6 (Sept. 2018): 931–40, https://doi.org/10.1177/1368430216677304, finding that "Reminding White Americans high in ethnic identification that non-White racial groups will outnumber Whites in the United States by 2042 caused them to become more concerned about the declining status and influence of White Americans as a group (i.e., experience group status threat), and caused them to report increased support for Trump and anti-immigrant policies, as well as greater opposition to political correctness." Additionally, see H. Robert Outten, et al., "Majority Group Members' Negative Reactions to Future Demographic Shifts Depend on the Perceived Legitimacy of Their Status: Findings from the United States and Portugal," *Frontiers in Psychology* 9, no.79 (Feb 2018), https://doi.org/10.3389/fpsyg.2018.00079. According to this study, "White Americans who perceived their status to be highly legitimate expressed greater intergroup threat, and negative feelings (anger and fear) toward minorities after exposure to projections with a large decline in the relative size of the White American population."

xx **Latinx factory worker is paid less** "Since 2000, the wage gap between Hispanic workers and their peers has remained practically unchanged: Hispanic men working full time made 14.9 percent less in hourly wages in 2016 compared to white men (compared to 17.8 percent in 2000), and Hispanic women made 33.1 percent less than white counterparts (compared to 35.1 percent in 2000)." Kari Paul, "Hispanic Workers Continue to Make Significantly Less than White Workers," *MarketWatch*, July 3, 2018, https://www.marketwatch.com/story/hispanic-workers-continue-to-make-significantly-less-than-white-workers-2018-07-03.

xx **rates are near thirty-year lows** Jonnelle Marte, "'We Haven't Made Any Progress': Black Homeownership Is Stuck Near 30-Year Lows," *Washington Post*, July 6, 2018, https://www.washingtonpost.com/business/economy/the-black-white-employment-gap-has-closed-but

-the-homeownership-gap-has-not-heres-why/2018/07/06/1c6943dc
-7ef6-11e8-b0ef-fffcabeff946_story.html.

xxi **African Americans just don't buy that** "Our research also suggests
that among whites, there's a lingering view that the American Dream
is a 'fixed pie,' such that the advancement of one group of citizens
must come at the expense of all the other groups. Whites told us they
see things as a zero-sum game: Any improvements for black Americans, they believe, are likely to come at a direct cost to whites. Black
respondents in our surveys, meanwhile, report believing that outcomes
for blacks can improve without affecting outcomes for white Americans." Michael I. Norton and Samuel R. Sommers, "White People
Think Racism Is Getting Worse. Against White People," *Washington
Post,* July 21, 2016, https://www.washingtonpost.com/
posteverything/wp/2016/07/21/white-people-think-racism-is
-getting-worse-against-white-people/. Based on Michael I. Norton
and Samuel R. Sommers, "Whites See Racism as a Zero-Sum Game
that They Are Now Losing," *Perspectives on Psychological Science* 6,
no. 3 (May 2011): 215–18.

xxii **ended up being a boon** Gavin Wright, *Sharing the Prize: The Economics of the Civil Rights Revolution in the American South* (Cambridge, MA: Belknap Press, 2013).

xxii **racial inequality topping the list** Edison Research November 2020
Exit Polls.

xxii **lied to Americans** Glenn Kessler, Salvador Rizzo and Meg Kelly,
"Trump Is Averaging More than 50 False or Misleading Claims
A Day," *Washington Post,* October 22, 2020, https://www
.washingtonpost.com/politics/2020/10/22/president-trump-is
-averaging-more-than-50-false-or-misleading-claims-day/.

xxii **white supremacist terror groups** See, for example, Cassie Miller and
Howard Graves, "When the Alt-Right Hits the Streets: Far-Right Political Rallies in the Trump Era," Southern Poverty Law Center, August 10, 2020, https://www.splcenter.org/20200810/when-alt-right
-hit-streets-far-right-political-rallies-trump-era.

xxii **mismanaged and downplayed** See, for example, Whitney Shefte and
Jorge Ribas, "America's Pandemic," *Washington Post,* October 27,
2020, https://www.washingtonpost.com/graphics/2020/national/
administrations-pandemic-documentary/.

## Chapter One: An Old Story: The Zero-Sum Hierarchy

3 **"the fragile middle class"** Teresa A. Sullivan et al., *The Fragile Middle Class: Americans in Debt* (New Haven, CT: Yale University Press,

2000). See also Maura Cheeks, "American Wealth Is Broken," *The Atlantic,* July 31, 2019, https://www.theatlantic.com/family/archive/2019/07/the-wealth-gap-taints-americas-success-stories/593719.

3   **notorious Robert Taylor public housing projects** Built in 1959 as the world's largest public housing project, the Taylor homes were soon subject to disinvestment by Chicago and fell into serious disrepair. By the 1980s, these projects were the site of drug and gang wars. Aaron Modica, "Robert R. Taylor Homes, Chicago, Illinois (1959–2005)," *BlackPast,* December 19, 2009, https://www.blackpast.org/african-american-history/robert-taylor-homes-chicago-illinois-1959-2005. See also "Robert Taylor Homes," *Chicago Gang History,* https://chicagoganghistory.com/housing-project/robert-taylor-homes.

4   **so many people sleeping** "Nationally between 1973 and 1993, 2.2 million low-rent units disappeared from the housing market while demand increased by 4.7 million units. Chicago has lost 11,500 units, with 117,000 households unable to find affordable housing. At present, Chicago faces losing 18,000 public housing units, which would displace 42,000 people." In Dr. John Hobbs, "Homelessness Is a Complex Issue," *Chicago Tribune,* February 14, 1999, https://www.chicagotribune.com/news/ct-xpm-1999-02-14-9902140071-story.html. The flight of working- and middle-class whites to the suburbs in the 1970s and '80s, along with investments in spaces such as the Magnificent Mile and Navy Pier, meant to attract wealthy taxpayers, contributed to and intensified the production of homelessness in Chicago. Police in Chicago conducted regular "sweeps" of Lower Wacker Drive every few weeks in the early 1990s in order to disperse the homeless who gathered there, with sanitation workers stealing their shelter and belongings. See Talmadge Wright, *Out of Place: Homeless Mobilizations, Subcities, and Contested Landscapes* (Albany, NY: SUNY Press, 1997), 124, 192.

4   **40 percent of adults** Breno Braga et al., "Working to Make Ends Meet During Good Economic Times," Urban Institute, February 2019, https://www.urban.org/sites/default/files/publication/99772/working_to_make_ends_meet_during_good_economic_times.pdf.

4   **Only about two out of three** About two-thirds of workers in the private sector have access to a retirement plan, overwhelmingly defined-contribution, not defined-benefit. "Data on Workers' Access to Retirement Plans and Take Up Rates," Pension Rights Center, 2019, http://www.pensionrights.org/node/3015; 47 percent of private employers offered health insurance benefits in 2019. "Percent of Private Sector Establishments that Offer Health Insurance to Employees (2019)," State Health Facts, KFF, n.d., https://www.kff.org/other/

state-indicator/percent-of-firms-offering-coverage/
?currentTimeframe=0&selectedRows=%7B%22wrapups%22:%
7B%22united-states%22:%7B%7D%7D%7D&sortModel=%7B
%22colId%22:%22Location%22,%22sort%22:%22asc%22%7D;
75 percent of private sector employees had access to paid sick days,
and 21 percent had access to paid family leave. "Employee Benefits in
the United States, March 2020," US Bureau of Labor Statistics, March
2020, https://www.bls.gov/news.release/ebs2.nr0.htm.

4    **Upward mobility** Someone born to less-educated parents has a better
chance of ending up in the top quarter of educational attainment in
all but three of the United States' wealthy peer countries. "Fair Progress? Economic Mobility Across Generations Around the World," The
World Bank, May 9, 2018, https://www.worldbank.org/en/topic/pov-
erty/publication/fair-progress-economic-mobility-across-generations
-around-the-world.

4    **the 350 biggest corporations** Lawrence Mishel and Julia Wolfe,
"CEO Compensation Has Grown 940% Since 1978," Economic Policy
Institute, August 14, 2019, https://www.epi.org/publication/ceo
-compensation-2018.

5    **CEO-to-worker pay gaps** Sahid Fawaz, "In 1965, the CEO–Worker
Pay Ratio Was 20 to 1," *Labor 411* (blog), February 17, 2020, http://
labor411.org/411-blog/in-1965-the-ceo-worker-pay-ratio-was-25-to-1
-in-2020-these-19-companies-pay-ceos-over-1000-to-1.

5    **The richest 1 percent** Alexandre Tanzi and Michael Sasso, "Richest
1% of Americans Close to Surpassing Wealth of the Middle Class,"
Bloomberg, November 9, 2019, https://www.bloomberg.com/news/
articles/2019-11-09/one-percenters-close-to-surpassing-wealth-of-u-s
-middle-class.

5    **a study by two Boston-based scholars** Michael I. Norton and Samuel
R. Sommers, "Whites See Racism as a Zero-Sum Game that They Are
Now Losing," *Perspectives on Psychological Science* 6, no. 3 (May
2011): 215–18.

5    **Harvard Business School** James B. Stewart, "How Harvard Business
School Has Reshaped American Capitalism," review of *The Golden
Passport: Harvard Business School, the Limits of Capitalism, and the
Moral Failure of the MBA Elite,* by Duff McDonald, *New York Times
Book Review,* April 24, 2017.

5    **white Tea Party movement** Of the 18 percent of Americans who identified as Tea Party supporters in a 2012 poll, 89 percent were white.
Brian Montopoli, "Tea Party Supporters: Who They Are and What
They Believe," *CBS News,* December 14, 2012, https://www.cbsnews.
com/news/tea-party-supporters-who-they-are-and-what-they-believe.

5   **from corporations** Phil Wahba, "The Number of Black CEOs in
the Fortune 500 Remains Very Low," *Fortune,* June 1, 2020, https://
fortune.com/2020/06/01/black-ceos-fortune-500-2020-african
-american-business-leaders.

5   **90 percent** A comprehensive research project from the Women Donors Network showed that "white men hold 65% of elected seats, although they are only 31% of the population—effectively constituting
a 'veto-proof minority' in our political system." See "2014–15 Demographics of Power," Who Leads Us? Women Donors Network, https://
wholeads.us/wp-content/uploads/2018/09/wholeads2014.pdf.

7   **it changed the amount of carbon** Alexander Koch et al., "Earth System Impacts of the European Arrival and Great Dying in the Americas after 1492," *Quaternary Science Reviews* 207 (March 2019): 13–36,
https://doi.org/10.1016/j.quascirev.2018.12.004.

8   **ill-gotten land for free** The Homestead Act of 1862 benefited more
than 1.5 million white families. By the time it ended in 1934, "more
than 270 million acres of western land had been transferred to individuals, almost all of whom were white. Nearly 10 percent of all the
land in the entire U.S. was given to homesteaders for little more than
a filing fee." Keri Leigh Merritt, "Land and the Roots of African-
American Poverty," *Aeon,* March 11, 2016, https://aeon.co/ideas/land
-and-the-roots-of-african-american-poverty.

8   **Colonial slavery** The United States perfected chattel slavery, but it
did not invent it. Rulers and elites in ancient Egypt, Greece, and
Rome had slaves, usually captives from conquests, and in medieval
western Europe, eastern Europeans ("slavs") were actually the most
common slaves. However, while slavery existed in ancient and medieval times, people in those eras didn't believe that humans deserved to
be enslaved because of some unchangeable "racial" status, a hallmark
of slavery in the United States. See, for example, Nell Irvin Painter,
*The History of White People* (New York: W. W. Norton, 2010).

8   **"Thomas Jefferson described"** Caitlin Rosenthal, "Slavery's Scientific Management: Accounting for Mastery," in *Slavery's Capitalism: A
New History of American Economic Development,* ed. Sven Beckert
and Seth Rockman (Philadelphia: University of Pennsylvania Press,
2016), 86.

8   **"less than they needed"** Edmund S. Morgan, *American Slavery,
American Freedom: The Ordeal of Colonial Virginia* (New York: W. W.
Norton, 1975), 309. Even clothing costs could be skimmed: Carter's
uncle made his enslaved workers partially pay for their clothes by selling from their cabin gardens (p. 310). Black people were also left to
provide for their own medical needs, from childbirth to illness (and

often forced to share their craft of midwifery or medicine with owners and local white people).

8   **life insurance on their slaves** Rachel L. Swarns, "Insurance Policies on Slaves: New York Life's Complicated Past," *New York Times*, December 18, 2016, https://www.nytimes.com/2016/12/18/us/insurance-policies-on-slaves-new-york-lifes-complicated-past.html.

9   **many northern corporations** Zoe Thomas, "The Hidden Links Between Slavery and Wall Street," *BBC News*, August 29, 2019, https://www.bbc.com/news/business-49476247.

9   **all the way up to 1846** Rather than emancipating slaves within the state, this act turned them into "apprentices for life." When the Civil War began, New Jersey slaveholders owned eighteen such apprentices for life. Geneva Smith, "Legislating Slavery in New Jersey," *Princeton and Slavery*, https://slavery.princeton.edu/stories/legislating-slavery-in-new-jersey.

9   **port cities in Rhode Island** Rhode Island's eighteenth-century economy was heavily dependent on the slave trade, both in human captives and the material goods of the "Triangle Trade," molasses and rum. Christy Clark-Pujara finds that 60 percent of all the slave ships that left North America came from Rhode Island. *Dark Work: The Business of Slavery in Rhode Island* (New York: NYU Press, 2016). See also Jay Coughtry, *The Notorious Triangle: Rhode Island and the African Slave Trade, 1700–1807* (Philadelphia, PA: Temple University Press, 1981).

9   **filled the Massachusetts textile mills** See, for example, Ronald Bailey, "The Other Side of Slavery: Black Labor, Cotton, and Textile Industrialization in Great Britain and the United States," *Agricultural History* 68, no. 2 (1994): 35–50, http://www.jstor.org/stable/3744401.

9   **capitalized the future Wall Street banks** Pedro Nicolaci da Costa, "America's First Bond Market Was Backed by Enslaved Human Beings," *Forbes*, September 1, 2019, https://www.forbes.com/sites/pedrodacosta/2019/09/01/americas-first-bond-market-was-backed-by-enslaved-human-beings/#2b55fc4a1888; David Teather, "Bank Admits It Owned Slaves," *Guardian*, January 21, 2005, https://www.theguardian.com/world/2005/jan/22/usa.davidteather.

9   **market value of $3 billion** Roger L. Ransom, "The Economics of the Civil War," Economic History Association, EH.net, https://eh.net/encyclopedia/the-economics-of-the-civil-war.

9   **New York merchants had gotten so rich** Peter Moskowitz, "New York City's Surprising Role Funding Slavery and Profiting Off the Civil War," *Vice*, August 6, 2016, https://www.vice.com/en_us/article/mvkgay/city-of-seditiion-new-york-citys-surprising-role-in-funding-slavery-and-the-civil-war.

9     **advocated that his city secede** John Lockwood and Charles Lockwood, "First South Carolina. Then New York?" *Opinionator* (blog), *New York Times,* January 6, 2011, https://opinionator.blogs.nytimes .com/2011/01/06/first-south-carolina-then-new-york.

10     **"At a time when most men"** Greg Grandin, *The Empire of Necessity: Slavery, Freedom, and Deception in the New World* (New York: Metropolitan, 2014), 7.

10     **people at the bottom** Nancy Isenberg, *White Trash: The 400-Year Untold History of Class in America* (New York: Viking, 2016), 17–21.

10     **Bacon's Rebellion** Heather McGhee, "Bacon's Rebellion, 1674–1679" in *400 Souls: A Community History of African America 1619–2019* (New York: One World, 2021).

10     **"basically uncivil"** Morgan, *American Slavery,* 329.

10     **"profits to the poor"** Morgan, *American Slavery,* 333.

11     **A 1669 Virginia colony law** Morgan, *American Slavery,* 312, from William W. Hening, ed., *The Statutes at Large: Being a Collection of All the Laws of Virginia,* vol. 2 (New York: R. & W. & G. Bartow, 1823), 270.

11     **posted on church doors** Morgan, *American Slavery,* 312.

11     **ads of black people seeking relatives** A collaboration between Villanova University's graduate history program and Mother Bethel African Methodist Episcopal Church in Philadelphia has created a digital library of such ads, "Last Seen: Finding Family After Slavery," http:// informationwanted.org.

12     **economic stake that white people** In an interview, Jones-Rogers notes, "Some of my preliminary data show that white women constituted approximately 40% of all the slave owners in my data sets. This is a figure that also holds in data collected by Catherine Hall at the University College London," in "Unmasked: Many White Women Were Southern Slave Owners, Too," *Berkeley News,* UC Berkeley, October 25, 2019, https://news.berkeley.edu/2019/10/25/white-women -slaveholders-q-a.

12     **independent of their husbands' assets** Stephanie E. Jones-Rogers, *They Were Her Property: White Women as Slave Owners in the American South* (New Haven, CT: Yale University Press, 2019), xiv.

12     **white mother rocking her chair** Jones-Rogers, *They Were Her Property,* 11.

12     **"To a large degree"** Morgan, *American Slavery,* 5.

13     **people from European communities** For example, Thomas Paine writes in *Common Sense* (1776), "Europe, and not England, is the parent country of America. This new world hath been the asylum for the persecuted lovers of civil and religious liberty from *every part* of Eu-

rope." *Common Sense and Other Writings* (New York: Modern Library, 2003), 21.

13   **Ten out of the eleven passages** David Waldstreicher, "How the Constitution Was Indeed Pro-Slavery," *The Atlantic,* September 19, 2015, https://www.theatlantic.com/politics/archive/2015/09/how-the -constitution-was-indeed-pro-slavery/406288.

13   **three-fifths of their enslaved** Article, 1 Section 2, of the U.S. Constitution reads, "Representatives and direct Taxes shall be apportioned among the several States which may be included within this Union, according to their respective Numbers, which shall be determined by adding to the whole Number of free Persons, including those bound to Service for a Term of Years, and excluding Indians not taxed, three fifths of all other Persons."

13   **nearly one-fifth of the population** According to the 1790 Census, the total population was 3,929,214, and the total black population was 757,208, which is 19.2 percent. "1790 Census: Return of the Whole Number of Persons Within the Several Districts of the United States," U.S. Census Bureau, https://www.census.gov/library/publications/ 1793/dec/number-of-persons.html.

14   **"if Lincoln is elected"** Lockwood and Lockwood, "First South Carolina. Then New York?"

14   **The idea of affirmative action** W. Carson Byrd, "Most White Americans Will Never Be Affected by Affirmative Action. So Why Do They Hate It So Much?" *Washington Post,* October 18, 2018, https://www .washingtonpost.com/nation/2018/10/19/most-white-americans-will -never-experience-affirmative-action-so-why-do-they-hate-it-so-much.

14   **Some white people even believe** Ashley C. Ford, "PSA: Black People Do Not Go to College for Free," *Refinery29,* August 2, 2017, https:// www.refinery29.com/en-us/2017/08/166293/no-free-college-for -black-people.

14   **wind up paying more for college** Judith Scott-Clayton and Jing Li, "Black-White Disparity in Student Loan Debt More than Triples After Graduation," Brookings Institution, October 20, 2016, https:// www.brookings.edu/research/black-white-disparity-in-student-loan -debt-more-than-triples-after-graduation.

15   **competing with another white person** "Using 1989 data from a representative sample of selective schools, former university presidents William Bowen and Derek Bok showed in their 1998 book, *The Shape of the River,* that eliminating racial preferences would have increased the likelihood of admission for white undergraduate applicants from 25 percent to only 26.5 percent." Goodwin Liu, "The Myth and Math of Affirmative Action," *Washington Post,* April 14, 2002, https://www.washingtonpost.com/archive/opinions/2002/04/14/the

-myth-and-math-of-affirmative-action/60096413-672b-4a4f-8dd1
-8d38a7f282e9.

15    **billionaire Rupert Murdoch** See David McKnight, *Rupert Murdoch:
      An Investigation of Political Power* (Australia: Allen & Unwin, 2012);
      Jane Mayer, "The Making of the Fox News White House," *New
      Yorker*, March 4, 2019, https://www.newyorker.com/magazine/2019/
      03/11/the-making-of-the-fox-news-white-house.

## Chapter Two: Racism Drained the Pool

17    **near the bottom of the list** General Government Spending (graph),
      OECD, https://data.oecd.org/gga/general-government-spending.htm.

17    **roads, bridges, and water systems get a D+** 2017 Infrastructure Re-
      port Card, American Society of Civil Engineers, https://www
      .infrastructurereportcard.org.

18    **The project encouraged advocates** "How to Talk About Government:
      A FrameWorks Message Memo," FrameWorks Institute, March 1,
      2006, pp. 9, 13, https://www.frameworksinstitute.org/publication/
      how-to-talk-about-government-a-frameworks-message-memo.

18    **count how many schools, libraries** See Tables XXXVI–XXXIX in
      Hinton Rowan Helper, *The Impending Crisis of the South: How to
      Meet It* (New York: Burdick Brothers, 1857), 288–89, https://docsouth
      .unc.edu/nc/helper/helper.html.

19    **The slave economy was a system** "In 1860, the states and counties
      with the largest proportion of slaves in their population also had the
      most unequal distribution of land holdings." Nathan Nunn, "Slavery,
      Inequality, and Economic Development in the Americas: An Examina-
      tion of the Engerman-Sokoloff Hypothesis" (October 2007): 28,
      https://scholar.harvard.edu/files/nunn/files/domestic_slavery.pdf.

19    **"Notwithstanding the fact"** Helper, *Impending Crisis*, 19. In Georgia,
      for example, in 1850 and 1860, more than two-thirds of all state legis-
      lators were slaveholders, although they accounted for less than a third
      of the free white population. See Jeffrey Robert Young, "Slavery in
      Antebellum Georgia," *New Georgia Encyclopedia*, October 20, 2003,
      https://www.georgiaencyclopedia.org/articles/history-archaeology/
      slavery-antebellum-georgia.

19    **at three hundred dollars per enslaved person** "The District of Co-
      lumbia Emancipation Act," Online Exhibits, National Archives, last
      modified April 5, 2019, https://www.archives.gov/exhibits/featured
      -documents/dc-emancipation-act.

20    **The value of northern land** Helper, *Impending Crisis*, 59.

20    **nine of the ten poorest states** 2018 Poverty Statistics, U.S. Census
      Bureau, s.v. "poverty by states."

20    **states with the least educational attainment** 2010 American Community Survey, s.v. "Educational Attainment," U.S. Census Bureau, https://data.census.gov/cedsci/table?q=educational%20attainment&t =Educational%20Attainment&g=0100000US.04000.001&tid= ACSST1Y2010.S1501&hidePreview=true.

20    **In 2007, economist Nathan Nunn** Nunn, "Slavery, Inequality."

20    **"societies that began"** Stanley L. Engerman and Kenneth L. Sokoloff, *Economic Development in the Americas Since 1500: Endowments and Institutions* (Cambridge, UK: Cambridge University Press, 2012), 36.

21    **The Homestead Act of 1862** Robert B. Williams, *The Privileges of Wealth: Rising Inequality and the Growing Racial Divide* (New York: Routledge, 2017), 71.

21    **Fewer than six thousand black families** Trina Williams Shanks, "The Homestead Act: A Major Asset-Building Policy in American History," in *Inclusion in the American Dream: Assets, Poverty, and Public Policy,* ed. Michael Sherraden (New York: Oxford University Press, 2005), 36.

21    **an estimated 46 million people** Shanks, "Homestead Act," 36.

21    **the American government told banks** Depression-era mortgage policy innovations included higher loan-to-value ratios reducing down payments from over 50 percent of purchase price to just 20 percent and fixed-rate, fully-amortizing mortgages. Dennis J. Ventry Jr., "The Accidental Deduction: A History and Critique of the Tax Subsidy for Mortgage Interest," *Law and Contemporary Problems* 73, no. 1 (Winter 2010): 247, https://scholarship.law.duke.edu/lcp/vol73/iss1/9.

21    **red "Do Not Lend" lines** See chapter 3, "Racial Zoning," in Richard Rothstein, *The Color of Law: A Forgotten History of How Our Government Segregated America* (New York: Liveright, 2017), 39–57.

22    **excluded the job categories** Ira Katznelson, *When Affirmative Action Was White: An Untold History of Racial Inequality in Twentieth-Century America* (New York: W. W. Norton, 2005), 22.

22    **few black veterans benefited** Shannon Luders-Manuel, "The Inequality Hidden Within the Race-Neutral G.I. Bill," *JSTOR Daily,* September 18, 2017, https://daily.jstor.org/the-inequality-hidden -within-the-race-neutral-g-i-bill. Edward Humes, "How the GI Bill Shunted Blacks into Vocational Training," *The Journal of Blacks in Higher Education* 53 (2006): 92–104.

22    **mortgage benefit in the GI Bill** Humes, "How the GI Bill."

22    **The federal government created suburbs** Alana Semuels, "The Role of Highways in American Poverty," *The Atlantic,* March 18, 2016, https://www.theatlantic.com/business/archive/2016/03/role-of -highways-in-american-poverty/474282.

22    **excluded from the program** Katznelson, *When Affirmative Action*, 22.

23    **"Let's build bigger"** Jeff Wiltse, *Contested Waters: A Social History of Swimming Pools in America* (Chapel Hill: University of North Carolina Press, 2007), 103.

23    **In 1953, a thirteen-year-old** Wiltse, *Contested Waters*, 154.

24    **white children stopped going** Fern Shen, "Once Baltimore's Only City Pool for Blacks, Pool #2 Endures as Art," *Baltimore Brew*, May 2, 2017, https://baltimorebrew.com/2017/05/02/once-baltimores-only -city-pool-for-blacks-pool-2-endures-as-art.

24    **The town of Warren, Ohio** Wiltse, *Contested Waters*, 159.

24    **town of Montgomery, West Virginia** Wiltse, *Contested Waters*, 162.

25    **In Montgomery, Alabama** A photograph of the Oak Park pool can be seen at the Alabama Department of Archives and History website, https://digital.archives.alabama.gov/digital/collection/photo/id/ 21497.

25    **"It was miserable"** Rose Hackman, "Swimming While Black: The Legacy of Segregated Public Pools Lives On," *Guardian*, August 4, 2015, https://www.theguardian.com/world/2015/aug/04/black -children-swimming-drownings-segregation.

25    **The entire public park system** Rebecca Retzlaff, "Desegregation of City Parks and the Civil Rights Movement: The Case of Oak Park in Montgomery, Alabama," *Journal of Urban History*, October 3, 2019, https://journals.sagepub.com/doi/10.1177/0096144219877636.

26    **New Orleans closed** Eli A. Haddow, "The Integration of Audubon Park's Pool and the Committee that Made It Happen," The Historic New Orleans Collection, June 4, 2019, https://www.hnoc.org/ publications/first-draft/integration-audubon-park%E2%80%99s-pool -and-committee-made-it-happen.

26    **In Winona, Mississippi** P. Caleb Smith, "Reflections in the Water: Society and Recreational Facilities, a Case Study of Public Swimming Pools in Mississippi," *Southeastern Geographer* 52, no. 1 (Spring 2012): 39–54.

26    **in nearby Stonewall** Adam Nossiter, "Unearthing a Town Pool, and Not for Whites Only," *New York Times*, September 18, 2006, https:// www.nytimes.com/2006/09/18/us/18pool.html.

26    **the Fairground Park pool** Wiltse, *Contested Waters*, 79.

26    **"bats, clubs, bricks and knives"** Wiltse, *Contested Waters*, 169.

27    **a white mob** Phillip O'Connor, "Pool Riot Pivotal in Race Relations," *St. Louis Post-Dispatch*, June 21, 2009, https://www.stltoday.com/ news/pool-riot-pivotal-in-race-relations-citys-decision-in-49-to -integrate-swimming-pools-sparked/article_914ec52e-4be8-5b09-ac98 -e71da7160cc6.html.

27    **logged just 10,000** Wiltse, *Contested Waters*, 178–79.

27    **The city closed the pool** In Pittsburgh, a similar scene played out around Sully's Pool, where white attendance plummeted after orders to integrate it were handed down. It was closed in 1977, then filled in and paved over. No memorial marks the spot. Linda Wilson Fuoco, "Black History Month: Local Activists, Black and White, Worked to Integrate Sully's Pool in South Park," *Pittsburgh Post-Gazette*, February 21, 2001, https://old.post-gazette.com/neigh_south/20010221spool2.asp.

27    **blessing of the U.S. Supreme Court** *Palmer v. Thompson*, 403 U.S. 217 (1971).

27    **"There was no evidence"** Quoted in U.S. Reports: *Palmer v. Thompson*, 403 U.S. 217 (1971), 217–18.

27    **"Petitioners' contention"** *Palmer v. Thompson*, 403 U.S. 217 (1971), 224–26.

27    **"Beginning in the mid-1950s"** Wiltse, *Contested Waters*, 180.

28    **In Washington, D.C.** Wiltse, *Contested Waters*, 193.

28    **two-hundred-dollar ownership fees and annual dues** Wiltse, *Contested Waters*, 194.

28    **According to the authoritative American National Elections Studies** Sean McElwee and Sarah Merchant data analysis for the author, April 2017, updated September 2020.

29    **group of mostly black activists demanding** The March's wage demand of $2.00 in 1963 would be $16.85 in 2020 dollars, more than twice the current minimum wage. See "What We Demand" in the March on Washington's program at https://www.crmvet.org/docs/mowprog.pdf.

29    **biological racism waned** Donald R. Kinder and Lynn Sanders, *Divided by Color: Racial Politics and Democratic Ideals* (University of Chicago Press, 1996), 97.

29    **"today, we say, prejudice"** Kinder and Sanders, *Divided by Color*, 115.

29    **They measured racial resentment** Kinder and Sanders, *Divided by Color*, 106–8.

29    **"although whites' support"** Kinder and Sanders, *Divided by Color*, 92.

30    **opposed racial public policies** Kinder and Sanders, *Divided by Color*, 117.

30    **The researchers couldn't explain** Kinder and Sanders, *Divided by Color*, 116.

30    **there was a sixty-point difference** Sean McElwee, data analysis for the author, April 2017, updated September 2020.

31    **when President Johnson accurately predicted** President Johnson

reportedly said to Bill Moyers upon signing the Civil Rights Act, "I think we just delivered the South to the Republican Party for a long time to come." While the Democrats still won some southern states in the following election, 1964, the regional realignment did happen. Even more consequentially, the majority of white Americans voted against the Democratic presidential nominee from then on. See Michael Oreskes, "Civil Rights Act Leaves Deep Mark on the American Political Landscape," *New York Times*, July 2, 1989, https://www .nytimes.com/1989/07/02/us/civil-rights-act-leaves-deep-mark-on -the-american-political-landscape.html.

31   **hit their peak as a percentage** In 1969, total U.S. tax revenues as a share of the economy were similar to those in Europe; today, they are lower than those in thirty out of the thirty-six OECD countries. See "Table 3.2. Total Tax Revenue as % of GDP, 1965–2014" download- able chart at "Tax Policy Analysis, Revenue Statistics—Tax ratio Changes Between 1965 and 2014," Tax Policy Analysis, OECD, oecd .org/ctp/tax-policy/revenue-statistics-ratio-change-all-years.htm.

32   **larger share of their incomes** See, for example, Andrew Van Dam, "Black Families Pay Significantly Higher Property Taxes than White Families, New Analysis Shows," *Washington Post*, July 2, 2020, https://www.washingtonpost.com/business/2020/07/02/black -property-tax; Eric Bronson, "Why Black Women Are Paying More in Taxes than Washington's Billionaires," *Firesteel* (blog), YWCA, March 3, 2020, https://www.ywcaworks.org/blogs/firesteel/tue -03032020-0910/why-black-women-are-paying-more-taxes -washingtons-billionaires; "Racial Disparities and the Income Tax System," Tax Policy Center, Urban Institute, January 30, 2020, https://apps.urban.org/features/race-and-taxes.

33   **"You start out in 1954"** Rick Perlstein, "Exclusive: Lee Atwater's In- famous 1981 Interview on the Southern Strategy," *The Nation*, No- vember 13, 2012, https://www.thenation.com/article/archive/ exclusive-lee-atwaters-infamous-1981-interview-southern-strategy.

33   **harping on the issue of welfare** Ian Haney López documents Rea- gan and the Republicans' anti-welfare messaging extensively in *Dog Whistle Politics: How Coded Racial Appeals Have Reinvented Racism and Wrecked the Middle Class* (New York: Oxford University Press, 2014) and *Merge Left: Fusing Race and Class, Winning Elections, and Saving America* (New York: The New Press, 2019).

33   **An emblematic line** Ronald Reagan, "Radio Address to the Nation on Welfare Reform," February 15, 1986, https://www.reaganlibrary.gov/ archives/speech/radio-address-nation-welfare-reform.

33   **tapped into an old stereotype** See David Pilgrim, "The Coon Carica-

ture," Jim Crow Museum, Ferris University, https://www.ferris.edu/jimcrow/coon, and Donald Bogle, *Toms, Coons, Mulattoes, Mammies, and Bucks: An Interpretive History of Blacks in American Films* (New York: Viking, 1973); and Micki McElya, *Clinging to Mammy: The Faithful Slave in Twentieth-Century America* (Cambridge, MA: Harvard University Press, 2007).

33    **white Americans constitute the majority** Isaac Shapiro, Danilo Trisi, and Raheem Chaudhry, "Poverty Reduction Programs Help Adults Lacking College Degrees the Most," Center on Budget and Policy Priorities, February 16, 2017, https://www.cbpp.org/research/poverty-and-inequality/poverty-reduction-programs-help-adults-lacking-college-degrees-the.

34    **"47 percent" version from millionaire Mitt Romney** Former Republican presidential nominee Mitt Romney was recorded saying that 47 percent of the country would vote for Obama, and he described that percentage of the electorate as those who paid no income tax and were dependent on government. Although he did not mention race, obviously Romney knew that the majority of black people was voting for Obama in 2012. As Ezra Klein pointed out, however, "For what it's worth, this division of 'makers' and 'takers' isn't true. Among the Americans who paid no federal income taxes in 2011, 61 percent paid payroll taxes—which means they have jobs and, when you account for both sides of the payroll tax, they paid 15.3 percent of their income in taxes, which is higher than the 13.9 percent that Romney paid. Another 22 percent were elderly." Ezra Klein, "Romney's Theory of the 'Taker Class' and Why It Matters," *Washington Post*, September 17, 2012, https://www.washingtonpost.com/news/wonk/wp/2012/09/17/romneys-theory-of-the-taker-class-and-why-it-matters.

34    **racially explicit Fox News version** See "'The Makers and the Takers': How Fox News Forges a Working-Class/Business-Class Political Alliance," chapter 4 in Reece Peck, *Fox Populism: Branding Conservatism as Working Class* (New York: Cambridge University Press, 2019), 155–84.

34    **In 2016, the majority** Peter Moore, "Racial Attitudes Differ More on Ideology than Class," YouGov, January 29, 2016, https://today.yougov.com/topics/politics/articles-reports/2016/01/29/racial-attitudes-differ-ideology-class.

34    **one out of six children** "The State of America's Children 2020: Child Poverty," Children's Defense Fund, https://www.childrensdefense.org/policy/resources/soac-2020-child-poverty.

34    **We could eliminate all poverty** Rachel West, "For the Cost of the Tax Bill, the U.S. Could Eliminate Child Poverty. Twice," *talk poverty*,

December 12, 2017, https://talkpoverty.org/2017/12/12/u-s
-eliminate-child-poverty-cost-senate-tax-bill/.

34  **The media's inaccurate portrayal of poverty** See Martin Gilens,
*Why Americans Hate Welfare: Race, Media, and the Politics of Anti-
poverty Policy* (Chicago, IL: University of Chicago Press, 1999). In another study, in 474 print news stories about poverty published between
1992 and 2010, editors chose to use photographs or illustrations of
black people more than half the time, even though black people were
only about a quarter of those in poverty during the studied period. See
Bas W. van Doorn, "Pre- and Post-Welfare Reform Media Portrayals
of Poverty in the United States: The Continuing Importance of Race
and Ethnicity," *Politics & Policy* 43, no. 1 (February 2015): 142–62.

35  **Reagan cut taxes on the wealthy** The 1981 and 1986 tax cuts lowered
the top marginal rate from 70 percent to 28 percent, and the 1986 reform raised the lowest bracket from 11 percent to 15 percent. See Federal Individual Income Tax Rates History, Nominal Dollars Income
Years 1913–2013 (table), Tax Foundation, https://files.taxfoundation
.org/legacy/docs/fed_individual_rate_history_nominal.pdf. The 1983
Social Security reform package raised payroll tax rates and required
self-employed people to pay both sides of the payroll tax, a change
that has grown more costly to lower-income workers, who are increasingly likely to be contingent, independent contractors today. The 1986
reform expanded interest deductions for homeowners and ended it for
credit card debt. While there were some tax increases over Reagan's
term that impacted the wealthy (various deductions were eliminated
to "broaden the base," and the capital gains and top income tax rates
were equalized), the net effect was a lower tax bill for the wealthy. See
Thomas L. Hungerford, Taxes and the Economy: An Economic Analysis of the Top Tax Rates Since 1945, Congressional Research Service,
September 14, 2012, http://graphics8.nytimes.com/news/business/
0915taxesandeconomy.pdf and https://www.nytimes.com/2017/12/
26/business/economy/tax-cuts-incomes.html.

35  **slashed domestic spending** For example, among other changes,
Reagan reduced child nutrition subsidies, raised Medicare deductibles,
cut back Amtrak subsidies, and tightened income eligibility rules for
food stamps. See David Kotz and Michelle Harlan, "Major Deficit-
Reduction Measures Enacted in Recent Years," CRS Report for Congress, September 8, 1994, pp. 4–5, Congressional Research Service,
https://www.everycrsreport.com/files/19940908_94-719
_eee13a7d0e01ed5a9a29c619c719b722a1092623.pdf.

35  **with the overwhelming support** Asma Khalid, "Republicans' White
Working-Class Trap: A Growing Reliance," NPR, January 18, 2016,

https://www.npr.org/2016/01/18/462027861/republicans-white
-working-class-trap-a-growing-reliance.

35  **That message is** See the 2020 Republican Party platform, "Restoring
the American Dream," https://gop.com/platform/restoring-the
-american-dream, and "Health Care," https://gop.com/issue/health
-care.

35  **46 percent of Republicans** Daniel Villarreal, "69 Percent of Americans Want Medicare for All, Including 46 Percent of Republicans,
New Poll Says," *Newsweek*, April 24, 2020, https://www.newsweek
.com/69-percent-americans-want-medicare-all-including-46-percent
-republicans-new-poll-says-1500187.

35  **nearly half of Republican voters** Sean McElwee, Data for Progress,
data analysis for the author, April 24, 2019.

36  **"The press and elites"** Stanley B. Greenberg et al., "The Very Separate World of Conservative Republicans: Why Republican Leaders
Will Have Trouble Speaking to the Rest of America," October 16,
2009, p. 1, https://democracycorps.com/wp-content/uploads/2009/
10/TheVerySeparateWorldofConservativeRepublicans101609.pdf.

36  **"They are actively rooting"** Greenberg et al., "Very Separate World," 5.

37  **"People may fail to report"** Eric D. Knowles et al., "Racial Prejudice
Predicts Opposition to Obama and His Health Care Reform Plan,"
*Journal of Experimental Psychology* 46, no. 2 (March 2010): 420.

37  **"Obama has a plan"** Mike Burns and Andy Newbold, "Rush Limbaugh Opens 2012 with More Race-Baiting Attacks," Media Matters
for America, January 1, 2012, https://www.mediamatters.org/rush
-limbaugh/rush-limbaugh-opens-2012-more-race-baiting-attacks.

37  **"Have we suddenly transported"** Glenn Beck was referring to the
case of Shirley Sherrod, a veteran civil rights activist and employee at
the U.S. Department of Agriculture, whom President Obama's USDA
secretary fired after Breitbart.com published a selectively edited video
of Sherrod that suggested she had discriminated against a white
farmer facing foreclosure. "I was struggling with the fact that so many
black people had lost their farm land," she says in the video. "And
here I was faced with having to help a white person save their land."
In fact, she did help the white farmer, who credited her with having
helped save his farm. Secretary Vilsack apologized. Sheryl Gay Stol-
berg, Shaila Dewan, and Brian Stelter, "With Apology, Fired Official
Is Offered a New Job," *New York Times*, July 21, 2020. For Beck's com-
mentary, see Christine Schwen, "Despite Claim that 'Context Matters,'
Beck Played Heavily Edited Sherrod Clip on Radio," Media Matters
for America, July 21, 2020, https://www.mediamatters.org/fox
-nation/despite-claim-context-matters-beck-played-heavily-edited
-sherrod-clip-radio.

38 **"I think Mr. Obama allows"** See "Bill O'Reilly: 'Historical Grievances' Like Slavery Shape Obama's Economic Thinking," Media Matters for America, July 19, 2012, https://www.mediamatters.org/bill
-oreilly/bill-oreilly-historical-grievances-slavery-shape-obamas
-economic-thinking.

38 **policies Obama was pushing** O'Reilly was responding to Obama's
comments in a 2012 campaign speech: "If you were successful, somebody along the line gave you some help. There was a great teacher
somewhere in your life. Somebody helped to create this unbelievable
American system that we have that allowed you to thrive. Somebody
invested in roads and bridges. If you've got a business, you didn't build
that. Somebody else made that happen. The internet didn't get invented on its own. Government research created the internet so that
all the companies could make money off the internet."

38 **less than 1 percent annual income growth** "Average household
earnings for the lowest-earning 90 percent of the income distribution
from 1979 to 2017 was 0.6 percent; annual wage growth was three
times as high, between 1947–1979." From John Schmitt, Elise Gould,
and Josh Bivens, "America's Slow-Motion Wage Crisis," Economic Policy Institute, September 13, 2018, https://www.epi.org/publication/
americas-slow-motion-wage-crisis-four-decades-of-slow-and-unequal
-growth-2/.

39 **"Absent race as an issue"** The authors also set out to ask how, after a
fifty-year period of stasis in tax rates before 1980, politicians could
continue decreasing tax rates on the rich amid rising inequality post-
1980. "Our analysis offers an answer to this question: the existence of
a non-economic dimension, such as race, changes the alignment of
voters in a significantly different way from that predicted by unidi-
mensional models" (p. 1049). "The effect of racism on redistribution
in the United States is large. We predict that the Republican Party
would have proposed a marginal tax rate of 40% in 1984–1988, absent
racism. Due to the existence of racism, however, the Republican Party
was able to propose a tax rate of 23.9% in this period; thus the effect
of racism on the tax rate is about 16.5% in 1984–1988 for the Republican Party. The effect of racism on the tax rate of the Democratic
Party is also large. Absent racism, we predict party D would have proposed a marginal tax rate of 49.9%; due to the existence of racism, it
proposed 37%. The fact that the total effect of racism appears to be
large for both parties implies that voter racism pushes both parties in
the United States significantly to the right on the economic issue"
(p. 1044). Woojin Lee and John E. Roemer, "Racism and Redistribution in the United States: A Solution to the Problem of American Ex-
ceptionalism," *Journal of Public Economics* 90 (2006): 1027–52.

## Chapter Three: Going Without

41    **land taken from Indigenous people** "*High Country News* recon-
      structed approximately 10.7 million acres taken from nearly 250
      tribes, bands and communities through over 160 violence-backed land
      cessions, a legal term for the giving up of territory." Robert Lee,
      "Morrill Act of 1862 Indigenous Land Parcels Database," *High Coun-
      try News*, March 2020, https://www.landgrabu.org. In 1890, Congress
      passed another Morrill Act to allow for segregated land grant colleges,
      creating nineteen black colleges in southern and border states. These
      public Historically Black Colleges and Universities were essential in
      the education of black Americans for the next century, though they
      were chronically underfunded by state legislatures. See Katherine I. E.
      Wheatle, "Neither Just Nor Equitable: Race in the Congressional De-
      bate of the Second Morrill Act of 1890," *American Educational His-
      tory Journal* 46, no. 2 (2019): 1–20.

41    **veterans made up 50 percent** "In the peak year of 1947, veterans ac-
      counted for 49 percent of college admissions." "About GI Bill: History
      and Timeline," U.S. Department of Veterans Affairs, modified No-
      vember 21, 2013, https://www.benefits.va.gov/gibill/history.asp.

41    **largely excluded from these opportunities** "The availability of ben-
      efits to black veterans had a substantial and positive impact on the ed-
      ucational attainment of those likely to have access to colleges and
      universities outside the South. Unfortunately, for those more likely to
      be limited to the South in their collegiate choices, the G.I. Bill exacer-
      bated rather than narrowed the economic and educational differences
      between blacks and whites." Sarah E. Turner and John Bound, "Clos-
      ing the Gap or Widening the Divide: The Effects of the G.I. Bill and
      World War II on the Educational Outcomes of Black Americans,"
      *Journal of Economic History* 63, no. 1 (March 2003): 172.

41    **six out of every ten dollars** Thomas G. Mortenson, "State Funding:
      A Race to the Bottom," *Presidency* 15, no. 1 (Winter 2012): 26.

41    **a federal Pell Grant** In the 1970s and '80s, Pell recipients had the
      majority of costs covered. Pell covered not only tuition, but also a sub-
      stantial amount of living costs. See "Pell Grant Funding History
      (1976 to 2010)," ACE Fact Sheet on Higher Education, American
      Council on Education, https://www.acenet.edu/Documents/
      FactSheet-Pell-Grant-Funding-History-1976-2010.pdf.

42    **public colleges were tuition-free** The City University of New York
      waived tuition until 1976, and the University of California system was
      created in 1868 with the mandate that "admission and tuition shall be
      free to all residents of the state." In California, public budget cuts

prompted an educational fee of $150 in 1970, and tuition and fees
have climbed since. See Michael Stone, "What Happened When
American States Tried Providing Tuition-Free College," *Time*, April 4,
2016, https://time.com/4276222/free-college. Also see Table 320,
"Average undergraduate tuition and fees and room and board
rates . . . ," Digest of Education Statistics, National Center for Education Statistics, https://nces.ed.gov/programs/digest/d07/tables/dt07
_320.asp.

42   **a return of three to four dollars** Michael Hout, "Social and Economic Returns to College Education in the United States," *Annual Review of Sociology* 38, no. 1 (2012): 379–400.

42   **Students of color comprised** Mark Huelsman, "The Unaffordable
Era: A 50-State Look at Rising College Prices and the New American
Student," Demos, February 22, 2018, p. 7, https://www.demos.org/
research/unaffordable-era-50-state-look-rising-college-prices-and-new
-american-student.

42   **State legislatures began to drastically cut** "While state spending on
higher education increased by $10.5 billion in absolute terms from
1990 to 2010, in relative terms, state funding of higher education declined. Real funding per public FTE dropped by 26.1 percent from
1990–1991 to 2009–2010. After controlling for inflation, states collectively invested $6.12 per $1,000 in personal income in 2010–2011,
down from $8.75 in 1990–1991, despite the fact that personal income
increased by 66.2 percent over that period." John Quinterno, "The
Great Cost Shift: How Higher Education Cuts Are Undermining the
Future Middle Class," Demos, March 2012, p. 2, https://www.demos
.org/sites/default/files/publications/TheGreatCostShift_Demos_0.pdf.

42   **has nearly tripled since 1991** "Average tuition at public 4-year colleges across the country is $9,970 a year in 2017, which is . . . two-and-
a-half times as high as the average ($3,790) in 1991." Huelsman,
"The Unaffordable Era," 11.

42   **$1.5 trillion in 2020** "Quarterly Report on Household Debt and
Credit, Q2 2020," Center for Microeconomic Data, Federal Reserve
Bank of New York, August 2020, https://www.newyorkfed.org/media
library/interactives/householdcredit/data/pdf/HHDC_2020Q2.pdf.

42   **at least 33 percent more** Author calculation of average four-year
public college student loan debt in 2018 of $26,946 under the Stan-
dard Repayment Plan over ten years with no deferments, missed payments, or extensions, with an APR of 6 percent, subsidized.

42   **double-digit interest on private loans** See "Interest Rates on Student
Loans," Debt.org, n.d., https://www.debt.org/students/financial-aid
-process/interest-rates.

43    **Eight out of ten black graduates** Mark Huelsman, "The Debt Divide: The Racial and Class Bias Behind the 'New Normal' of Student Borrowing," Demos, May 19, 2015, p. 1, https://www.demos.org/research/debt-divide-racial-and-class-bias-behind-new-normal-student-borrowing. Between the lack of wealth and the wage gap, managing student debt is a financial catastrophe for black borrowers. An astonishing 55 percent of black men default on a loan within twelve years of starting college, and black women borrowers owe 113 percent of their original loan balance twelve years after starting school (compared to 56 percent for white male borrowers). Over 20 percent of black college *graduates* default, a rate five times as high as white bachelor's recipients. See also Mark Huelsman, "Debt to Society: The Case for Bold, Equitable Student Loan Cancellation and Reform," Demos, June 6, 2019, pp. 5–15, https://www.demos.org/research/debt-to-society.

43    **white high school dropouts** The average household wealth of a white person without a high school diploma was $34,700; that of a black person with a college degree was $23,400. Darrick Hamilton, William Darity Jr., Anne E. Price, Vishnu Sridharan, Rebecca Tippett, "Umbrellas Don't Make It Rain: Why Studying and Working Hard Isn't Enough for Black Americans," Insight Center for Community Economic Development, p. 5.

43    **it has now reached 63 percent** Huelsman, "The Debt Divide," 2.

43    **student debt payments are stopping us** Alvaro Mezza et al., "Can Student Loan Debt Explain Low Homeownership Rates for Young Adults?" *Consumer & Community Context* 1, no. 1 (January 2019), https://www.federalreserve.gov/publications/files/consumer-community-context-201901.pdf.

43    **even contributing to delays in marriage** Summer and Student Debt Crisis, "Buried in Debt: A National Survey Report on the State of Student Loan Borrowers in 2018," November 1, 2018, https://www.meetsummer.org/share/Summer-Student-Debt-Crisis-Buried-in-Debt-Report-Nov-2018.pdf.

43    **half the retirement savings** Matthew S. Rutledge, "Do Young Adults with Student Debt Save Less for Retirement?" *Issue in Brief*, No. 18–13 (June 2018), Center for Retirement Research at Boston College, https://crr.bc.edu/wp-content/uploads/2018/06/IB_18-13.pdf.

44    **A third of developed countries** Figure is annual tuition price. See "Indicator C5. How Much Do Tertiary Students Pay and What Public Support Do They Receive?" Education at a Glance 2019, OECD, p. 316, https://read.oecd-ilibrary.org/education/education-at-a-glance-2019_f8d7880d-en#page316.

44  **older, college-educated (white) Republicans** 85 percent of over-sixty-five college graduate Republicans oppose free college. See Hannah Hartig, "Democrats Overwhelmingly Favor Free College Tuition, While Republicans Are Divided by Age, Education," Fact Tank, Pew Research Center, February 21, 2020, https://www.pewresearch.org/fact-tank/2020/02/21/democrats-overwhelmingly-favor-free-college-tuition-while-republicans-are-divided-by-age-education.

44  **began voting for ballot initiatives** "Proposition 14 . . . aimed to roll back recently enacted civil rights laws forbidding racial discrimination in the sale or rental of housing. . . . The most infamous include Proposition 187, the so-called 'Save Our State' referendum . . . that sought to ban undocumented immigrants from schools, hospitals, and public assistance. Also infamous is Proposition 209, the cynically titled California Civil Rights Initiative successfully promoted by Ward Connerly in 1996 to end affirmative action in California in schools and universities, contracting, and state hiring. . . . [O]thers include Proposition 21 (1972), seeking to block school integration; Proposition 1 (1979), ending busing to promote school integration; Proposition 63 (1986), declaring English the official language of California; Proposition 165 (1992), seeking to slash welfare benefits, particularly to mothers; Proposition 184 (1994), adopting a three-strikes provision in criminal sentencing; Proposition 227 (1998) curtailing bilingual education; and Proposition 54 (2003), which sought to end the collection of racial data." Ian Haney López, "California Dog Whistling," University of California Othering and Belonging Institute, April 18, 2018, https://belonging.berkeley.edu/california-dog-whistling.

44  **Proposition 13 drastically limited** "When adjusted for inflation, California spent about $7,400 per pupil in 1977, about $1,000 above the national average, according to data collected by the National Center for Education Statistics. . . . [In 2016] California [ranked] 41st in the nation in per pupil spending, when taking into account cost of living in each state. . . . California would need to boost K–12 funding by 32 percent, or about $22 billion, in order for the state to meet its education targets." Vanessa Rancaño, "How Proposition 13 Transformed Neighborhood Public Schools Throughout California," KQED, October 5, 2018, https://www.kqed.org/news/11701044/how-proposition-13-transformed-neighborhood-public-schools-throughout-california.

45  **Between 1979 and 2019** Amy Rose, "The Cost of College, Then and Now," California Budget & Policy Center, April 30, 2019, https://calbudgetcenter.org/blog/the-cost-of-college-then-and-now/. Fortunately, California passed a law in 2017 offering two years of tuition-free community college, excluding the four-year institutions of

the California State University and University of California systems.
See Cecilia Rios-Aguilar and Austin Lyke, "The California College
Promise," Policy Analysis for California Education, March 2020,
https://edpolicyinca.org/publications/california-college-promise.

45    **Dog whistling was ever-present** Haney López, "California Dog
Whistling."

45    **Conservative columnist William Safire** William Safire, "Taxpayers'
Revolt," *New York Times,* February 27, 1978, https://www.nytimes
.com/1978/02/27/archives/taxpayers-revolt-essay.html?searchResult
Position=2.

45    **a constitutional amendment severely limiting taxes** TABOR has
wreaked havoc on Colorado's state and local governments, requiring
complex workarounds to maintain adequate services. Voters passed an
amendment to suspend it for five years in 2005. See "Policy Basics:
Taxpayer Bill of Rights (TABOR)," Center on Budget and Policy Priorities, updated November 5, 2019, https://www.cbpp.org/research/
state-budget-and-tax/policy-basics-taxpayer-bill-of-rights-tabor; Iris J.
Lav and Erica Williams, "A Formula for Decline: Lessons from Colorado for States Considering TABOR," Center on Budget and Policy
Priorities, updated March 15, 2010, https://www.cbpp.org/research/
a-formula-for-decline-lessons-from-colorado-for-states-considering
-tabor.

45    **forty-seventh place in higher education investments** Colorado is
forty-seventh in state higher education funding, as measured against
the state's ability to pay as reflected in personal income. "State Higher
Education Finance: FY 2018," State Higher Education Executive Officers Association, p. 44, https://sheeomain.wpengine.com/wp-content/
uploads/2019/04/SHEEO_SHEF_FY18_Report.pdf.

45    **tripling their expenditures** "Police and Corrections Expenditures,"
State and Local Finance Initiative, Urban Institute, https://www
.urban.org/policy-centers/cross-center-initiatives/state-and-local
-finance-initiative/state-and-local-backgrounders/police-and
-corrections-expenditures#Question3Police.

45    **spending more on jails and prisons** Christopher Ingraham, "The
States that Spend More Money on Prisoners than College Students,"
*Washington Post,* July 7, 2016, https://www.washingtonpost.com/
news/wonk/wp/2016/07/07/the-states-that-spend-more-money-on
-prisoners-than-college-students.

46    **federal government cut back massively** The Housing and Urban
Development budget authority went from 1.41 percent of GDP to just
0.25 percent of GDP from 1978 to 2018. See "Budget Trends," Federal
Budget & Spending, National Low Income Housing Coalition, https://
nlihc.org/federal-budget-and-spending.

46    **exceeded the total number of arrests** Christopher Ingraham, "More People Were Arrested Last Year over Pot than for Murder, Rape, Aggravated Assault, and Robbery Combined," *Washington Post*, September 26, 2017, https://www.washingtonpost.com/news/wonk/wp/2017/09/26/more-people-were-arrested-last-year-over-pot-than-for-murder-rape-aggravated-assault-and-robbery-combined.

46    **six times as likely** Betsy Pearl, "Ending the War on Drugs: By the Numbers," Center for American Progress, June 27, 2018, p. 1, https://www.americanprogress.org/issues/criminal-justice/reports/2018/06/27/452819/ending-war-drugs-numbers.

46    **about one hundred to one** Deborah J. Vagins and Jesselyn McCurdy, "Cracks in the System: Twenty Years of the Unjust Federal Crack Cocaine Law," American Civil Liberties Union, October 2006, https://www.aclu.org/other/cracks-system-20-years-unjust-federal-crack-cocaine-law. In 2010, Congress passed the Fair Sentencing Act, which reduced the disparity to eighteen to one. See "Fair Sentencing Act," ACLU, https://www.aclu.org/issues/criminal-law-reform/drug-law-reform/fair-sentencing-act.

46    **more common among white people** "From 2000 to 2009, the black imprisonment rate for drug offenses fell by 16 percent. For white people, it climbed by nearly 27 percent, according to BJS. . . . Starting around 2000, whites started going to prison more often for property offenses: robbery, burglary, theft, motor vehicle theft, forgery, counterfeiting and selling or buying stolen property, often categorized as crimes of poverty. From 2000 to 2009, black incarceration for those crimes dropped nine percent, the BJS numbers show. It went up by 21 percent for whites." Eli Hager, "A Mass Incarceration Mystery," *Justice Lab*, The Marshall Project, December 15, 2017, https://www.themarshallproject.org/2017/12/15/a-mass-incarceration-mystery. See also John Gramlich, "The Gap Between the Number of Blacks and Whites in Prison Is Shrinking," Fact Tank, Pew Research Center, April 30, 2019, https://www.pewresearch.org/fact-tank/2019/04/30/shrinking-gap-between-number-of-blacks-and-whites-in-prison.

46    **"Mostly white and politically conservative counties"** Josh Keller and Adam Pearce, "A Small Indiana County Sends More People to Prison than San Francisco and Durham, N.C., Combined. Why?" The Upshot, *New York Times*, September 2, 2016, https://www.nytimes.com/2016/09/02/upshot/new-geography-of-prisons.html.

47    **By 2018, an estimated 130** "What Is the U.S. Opioid Epidemic?," U.S. Department of Health and Human Services, modified on September 4, 2019, https://www.hhs.gov/opioids/about-the-epidemic/index.html.

47    **"We recently polled"** "New Data Shows COVID-19 and Economic Downturn Crushing Student Loan Borrowers," Student Debt Crisis,

https://studentdebtcrisis.org/student-debt-covid-survey; and email conversation between Natalia Abrams and author, September 1, 2020.

47 **"I'm watching everyone"** Josh Frost testimonial, "Real Student Debt Stories," Student Debt Crisis, July 11, 2018, https://studentdebt crisis.org/read-student-debt-stories.

48 **"This is madness"** Emilie Scott testimonial, "Real Student Debt Stories," Student Debt Crisis, May 20, 2018, https://studentdebtcrisis.org/read-student-debt-stories.

48 **senior citizens who still owe** Kelly McLaughlin, "3 Million Senior Citizens in the U.S. Are Still Paying Off Their Student Loans," *Insider,* May 3, 2019, https://www.insider.com/americans-over-60-paying-student-loans-2019-5?utm_source=copy-link&utm_medium=referral&utm_content=topbar; data on impact of debt on medical care and Social Security garnishment in "Snapshot of Older Consumers and Student Loan Debt," Consumer Financial Protection Bureau, January 2017, https://files.consumerfinance.gov/f/documents/201701_cfpb_OA-Student-Loan-Snapshot.pdf.

48 **still being sued for $60,000** It's not possible for Settle to discharge the $60,000 despite his insolvency, because of the bankruptcy reform bill that Demos opposed in 2005.

48 **"I want the entire country"** Robert C. Settle Jr. testimonial, "Real Student Debt Stories," Student Debt Crisis, March 4, 2016, https://studentdebtcrisis.org/read-student-debt-stories.

48 **more affordable, less complex, more secure** See Figure 1 at "Public Opinion on Single-Payer, National Health Plans, and Expanding Access to Medicare Coverage," KFF, Henry Kaiser Family Foundation, May 27, 2020, https://www.kff.org/slideshow/public-opinion-on-single-payer-national-health-plans-and-expanding-access-to-medicare-coverage.

48 **pay more individually** "Slaying the 'Fee-for-Service Monster' of American Healthcare," *Hidden Brain,* NPR, September 7, 2020, https://www.npr.org/transcripts/908728981. And on the idea that Medicare for All saves money, see Diane Archer, "22 Studies Agree: 'Medicare for All' Saves Money," *The Hill,* February 24, 2020, https://thehill.com/blogs/congress-blog/healthcare/484301-22-studies-agree-medicare-for-all-saves-money.

48 **and as a nation** "U.S. health care spending in 2016 totaled 17.2 percent of GDP, compared to just 8.9 percent for the OECD median. Not only does the U.S outspend other OECD countries, on the whole it has less access to many health care resources." See "U.S. Health Care Spending Highest Among Developed Countries," Bloomberg School of Public Health, Johns Hopkins University, January 7, 2019, https://

www.jhsph.edu/news/news-releases/2019/us-health-care-spending
-highest-among-developed-countries.html#:~:text=U.S.%20health
%20care%20spending%20in,to%20many%20health%20care%20
resources.

48    **have worse health outcomes** "The U.S. spends more on health care as
a share of the economy—nearly twice as much as the average OECD
country—yet has the lowest life expectancy and highest suicide rates
among the 11 nations. The U.S. has the highest chronic disease burden
and an obesity rate that is two times higher than the OECD average.
Compared to peer nations, the U.S. has among the highest number of
hospitalizations from preventable causes and the highest rate of avoid-
able deaths." Roosa Tikkanen and Melinda K. Abrams, "U.S. Health
Care from a Global Perspective, 2019: Higher Spending, Worse Outcomes?," The Commonwealth Fund, January 30, 2020, https://www
.commonwealthfund.org/publications/issue-briefs/2020/jan/us
-health-care-global-perspective-2019.

48    **all of whom have some version** "Universal Health Coverage and
Health Outcomes: Final Report," OECD, July 22, 2016, p. 9, https://
www.oecd.org/els/health-systems/Universal-Health-Coverage-and
-Health-Outcomes-OECD-G7-Health-Ministerial-2016.pdf. See also
"America Is a Health-Care Outlier in the Developed World," *The
Economist*, April 26, 2018, https://www.economist.com/special
-report/2018/04/26/america-is-a-health-care-outlier-in-the
-developed-world.

49    **successful economically** "America's Public Medicare Program
Costs Less and Is More Efficient than Private Health Insurance,"
Scholars Strategy Network, February 8, 2017, https://scholars.org/
contribution/americas-public-medicare-program-costs-less-and-more
-efficient-private-health. See also Bill Brody, "Is Medicare Cost Effective?," Crossroads, Johns Hopkins Medicine, June 13, 2003, https://
www.hopkinsmedicine.org/about/Crossroads/06_13_03.html. Glenn
Kessler complicates this a little more in "Medicare, Private Insurance
and Administrative Costs: A Democratic Talking Point," Fact Checker,
*Washington Post*, September 19, 2017, https://www.washingtonpost
.com/news/fact-checker/wp/2017/09/19/medicare-private
-insurance-and-administrative-costs-a-democratic-talking-point.

49    **popular with its beneficiaries** Seventy-five percent of seniors are satisfied with Medicare. Les Masterson, "Seniors Love Medicare, but Are
Pessimistic about Its Long-term Future," HealthcareDive, February
20, 2019, https://www.healthcaredive.com/news/seniors-love
-medicare-but-are-pessimistic-about-its-long-term-future/548721/.

49    **polled with majority support** See survey toplines in Kaiser Health

Tracking Poll, March 2012, p. 9, https://www.kff.org/wp-content/uploads/2013/01/8285-t.pdf.

49  **"a farm boy"** Jill Quadagno, *One Nation, Uninsured* (Oxford: Oxford University Press, 2006), 29.

50  **The accusation of socialism** See, for example, Jeff Woods, *Black Struggle, Red Scare: Segregation and Anti-Communism in the South, 1948–1968* (Baton Rouge: Louisiana State University Press, 2004); and Yasuhiro Katagiri, *Black Freedom, White Resistance, and Red Menace: Civil Rights and Anticommunism in the Jim Crow South* (Baton Rouge: Louisiana State University Press, 2014).

50  **"a front and tool"** Katagiri, *Black Freedom*, 101.

50  **"collected every photo"** Quadagno, *One Nation, Uninsured*, 42.

50  **by more than sixty thousand votes** See Howell Raines, "Legendary Campaign: Pepper vs. Smathers in '50," *New York Times*, February 24, 1983, https://www.nytimes.com/1983/02/24/us/legendary-campaign-pepper-vs-smathers-in-50.html.

51  **Harry Truman could not get** In fact, the segregationist caucus protested Truman's 1948 Democratic convention, seceding into its own States' Rights Democratic Party, whose platform railed against "centralized bureaucratic government." See Platform of the States Rights Democratic Party (August 14, 1948), American Presidency Project, University of California at Santa Barbara, https://www.presidency.ucsb.edu/node/273454.

51  **"If national health insurance"** Quadagno, *One Nation, Uninsured*, 34.

51  **Johnson's Congress conceded** Medicaid was built on Kerr-Mills, an American Medical Association–backed 1960 block grant program that Congress passed in part to blunt momentum on a universal medical benefit that was introduced by Rep. Aime Forand (D-RI) and opposed by southern Democrats. "By linking Medicaid eligibility to AFDC, the federal government left most decision-making power vested in the hands of states. . . . The states set the terms of entry into Medicaid, allowing them to select the benefits that would be offered, decree how much health care providers would be compensated, and (discriminatorily) determine which groups would be covered." Jamila Michener, *Fragmented Democracy: Medicaid, Federalism, and Unequal Politics* (New York: Cambridge University Press, 2018), 69–70.

51  **all Americans living in poverty by 1970** Charles N. Oberg and Cynthia Longseth Polich, "Medicaid: Entering the Third Decade," *Health Affairs* (Fall 1988): 91.

51  **the Robert Wood Johnson Foundation estimated** Oberg and Polich, "Medicaid," 90. After growing in its first decade, the program suffered from deliberate cutbacks in the "period of retrenchment" from 1976

to 1985. Growing poverty rates, particularly among children, and tighter eligibility rules that varied across the states limited the program's effectiveness. Reagan's 1981 budget cuts made 442,000 working poor families ineligible for Medicaid. Oberg and Polich, "Medicaid," 81.

52    **number of uninsured skyrocketed** The uninsured rate among the nonelderly population shot up from 12 to 17.2 percent over the course of the 1980s. "Uninsured Rate Among the Nonelderly Population, 1972–2018," Charts & Slides, KFF, August 28, 2018, https://www.kff .org/uninsured/slide/uninsured-rate-among-the-nonelderly -population-1972-2018. See also Katharine R. Levit, Gary L. Olin, and Suzanne W. Letsch, "Americans' Health Insurance Coverage, 1980–91," *Health Care Financing Review* 14, no. 1 (Fall 1992): 31–57, https:// www.ncbi.nlm.nih.gov/pmc/articles/PMC4193314.

52    **record turnout among black voters** Two-thirds of eligible black voters voted in 2008 and in 2012. President Obama won 80 percent of the votes of Americans of color and 39 percent of white voters in 2008. Paul Taylor, "The Growing Electoral Clout of Blacks Is Driven by Turnout, Not Demographics," Pew Social & Demographic Trends, Pew Research Center, December 26, 2012, p. 2, https://www .pewresearch.org/wp-content/uploads/sites/3/2013/01/2012_Black _Voter_Project_revised_1-9.pdf.

52    **federal subsidies for moderate- to middle-income purchasers** "In 2020, the subsidy range in the continental U.S. is from $12,490 for an individual and $25,750 for a family of four at 100% FPL, to $49,960 for an individual and $103,000 for a family of four at 400% FPL." "Explaining Health Care Reform: Questions About Health Insurance Subsidies," Health Reform, KFF, January 16, 2020, https://www.kff .org/health-reform/issue-brief/explaining-health-care-reform -questions-about-health.

52    **a federal "public option"** Robert Pear and Jackie Calmes, "Senators Reject Pair of Public Option Proposals," *New York Times,* September 29, 2009, https://www.nytimes.com/2009/09/30/health/policy/ 30health.html. A public option would offer people the choice of federal, not-for-profit insurance coverage, in competition with and at a lower price than private insurance options in the ACA marketplace. It would be a voluntary public plan aimed at demonstrating through market choice the advantages of public insurance, rather than a single-payer plan such as Medicare for All, which would replace the private insurance market. See Helen A. Halpin and Peter Harbage, "The Origins and Demise of the Public Option," *Health Affairs* 29, no. 6 (June 2010), https://doi.org/10.1377/hlthaff.2010.0363.

52    **collective bargaining to lower** Brett Norman and Sarah Karlin-

Smith, "The One that Got Away: Obamacare and the Drug Industry," *Politico*, July 13, 2016, https://www.politico.com/story/2016/07/obamacare-prescription-drugs-pharma-225444.

52    **insurer never made it to a vote** The public option continued to be a large part of the debate through the fall of 2009: "Senate Democrats were engaged in a highly contentious debate throughout the fall of 2009, and the political life of the public option changed almost daily. The debate reached a critical impasse in November 2009, when Sen. Joseph Lieberman (I-CT), who usually caucuses with the Democrats, threatened to filibuster the Senate bill if it included a public option." Halpin and Harbage, "The Origins and Demise." See also Max Fisher, "Why Obama Dropped the Public Option," *The Atlantic*, February 24, 2010, https://www.theatlantic.com/politics/archive/2010/02/why-obama-dropped-the-public-option/346546. The Sanders bill on Medicare for All didn't go further than being introduced. See American Health Security Act of 2009, 111th Cong., § 703 (2009–2010), https://www.congress.gov/bill/111th-congress/senate-bill/703. For more on the introduction of the bill and its contents, see "Sen. Bernie Sanders Introduces Single Payer Bill," PNHP, March 26, 2009, https://pnhp.org/news/sen-bernie-sanders-introduces-single-payer-bill; also Bernie Sanders, "Floor Speech on Single-Payer Amendment," December 16, 2009, https://www.sanders.senate.gov/newsroom/press-releases/floor-speech-on-single-payer-amendment.

52    **White support remained under 40 percent** According to the Kaiser Family Foundation's regular ACA tracking poll, the Obama-era high point of white approval was soon after the bill became law, in July 2010; the low point was December 2013, at just 26 percent approval, and it did not climb to above 40 percent until after Obama left office. As of July 2020, it has never reached majority white support. "KFF Health Tracking Poll: The Public's Views on the ACA," Health Reform, KFF, September 10, 2020, https://www.kff.org/interactive/kff-health-tracking-poll-the-publics-views-on-the-aca/#?total&response=Favorable&group=Race%2520%252F%2520Ethnicity::White.

52    **racial resentment among white people spiked** See Donald R. Kinder and Allison Dale-Riddle, *The End of Race? Obama, 2008, and Racial Politics in America* (New Haven, CT: Yale University Press, 2011); and Michael Tesler and David O. Sears, *Obama's Race: The 2008 Election and the Dream of a Post-Racial America* (Chicago: University of Chicago Press, 2010).

53    **"Racial attitudes"** Deborah Baum, "Michael Tesler," *News from Brown*, Brown University, https://news.brown.edu/new-faculty/social-sciences/michael-tesler.

53    **"The experiments"** Other research has found that because Hillary
      Clinton was most strongly associated with President Clinton's pro-
      posal, gendered attitudes played a role in public opinion in the 1990s.
      See Nicholas J. G. Winter, *Dangerous Frames: How Ideas About Race
      and Gender Shape Public Opinion* (Chicago: University of Chicago
      Press, 2008).

53    **"In sum"** Knowles et al., "Racial Prejudice Predicts," 420.

53    **"This is a civil rights bill"** Kate Conway, "Limbaugh Declares
      Health Care Reform 'a Civil Rights Bill' and 'Reparations,'" Media
      Matters for America, February 22, 2010, https://www.mediamatters
      .org/rush-limbaugh/limbaugh-declares-health-care-reform-civil
      -rights-bill-and-reparations. The "un-American" line of attack from
      the Truman days remained salient as well. Benjamin Knoll and Jordan
      Shewmaker also found that the healthcare reform battle activated
      "the perception that a traditional American culture and way of life
      needs to be protected against foreign influence." The more nativist
      fears a person held, the greater the likelihood that he would oppose
      ensuring every American affordable health insurance. The reason?
      The authors blamed political elites who primed nativist thinking by
      referring to the proposal as "un-American" and "socialist." They also
      noted that just as Obama being black made Obamacare less popular
      with racially resentful whites, the misperception that Obama was for-
      eign contributed to nativist whites rejecting his healthcare plan. Ben-
      jamin Knoll and Jordan Shewmaker, "Research Suggests Nativism
      Drives Opposition to Health Care Reform," *HuffPost Politics*, Febru-
      ary 19, 2014, https://www.huffpost.com/entry/research-suggests
      -nativis_b_4804267?utm_source=feedburner.

53    **120 rural hospitals have closed** The Chartis Center for Rural Health,
      "The Rural Health Safety Net Under Pressure: Rural Hospital Vulner-
      ability," February 2020, p. 1, https://www.chartis.com/forum/
      insight/the-rural-health-safety-net-under-pressure-rural-hospital
      -vulnerability/.

53    **One thing that all of the states** Chartis Center, "Rural Health Safety
      Net," 2.

54    **The state has half the hospitals** "Twenty-Five Things to Know
      About Texas Rural Hospitals," PDF, Texas Organization of Rural &
      Community Hospitals (TORCH), February 2017, https://capitol.texas
      .gov/tlodocs/85R/handouts/C2102017030910301/be43111d-e0d4
      -4de3-bc7d-935d111daced.pdf.

54    **In 2013, an eighteen-month-old died** "Loss of East Texas Town's
      Hospital Hits Home After Toddler Chokes, Dies," *Dallas Morning
      News*, September 28, 2013, https://www.dallasnews.com/news/

investigations/2013/09/29/loss-of-east-texas-towns-hospital-hits
-home-after-toddler-chokes-dies.

55 **1.5 million Texas citizens** The Kaiser Family Foundation estimated
that expansion would reach 1.5 million Texans, or 30 percent of the
currently estimated nonelderly uninsured. "Who Could Medicaid
Reach with Expansion in Texas," fact sheet, KFF, n.d., http://files.kff
.org/attachment/fact-sheet-medicaid-expansion-TX.

55 **mostly white and male** "In a state where people of color are in the
majority, almost two out of every three lawmakers are white. And not
even a quarter of them are women." Only 4 percent of Republicans in
both chambers identify as nonwhite. Alexa Ura and Darla Cameron,
"In Increasingly Diverse Texas, the Legislature Remains Mostly
White and Male," *Texas Tribune,* January 10, 2019, https://apps
.texastribune.org/features/2019/texas-lawmakers-legislature
-demographics.

55 **the state provides their health insurance** See "Health Benefits for
Active Employees," Employees Retirement System of Texas, n.d.,
https://ers.texas.gov/Active-Employees/Health-Benefits.

55 **don't offer coverage** Forty percent of firms with "many" low-wage
workers, measured as below $22,000 annually, offered healthcare ben-
efits to employees in the 2008 KFF survey. This may have overrepresented how many low-wage workers were offered benefits, given that
many are contractors and not employees at all. See *Employer Health
Benefits: 2008 Annual Survey,* Kaiser Family Foundation and Health
Research & Educational Trust, 2008, https://www.kff.org/wp
-content/uploads/2013/04/7790.pdf.

55 **an average of $4,000 a year** "Health Care Costs and Election 2008,"
Health Costs, KFF, October 14, 2008, https://www.kff.org/health
-costs/issue-brief/health-care-costs-and-election-2008/#back4.

55 **$8,532 for a family of three** Rachel Garfield, Kendal Orgera, and An-
thony Damico, "The Coverage Gap: Uninsured Poor Adults in States
that Do Not Expand Medicaid," Medicaid, KFF, January 14, 2020,
https://www.kff.org/medicaid/issue-brief/the-coverage-gap
-uninsured-poor-adults-in-states-that-do-not-expand-medicaid.

56 **these are the paltry annual amounts** These states cap eligibility for
parents at between 17 percent (Texas, though it uses a specific formula
based on monthly dollar amounts) and 35 percent (Georgia) of the
federal poverty level for a parent in a family of three, which is $21,270
in 2020. There are higher thresholds for pregnant women as required
by federal law. See "Medicaid Income Eligibility Limits for Adults as
a Percent of the Federal Poverty Level," State Health Facts, KFF, January 1, 2020, https://www.kff.org/health-reform/state-indicator/

medicaid-income-eligibility-limits-for-adults-as-a-percent-of-the
-federal-poverty.

56    **adults without children** Garfield et al., "The Coverage Gap."

56    **almost all the states of the former Confederacy** See "Status of State
Action on the Medicaid Expansion Decision," State Health Facts, KFF,
August 17, 2020, https://www.kff.org/health-reform/state-indicator/
state-activity-around-expanding-medicaid-under-the-affordable-care
-act/?currentTimeframe=0&sortModel=%7B%22colId%22:%22
Location%22,%22sort%22:%22asc%22%7D. See also Samantha Artiga, Anthony Damico, and Rachel Garfield, "The Impact of the
Coverage Gap for Adults in States Not Expanding Medicaid by Race
and Ethnicity," Racial Equity and Health Policy, KFF, October 26,
2015, https://www.kff.org/disparities-policy/issue-brief/the-impact
-of-the-coverage-gap-in-states-not-expanding-medicaid-by-race-and
-ethnicity.

56    **still the largest share** Artiga, Damico, and Garfield, "The Impact of
the Coverage Gap."

56    **4.4 million working Americans** "Who Could Get Covered Under
Medicaid Expansion? State Fact Sheets," Medicaid, KFF, January 23,
2020, https://www.kff.org/medicaid/fact-sheet/uninsured-adults-in
-states-that-did-not-expand-who-would-become-eligible-for-medicaid
-under-expansion.

57    **"What we've experienced"** Noam N. Levey, "Racial Gaps in Healthcare Still Cost Black Lives, Though Obamacare Narrowed Them," *Los
Angeles Times,* May 11, 2020, https://www.latimes.com/politics/
story/2020-05-11/obamacare-impact-on-civil-rights.

57    **polled higher than Obamacare** In February 2020, 61 percent of people in states that had not expanded Medicaid supported expansion, for
example, whereas ACA popularity has never topped 55 percent and
was less than 50 percent until 2017. See, respectively, Figure 4 in
"Data Note: 5 Charts About Public Opinion on Medicaid," Polling,
KFF, February 28, 2020, https://www.kff.org/medicaid/poll-finding/
data-note-5-charts-about-public-opinion-on-medicaid; and "KFF
Health Tracking Poll: The Public's Views on the ACA," Health Reform, KFF, updated September 10, 2020, https://www.kff.org/
interactive/kff-health-tracking-poll-the-publics-views-on-the-aca.

57    **Medicaid expansion had robust support** Colleen M. Grogan and
Sunggeun (Ethan) Park, "The Racial Divide in State Medicaid Ex-
pansions," *Journal of Health Politics, Policy and Law* 42, no. 3 (June
2017): 542.

57    **Across the country, state-level support** Grogan and Park, "The Racial Divide," p. 552.

57    **"as the percent"** Grogan and Park, "The Racial Divide," p. 553.

58    **majority-people-of-color state** "Quick Facts: Texas," U.S. Census Bureau, https://www.census.gov/quickfacts/TX.

58    **two-thirds white and three-quarters male** Ura and Cameron, "In Increasingly Diverse Texas."

58    **one out of every five** "Health Insurance Coverage of Nonelderly 0-64 (2018)," State Health Facts, KFF, n.d., https://www.kff.org/other/state-indicator/nonelderly-0-64/?currentTimeframe=0&selectedRows=%7B%22states%22:%7B%22texas%22:%7B%7D%7D%7D&sortModel=%7B%22colId%22:%22Location%22,%22sort%22:%22asc%22%7D.

58    **highest uninsured rate for families** John S. Kiernan, "2020's State Uninsured Rates," *Wallet* (blog), WalletHub, October 10, 2019, https://wallethub.com/edu/uninsured-rates-by-state/4800.

58    **Texans without any healthcare coverage** "Distribution of the Nonelderly Uninsured by Race/Ethnicity (2018)," State Health Facts, KFF, n.d., https://www.kff.org/uninsured/state-indicator/distribution-by-raceethnicity-2/?dataView=1&currentTimeframe=0&selectedRows=%7B%22states%22:%7B%22texas%22:%7B%7D%7D%7D&sortModel=%7B%22colId%22:%22Location%22,%22sort%22:%22asc%22%7D.

60    **"And he would just say"** On Abbott's strategy, see Dan Frosch and Jacob Gershman, "Abbott's Strategy in Texas: 44 Lawsuits, One Opponent: Obama Administration," *Wall Street Journal*, June 24, 2016, https://www.wsj.com/articles/abbotts-strategy-in-texas-44-lawsuits-one-opponent-obama-administration-1466778976.

62    **He founded the country's premier** See "Our History" and "WIC (Women, Infants and Children)," Food Research & Action Center (FRAC), n.d., https://frac.org/about/our-history and https://frac.org/programs/wic-women-infants-children.

64    **Once a northern Tea Party hotbed** The rural areas of Minnesota were home to many Tea Party members, and one of its leaders, Michele Bachmann, also hailed from the state. See MPR News Staff, "Reflecting on the Tea Party's Legacy in Minnesota," MPR News, December 8, 2016, https://www.mprnews.org/story/2016/12/08/reflecting-on-the-tea-partys-legacy-in-mn.

64    **growing Latinx and African Muslim population** Capitol Preservation Commission Subcommittee on Art, "Minnesota Now, Then, When . . . An Overview of Demographic Change," Minnesota State Demographic Center, April 2015, https://mn.gov/admin/assets/2015-04-06-overview-MN-demographic-changes_tcm36-74549.pdf.

64    **adopted the Greater Than Fear messaging** Jacob Swenson-Lengyel,

"Building Narrative Infrastructure in Minnesota," Narrative Initiative, August 2019, https://narrativeinitiative.org/resource/building-narrative-infrastructure-in-minnesota.

65  **"honest investments"** Rep. Melissa Hortman, "Minnesota House DFL Releases Framework for Minnesota Values Budget," Legislative News and Views, Minnesota House of Representatives website, March 25, 2019, https://www.house.leg.state.mn.us/members/profile/news/12266/24930.

## Chapter Four: Ignoring the Canary

68  **class-action predatory lending lawsuit** *Tomlin v. Dylan Mortgage, Inc.*, 2000 NCBC 9, https://www.nccourts.gov/assets/documents/opinions/2000%20NCBC%209.pdf?BFsAGywldLKzDs2foGqANXYmy6hbwgZr. Details in the pages come from the complaint, on file with the author, and the opinion.

69  **the majority of subprime loans** The 2007 analysis of the $2.5 trillion in subprime loans since 2000 showed that in 2000, the share of subprime loan holders with prime credit scores was 41 percent; by 2005, 55 percent; by 2006, 61 percent. Rick Brooks and Ruth Simon, "Subprime Debacle Traps Even Very Credit-Worthy; As Housing Boomed, Industry Pushed Loans to a Broader Market," *Wall Street Journal*, December 3, 2007, https://www.wsj.com/articles/SB119662974358911035.

70  **The public policy justification** See, e.g., U.S. Department of Housing and Urban Development, *Subprime Markets, the Role of GSEs, and Risk-Based Pricing*, March 2002, "Section 2: What Is Subprime Lending and Who Does it Serve," p. 4, https://www.huduser.gov/publications/pdf/subprime.pdf.

70  **marketed to existing homeowners** "Roughly two-thirds of subprime loans in the early 2000s were made not to new home purchasers but to individuals who already owned their homes and were refinancing them," Justin P. Steil, Len Albright, Jacob S. Rugh, and Douglas S. Massey, "The Social Structure of Mortgage Discrimination," *Housing Studies* 33, no. 5 (2018): 759–76, https://doi.org/10.1080/02673037.2017.1390076.

70  **loans issued in majority-black neighborhoods** Randall M. Scheessele, "Black and White Disparities in Subprime Mortgage Refinance Lending," U.S. Department of Housing and Urban Development, p. 3, https://www.huduser.gov/Publications/pdf/workpapr14.pdf.

70  **three times as likely as whites** Algernon Austin, "A Good Credit Score Did Not Protect Latino and Black Borrowers," Economic Policy

Institute, January 19, 2012, http://www.epi.org/publication/latino
-black-borrowers-high-rate-subprime-mortgages. See also Jacob W.
Faber, "Racial Dynamics of Subprime Mortgage Lending at the
Peak," Housing Policy Debate, 2013, 23:2, 328–49, https://doi.org/10
.1080/10511482.2013.771788; William P. Apgar Jr., Christopher E.
Herbert, and Priti Mathur, "Risk or Race: An Assessment of Subprime
Lending Patterns in Nine Metropolitan Areas," Office of Policy De-
velopment and Research, U.S. Department of Housing and Urban
Development, August 2009, p. 2, https://www.huduser.gov/portal/
publications/pdf/risk_race_2011.pdf.

70    **A 2014 review of the pre-crash mortgage market** Patrick Bayer,
Fernando Ferreira, and Stephen L. Ross, "What Drives Racial and
Ethnic Differences in High-Cost Mortgages? The Role of High-Risk
Lenders," *The Review of Financial Studies* 31, no. 1 (January 1, 2018):
175–205, https://doi.org/10.1093/rfs/hhx035.

74    **$19.2 trillion in lost household** "The Financial Crisis Response in
Charts," U.S. Department of the Treasury, April 2012, https://www
.treasury.gov/resource-center/data-chart-center/Documents/
20120413_FinancialCrisisResponse.pdf.

74    **four hundred thousand fewer homeowners** Alana Semuels, "The
Never-Ending Foreclosure," *The Atlantic*, December 1, 2017, https://
www.theatlantic.com/business/archive/2017/12/the-neverending
-foreclosure/547181.

74    **shrinking from 69 percent** "Homeownership Rates for the United
States (2017)," U.S. Census Bureau, at Economic Research, Federal Reserve Bank of St. Louis, September 21, 2020, https://fred.stlouisfed
.org/series/USHOWN.

74    **typical family in their prime years** William R. Emmons et al., "A
Lost Generation? Long-lasting Wealth Impacts of the Great Recession
on Young Families," in the Demographics of Wealth: 2018 Series,
Federal Reserve Bank of St. Louis, May 2018, pp. 6–17, https://www
.stlouisfed.org/~/media/Files/PDFs/HFS/essays/HFS_essay_2
_2018.pdf?la=en.

74    **5.6 million foreclosed homes** "United States Residential Foreclosure
Rates: Ten Years Later," CoreLogic, March 2017, https://www
.corelogic.com/research/foreclosure-report/national-foreclosure
-report-10-year.pdf.

75    **an estimated $2.2 trillion** "2013 Update: The Spillover Effects of
Foreclosures," Center for Responsible Lending, August 19, 2013,
https://www.responsiblelending.org/research-publication/2013
-spillover-costs-foreclosure.

75    **in Detroit, a surge** Corey Williams and Mike Householder, "Home

Demolitions in Detroit May Create New Problem: Lead-Tainted Dust," *Detroit Free Press,* July 20, 2018, https://www.freep.com/ story/news/local/michigan/detroit/2018/07/20/detroit-home -demolitions-lead-dust/805770002.

75   **One study identified home foreclosures** Jason N. Houle and Michael T. Light, "The Home Foreclosure Crisis and Rising Suicide Rates, 2005 to 2010," *American Journal of Public Health* 104, no. 6 (June 2014), https://www.ncbi.nlm.nih.gov/pmc/articles/PMC4062039.

75   **another found that the Great Recession** Claire Margerison-Zilko et al., "Health Impacts of the Great Recession: A Critical Review," *Current Epidemiology Reports* 3, no. 1 (February 2016): 81–91, https://doi.org/10.1007/s40471-016-0068-6.

75   **In 2017, an examination** Kenneth Shores and Matthew Steinberg, "The Impact of the Great Recession on Student Achievement: Evidence from Population Data," August 31, 2017, https://dx.doi.org/10 .2139/ssrn.3026151.

75   **8.7 million jobs were destroyed** "Chart Book: The Legacy of the Great Recession," Center on Budget and Policy Priorities, June 6, 2019, https://www.cbpp.org/research/economy/chart-book-the -legacy-of-the-great-recession.

77   **679,923 Americans to experience foreclosure** "United States Residential Foreclosure Rates," CoreLogic.

79   **The exclusion of free people of color** Lisa Rice, "An Examination of Civil Rights Issues with Respect to the Mortgage Crisis: The Effects of Predatory Lending on the Mortgage Crisis," U.S. Commission on Civil Rights Public Briefing, March 20, 2009, http://nationalfair housing.org/wp-content/uploads/2017/04/US-Commission-on-Civil -Rights-Statement-of-LR-on-Predatory-Lending-Final . . . -1.pdf.

80   **the birth of redlining** See "Introduction," Mapping Inequality: Redlining in New Deal America, https://dsl.richmond.edu/ panorama/redlining/#loc=8/35.648/-66.984&text=intro. See also Rothstein, *The Color of Law,* 63–65, 97, 108, 113. Assessment quotation from "Chicago, IL: D1 Description and Characteristics of Area," Mapping Inequality, https://dsl.richmond.edu/panorama/redlining/ #loc=9/41.946/-88.385&city=chicago-il&area=D1. The assessments incorporated judgments of Jewish, "Asiatic," and European immigrant residents' impact on neighborhood quality, as well. ("This is a very mixed district of congested appearance and changing character. The population is largely lower class Jewish, but there is at the present time a moderate infiltration of Polish families. The favorable influence of this population shift is minimized by threatening negro infiltration along the eastern edge.") "Chicago, IL: D28 Description and

Characteristics of Area," Mapping Inequality, https://dsl.richmond
.edu/panorama/redlining/#loc=9/41.946/-88.385&city=chicago-il&
area=D28.

81    **typical white family in America had** Author analysis of Survey of
Consumer Finances (SCF), Federal Reserve, 2016, https://www
.federalreserve.gov/econres/scfindex.htm.

81    **vast increase in home ownership** Historical Census of Housing Tables, U.S. Census Bureau, https://www.census.gov/housing/census/
data/ownerchar.html.

81    **fewer than 2 percent** Rice, "Examination of Civil Rights Issues," 6.
The 1.2 million black World War II veterans were largely excluded
from the GI Bill's benefits as well. Erin Blakemore, "How the GI Bill's
Promise Was Denied to a Million Black WWII Veterans," History
Channel, June 21, 2019, https://www.history.com/news/gi-bill-black
-wwii-veterans-benefits.

81    **it would take another twenty-four years** Richard Rothstein, "A
Comment on Bank of America/Countrywide's Discriminatory Mortgage Lending and Its Implications for Racial Segregation," Economic
Policy Institute, January 23, 2012, https://www.epi.org/publication/
bp335-boa-countrywide-discriminatory-lending.

82    **they owned nothing** Richard Rothstein, "How Government Policies
Cemented the Racism that Reigns in Baltimore," *The American Prospect*, April 29, 2015, http://prospect.org/article/how-government
-policies-cemented-racism-reigns-baltimore.

82    **These local groups were backed** "CRA: Community Reinvestment
Act and the Financial Modernization Movement," Leadership Conference on Civil Rights and Leadership Conference Education Fund,
p. 20, http://www.protectcivilrights.org/pdf/reports/healthy
_communities/cra_report_chapters.pdf.

82    **For example, a 1974 survey** "CRA: Community Reinvestment
Act," 20.

82    **In 1978, two of the earliest** The complaint in Brooklyn convinced
the FDIC to issue its first bank branch denial under the CRA and resulted in an agreement between the delinquent bank and local community groups for a $25 million investment in loans. "Building
Healthy Communities," Leadership Conference on Civil Rights, p. 34,
http://www.protectcivilrights.org/pdf/reports/healthy_communities/
cra_report_chapters.pdf; "Enforcing Anti-Redlining Policy Under the
Community Reinvestment Act," Federal Reserve Bank of San Francisco, 1982, https://www.frbsf.org/economic-research/files/82-2_19
-34.pdf.

83    **Congress declined to amend the law** *Marquette National Bank of*

*Minneapolis v. First of Omaha Service Corp.,* 439 U.S. 299 (1978). The ensuing wave of deregulation included revoking protections against exorbitant mortgage interest rates and government control over variable interest rates and "balloon" payments (mortgage bills that dramatically increase after a set period of time). Rice, "Examination of Civil Rights Issues," 7.

83    **produced the most profits, supplanting manufacturing** Heather McGhee and Tamara Draut, "Why We Need an Independent Consumer Protection Agency Now," Demos, n.d., http://www.demos.org/sites/default/files/publications/BRIEF_WhyWeNeed_CFPA_Demos.pdf.

83    **became the biggest spender in politics** Author calculations using Center for Responsive Politics Data 1990–1998. See generally "Financial/Insurance/Real Estate" Sector Profile, OpenSecrets, https://www.opensecrets.org/industries/indus.php?Ind=F.

83    **there was no single regulator** This was the insight that led Professor Elizabeth Warren to design the Consumer Financial Protection Bureau, which was created as part of the Dodd-Frank Wall Street Reform and Consumer Protection Law of 2010.

84    **Doris Dancy became a witness** All quotes from Memphis employees come from their declarations in the *U.S. District Court case City of Memphis and Shelby County v. Wells Fargo Bank et al.,* No. 09-2857-STA (W.D. Tenn. 2011), http://www.relmanlaw.com/docs/Declarations-Memphis.pdf.

86    **"My pay was based on commissions"** All quotes from Baltimore employees come from their declarations in the *U.S. District Court case Mayor and City Council of Baltimore v. Wells Fargo Bank et al.,* Civil Case No. JFM-08-62 (D. Md. 2011), http://www.relmanlaw.com/docs/Baltimore-Declarations.pdf.

87    **Countrywide Financial Corporation agreed** "Justice Department Reaches $335 Million Settlement to Resolve Allegations of Lending Discrimination by Countrywide Financial Corporation," press release, U.S. Department of Justice, December 21, 2011, https://www.justice.gov/opa/pr/justice-department-reaches-335-million-settlement-resolve-allegations-lending-discrimination.

87    **According to an analysis** "Justice Department Reaches $335 Million Settlement."

87    **eight times more likely** Jordan Weissmann, "Countrywide's Racist Lending Practices Were Fueled by Greed," *The Atlantic,* December 23, 2011, https://www.theatlantic.com/business/archive/2011/12/countrywides-racist-lending-practices-were-fueled-by-greed/250424.

87    **shrank the wealth of the median** Rothstein, "A Comment."

87    **officials took more than nine thousand** McGhee and Draut, "Why
      We Need."

88    **"the one entity"** National Commission on the Causes of the Financial
      and Economic Crisis in the United States, *Financial Crisis Inquiry Re-
      port*, 9.

88    **took no action at all** McGhee and Draut, "Why We Need."

88    **there was a blindness** In a 2005 speech, Federal Reserve chairman
      Alan Greenspan praised the lending industry's ability to "quite effi-
      ciently judge the risk posed by individual applicants and to price that
      risk appropriately." Federal Reserve Board, "Remarks by Chairman
      Alan Greenspan," April 8, 2005, https://www.federalreserve.gov/
      boarddocs/speeches/2005/20050408/default.htm; see also Kat Aaron,
      "Predatory Lending: A Decade of Warnings," Center for Public Integ-
      rity, updated May 19, 2014, https://publicintegrity.org/inequality
      -poverty-opportunity/predatory-lending-a-decade-of-warnings.

89    **From 1998 to 2006, the majority** NCRC, "CRA Myth and Fact," Na-
      tional Community Reinvestment Coalition, September 24, 2008,
      https://ncrc.org/cra-myth-and-fact-2.

89    THEY GAVE YOUR MORTGAGE Ann Coulter, "They Gave Your Mortgage
      to a Less Qualified Minority," September 24, 2008, http://www
      .anncoulter.com/columns/2008-09-24.html.

89    **"What does it mean when"** Jeff Jacoby, "Frank's Fingerprints Are All
      Over the Financial Crisis," *Boston Globe*, September 28, 2008, http://
      archive.boston.com/bostonglobe/editorial_opinion/oped/articles/
      2008/09/28/franks_fingerprints_are_all_over_the_financial_fiasco.

89    **"a no-win situation"** Jeff Jacoby, "How Government Makes Things
      Worse," *Boston Globe*, March 9, 2008, http://archive.boston.com/
      bostonglobe/editorial_opinion/oped/articles/2008/03/09/how
      _government_makes_things_worse.

89    **Michael Bloomberg told a Georgetown University audience** Matt
      Stevens, "Bloomberg Once Linked 2008 Crisis to End of Redlining
      Bias in Home Loans," *New York Times,* February 13, 2020, https://
      www.nytimes.com/2020/02/13/us/politics/michael-bloomberg
      -redlining.html. For video and full transcript, see "Urban Economics,"
      C-SPAN, September 17, 2008, at 18:30, https://www.c-span.org/
      video/?281174-1/urban-economics.

90    **conservatives were quick to blame** "Conservative critics have argued
      that the need to meet CRA requirements pushed lenders to loosen
      their lending standards leading up to the housing crisis, effectively in-
      centivizing the extension of credit to undeserved borrowers and fuel-
      ing an unsustainable housing bubble. Yet, the evidence does not
      support this narrative." Colin McArthur and Sarah Edelman, "Don't

Blame Federal Housing Programs for Wall Street's Recklessness,"
Center for American Progress, April 13, 2017, https://www.american
progress.org/issues/economy/reports/2017/04/13/430424/2008
-housing-crisis/.

90    **"some portion of the problem"** Ronald Utt, "The Subprime Mortgage Market Collapse: A Primer on the Causes and Possible Solutions," Heritage Foundation, April 22, 2008, https://www.aei.org/
articles/a-crisis-caused-by-housing-policies-not-lack-of-regulation/.

90    **Calling that conclusion** Peter J. Wallison, "A Crisis Caused by Housing Policies, Not Lack of Regulation," American Enterprise Institute,
October 30, 2017, http://www.aei.org/publication/a-crisis-caused-by
-housing-policies-not-lack-of-regulation.

90    **And so many pundits blamed** National Commission on the Causes of
the Financial and Economic Crisis in the United States, *Financial Crisis Inquiry Report,* 219–21, xxvii.

91    **a man named Roland Arnall** Bethany McLean, "The Man that Got
Away," *Slate,* June 29, 2011, https://slate.com/business/2011/06/
subprime-prosecutions-why-the-government-hunts-small-game.html.

91    **"the recovery that we got"** "Median net worth fell about 30 percent
for all groups during the Great Recession. However, for black and Hispanic families, net worth continued to fall an additional 20 percent in
the 2010–13 period, while white families' net worth was essentially
unchanged." Lisa J. Dettling, Joanne W. Hsu, Lindsay Jacobs, Kevin B.
Moore, and Jeffrey P. Thompson, "Recent Trends in Wealth-Holding
by Race and Ethnicity: Evidence from the Survey of Consumer Finances," Federal Reserve Board of Governors, September 27, 2017,
https://www.federalreserve.gov/econres/notes/feds-notes/
recent-trends-in-wealth-holding-by-race-and-ethnicity-evidence-
from-the-survey-of-consumer-finances-20170927.htm; for a critical assessment of the Obama Administration foreclosure prevention policies, see David Dayden, "Obama Failed to Mitigate America's
Foreclosure Crisis," *The Atlantic,* December 14, 2016, https://www
.theatlantic.com/politics/archive/2016/12/obamas-failure-to
-mitigate-americas-foreclosure-crisis/510485/.

92    **In a study conducted** Matthew D. Luttig, Christopher M. Federico,
and Howard Levine, "Supporters and Opponents of Donald Trump
Respond Differently to Racial Cues: An Experimental Analysis," *Research and Politics* (October–December 2017): 1–8, https://doi.org/10
.1177/2053168017737411.

92    **the secret was mortgage *securitization*** Jacob S. Rugh and Douglas S. Massey, "Racial Segregation and the American Foreclosure Crisis," *American Sociological Review* 75, no. 5 (October 2010): 630,

https://doi.org/10.1177/0003122410380868; and James Lardner, "Beyond the Mortgage Meltdown: Addressing the Current Crisis, Avoiding a Future Catastrophe," Demos, 2008, p. 19, https://www.demos.org/sites/default/files/publications/Beyond%20the%20Mortgage%20Meltdown.pdf.

92    **a lighthearted acronym** National Commission on the Causes of the Financial and Economic Crisis in the United States, *Financial Crisis Inquiry Report*, 8.

93    **The average FICO credit score** National Commission on the Causes of the Financial and Economic Crisis in the United States, *Financial Crisis Inquiry Report*, 107.

93    **More than half of the $2.5 trillion** Brooks and Simon, "Subprime Debacle Traps Even Very Credit-Worthy."

94    **more than 20 percent** Mara der Hovanesian, "Nightmare Mortgages," *Bloomberg News*, September 11, 2006, https://www.bloomberg.com/news/articles/2006-09-10/nightmare-mortgages.

94    **fall by over 30 percent** Michele Lerner, "10 Years Later: How the Housing Market Has Changed Since the Crash," *Washington Post*, October 4, 2018, https://www.washingtonpost.com/news/business/wp/2018/10/04/feature/10-years-later-how-the-housing-market-has-changed-since-the-crash/?utm_term=.b5da5edc779a.

96    **over two-thirds will probably never own** Laura Kusisto, "Many Who Lost Homes to Foreclosure in Last Decade Won't Return," *Wall Street Journal*, April 20, 2015, https://www.wsj.com/articles/many-who-lost-homes-to-foreclosure-in-last-decade-wont-return-nar-1429548640.

97    **the brothers Lehman, slave owners** Joseph Wechsberg, *The Merchant Bankers* (Boston: Little, Brown, 1966), 297–300.

98    **would not have existed without it** Dozens of other U.S. financial companies, some extinct but others still operating, had roots in the slave trade. New York Life, for example, sold life insurance for enslaved people: to benefit not the slaves' families, but their owners. A few companies, like JPMorgan Chase, Aetna, and Wachovia (a predecessor to Wells Fargo), have apologized for their role. Others, like AIG subsidiary US Life, refuse to address their historic ties to slavery. Rachel L. Swarns, "Insurance Policies on Slaves: New York Life's Complicated Past," *New York Times*, December 18, 2016, https://www.nytimes.com/2016/12/18/us/insurance-policies-on-slaves-new-york-lifes-complicated-past.html.

98    **the highest returns in its history** Nick L. Lioudis, "The Collapse of Lehman Brothers: A Case Study," *Investopedia*, updated November 26, 2019, https://www.investopedia.com/articles/economics/09/lehman-brothers-collapse.asp.

98   **Lehman's CFO asserted boldly** Lioudis, "The Collapse of Lehman Brothers."

98   **underwrite more mortgage-backed securities** Lioudis, "The Collapse of Lehman Brothers."

99   **more borrowers had their just resolution** The Tomlins' subprime loan came early in the development of the nonbank lender market, and Chase (later HomeGold) failed to do what most subprime lenders would learn to do—structure the loan to avoid the triggers of the 1994 HOEPA antipredatory lending law. According to Mal Maynard, because the class action included many loans that were illegal under HOEPA, there was a greater chance of prevailing in court. HOEPA was unable to prevent the predatory mortgage crisis of the mid-1990s and 2000s because of numerous loopholes. For more on HOEPA's limitations, see Elizabeth Renuart, "Testimony Before the Board of Governors of the Federal Reserve Regarding Home Equity Lending and HOEPA," August 4, 2000, https://www.nclc.org/images/pdf/foreclosure_mortgage/archive/hoepa_f1.pdf.

## Chapter Five: No One Fights Alone

I have chosen to change the names of Nissan workers at the worker center for their protection. Chip Wells's story has been made public in the media, so his name appears unchanged.

103   **On August 4, 2017, a group of workers** Noam Scheiber, "Racially Charged Nissan Vote Is a Test for U.A.W. in the South," *New York Times,* August 2, 2017, https://www.nytimes.com/2017/08/02/business/economy/nissan-united-auto-workers-mississippi.html; Noam Scheiber, "Nissan Workers in Mississippi Reject Union Bid by U.A.W.," *New York Times,* August 5, 2017, https://www.nytimes.com/2017/08/05/business/nissan-united-auto-workers-union.html.

106   **full-time "temps" for more than five years** Jeff Amy, "Former Contract Workers Key in Canton Nissan Union Vote," *Clarion Ledger,* July 25, 2017, http://www.clarionledger.com/story/business/2017/07/25/former-contract-workers-key-canton-nissan-union-vote/507770001. See also Scott Tong, "How Temp Workers Became the Norm in America," *Marketplace,* November 25, 2018, https://www.marketplace.org/2018/11/15/how-great-recession-helped-normalize-use-temp-workers.

107   **as high as 40 percent** "When an Election Is Neither Free Nor Fair: Nissan and the 2017 Union Election in Mississippi," UAW Briefing Paper, October 25, 2017, p. 2, https://uaw.org/wp-content/uploads/2017/09/Nissan-Report-3.pdf.

109     **as threats to their livelihood** See, for example, Jacqueline Jones, *American Work: Four Centuries of Black and White Labor* (New York: W. W. Norton, 1998).

109     **stratification only helped the employer** David Roediger writes, "As late as 1907 the pioneering labor economist John R. Commons regarded not scientific management but 'playing one race against the other' as the only 'symptom of originality' in US management." *Working Toward Whiteness: How America's Immigrants Became White* (New York: Basic Books, 2005), 72–73.

109     **questionable categories of "bankers, land speculators"** "Such men (the gender was assumed) either preyed on human weaknesses or made a lucrative income without having to work very hard for it. Certainly no sweat begrimed their well-fed countenances." Michael Kazin, *The Populist Persuasion* (Ithaca, NY: Cornell University Press, 1995), 35.

109     **"Why should working men"** *Journal of United Labor,* Washington, D.C., August 15, 1880.

109     **journalist in 1886 Charleston** Philip S. Foner, "The Knights of Labor," *The Journal of Negro History* 53, no. 1 (January 1968): 70.

109     **"When everything else"** *John Swinton's Paper,* May 16, 1886, quoted in Foner, "The Knights of Labor," 70.

110     **"It is generally considered"** "Colored Knight Ferrell, Race Prejudice Aroused in Richmond; The Knights Condemned for Abusing Southern Hospitality," *New York Times,* October 7, 1886.

110     **estimated one-third to one-half** Philip S. Foner, *Organized Labor and the Black Worker, 1619–1973* (New York: Picador, 1974), 49.

110     **reign lasted only a decade** Alana Semuels, " 'Segregation Had to Be Invented,' " *The Atlantic,* February 17, 2017.

110     **essentially militarized** "But after 1877 American labor relations were the most violent in the Western world with the exception of Russia. It is one of those superficial paradoxes of history that the most democratic and the most despotic countries in the Western world would have the most violent labor clashes. The strongly held American belief in the right of business owners to have complete control over their property, along with business dominance of both political parties and a history of violence in dealing with Native Americans and slaves, not to mention the horrendous casualty rate in the Civil War, made the pitched labor battles seem as normal and expectable to most Americans as they were to Russians with their totally different history. Between 1877 and 1900, American presidents sent the U.S. Army into 11 strikes, governors mobilized the National Guard in somewhere between 118 and 160 labor disputes," G. William Domhoff, "The Rise

and Fall of Labor Unions in the U.S.: From the 1830s until 2012," *Power in America, Who Rules America?*, http://whorulesamerica.net/power/history_of_labor_unions.html.

110    **to exclude black workers** For decades, craft unions had excluded black workers despite the official policy of both the National Labor Union and the AFL being of nondiscrimination. Isaac Myers, a ship caulker from Baltimore, created an alternative to the National Labor Union, the Colored National Labor Union. Frederick Douglass became the president of the CNLU in 1872. See Jones, *American Work*, 295; and "A House Divided: African American Workers Struggle Against Segregation," Unions Making History in America, University of Maryland Libraries, https://www.lib.umd.edu/unions/social/african -americans-rights.

110    **In the 1920s, the leaders** See Roediger, *Working Toward Whiteness*, 78–82.

110    **as synonymous with strike breakers** Warren C. Whatley, "African-American Strikebreaking from the Civil War to the New Deal," *Social Science History* 17, no. 4 (1993): 525–58.

111    **explicit commitment to interracial unity** Robert H. Zieger, *The CIO, 1935–1955* (Chapel Hill: University of North Carolina Press, 1997), 83–84.

111    **"Probably the greatest"** W.E.B. Du Bois, "Race Relations in the United States, 1917–1947," *Phylon* IX (Third Quarter 1948): 234–47, quoted in Michael Goldfield, "Race and the CIO: The Possibilities for Racial Egalitarianism during the 1930s and 1940s," *International Labor and Working-Class History* 44 (Fall 1993): 1–32. Du Bois also wrote, however, of the realities of white racial programming, even among union workers: "The white laborer has been trained to dislike and fear black labor; to regard the Negro as an unfair competitor, able and willing to degrade the price of labor; and even if the Negro prove a good union man, his treatment as an equal would involve equal status, which the white laborer through his long cultural training bitterly resents as a degradation of his own status. Under these circumstances the American Negro faces in the current labor movement, especially in the A F of L and also even in the CIO, the current racial patterns of America." *Dusk of Dawn* (1940; New York: Oxford University Press, 2014), 104.

111    **reaching a high-water mark** Josh Bivens et al., "How Today's Unions Help Working People," Economic Policy Institute, August 24, 2017, https://www.epi.org/publication/how-todays-unions-help-working -people-giving-workers-the-power-to-improve-their-jobs-and-unrig -the-economy.

111    **one out of every three workers** Bivens et al., "How Today's
       Unions," 72.

112    **classified as "low-wage"** "More than 53 million people—44% of all
       workers aged 18–64—are low-wage workers by our criteria. They earn
       median hourly wages of $10.22 and median annual earnings of
       $17,950." Martha Ross and Nicole Bateman, "Meet the Low-Wage
       Workforce," Metropolitan Policy Program, Brookings Institution, No-
       vember 2019, https://www.brookings.edu/wp-content/uploads/
       2019/11/201911_Brookings-Metro_low-wage-workforce_Ross
       -Bateman.pdf.

112    **Less than half** "Percent of Private Sector Establishments that
       Offer Health Insurance to Employees (2019)," State Health Facts,
       KFF, n.d., https://www.kff.org/other/state-indicator/percent-of-firms
       -offering-coverage/?currentTimeframe=0&selectedRows=%7B
       %22wrapups%22:%7B%22united-states%22:%7B%7D%7D%7D&
       sortModel=%7B%22colId%22:%22Location%22,%22sort%22:
       %22asc%22%7D.

112    **Only 12 percent** "How Many Workers Participate in Workplace Re-
       tirement Plans?" Pension Rights Center, July 15, 2019, http://www
       .pensionrights.org/publications/statistic/how-many-american
       -workers-participate-workplace-retirement-plans.

112    **1950s peak** See Figure 1 in David Madland and Malkie Wall, "The
       Middle Class Continues to Struggle as Union Density Remains Low,"
       Center for American Progress Action Fund, September 10, 2019,
       https://www.americanprogressaction.org/issues/economy/news/
       2019/09/10/175024/middle-class-continues-struggle-union-density
       -remains-low.

112    **one out of every sixteen** Bureau of Labor Statistics, "Union Mem-
       bers—2019," news release, U.S. Department of Labor, January 22,
       2020, https://www.bls.gov/news.release/pdf/union2.pdf. See Table 3:
       The union membership rate of public-sector workers (33.6 percent)
       continued to be more than five times higher than the rate of private-
       sector workers (6.2 percent).

112    **has directly tracked the share** Henry Farber et al., "Unions and In-
       equality Over the Twentieth Century: New Evidence from Survey
       Data," Working Paper 24587, National Bureau of Economic Research,
       May 2018, http://www.nber.org/papers/w24587.

112    **to the richest Americans** Juliana Menasce Horowitz, Ruth Igielnik,
       and Rakesh Kochhar, "Trends in Income and Wealth Inequality," Pew
       Research Center, January 9, 2020, https://www.pewsocialtrends.org/
       2020/01/09/trends-in-income-and-wealth-inequality.

112    **increased in step** "As Unions Decline, Inequality Becomes More Ex-

treme," chart, in "Income Inequality in the United States," Inequality
.Org, Institute for Policy Studies, n.d., https://inequality.org/facts/
income-inequality/#ceo-worker-pay-gaps.

112 **over 13 percent higher wages** Bivens et al., "How Today's Unions,"
29n20.

112 **In Houston in 2006** Steven Greenhouse, "Janitors' Union, Recently
Organized, Strikes in Houston," *New York Times,* November 3, 2006,
https://www.nytimes.com/2006/11/03/us/03labor.html; Steven
Greenhouse, "Cleaning Companies in Accord with Striking Houston
Janitors," *New York Times,* November 3, 2006, https://www.nytimes
.com/2006/11/21/us/21janitor.html.

112 **In Las Vegas** Steven Greenhouse, "ORGANIZED; Local 226, 'the Cu-
linary,' Makes Las Vegas the Land of the Living Wage," *New York
Times,* June 3, 2004, https://www.nytimes.com/2004/06/03/us/
organized-local-226-the-culinary-makes-las-vegas-the-land-of-the
-living-wage.html.

112 **earned four dollars more per hour** See Bivens et al., "How Today's
Unions," 33n60.

112 **and more benefits** Bivens et al., "How Today's Unions," 29n26.

112 **thanks to union bargaining** Fiona Simmons, "Las Vegas Unions
Agree on Health Benefits for Casino Employees," *Gambling News,*
September 2, 2020, https://www.gamblingnews.com/news/las-vegas
-unions-agree-on-health-benefits-for-casino-employees.

113 **Economists have calculated** "When union density is high, *nonunion*
workers benefit from higher wages. When the share of workers who
are union members is relatively high, as it was in 1979, wages of nonunion workers are higher. For example, had union density remained at
its 1979 level, weekly wages of nonunion men in the private sector
would be 5 percent higher (that's an additional $2,704 in earnings for
year-round workers), while wages for nonunion men in the private
sector without a college education would be 8 percent, or $3,016 per
year, higher. (These estimates look at what wages would have been in
2013 had union density remained at its 1979 levels)." Bivens et al.,
"How Today's Unions," 9–10.

113 **risen by 190 percent** Bivens et al., "How Today's Unions," 29n19.

113 **suffer from infighting** Steven Greenhouse, "Infighting Distracts
Unions at Crucial Time," *New York Times,* July 9, 2009, https://www
.nytimes.com/2009/07/09/business/09labor.html.

113 **misusing corporate and union funds** Neal E. Boudette, "Ex-Fiat
Chrysler Executive Accused of Siphoning Millions with Union
Leader," *New York Times,* July 26, 2017, https://www.nytimes.com/
2017/07/26/business/ex-fiat-chrysler-executive-accused-of

-siphoning-millions-with-union-leader.html; most recently, see Neal
E. Boudette and Noam Scheiber, "Dennis Williams, Former U.A.W.
Leader, Is Accused of Conspiracy," *New York Times*, August 27, 2020,
https://www.nytimes.com/2020/08/27/business/uaw-dennis
-williams.html.

114   **strike of 1981** "1981 Strike Leaves Legacy for American Workers,"
*Morning Edition*, NPR News, August 3, 2006, https://www.npr.org/
2006/08/03/5604656/1981-strike-leaves-legacy-for-american
-workers.

114   **eleven thousand striking controllers** Joseph A. McCartin, *Collision
Course: Ronald Reagan, the Air Traffic Controllers, and the Strike that
Changed America* (New York: Oxford University Press, 2011).

114   **chairman Paul Volcker's** Bill Medley, "Volcker's Announcement of
Anti-Inflation Measures," Federal Reserve History, September 2013,
https://www.federalreservehistory.org/essays/anti_inflation
_measures.

114   **labor's breaking point** Kimberly Phillips-Fein, "How Employers
Broke Unions by Creating a Culture of Fear," *Washington Post*, August
2, 2016, https://www.washingtonpost.com/news/in-theory/wp/
2016/08/02/how-employers-broke-unions-by-creating-a-culture-of
-fear.

114   **illegally fired workers for union activity** Celine McNicholas et al.,
"Unlawful," Economic Policy Institute, December 11, 2019, https://
www.epi.org/publication/unlawful-employer-opposition-to-union
-election-campaigns.

114   **despite federal protections** Bivens et al., "How Today's Unions,"
34n81.

114   **the majority of businesses** Bivens et al., "How Today's Unions,"
35n84.

114   **The Nissan employees attested** Beginning in mid-July, Nissan supervisors pressured employees with antiunion messages in group and
one-on-one meetings. The company broadcast antiunion videos inside
the plant instructing workers to "Vote no" and launched a sizable
antiunion cable-television buy in the central Mississippi media
market. Nissan made implied threats to close the Canton plant if
workers unionized and threatened employees with layoffs if they
unionized—similar to the unfair labor practices previously alleged
by the NLRB. See "Nissan Threats, Intimidation Tilt Outcome of
Union Election in Mississippi," news release, UAW, August 4, 2017,
https://uaw.org/nissan-threats-intimidation-tilt-outcome-union
-election-mississippi.

114   **National Labor Relations Board issued** See Scheiber, "Racially

Charged Nissan Vote," and "NLRB Issues New Unfair Labor Practice Complaint Against Nissan," news release, UAW, July 31, 2017, https://uaw.org/nlrb-issues-new-unfair-labor-practice-complaint-nissan.

114    **42,400 factories in just eight years** Richard McCormack, "The Plight of American Manufacturing," *American Prospect,* December 21, 2009, https://prospect.org/article/plight-american-manufacturing.

115    **total value of our exports** Grant Suneson, "These Are the 25 Richest Countries in the World," *USA Today,* July 8, 2019, https://www.usatoday.com/story/money/2019/07/07/richest-countries-in-the-world/39630693.

115    **But other countries** Niall McCarthy, "Which Countries Have the Highest Levels of Union Membership?" *Forbes,* June 20, 2017, https://www.forbes.com/sites/niallmccarthy/2017/06/20/which-countries-have-the-highest-levels-of-labor-union-membership-infographic/#fbb85a233c04; Dylan Matthews, "Europe Could Have the Secret to Saving America's Unions," *Vox,* April 17, 2017, https://www.vox.com/policy-and-politics/2017/4/17/15290674/union-labor-movement-europe-bargaining-fight-15-ghent.

115    **According to Gallup** In 1959, the approval rate was at 73 percent. It hovered right around 70 percent until 1965, when it began to decline. Jeff Jones and Lydia Saad, "Gallup Poll Social Series: Work and Education," Gallup, August 2–6, 2017, http://www.gallup.com/file/poll/217334/Labor%20Unions%20(Trends).pdf.

115    **supporting the March on Washington** Ross Eisenbrey, "Key Goals of 1963 March on Washington for Jobs and Freedom Are Still Unmet," *Working Economics Blog,* Economic Policy Institute, August 28, 2012, https://www.epi.org/blog/key-goals-1963-march-washington-jobs-freedom/1347049061000; Michael Kazin, "The White Man Whose 'March on Washington' Speech You Should Remember Too," *New Republic,* August 21, 2013, https://newrepublic.com/article/114408/march-washington-50th-anniversary-walter-reuthers-speech.

115    **unionized capital of American manufacturing** Mike Smith, " 'Let's Make Detroit a Union Town': The History of Labor and the Working Class in the Motor City," *Michigan Historical Review* 27, no. 2 (Fall 2001): 157–73.

115    **epicenter of black cultural and economic power** See Herb Boyd, *Black Detroit: A People's History of Self-Determination* (New York: HarperCollins, 2017).

115    **white people were abandoning** Ross Eisenbrey, "Detroit's Bankruptcy Reflects a History of Racism," *Working Economics Blog,* Eco-

354       NOTES TO CHAPTER FIVE: NO ONE FIGHTS ALONE

nomic Policy Institute, February 25, 2014, https://www.epi.org/blog/
detroits-bankruptcy-reflects-history-racism.

115    **White men began to leave** Marilyn Salenger, "White Flight and De-
       troit's Decline," *Washington Post,* July 21, 2013, https://www.washington
       post.com/opinions/marilyn-salenger-white-flight-and-detroits-decline/
       2013/07/21/7903e888-f24a-11e2-bdae-0d1f78989e8a_story.html; Mi-
       chael Jackman, "White Flight Did Not Begin in 1967," *Detroit Metro
       Times,* July 19, 2017, https://www.metrotimes.com/detroit/white
       -flight-did-not-begin-in-1967/Content?oid=4618876.

115    **Over time, a slightly higher share** Natalie Spievack, "Can Labor
       Unions Help Close the Black-White Wage Gap?" *Urban Wire* (blog),
       Urban Institute, February 1, 2019, https://www.urban.org/urban
       -wire/can-labor-unions-help-close-black-white-wage-gap; Bureau of
       Labor Statistics, "Union Members—2019."

115    **government neutrality in union drives** Between 1955 and 1984, al-
       most all states passed laws about public-sector bargaining, and most of
       those were pro-bargaining, requiring governments to meet with or ne-
       gotiate with unions. See Henry S. Farber, "The Evolution of Public
       Sector Bargaining Laws," in *When Public Sector Workers Unionize,* eds.
       Richard B. Freeman and Casey Ichniowski (Chicago: University of
       Chicago Press, 1988), 132–33, http://www.nber.org/chapters/c7906.

116    **more than five times higher** The union membership rate of public-
       sector workers (34.4 percent) is more than five times higher than that
       of private-sector workers (6.5 percent). See Bureau of Labor Statistics,
       "Union Members—2019."

116    **all-time lowest approval of unions** Jones and Saad, "Gallup Poll So-
       cial Series: Work and Education."

116    **White approval of unions** "Our analysis of the February 2010 Pew
       Survey showed that support for unions fell dramatically among Amer-
       icans of all races, though respondents of color continued to have more
       favorable views of unions than whites. Support among blacks fell 11
       points between 2007 and 2010, from 80 percent to 69 percent. Among
       Hispanics, it fell 22 points, from 82 percent to 60 percent. And support
       among whites fell by 15 points, from 60 percent to 45 percent." David
       Madland and Karla Walter, "Why Is the Public Suddenly Down on
       Unions?" Center for American Progress Action Fund, July 20, 2010,
       https://www.americanprogressaction.org/issues/economy/reports/
       2010/07/20/8046/why-is-the-public-suddenly-down-on-unions. As
       research has demonstrated, the suspicion that a black president would
       tilt government toward black people at the expense of whites was
       prevalent during the Obama administration; racial resentment tinged
       white opinion on issues like foreclosure assistance, taxes, the Recovery
       Act's food stamps and unemployment insurance, and healthcare.

116    **"[Obama] doesn't see himself"** Mike Burns and Andy Newbold,
       "Rush Limbaugh Opens 2012 with More Race-Baiting Attacks,"
       Media Matters for America, January 12, 2012, https://www
       .mediamatters.org/rush-limbaugh/rush-limbaugh-opens-2012-more
       -race-baiting-attacks.

116    **began to consider unions the enemy** Steven Greenhouse, "When Re-
       publicans and Unions Got Along," *New York Times,* September 6,
       2020, https://www.nytimes.com/2020/09/06/opinion/labor-unions
       -republicans.html. White approval of unions has rebounded in the
       Trump era, to 64 percent in August 2020, though Republican support
       for unions is still underwater, at 45 percent approving and 52 percent
       disapproving. See "Gallup Poll Social Series: Work and Education,"
       Gallup, July 30–August 12, 2020, https://news.gallup.com/file/poll/
       319058/200903Unions.pdf.

116    **fight song, "Solidarity Forever"** The lyrics for the song can be found
       at "Solidarity Forever," Industrial Workers of the World, https://
       archive.iww.org/history/icons/solidarity_forever.

117    **After World War II, the CIO** See chapter 3, "The 'Holy Crusade,'" in
       Barbara S. Griffith, *The Crisis of American Labor: Operation Dixie
       and the Defeat of the CIO* (Philadelphia, PA: Temple University Press,
       1988), 22–45.

118    **Operation Dixie failed spectacularly, and racism** See "Organiza-
       tional History," Operation Dixie: The CIO Organizing Committee Pa-
       pers on Microfilm, Kheel Center for Labor-Management
       Documentation and Archives, Cornell University Library, https://rmc
       .library.cornell.edu/EAD/htmldocs/KCL05747mf.html.

118    **"there was no Negro problem"** Zieger, *The CIO,* 234.

118    **CIO unofficially admitted defeat** Zieger, *The CIO,* 238.

118    **even lower than the federal one** See "Georgia," State Minimum
       Wage Laws, Wage and Hour Division, U.S. Department of Labor, up-
       dated September 1, 2020, https://www.dol.gov/agencies/whd/
       minimum-wage/state#ga.

118    **and in the U.S. South** By region, those living in the South are less
       likely than those living elsewhere in the country to hold favorable
       views of unions: 41 percent of southerners view labor unions favor-
       ably, while 42 percent hold an unfavorable view. In the three other re-
       gions of the country, more hold favorable than unfavorable views of
       unions. "Mixed Views of Impact of Long-Term Decline in Union
       Membership," Pew Research Center, April 27, 2015, https://www
       .pewresearch.org/politics/2015/04/27/mixed-views-of-impact-of
       -long-term-decline-in-union-membership.

119    **grew by 13.5 percent** Howard Schneider, "U.S. South, Not Just Mex-
       ico, Stands in Way of Rust Belt Jobs Revival," Reuters, April 7, 2017,

https://www.reuters.com/article/us-usa-trump-south-insight/u-s
-south-not-just-mexico-stands-in-way-of-rust-belt-jobs-revival
-idUSKBN1790HO.

119 **primarily in the nonunionized South** The South with a few exceptions: see "Operations by State," Toyota, https://www.toyota.com/
usa/operations/map.html.

119 **South for the low wages** Kim Hill and Emilio Brahmst, "The Auto
Industry Moving South: An Examination of Trends," Center for Auto-
motive Research, December 15, 2003, https://www.cargroup.org/wp
-content/uploads/2017/02/The-Auto-Industry-Moving-South-An
-Examination-of-Trends.pdf.

119 **the worse it got** Harold Meyerson, "How the American South Drives
the Low-Wage Economy," *American Prospect,* July 6, 2015, https://
prospect.org/article/how-american-south-drives-low-wage-economy.

119 **largest private employer by far** Walmart employs 1.5 million Americans. See "Company Facts," Walmart, https://corporate.walmart
.com/newsroom/company-facts.

119 **local wages and benefits tumbled** Wages in a county after a Walmart
had been operating for eight years were lower across the board by almost 5 percent, according to David Neumark, Junfu Zhang, and Stephen Ciccarella Jr., "The Effects of Wal-Mart on Local Labor
Markets," Working Papers 060711, Department of Economics, University of California–Irvine, https://ideas.repec.org/p/irv/wpaper/
060711.html. Wages and health coverage declined for retail workers
upon the opening of Walmarts, according to Arindrajit Dube, T. William Lester, and Barry Eidlin, "Firm Entry and Wages: Impact of
Wal-Mart Growth on Earnings Throughout the Retail Sector," Institute of Industrial Relations Working Paper No. iirwps-126-05, August
7, 2007, https://ssrn.com/abstract=841684. Responding to massive
worker organizing, tighter labor markets, and public pressure in the
past half decade, Walmart has begun to raise pay and promote career
ladders and promotions for hourly workers, though it remains unorganized and low-wage. Meyerson, "How the American South."

119 **slashed the regional difference in half** See Moody's Analytics data
cited in Meyerson, "How the American South."

119 **"the South today shares"** Meyerson, "How the American South."

121 **"There probably are not today"** W.E.B. Du Bois, *Black Reconstruction in America* (1935; New York: Free Press, 1998), 700.

123 **One of the most influential Irish** David R. Roediger, *The Wages of
Whiteness* (New York: Verso, 1991), 134–38; Frederick Douglass
quoted an O'Connell speech in Ireland, "I have been assailed for attacking the American institution, as it is called,—Negro slavery. I am
not ashamed of that attack. I do not shrink from it. I am the advocate

of civil and religious liberty, all over the globe, and wherever tyranny exists, I am the foe of the tyrant; wherever oppression shows itself, I am the foe of the oppressor; wherever slavery rears its head, I am the enemy of the system, or the institution, call it by what name you will." Letter from Frederick Douglass to William Lloyd Garrison, October 24, 1845, in *Frederick Douglass in Ireland, in His Own Words*, ed. Christine Kinealy (New York: Routledge, 2018).

123 **"Irish attacks on blacks"** Michael Miller Topp, "Racial and Ethnic Identity in the United States, 1837–1877," in *The Columbia Documentary History of Race and Ethnicity in America*, ed. Ronald H. Bayor (New York: Columbia University Press, 2004), 277.

123 **decreased by 20 percent afterward** Albon P. Man Jr., "Labor Competition and the New York Draft Riots of 1863," *The Journal of Negro History* 36, no. 4 (October 1951): 375–405.

124 **"Herrenvolk republicanism"** Roediger, *Wages of Whiteness*, 60.

125 **Norton and his colleagues** Ilyana Kuziemko et al., " 'Last-Place Aversion': Evidence and Redistributive Implications," *The Quarterly Journal of Economics* 129, no. 1 (2014): 105–49.

125 **"and thus those most likely"** Kuziemko et al., " 'Last-Place Aversion,' " 107.

125 **"Last-place aversion suggests"** Kuziemko et al., " 'Last-Place Aversion,' " 107.

125 **Workers heard this messaging** Chris Brooks, "Why Did Nissan Workers Vote No?" *Labor Notes,* August 11, 2017, https://www.labornotes.org/2017/08/why-did-nissan-workers-vote-no.

128 **favors Nissan got in the statehouse** The workers referenced a recent set of tax breaks and incentives for a Nissan supplier moving to the county, which totaled more than $1 million. Dennis Moore, "Japanese Company Adds 100 Jobs to Madison County Operation," *Mississippi Today,* July 17, 2017, https://mississippitoday.org/2017/07/17/japanese-company-adds-100-jobs-to-madison-county-operation/; Overall, Good Jobs First calculated over $1 billion in incentives from the state to Nissan. "A Good Deal for Mississippi?," Good Jobs First, May 2013, http://www.goodjobsfirst.org/sites/default/files/docs/pdf/nissan_report.pdf.

129 **slogans like "One-two-three-four"** "New York Fast Food Workers in Historic Strike for $15 an Hour," Real News Network, November 30, 2012, https://www.youtube.com/watch?v=kW9Ak00ejPU.

129 **had gone precisely nowhere** See, for example, "State Minimum Wage Rates," Labor Law Center, https://www.laborlawcenter.com/state-minimum-wage-rates. The first "state" to pass the ten-dollar threshold was the District of Columbia, three years later in 2015.

129 **had spread across the country** Wendi C. Thomas, "How New York's

'Fight for $15' Launched a Nationwide Movement," *American Prospect*, January 4, 2016, https://prospect.org/economy/new-york-s-fight-15-launched-nationwide-movement.

129 **a $15-an-hour victory** David Rolf, *The Fight for Fifteen: The Right Wage for a Working America* (New York: New Press, 2016), 110.

130 **poverty wage for the Seattle area** Rolf, *The Fight for Fifteen*, 102.

130 **streets of sixty cities teemed** Alanna Petroff and James O'Toole, "Wave of Fast Food Strikes Hits 60 Cities," CNN Money, August 29, 2013, https://money.cnn.com/2013/08/29/news/fast-food-strikes/index.html.

130 **first American city to raise** Rolf, *The Fight for Fifteen*, 159.

131 **raised him on a Hardee's paycheck** Steven Greenhouse, "Strong Voice in 'Fight for 15' Fast-Food Wage Campaign," *New York Times*, December 4, 2014, https://www.nytimes.com/2014/12/05/business/in-fast-food-workers-fight-for-15-an-hour-a-strong-voice-in-terrance-wise.html.

131 **testifying before the U.S. Congress** See Fight for $15, "#FightFor15 Leader Terrence Wise Testifies on Raise the Wage Act," Facebook, February 8, 2019, https://www.facebook.com/watch/?v=531773327344136.

134 **chapters cross-organized with Black Lives Matter** Justin Miller, "Fight for 15 and Black Lives Matter Join Forces on Anniversary of MLK's Death," *American Prospect*, April 4, 2017, https://prospect.org/article/anniversary-mlk-death-fight-15-and-black-lives-matter-join-forces.

134 **The advocates sued** John Blake, "The Fight for $15 Takes on the 'Jim Crow' Economy," CNN, April 13, 2018, https://edition.cnn.com/2018/04/13/us/fight-for-15-birmingham/index.html.

134 **the twenty-one states** State Minimum Wage Laws, Wage and Hour Division, U.S. Department of Labor, updated September 1, 2020, https://www.dol.gov/agencies/whd/minimum-wage/state.

134 **largest African American populations** Sonya Rastogi et al., "The Black Population: 2010," 2010 Census Briefs, C2010BR-06, September 2011, https://www.census.gov/prod/cen2010/briefs/c2010br-06.pdf.

135 **largest group to benefit** Laura Huizar and Tsedeye Gebreselassie, "What a $15 Minimum Wage Means for Women and Workers of Color," National Employment Law Project, December 2016, p. 2, https://www.nelp.org/wp-content/uploads/Policy-Brief-15-Minimum-Wage-Women-Workers-of-Color.pdf.

136 **win the support of whites** Leslie Davis and Hannah Hartig, "Two-Thirds of Americans Favor Raising Federal Minimum Wage to $15 an Hour," Fact Tank, Pew Research Center, July 30, 2019, https://www

.pewresearch.org/fact-tank/2019/07/30/two-thirds-of-americans
-favor-raising-federal-minimum-wage-to-15-an-hour. In 2019, 60 percent of white Americans supported raising the federal minimum wage
to fifteen dollars.

136  **they won a statewide $15 minimum wage** "New York State's Mini-
mum Wage," New York State, https://www.ny.gov/new-york-states
-minimum-wage/new-york-states-minimum-wage.

136  **So, too, did workers in states including** See, for example, Ovetta
Wiggins and Rachel Chason, "Maryland Adopts $15 Minimum Wage
by 2025 as Lawmakers Reject Hogan's Veto," *Washington Post,*
March 28, 2019, https://www.washingtonpost.com/local/md
-politics/maryland-house-rejects-hogan-veto-of-15-minimum-wage
-senate-to-vote-next/2019/03/28/88c240e0-5152-11e9-a3f7
-78b7525a8d5f_story.html; "454 CMR 27.00: Minimum Wage," Mass.
Gov, December 16, 2016, https://www.mass.gov/regulations/454
-CMR-2700-minimum-wage.

136  **$68 billion more** Yannet Lathrop, "Impact of the Fight for $15: $68
Billion in Raises, 22 Million Workers," National Employment Law
Project, November 29, 2018, https://www.nelp.org/publication/
impact-fight-for-15-2018.

136  **all the terms of business** You get identical customer experiences at
McDonald's restaurants across the country, and that's because the corporate parent controls the scripts that workers use and how they dress
and monitor in real time how much they work and sell. Patricia
Smith, "McDonald's Cannot Dodge Its Illegal Treatment of Franchise
Workers," National Employment Law Project, December 27, 2017,
https://www.nelp.org/commentary/mcdonalds-cannot-dodge-its
-illegal-treatment-of-franchise-workers.

## Chapter Six: Never a Real Democracy

140  **"I believe if you can't have"** ACLU Videos, "Larry's Fight to Vote
Goes to the Supreme Court," YouTube, 2:27, January 8, 2018, https://
www.youtube.com/watch?v=BVIiRNLHgfM.

140  **political scientist Larry M. Bartels found** "I find that substantial
numbers of Republicans endorse statements contemplating violations
of key democratic norms, including respect for the law and for the
outcomes of elections and eschewing the use of force in pursuit of political ends. The strongest predictor by far of these antidemocratic attitudes is ethnic antagonism—especially concerns about the political
power and claims on government resources of immigrants, African-
Americans, and Latinos. The strong tendency of ethnocentric Repub-

licans to countenance violence and lawlessness, even prospectively and hypothetically, underlines the significance of ethnic conflict in contemporary US politics." Larry M. Bartels, "Ethnic Antagonism Erodes Republicans' Commitment to Democracy," *PNAS* 117, no. 37 (August 2020): 22752–59, https://doi.org/10.1073/pnas.2007747117.

141    **majority of white men were excluded** See for example "Voting Rights: A Short History," Carnegie Corporation of New York, November 18, 2019, https://www.carnegie.org/topics/topic-articles/voting-rights/voting-rights-timeline.

141    **original thirteen states limited the franchise** "The Founders and the Vote," Elections, Library of Congress, Washington, D.C., https://www.loc.gov/classroom-materials/elections/right-to-vote/the-founders-and-the-vote. See also "Table A.2: Property and Taxpaying Requirements for Suffrage: 1970–1855," in Alexander Keyssar, *The Right to Vote: The Contested History of Democracy in the United States* (New York: Basic Books, 2009), 308.

141    **equality and democracy** It has become popular on the right to reject the aspiration to democracy altogether in the face of demographic change and equalization of the franchise. The right asserts instead that we are a republic, given that we do not have direct democracy; however, democracies can and usually do function through elected representatives.

141    **the Three-fifths Compromise** Article I, Sec. 2 of the U.S. Constitution reads, "Representatives and direct taxes shall be apportioned among the several states which may be included within this Union, according to their respective numbers, which shall be determined by adding to the whole number of free persons, including those bound to service for a term of years, and excluding Indians not taxed, three-fifths of all other persons."

141    **give those states an advantage** "The remaining mode was an election by the people or rather by the qualified part of them, at large: With all its imperfections he liked this best." However, "the second difficulty arose from the disproportion of qualified voters in the N. & S. States, and the disadvantages which this mode would throw on the latter." James Madison, Madison Debates, July 25, 1787, The Avalon Project, Yale Law School, https://avalon.law.yale.edu/18th_century/debates_725.asp.

141    **region had thirteen extra electors** Sean Illing, "The Real Reason We Have an Electoral College: To Protect Slave States," *Vox*, November 12, 2016, https://www.vox.com/policy-and-politics/2016/11/12/13598316/donald-trump-electoral-college-slavery-akhil-reed-amar.

142    **white people who live in larger** "While votes are roughly proportionately distributed, since even the smallest states are guaranteed

three votes, the people in these states end up being overrepresented in the Electoral College. For example, in Wyoming, there is an electoral vote for every 195,000 residents, in North Dakota there is one for every 252,000, and in Rhode Island one for every 264,000. On the other hand, in California there is an electoral vote for every 711,000 residents, in Florida one for every 699,000, and in Texas one for every 723,000. The states that are overrepresented in the Electoral College also happen to be less diverse than the country as a whole." Lara Merling and Dean Baker, "In the Electoral College White Votes Matter More," Center for Economic and Policy Research, November 14, 2016, https://www.cepr.net/in-the-electoral-college-white-votes-matter-more.

142   **reconsider the property limitations** The developing manufacturing economy, led by cotton and textiles, meant that there were millions more men without property but with money, toiling in the class between servant and landowner, earning wages in factories and working jobs as mechanics, merchants, blacksmiths, and the like. The pressure built during the War of 1812 as many of these men fought for a government in which they had no voice.

142   **tenuous voting rights of free black citizens** In addition, almost all northern states denied free black citizens the other crucial mark of citizenship in a democracy: the right to be jurors or witnesses. C. Vann Woodward, *The Strange Career of Jim Crow* (1955; New York: Oxford University Press, 2002), 20.

142   **only 6 percent** Keyssar, *The Right to Vote*, 308.

142   **They just needed to be white** By giving the vote to all white men while disenfranchising free black men, states deemed the voice of the poorest white man worthier than that of the wealthiest man of color. New York eliminated its property requirement for white men in 1821 but kept it for free men of color, who couldn't vote unless they were wealthy, possessing property worth $250. Keyssar, *The Right to Vote*, 308.

142   **white-skinned immigrants didn't even need** "From the early 19th century until the 1920s, non-citizens could vote in many states, where voting rights were extended to immigrants who had resided in the United States for three years and declared their intent to become citizens." Alexander Keyssar, "What Struggles over the Right to Vote Reveal About American Democracy," Scholars Strategy Network, May 1, 2012, https://scholars.org/contribution/what-struggles-over-right-vote-reveal-about-american-democracy. It's worth noting that, at the time, the only immigrants who could naturalize as citizens were "free white persons."

142   **John Wilkes Booth** Doris Kearns Goodwin, *Team of Rivals: The Polit-*

*ical Genius of Abraham Lincoln* (New York: Simon & Schuster, 2005), 728.

143    **registering seven hundred thousand recently freed** Ari Berman, *Give Us the Ballot: The Modern Struggle for Voting Rights in America* (New York: Farrar, Straus and Giroux, 2015), 16.

143    **In Colfax, Louisiana** In November 1872, a pro-Reconstructionist Republican candidate supported by black voters, William Pitt Kellogg, won a gubernatorial race that was so fiercely disputed that both candidates claimed victory, and President Grant had to send federal troops to support Kellogg. (Henry Louis Gates Jr., "What Was the Colfax Massacre?" *The Root,* July 29, 2013, https://www.theroot.com/what-was-the-colfax-massacre-1790897517.) The following spring, Kellogg's opponents formed a paramilitary group called the White League, which, like the Ku Klux Klan, used violence to terrorize black citizens and their white Republican supporters. (Danny Lewis, "The 1873 Colfax Massacre Crippled the Reconstruction Era," *Smithsonian Magazine,* April 13, 2016, https://www.smithsonianmag.com/smart-news/1873-colfax-massacre-crippled-reconstruction-180958746.) In early April, intermittent fighting broke out in Colfax Parish between Kellogg's white opponents and black supporters over control of the courthouse, the seat of civic life and the repository where the election results were held (in Lewis, "The 1873 Colfax Massacre"). More than a hundred black residents began to camp out in the courthouse to protect it. On April 13, members of the White League, armed with guns, knives, and a cannon, went to war against the black defenders of the courthouse, in what one white leader called "a struggle for white supremacy" (in Gates, "What Was the Colfax Massacre?"). Outnumbered and outgunned, the defenders fought back but were forced to yield when the opponents set fire to the courthouse. The White League then slaughtered every black person they found, even those waving white cloths of surrender. Historians are not sure of the number, but somewhere between 60 and 150 black men and 3 white men were killed in what came to be known as the Colfax Massacre, one of the most violent episodes of the Reconstruction era. Nine members of the white mob were tried, but the charges were dropped by the U.S. Supreme Court in its infamous 1876 decision in *United States v. Cruikshank,* which held that the federal government had no role in protecting citizens from racist attacks by individuals or groups—only by the state. See Adam Serwer, "The Supreme Court Is Headed Back to the 19th Century," *The Atlantic,* September 14, 2018, https://www.theatlantic.com/ideas/archive/2018/09/redemption-court/566963.

143   **Indigenous Americans** See Laughlin McDonald, *American Indians and the Fight for Equal Voting Rights* (Norman: University of Oklahoma Press, 2014). Native American voting rights are still under attack. See James T. Tucker et al., *Obstacles at Every Turn: Barriers to Political Participation Faced by Native American Voters*, Native American Voting Rights Coalition, June 2020, https://vote.narf.org/wp-content/uploads/2020/06/obstacles_at_every_turn.pdf.

143   **alliances sometimes known as "Fusion"** Helen G. Edmonds, *The Negro and Fusion Politics in North Carolina, 1894–1901* (Chapel Hill: University of North Carolina Press, 2013), 220.

143   **violent intimidation to those who didn't** See, for example, the racial terror organization the Red Shirts in North Carolina, in Edmonds, *The Negro and Fusion Politics*, 163–64.

143   **Mississippi implemented** Lawrence Goldstone, "America's Relentless Suppression of Black Voters," *New Republic,* October 24, 2018, https://newrepublic.com/article/151858/americas-relentless-suppression-black-voters.

144   **In some places, grandfather clauses** Tova Wang, *The Politics of Voter Suppression* (Ithaca, NY: Cornell University Press, 2012), 18.

144   **a scant 18 percent** Carol Anderson, *One Person, No Vote: How Voter Suppression Is Destroying Our Democracy* (New York: Bloomsbury, 2018), 10. (The Twenty-fourth Amendment prohibited poll taxes in federal elections in 1964, and court decisions struck down the remaining state poll taxes by 1966.)

144   **The requirement that we register** Keyssar, *The Right to Vote*, 52.

144   **"voter registration has thus been"** Daniel P. Tokaji, "Voter Registration and Election Reform," *William and Mary Bill of Rights Journal* 17, no. 2 (December 2008): 461.

144   **nearly 20 percent of eligible voters** Laura Williamson et al., "Toward a More Representative Electorate: The Progress and Potential of Voter Registration Through Public Assistance Agencies," Demos, December 18, 2018, https://www.demos.org/publication/toward-more-representative-electorate-progress-and-potential-voter-registration-through-.

144   **Over six million Americans are prohibited** Christopher Uggen et al., "6 Million Lost Voters: State-Level Estimates of Felony Disenfranchisement, 2016," The Sentencing Project, October 6, 2016, https://www.sentencingproject.org/publications/6-million-lost-voters-state-level-estimates-felony-disenfranchisement-2016. See also Jacey Fortin, "Can Felons Vote? It Depends on the State," *New York Times,* April 21, 2018, https://www.nytimes.com/2018/04/21/us/felony-voting-rights-law.html.

145    **"Some crimes were specifically defined"** Michelle Alexander, *The New Jim Crow: Mass Incarceration in the Age of Colorblindness* (New York: The New Press, 2012), 192.

145    **These included petty theft** Tim Elfrink, "The Long, Racist History of Florida's Now-Repealed Ban on Felons Voting," *Washington Post*, November 7, 2018, https://www.washingtonpost.com/nation/ 2018/11/07/long-racist-history-floridas-now-repealed-ban-felons -voting/?utm_term=.1653b54f0e20.

145    **Mississippi designated crimes** During the 1870s–1880s, an estimated 95 percent of people in Florida prison camps were black men. A captain in one of the camps at that time noted, "It was possible to send a negro to prison on almost any pretext, but difficult to get a white man there." The 1868 law was reaffirmed in 1968 against a backdrop of heightened racial conflict and repression during the civil rights movement. "History of Florida's Felony Disenfranchisement Provision," Brennan Center for Justice and Florida Rights Restoration Coalition, March 2006, https://www.brennancenter.org/sites/default/files/ legacy/d/download_file_38222.pdf.

145    **one in fifty-six non-black voters is impacted** "Felony Disenfranchisement," The Sentencing Project, https://www.sentencingproject .org/issues/felony-disenfranchisement.

145    **In Florida, voters in 2018 overturned** Philip Bump, "Allowing Felons to Vote Likely Would Have Changed the Result in Florida's Senate Race," *Washington Post*, November 8, 2018, https://www.washington post.com/politics/2018/11/08/allowing-felons-vote-would-likely -have-changed-result-floridas-senate-race/?utm_term=.92afab953729; Kevin Morris, "A Transformative Step for Democracy in Florida," Brennan Center for Justice, November 6, 2018, https://www.brennan center.org/blog/transformative-step-democracy-florida.

146    **passed with 65 percent** Samantha J. Gross, "Florida Voters Approve Amendment 4 on Restoring Felons' Voting Rights," *Miami Herald*, November 6, 2018, https://www.miamiherald.com/news/politics -government/election/article220678880.html.

146    **nearly impossible for returning citizens** Amy Gardner and Lori Rozsa, "In Florida, Felons Must Pay Court Debts Before They Can Vote," *Washington Post*, May 13, 2020, https://www.washingtonpost .com/politics/in-florida-felons-must-pay-court-debts-before-they -can-vote-but-with-no-system-to-do-so-many-have-found-it -impossible/2020/05/13/08ed05be-906f-11ea-9e23-6914ee410a5f _story.html.

146    **"there is no database"** *Kelvin Leon Jones v. Governor of Florida*, 20-12003 (11th Cir. 2020), p. 109, https://media.ca11.uscourts.gov/ opinions/pub/files/202012003.enb.pdf.

146 **paid up before they can vote** Lori Rozsa, "Federal Appeals Court Blocks Hundreds of Thousands of Felons in Florida Who Still Owe Fines and Fees from Voting," *Washington Post,* September 11, 2020, https://www.washingtonpost.com/politics/florida-felon -voting/2020/09/11/9a6b5d3a-f45e-11ea-bc45-e5d48ab44b9f_story .html.

147 **nearly 97 percent of Australians** Tacey Rychter, "How Compulsory Voting Works: Australians Explain," *New York Times,* October 22, 2018, https://www.nytimes.com/2018/10/22/world/australia/ compulsory-voting.html.

147 **compared to about 70 percent** "Reported Voting and Registration, by Race, Hispanic Origin, Sex, and Age, for the United States: November 2016," U.S. Census Bureau, https://www2.census.gov/programs -surveys/cps/tables/p20/580/table02_1.xlsx.

147 **about 93 and 91 percent, respectively** Alexis Chemblette, "These Countries with Nearly 100 Percent Voter Participation Put the US to Shame," *Vice,* October 25, 2017, https://impact.vice.com/en_us/ article/ne3n9b/these-countries-with-nearly-100-percent-voter- participation-put-the-us-to-shame.

147 **deeply uncertain** Robert P. Jones et al., "American Democracy in Crisis: The Challenges of Voter Knowledge, Participation, and Polarization," PRRI, July 17, 2018, https://www.prri.org/research/ American-democracy-in-crisis-voters-midterms-trump-election-2018.

147 **Oregon, for example, was judged** Quan Li et al., "Cost of Voting in the American States," *Election Law Journal* (September 2018): 234–47, https://doi.org/10.1089/elj.2017.0478. Oregon is less than 3 percent black.

147 **add eligible voters to the rolls** Sixteen states and Washington, D.C., now use this technology. "Automatic Voter Registration, a Summary," Brennan Center for Justice, July 10, 2019, https://www.brennan center.org/our-work/research-reports/automatic-voter-registration -summary.

148 **highest percentage of black citizens** The District of Columbia is actually the jurisdiction with the highest percentage of African Americans, but (not unrelatedly), statehood for D.C. has failed to pass the U.S. Congress.

148 **dead last of the fifty states** Quan Li et al., "Cost of Voting." Mississippi has no open early voting period; no online registration; narrow absentee ballot permissions, which the state broadened only slightly to account for the COVID-19 pandemic; lifetime felony conviction bans unless you're pardoned or have your voting rights restored by either the governor or a two-thirds vote of the legislature, and strict ID requirements for registration and voting.

148   *Shelby County v. Holder* Meagan Hatcher-Mays, "NY Times Misses
       Link Between Anti-Civil Rights Zealot and Right-Wing's 'Dark
       Money ATM,'" Media Matters for America, April 8, 2014, https://
       www.mediamatters.org/new-york-times/ny-times-misses-link
       -between-anti-civil-rights-zealot-and-right-wings-dark-money-atm.

148   **"target[ed] African Americans with almost surgical precision"**
       *N.C. State Conference of the NAACP v. McCrory,* 831 F.3d 204
       (4th Cir. 2016), https://casetext.com/case/nc-state-conference-of-the
       -naacp-v-mccrory-4.

148   **Texas introduced a voter ID law** "Written Testimony of Chiraag
       Bains to the House On H.R. 1, the For the People Act," Demos, Febru-
       ary 14, 2019, https://www.demos.org/publication/written-testimony
       -chiraag-bains-house-hr-1-people-act.

148   **Alabama demanded photo IDs** Maggie Astor, "Seven Ways Alabama
       Has Made It Harder to Vote," *New York Times,* June 23, 2018, https://
       www.nytimes.com/2018/06/23/us/politics/voting-rights-alabama
       .html.

149   **twenty-three states raised new barriers** Eric Badner, "Discrimina-
       tory Voter Laws Have Surged in Last 5 Years, Federal Commission
       Finds," CNN Politics, September 12, 2018, https://www.cnn
       .com/2018/09/12/politics/voting-rights-federal-commission-election/
       index.html.

149   **Although about 11 percent** Keesha Gaskins and Sundeep Iyer, "The
       Challenge of Obtaining Voter Identification," Brennan Center for Jus-
       tice, July 18, 2012, https://www.brennancenter.org/publication/
       challenge-obtaining-voter-identification; Sari Horwitz, "Getting a
       Photo ID So You Can Vote Is Easy. Unless You're Poor, Black, Latino or
       Elderly," *Washington Post,* May 23, 2016, https://www.washington
       post.com/politics/courts_law/getting-a-photo-id-so-you-can-vote-is
       -easy-unless-youre-poor-black-latino-or-elderly/2016/05/23/
       8d5474ec-20f0-11e6-8690-f14ca9de2972_story.html?utm_term
       =.9911008ca3b1.

149   **by 2020, six states** "Voter Identification Requirements—Voter ID
       Laws," National Conference of State Legislatures, August 25, 2020,
       http://www.ncsl.org/research/elections-and-campaigns/voter-id
       .aspx.

149   **about 5 percent of white people** Vanessa M. Perez, "Americans with
       Photo ID: A Breakdown of Demographic Characteristics," Project
       Vote, February 2015, http://www.projectvote.org/wp-content/
       uploads/2015/06/AMERICANS-WITH-PHOTO-ID-Research
       -Memo-February-2015.pdf.

149   **"Why would I want to vote"** Wade Goodwyn, "Texas' Voter ID Law
       Creates a Problem for Some Women," *All Things Considered,* NPR,

October 30, 2013, https://www.npr.org/2013/10/30/241891800/
texas-voter-id-law-creates-a-problem-for-some-women; Aviva Shen,
"Texas Judge Almost Blocked from Voting Because of New Voter ID
Law," Think Progress, October 23, 2013, https://archive.thinkprogress
.org/texas-judge-almost-blocked-from-voting-because-of-new-voter-id
-law-b533a451f312/.

149  **fellow Texan Anthony Settles** See Horwitz, "Getting a Photo ID So
You Can Vote Is Easy."

150  **Hargie Randell** Horwitz, "Getting a Photo ID So You Can Vote Is
Easy." Randell's lawyer was finally able to prove to a DPS supervisor
that there was a clerical error.

150  **to eliminate two hundred thousand registered Ohio voters** Chris
Bury, "Why Ohio Has Purged at Least 200,000 from the Voter Rolls,"
*PBS NewsHour,* July 31, 2016, https://www.pbs.org/newshour/show/
inside-ohios-fight-voting-rules.

150  **In 2012, Ohio went to the trouble** Oral argument transcript in *Husted v. A. Philip Randolph Institute,* 584 U.S. ___ (2018), p. 47, https://
www.supremecourt.gov/oral_arguments/argument_transcripts/
2017/16-980_5426.pdf.

151  **about three out of every one hundred** Oral argument transcript in
*Husted v. A. Philip Randolph Institute,* 584 U.S. ___ (2018), p. 73,
https://www.supremecourt.gov/oral_arguments/argument_
transcripts/2017/16-980_5426.pdf.

151  **1.2 million never responded** Phil Keisling, "A Better Path to Accurate Voter Rolls," Governing the States and Localities, October 3, 2018,
http://www.governing.com/columns/smart-mgmt/col-better-path
-more-accurate-voter-rolls-postcard.html.

151  **Or perhaps the process was working** Greg Palast, "The GOP's
Stealth War Against Voters," *Rolling Stone,* August 24, 2016, https://
www.rollingstone.com/politics/politics-features/the-gops-stealth-war
-against-voters-247905.

151  **"I've lived in Ohio"** ACLU Videos, "Larry's Fight to Vote Goes to the
Supreme Court," YouTube, 2:27, January 8, 2018, https://www
.youtube.com/watch?v=BVIiRNLHgfM.

152  **"I thought, 'Well, jeez'"** Bury, "Why Ohio Has Purged."

152  **no other state initiated a purge** Chiraag Bains, "You Have the Right
to Vote. Use It or Lose It, the Supreme Court Says," *Washington Post,*
June 13, 2018, https://www.washingtonpost.com/opinions/vote-or-be
-purged-thats-wrong/2018/06/13/5e9730d6-6f27-11e8-afd5
-778aca903bbe_story.html.

152  **"In the United States, if you don't"** Bains, "You Have the Right to
Vote."

153  **an affirmative right to vote** The Constitution's voting rights amend-

ments have prohibited states from using certain enumerated conditions such as race as bases for denying the vote, but an affirmative
right would require states to meet a high bar of justification for any
burden on citizens' voting freedoms. See Laura Williamson and
Brenda Wright, "Right to Vote: The Case for Expanding the Right to
Vote in the U.S. Constitution," Demos, August 26, 2020, https://www
.demos.org/policy-briefs/right-vote-case-expanding-right-vote-us
-constitution.

153   **states purged almost 16 million voters** Jonathan Brater et al.,
"Purges: A Growing Threat to the Right to Vote," Brennan Center for
Justice, July 20, 2018, https://www.brennancenter.org/publication/
purges-growing-threat-right-vote.

153   **Some 7 percent of Americans report** Jones et al., "American Democracy in Crisis." Black and Latino voters are about twice as likely (10
and 11 percent, respectively) as white voters (5 percent) to be purged.

153   **"It appears as if what"** Oral argument transcript in *Husted v.
A. Philip Randolph Institute,* 584 U.S. ___ (2018), p. 18, https://www
.supremecourt.gov/oral_arguments/argument_transcripts/2017/16
-980_5426.pdf.

154   **American Legislative Exchange Council** More than half of the
sixty-two anti-voting bills sponsored in 2011–12 were sponsored by
ALEC conference attendees. See Ethan Magoc, "Flurry of Voter ID
Laws Tied to Conservative Group ALEC," NBC News, August 21,
2012, http://investigations.nbcnews.com/_news/2012/08/21/
13392560-flurry-of-voter-id-laws-tied-to-conservative-group-alec.

154   **Project on Fair Representation** Edward Blum, founder and director
of the Project on Fair Representation, is the strategist behind attacks
on affirmative action and the Voting Rights Act. Morgan Smith, "One
Man Standing Against Race-Based Laws," *New York Times,* February 24, 2012, https://www.nytimes.com/2012/02/24/us/edward
-blum-and-the-project-on-fair-representation-head-to-the-supreme
-court-to-fight-race-based-laws.html.

154   **Public Interest Legal Foundation** "Public Interest Legal Foundation
Drops Meritless Voter Purge Lawsuit Against Detroit," Brennan Center
for Justice, June 30, 2020, https://www.brennancenter.org/our-work/
analysis-opinion/public-interest-legal-foundation-drops-meritless-voter
-purge-lawsuit; Amadou Diallo, "Who's Funding Voter Suppression,"
Al-Jazeera America, February 12, 2016, http://america.aljazeera.com/
articles/2016/2/12/whos-funding-voter-suppression.html.

154   **group of radical right-wing millionaires** The Bradley Foundation
supported the Project on Fair Representation's crusades against affirmative action and the Voting Rights Act. Brendan Fischer, "For Bradley Foundation, Challenging Affirmative Action & Voting Rights Is

Part of Long-Term Crusade," PR Watch, The Center for Media and Democracy, June 27, 2013, https://www.prwatch.org/news/2013/06/ 12142/bradley-foundation-challenging-affirmative-action-voting -rights-part-long-term-cr. DonorsTrust is a nondisclosed pooled fund that has been heavily funded by the Koch brothers. Andy Kroll, "Exposed: The Dark-Money ATM of the Conservative Movement," *Mother Jones,* February 5, 2013, https://www.motherjones.com/ politics/2013/02/donors-trust-donor-capital-fund-dark-money-koch -bradley-devos. See also Eliza Newlin Carney, "The GOP's Weapon of Suppression: Voter Purges," *American Prospect,* December 15, 2017, https://prospect.org/article/gop%E2%80%99s-weapon-suppression -voter-purges. (There are also hundreds of organized wealthy donors to progressive causes, of course. I personally have raised money from wealthy individuals and foundations to fund the nonprofits at which I have played a leadership role; I have also volunteered on the boards of the Rockefeller Brothers Fund and the Open Society Foundation U.S. Programs. The agenda of these progressive donors and foundations, however, includes reforms that would run against the narrow self-interest of the donors and wealthy people in general, including support for more regulation, higher taxation, and stricter campaign finance reform. The Koch network's philanthropic interests generally further their financial interests, at great cost to the public interest and the planet.)

154   **"the Koch brothers"** For more about the Koch brothers, see Tim Dickinson, "Inside the Koch Brothers' Toxic Empire," *Rolling Stone,* September 14, 2014, https://www.rollingstone.com/politics/politics-- news/inside-the-koch-brothers-toxic-empire-164403; and Jane Mayer, " 'Kochland' Examines How the Koch Brothers Made Their Fortune and the Influence It Bought," *The New Yorker,* August 13, 2019, https://www.newyorker.com/news/daily-comment/kochland -examines-how-the-koch-brothers-made-their-fortune-and-the -influence-it-bought.

155   **That's why the hundreds of millionaires** Six hundred thirty-four donors attended the 2019 Koch Network convention, pledging a minimum of $100,000 each. Sally Ho, "Muted Political Tone at Largest Koch Donor Network Meeting," Associated Press, January 26, 2019, https://apnews.com/2930f1f88d4d4d60b3f3880e4be8dbf1.

155   **spurred more than one hundred pieces** "New Voting Restrictions in America," Brennan Center for Justice, October 1, 2019, https://www .brennancenter.org/our-work/research-reports/new-voting -restrictions-america.

155   **launched dozens of lawsuits** Hatcher-Mays, "NY Times Misses Link"; Lateshia Beachum, "Kochs Key Among Small Group Quietly Funding Legal Assault on Campaign Finance Regulation," Center for

Public Integrity, November 15, 2017, https://publicintegrity.org/
federal-politics/kochs-key-among-small-group-quietly-funding-legal
-assault-on-campaign-finance-regulation.

155    **invested in technology** Andy Kroll, "Meet the Fortune 500 Companies Funding the Political Resegregation of America," *Mother Jones*,
November 21, 2014, https://www.motherjones.com/politics/2014/
11/rslc-redistricting-fortune-500-political-resegregation.

155    **James Buchanan was awarded** Robert D. McFadden, "James M. Buchanan, Economic Scholar and Nobel Laureate, Dies at 93," *New York
Times*, January 10, 2013, https://www.nytimes.com/2013/01/10/
business/economy/james-m-buchanan-economic-scholar-dies-at-93
.html.

155    **resist desegregating public schools** Many economists in the libertarian school, often funded by and aligned with the Koch Network, have
taken issue with Nancy MacLean's *Democracy in Chains*. The primary
refutation relevant here is that Buchanan was not a segregationist. Buchanan was of the common "free association" school, which believed
that whites and blacks should associate with whomever they chose—
a tidy equivalence that falls apart when black people want to associate
with white people or white institutions that refuse them. MacLean
critics Art Carden (who admits that he is "as Koched up as they
come"), Vincent Geloso, and Phillip W. Magness write, "[Buchanan's]
views on segregation emerged from the efficiency arguments of the
mid-century Chicago School rather than any pro-segregation, pro-
discrimination, or otherwise racially conservative southern source"
(p. 18). I can't imagine that this distinction would have made a difference to the thousands of black schoolchildren in Virginia pushed out
of closed schools during "Massive Resistance," the policy the state of
Virginia adopted in opposition to *Brown*. Buchanan later reversed his
stance on school privatization, but the intellectual pairing of libertarian ideas and opposition to government action to promote civil rights
endured. Another prominent libertarian economist has defended
MacLean's characterization of Buchanan's antidemocratic antigovernment beliefs. See Michael Chwe, "The Beliefs of Economist James
Buchanan Conflict with Basic Democratic Norms," *Washington Post*,
July 25, 2017, https://www.washingtonpost.com/news/monkey-cage/
wp/2017/07/25/the-beliefs-of-economist-james-buchanan-conflict
-with-basic-democratic-norms-heres-why/. He writes, "I do not know
their intentions, but Buchanan and Nutter's argument for school
privatization gave intellectual validation to whites who wanted to exclude blacks from their schools." The most complete account of
Nutter and Buchanan's segregationist view to date comes from

Daniel Peter Kuehn, "Accommodation Within the Broad Structure of Voluntary Society: Buchanan and Nutter on School Segregation," SSRN, December 30, 2018, p. 44, https://ssrn.com/abstract=3308162.

155  **Buchanan and his co-author** G. Warren Nutter and James M. Buchanan, "Different School Systems Are Reviewed," *Richmond Times-Dispatch*, April 12, 1959, https://delong.typepad.com/nutter _buchanan_richmond1.pdf.

156  **64 percent of Americans** Howard Schneider and Chris Kahn, "Majority of Americans Favor Wealth Tax on Very Rich: Reuters/Ipsos Poll," Reuters, January 10, 2020, https://www.reuters.com/article/us -usa-election-inequality-poll/majority-of-americans-favor-wealth-tax -on-very-rich-reuters-ipsos-poll-idUSKBN1Z9141.

156  **70 percent want** Matthew Yglesias, "A Huge Boost in Infrastructure Spending Is Very Popular—If Rich People Pay for It," *Vox*, May 21, 2020, https://www.vox.com/2020/5/21/21262211/infrastructure -spending-poll-stimulus.

156  **56 percent support** "Public Opinion on Single-Payer National Health Plans and Expanding Access to Medicare Coverage," Charts & Slides, KFF, May 27, 2020, https://www.kff.org/slideshow/public-opinion-on -single-payer-national-health-plans-and-expanding-access-to -medicare-coverage.

156  **They used images** Wealthy donors paid for 140 billboards in black neighborhoods in Ohio and Wisconsin weeks before the 2012 election warning that voter fraud is a felony. Daniel Bice, "Bradley Foundation Helped Pay for 2010 Voter Fraud Signs," *Milwaukee-Wisconsin Journal Sentinel*, October 31, 2012, http://archive.jsonline.com/blogs/ news/176675811.html.

156  **to be virtually nonexistent** "Debunking the Voter Fraud Myth," Brennan Center for Justice, January 31, 2017, https://www.brennan- center.org/analysis/debunking-voter-fraud-myth.

156  **particularly among white Republicans** Support for photo ID requirements to address voter fraud has become Republican party dogma; studies also show that support rises among white people with higher racial resentment, those who have strong implicit biases, and those who are primed with images of black poll workers and black voters. Paul Gronke, et al., "Voter ID Laws: A View from the Public," *Social Science Quarterly* 100, no. 1 (February 2019): 219, https://doi .org/10.1111/ssqu.12541.

156  **becomes more tolerable** Sixty-seven percent of Americans believe that too few people voting is a problem, majorities in both parties. Jones et al., "American Democracy in Crisis."

156  **Paul Weyrich** He cofounded the Heritage Foundation and the Ameri-

can Legislative Exchange Council, among other conservative organizations, and is credited with coining the phrase "moral majority." Bruce Weber, "Paul Weyrich, 66, a Conservative Strategist, Dies," *New York Times*, December 18, 2008, https://www.nytimes.com/2008/12/19/us/politics/19weyrich.html; Rachel Weiner, "How ALEC Became a Political Liability," *Washington Post*, April 24, 2012, https://www.washingtonpost.com/blogs/the-fix/post/how-alec-became-a-political-liability/2012/04/24/gIQA3QnyeT_blog.html.

156    **"I don't want everybody to vote"** Paul Weyrich, "I Don't Want Everybody to Vote," YouTube, 0:40, June 8, 2007, https://www.youtube.com/watch?v=8GBAsFwPglw.

158    **Name all the signers** Doug Clark, "The 'Literacy Test' that Henry Frye Failed," *Greensboro News & Record*, May 16, 2013, https://www.greensboro.com/townnews/politics/the-literacy-test-that-henry-frye-failed/article_8709f91e-be4b-11e2-bdc1-0019bb30f31a.html.

158    **In 1962, only 36 percent** "Voting Right Act of 1965," North Carolina History Project, https://northcarolinahistory.org/encyclopedia/voting-rights-act-of-1965.

158    **Throughout the South, about one million** Anderson, *One Person, No Vote*, 27.

158    **to become the chief justice** "Henry Frye: First African-American on the N.C. Supreme Court," North Carolina Department of Natural and Cultural Resources, https://www.ncdcr.gov/blog/2017/02/03/henry-frye-first-african-american-on-the-n-c-supreme-court.

158    **participation of lower-income white voters** Atiba Ellis, "The Cost of the Vote: Poll Taxes, Voter Identification Laws, and the Price of Democracy," *Denver University Law Review* 86, no. 3 (2009): 1023–68, https://www.researchgate.net/publication/272023853_The_Cost_of_the_Vote_Poll_Taxes_Voter_Identification_Laws_and_the_Price_of_Democracy.

158    **the poll tax requirement** At the time leading up to the Twenty-fourth Amendment's ratification, the poll tax prevented some four million people from voting in this country. See "White Only: Jim Crow in America," *Separate Is Not Equal: Brown v. Board of Education*, National Museum of American History, Smithsonian Institution, Washington, D.C., https://americanhistory.si.edu/brown/history/1-segregated/white-only-1.html. The Twenty-fourth Amendment made poll taxes unconstitutional, though some have compellingly argued that current hurdles to voting for low-income people constitute a tax (not to mention the 2020 Florida criminal legal system fees requirement). See Valencia Richardson, "Voting While Poor: Reviving the 24th Amendment and Eliminating the Modern-Day Poll Tax,"

*Georgetown Journal on Poverty Law and Policy* 27, no. 3 (Spring 2020): 451–68, https://www.law.georgetown.edu/poverty-journal/wp-content/uploads/sites/25/2020/06/05-Richardson_Final_Proof.pdf.

158 **the courts upheld it** *Breedlove v. Suttles,* 302 U.S. 277 (1937); *Butler v. Thomson,* 97 F. Supp. 17 (E.D. Va. 1951).

159 **V. O. Key described in 1949** Wright, *Sharing the Prize,* 56, referring to V. O. Key's *Southern Politics in State and Nation* (1949) at pp. 1–18.

159 **they won investments** Wright, *Sharing the Prize,* ebook, Chapter six, "The Economic Consequences of Voting Rights."

159 **This was the case** Stephen G. Katsinas, "Albert Brewer Was a Workhorse for Education," Advance Local Media, March 6, 2019, https://www.al.com/opinion/2017/02/albert_brewer_was_a_workhorse.html.

160 **a Koch brothers–founded libertarian group** The group, Americans for Prosperity, denied financial involvement in the 2009 Wake County school board elections. However, media outlets have reported the group's involvement through "significant financial contributions as well as other support." A *Newsweek* article reported that Americans for Prosperity was involved in volunteer work on the campaign, and voter education work. Additionally, Koch-allied Art Pope, a wealthy conservative businessman in the state with financial ties to Americans for Prosperity (who served on the organization's board of directors), donated more than $15,000 to the Wake County GOP, which utilized the funds for conservative candidates' school board campaigns in 2009. Trymaine Lee, "The Koch Brothers and the Battle Over Integration in Wake County's Schools," *HuffPost,* August 15, 2011, updated October 14, 2011, https://www.huffpost.com/entry/the-battle-for-wake-count_n_926799; Ben Adler, "Weak Tea Party Connection to Wake County, N.C. School Board," *Newsweek,* January 21, 2011, https://www.newsweek.com/weak-tea-party-connection-wake-county-nc-school-board-21053; Jane Mayer, "State for Sale," *New Yorker,* October 3, 2011, https://www.newyorker.com/magazine/2011/10/10/state-for-sale.

160 **to give more than $3.5 million** The pre-decision limit was $132,000 in 2014. "What Is McCutcheon v. FEC?," Demos, April 8, 2014, https://www.demos.org/research/what-mccutcheon-v-fec.

160 **for corporations and unions to spend** Liz Kennedy, "10 Ways Citizens United Endangers Democracy," Demos, January 19, 2012, https://www.demos.org/policy-briefs/10-ways-citizens-united-endangers-democracy.

160     **for secret money to sway elections** "SpeechNow v. FEC—The Case that Created Super PACs, and Our Challenge," Free Speech for Free People, January 27, 2018, https://freespeechforpeople.org/speechnow -v-fec-case-created-super-pacs-challenge.

161     **"Economic elites and organized groups"** Martin Gilens and Benjamin I. Page, "Testing Theories of American Politics: Elites, Interest Groups, and Average Citizens," *Perspectives on Politics* 12, no. 3 (September 2014): 564–81, https://www.cambridge.org/core/journals/ perspectives-on-politics/article/testing-theories-of-american-politics -elites-interest-groups-and-average-citizens/62327F513959D0A304D 4893B382B992B.

161     **"senators' [policy] preferences diverge"** Michael J. Barber, "Representing the Preferences of Donors, Partisans, and Voters in the U.S. Senate," *Public Opinion Quarterly* 80, no. 1 (March 2016): 225–49, https://doi.org/10.1093/poq/nfw004.

161     **"in the bottom one-third"** Larry Bartels, *Unequal Democracy: The Political Economy of the New Gilded Age* (Princeton, NJ: Princeton University Press, 2008), 285.

161     **Since the early 1970s** "Fundraising Wasn't for the Forefathers," Center for Responsive Politics, February 22, 2007, https://www.open secrets.org/news/2007/02/fundraising-wasnt-for-the-fore; "Donor Demographics 2018," Center for Responsive Politics, Open Secrets, https://www.opensecrets.org/elections-overview/donor-demographics ?cycle=2018&display=G.

161     **of donors who gave more** Sean McElwee, "Whose Voice, Whose Choice? The Distorting Influence of the Political Donor Class in Our Big-Money Elections," Demos, December 8, 2016, https://www .demos.org/publication/whose-voice-whose-choice-distorting -influence-political-donor-class-our-big-money-electi.

161     **"They are overwhelmingly white"** Nicholas Confessore, Sarah Cohen, and Karen Yourish, "The Families Funding the 2016 Presidential Election," *New York Times*, October 10, 2015, https://www .nytimes.com/interactive/2015/10/11/us/politics/2016-presidential -election-super-pac-donors.html.

162     **Two-thirds of Americans consider** Jones et al., "American Democracy in Crisis," 13.

162     **After a history of high-profile corruption** "Welcome to Corrupticut: A Look Back at the History of Corrupt Politics in Connecticut," *Hartford Courant*, June 25, 2019, https://www.courant.com/politics/capitol -watch/hc-pol-political-corruption-in-connecticut-20190625 -ur5fnxn7ibamdnwjlhyny5elpe-story.html; "Connecticut's Landmark Pay-to-Play Law," Brennan Center for Justice, February 1, 2009,

https://www.brennancenter.org/our-work/research-reports/
connecticuts-landmark-pay-play-law.

162   **The Connecticut Citizens' Election Program offered** The reform
      included a ban on lobbyist contributions and a voluntary public fi-
      nancing program for campaigns. The limit has since been increased to
      $270. See "Welcome to the Citizens' Election Program," Connecticut
      State Elections Enforcement Commission, https://seec.ct.gov/Portal/
      CEP/CEPLanding.

162   **"I announced my reelection bid"** J. Mijin Cha and Miles Rapoport,
      "Fresh Start: The Impact of Public Financing in Connecticut,"
      Demos, April 2013, p. 7, https://www.demos.org/sites/default/files/
      publications/FreshStart_PublicFinancingCT_0.pdf.

162   **less sway over legislators'** The former Speaker of the Connecticut
      House, Chris Donovan, observed, "Newer legislators have a new
      attitude towards lobbyists. There is a different perception that lobby-
      ists are not such big players. You are much less worried about a
      lobbyist amassing funds against you." Cha and Rapoport, "Fresh
      Start," 10.

162   **"Public financing definitely made"** Cha and Rapoport, "Fresh
      Start," 13.

162   **"the candidate who wasn't supposed"** Piper Fund, "Senator Gary
      Holder-Winfield on the Benefits of Public Financing in CT," You-
      Tube, 3:36, January 13, 2016, https://www.youtube.com/watch?v=
      4RgElV5WAUI.

162   **"I didn't come from money"** DeNora Getachew and Ava Mehta, eds.,
      "Breaking Down Barriers: The Faces of Small Donor Public Financ-
      ing," Brennan Center for Justice, 2016, p. 12,
      https://www.brennancenter.org/sites/default/files/publications/
      Faces_of_Public_Financing.pdf.

163   **a raft of popular public-interest bills** Cha and Rapoport, "Fresh
      Start," 15–16.

163   **Despite regular efforts to curtail it** Karen Hobert Flynn, "The Citi-
      zens Election Program Is at Risk Again," *Connecticut Mirror,* Janu-
      ary 3, 2018, https://ctmirror.org/category/ct-viewpoints/the-citizens
      -election-program-is-at-risk-again.

163   **73 percent of whom opted into** "Small Donor Solutions for Big
      Money: The 2014 Elections and Beyond," Public Campaign, Novem-
      ber 21, 2014, https://everyvoice.org/wp-content/uploads/2015/04/
      2014SmallDonorReportJan13.pdf.

163   **has national popular support as well** Seventy-two percent of likely
      voters in 2015 supported small-donor public financing of federal elec-
      tions. Laura Friedenbach, "New Poll: Broad Support for Small-Donor

Driven Solutions to Money in Politics," Every Voice, December 17, 2015, https://everyvoice.org/press-release/new-poll-small-donor -driven-solutions.

163    **"Yeah, we are using"** Piper Fund, "Senator Gary Holder-Winfield."

## Chapter Seven: Living Apart

168    **a suburb famous for its integration** When I was in middle school, my father lived in Oak Park, Illinois, one of the more diverse and in- tegrated suburbs in the nation. Emily Badger, "How Race Still Influ- ences Where We Choose to Live," *Washington Post*, July 17, 2015, https://www.washingtonpost.com/news/wonk/wp/2015/07/17/how -race-still-influences-where-we-chose-to-live/?utm_term= .412391a8e90b.

168    **four times as many Asian American students** Berkeley Law School, Law School Numbers, http://berkeley.lawschoolnumbers.com.

168    **most segregated people in America** White people "are most likely to live in racially homogenous communities and least likely to come into contact with people unlike themselves. By this measure, whites are the most isolated of racial groups." Thomas J. Sugrue, "Less Separate, Still Unequal: Diversity and Equality in 'Post-Civil Rights' America," *Our Compelling Interests: The Value of Diversity for Democracy and a Prosperous Society*, ed. Earl Lewis and Nancy Cantor (Princeton, NJ: Princeton University Press, 2016). See also Aaron Williams and Ar- mand Emamdjomeh, "America Is More Diverse than Ever—But Still Segregated," *Washington Post*, May 10, 2018, https://www.washington post.com/graphics/2018/national/segregation-us-cities/.

169    **at least 75 percent white** The typical African American, by contrast, lives in a 45 percent black neighborhood. John R. Logan and Brian Stults, "The Persistence of Segregation in the Metropolis: New Find- ings from the 2010 Census," US2010 Project, March 24, 2011, pp. 2–3, https://s4.ad.brown.edu/Projects/Diversity/Data/Report/report2 .pdf.

169    **limited or barred free black people** Woodward, *The Strange Career of Jim Crow*, 19; Alana Semuels, "The Racist History of Portland, the Whitest City in America," *The Atlantic*, July 22, 2016, https://www .theatlantic.com/business/archive/2016/07/racist-history-portland/ 492035.

169    **In the North** Of course, it was the racism that allowed white employ- ers to pay black people less, which enabled other white people to see them as wage-suppressing competition. For more on the job competi- tion and status dynamics between the white and black northern

working classes, see David Roediger, *Working Toward Whiteness: How America's Immigrants Became White* (New York: Basic Books, 2005).

169 **Civil Rights Act in 1875** The law provided "That all persons within the jurisdiction of the United States shall be entitled to the full and equal enjoyment of the accommodations, advantages, facilities, and privileges of inns, public conveyances on land or water, theaters, and other places of public amusement; subject only to the conditions and limitations established by law, and applicable alike to citizens of every race and color, regardless of any previous condition of servitude."

170 **"salt-and-pepper" integration** Alana Semuels, " 'Segregation Had to Be Invented,' " *The Atlantic*, February 17, 2017, https://www.the-atlantic.com/business/archive/2017/02/segregation-invented/517158.

170 **This time, they reasoned** See Semuels, " 'Segregation Had to Be Invented.' "

170 **struck down America's first Civil Rights Act** Civil Rights Cases, 109 US 3 (1883). The 8–1 majority opinion reasoned that the Reconstruction amendments did not empower Congress to regulate "private" behavior, only state action. Justice Harlan's dissent stressed the public function of private businesses such as railroads and invoked a still-dormant reading of the "Privileges and Immunities" clause of the Fourteenth Amendment as a potential basis for broad federal action to guarantee equal rights.

170 **"Jim Crow laws put"** Woodward, *Strange Career*, 108.

170 **Any white person was now deputized** See Carol Anderson, *White Rage: The Unspoken Truth of Our Racial Divide* (New York: Bloomsbury, 2016).

170 **For the next eighty years** Todd Lewan and Dolores Barclay, " 'When They Steal Your Land, They Steal Your Future,' " *Los Angeles Times*, December 2, 2001, https://www.latimes.com/archives/la-xpm-2001-dec-02-mn-10514-story.html.

170 **looked to America's laws** James Whitman, *Hitler's American Model: The United States and the Making of Nazi Race Law* (Princeton, NJ: Princeton University Press, 2017); George M. Fredrickson, *Racism: A Short History* (Princeton, NJ: Princeton University Press, 2002).

170 **federal government supported housing segregation** Under the purportedly progressive New Deal, the federal government further cemented segregation as a nationwide rule, building thousands of units of public housing for workers on a segregated basis even in cities that previously had no segregation rules. Out of the Great Depression

came the federal Home Owners' Loan Corporation, created to shore up the housing market by making mortgages affordable to the masses. The government deemed (with no empirical evidence) that black and ethnic immigrant neighborhoods would be a poor credit risk, so created racial population neighborhood maps of 239 cities to designate those areas as "hazardous" (shading them red in a process known as "redlining"). See Rothstein, *Color of Law.* Surveyor assessments of the neighborhood's racial and ethnic population, as well as amenities and current prices, led to a color-coding system that designated green for best, blue for "still desirable," yellow for "definitely declining," and red for "hazardous." See Mapping Inequality: Redlining in New Deal America, https://dsl.richmond.edu/panorama/redlining/#loc= 5/39.1/-94.58.

171    **Supreme Court ruled in 1948** *Shelley v. Kraemer,* 334 US 1 (1948).

171    **Planners for the Interstate Highway System** See, for example, Kevin M. Cruse, "Traffic," in *The 1619 Project, New York Times Magazine,* August 18, 2019, pp. 48–49, https://www.nytimes.com/interactive/ 2019/08/14/magazine/traffic-atlanta-segregation.html; Raymond A. Mohl, "The Interstates and the Cities: The U.S. Department of Transportation and the Freeway Revolt, 1966–1973," *Journal of Policy History* 20, no. 2 (2008): 193–226, https://www.cambridge.org/core/ journals/journal-of-policy-history/article/interstates-and-the-cities -the-us-department-of-transportation-and-the-freeway-revolt-- 19661973/4FE236EB30F98269D9931788AD7CCA47.

171    **is responsible for as much as half** "Indeed, looking across entire neighborhoods (not just across narrow boundaries), our findings suggest that the maps could account for between 15 and 30 percent of the D-C [the letter grades for quality ratings assigned to different neighborhoods] gap in share African-American and homeownership and 40 percent of the gap in house values over the 1950 to 1980 period. The maps account for roughly half of the homeownership and house value gaps along the C-B borders over the same period," p. 4, in Daniel Aaronson et al., "The Effects of the 1930s HOLC 'Redlining' Maps," Working Paper no. 2017-12, Federal Reserve Bank of Chicago, revised August 2020, https://www.chicagofed.org/publications/working -papers/2017/wp2017-12.

171    **Supreme Court invalidated city ordinances** *Buchanan v. Warley,* 245 US 60 (1917).

171    **rushed to adopt "exclusionary zoning" laws** "In 1916, only eight cities in the country had zoning ordinances. By 1936, 1,246 cities had put such ordinances on the books." Elizabeth Winkler, " 'Snob Zoning' Is Racial Housing Segregation by Another Name," *Washington Post,*

September 25, 2017, https://www.washingtonpost.com/news/wonk/
wp/2017/09/25/snob-zoning-is-racial-housing-segregation-by
-another-name/?utm_term=.93b0a6ee215a.

172    **laid across 75 percent** A June 2019 *New York Times* Upshot analysis
found that, for example, Minneapolis had detached single-family
housing restrictions on 70 percent of its metro area land; San Jose restricted 94 percent; Portland, OR, 77 percent; and Charlotte, NC, 84
percent. Emily Badger and Quoctrung Bui, "Cities Start to Question
an American Ideal: A House with a Yard on Every Lot," *New York
Times,* June 18, 2019, https://www.nytimes.com/interactive/2019/
06/18/upshot/cities-across-america-question-single-family-zoning
.html. In December 2018, Minneapolis voted to end its single-family
zoning restrictions, citing the racist history of intentional housing segregation. See Minneapolis 2040 urban plan, https://minneapolis2040
.com/goals/affordable-and-accessible-housing.

172    **Exclusionary zoning rules limit** Elliott Anne Rigsby, "Understanding Exclusionary Zoning and Its Impact on Concentrated Poverty,"
The Century Foundation, June 23, 2016, https://tcf.org/content/
facts/understanding-exclusionary-zoning-impact-concentrated
-poverty.

172    **In 1977, the Supreme Court failed** *Village of Arlington Heights v.
Metropolitan Housing Development Corp,* 429 US 252 (1977).

173    **when you bought on contract** According to Richard Rothstein, in the
1960s "approximately 85 percent of all property purchased by African
Americans in Chicago had been sold to them on contract," in *The
Color of Law,* 98.

173    **Chicago is one** Alana Semuels, "Chicago's Awful Divide," *The Atlantic,* March 28, 2018, https://www.theatlantic.com/business/archive/
2018/03/chicago-segregation-poverty/556649.

173    **1948 racial covenant Supreme Court decision** *Shelley v. Kraemer,*
334 US 1 (1948).

173    **80 percent of the city** "Understanding Fair Housing," U.S. Commission on Civil Rights, 1973, Washington, D.C., https://files.eric.ed.gov/
fulltext/ED075565.pdf.

174    **over 90 percent African American** See "City of Chicago Community
Areas, 1910–1990s," http://i.imgur.com/xZoKnTa.gif.

175    **majority of white Americans said** "Reactions to the Shooting in Ferguson, Mo., Have Sharp Racial Divides," *New York Times*/CBS News
Poll, *New York Times,* August 21, 2014, https://www.nytimes.com/
interactive/2014/08/21/us/ferguson-poll.html.

175    **21 percent "seldom or never" interacted** Maxine Najle and Robert P.
Jones, "American Democracy in Crisis: The Fate of Pluralism in a

Divided Nation," PRRI, February 19, 2019, https://www.prri.org/
research/american-democracy-in-crisis-the-fate-of-pluralism-in-a
-divided-nation.

175   **three-quarters of white people reported** Daniel Cox et al., "IV. Racial Homogeneity of Whites' Social Networks," in "Race, Religion,
and Political Affiliation of Americans' Core Social Networks," PRRI,
August 3, 2016, https://www.prri.org/research/poll-race-religion
-politics-americans-social-networks.

175   **This white isolation continues** Alvin Chang, "White America Is Quietly Self-Segregating," *Vox,* July 31, 2018, https://www.vox.com/
2017/1/18/14296126/white-segregated-suburb-neighborhood
-cartoon.

175   **"Approximately ninety-four percent of the cases"** Linda R. Tropp,
"Benefits of Contact Between Racial and Ethnic Groups: A Summary
of Research Findings," Testimony in Support of New York City
School Diversity Bills, Hearing on Diversity in New York City Schools,
December 11, 2014, http://school-diversity.org/wp-content/uploads/
2014/09/Tropp-written-testimony-for-New-York-City-Schools-12
-2014.pdf.

175   **In their study, white people** Accordingly, while black and Latinx
people search in neighborhoods that match their stated ethnic mix,
they end up in neighborhoods with larger minority populations than
they desired. See "Racial Residential Segregation and the Housing
Search Process," *Research Spotlight: Maria Krysan* (newsletter), Institute of Government and Public Affairs, University of Illinois, December 3, 2015, https://igpa.uillinois.edu/sites/igpa.uillinois.edu/files/
reports/Research-Spotlight-Krysan_Housing-Search.pdf.

176   **"both the racially mixed"** The experiment showed a range of social
class cues, and higher-class-appearing neighborhoods were rated more
highly by black and white respondents. However, race impacted white
respondents' ratings even within each social class category. See Maria
Krysan et al., "Does Race Matter in Neighborhood Preferences? Results from a Video Experiment," *American Journal of Sociology* 115,
no. 2 (September 2009): 527–59, doi:10.1086/599248.

176   **White people are surely losing something** Meanwhile, white avoid-
ance of black neighborhoods in a housing market still dominated by
white wealth costs black homeowners an average of $48,000 each, ac-
cording to a Brookings Institution–Gallup study that looked at identical properties in majority-black and all-white neighborhoods, with the
effect of racial bias isolated from other rationales, "such as the structural characteristics of the buildings and access to good schools, good
jobs and good stores." As with all aspects of racism, the targeted com-

munities bear the brunt—but you don't have to look far to find the collateral damage to the rest of society. See Christopher Ingram, "How White Racism Destroys Black Wealth," *Washington Post*, November 28, 2018, https://www.washingtonpost.com/business/2018/11/28/how-white-racism-destroys-black-wealth; and Andre Perry et al., "The Devaluation of Assets in Black Neighborhoods: The Case of Residential Property," Metropolitan Policy Program, Brookings Institution, November 2018, https://www.brookings.edu/wp-content/uploads/2018/11/2018.11_Brookings-Metro_Devaluation-Assets-Black-Neighborhoods_final.pdf.

177 **They analyzed quality-of-life indicators** *The Cost of Segregation* calculated the degree of segregation in the country's one hundred most populous cities or commuting zones and measured quality-of-life indicators that could be impacted by segregation (for example, income levels suppressed by greater distances between employees and jobs; educational attainment associated with segregated and/or resource-constrained schools; life expectancy flowing from inequitable healthcare access and pollution). The research team then controlled for factors besides segregation that could have contributed to the outcomes, from degree of inequality to population size. Finally, they accounted for city-specific variables across all one hundred locations. Gregory Acs et al., *The Cost of Segregation: National Trends and the Case of Chicago, 1990–2010*, Urban Institute and Metropolitan Planning Council of Chicago, March 2017, pp. 9–11, https://www.urban.org/sites/default/files/publication/89201/the_cost_of_segregation_final_0.pdf.

177 **segregation is correlated with billions** See the Cost of Segregation website, Metropolitan Planning Council of Chicago, https://www.metroplanning.org/costofsegregation/cost.aspx.

178 **more likely to direct pollutants** Paul Mohai and Robin Saha, "Which Came First, People or Pollution? Assessing the Disparate Siting and Post-Siting Demographic Change Hypotheses of Environmental Justice," *Environmental Research Letters* 10, no. 11 (November 2015), https://doi.org/10.1088/1748-9326/10/11/115008.

178 **less able to band together** Kendra Pierre-Louis, "Dr. King Said Segregation Harms Us All. Environmental Research Shows He Was Right," *New York Times*, April 3, 2018, https://www.nytimes.com/2018/04/03/climate/mlk-segregation-pollution.html.

178 **"The way we talk about"** Robin DiAngelo, *What Does It Mean to Be White? Developing White Racial Literacy* (New York: Counterpoints, 2016), 188.

179 **schools are financed primarily** K–12 public school revenue is about

evenly split between local funds and state funds. "K–12 schools in every state rely heavily on state aid. On average, 47 percent of school revenues in the United States come from state funds. Local governments provide another 45 percent; the remaining 8 percent comes from the federal government." Michael Leachman and Eric Figueroa, "K–12 School Funding Up in Most 2018 Teacher-Protest States, but Still Well Below Decade Ago," Center on Budget and Policy Priorities, March 6, 2019, https://www.cbpp.org/research/state-budget-and-tax/k-12-school-funding-up-in-most-2018-teacher-protest-states-but-still.

179     **an average of $2,226 more** "Nonwhite School Districts Get $23 Billion Less than White Districts Despite Serving the Same Number of Students," EdBuild, February 2019, https://edbuild.org/content/23-billion.

179     **are children of color** "Indicator 6: Elementary and Secondary Enrollment," *Status and Trends in the Education of Racial and Ethnic Groups*, National Center for Education Statistics, updated February 2019, https://nces.ed.gov/programs/raceindicators/indicator_rbb.asp.

179     **The boom in private schools** "A History of Private Schools & Race in the American South," Southern Education Foundation, https://www.southerneducation.org/publications/historyofprivateschools.

180     **almost half of private school kids** Emma Brown, "The Overwhelming Whiteness of U.S. Private Schools, in 6 Maps and Charts," *Washington Post*, March 29, 2016, https://www.washingtonpost.com/news/education/wp/2016/03/29/the-overwhelming-whiteness-of-u-s-private-schools-in-six-maps-and-charts/?utm_term=.de784181ce5a.

180     **cost 58 percent more** Michael Sklarz et al., "Housing Values & School Quality," Collateral Analytics, April 17, 2018, https://collateralanalytics.com/housing-values-school-quality.

180     **77 percent more expensive** The study looked at standardized test scores of elementary schools for zip codes in which at least one school had a score average at least 33 percent higher than the statewide average. "Home Values 77 Percent Higher in Zip Codes with Good Schools than in Zip Codes Without Good Schools," Realtytrac, August 3, 2016, https://www.realtytrac.com/news/2016-schools-and-housing-report.

180     **65 percent of the zip codes** Lack of affordability is defined as "average wage earners would need to spend more than one-third of their income to buy a median-priced home." "Homes Not Affordable for Average Wage Earners in 65 Percent of Zip Codes with Good Schools," Realtytrac, November 18, 2015, https://www.realtytrac.com/news/realtytrac-2015-good-schools-and-affordable-homes/.

180     **CNN covered that study** Jeanne Sahadi, "You Probably Can't Afford

to Live Near Good Schools," CNN Money, November 9, 2015, https://
money.cnn.com/2015/11/19/real_estate/neighborhoods-good-schools
-affordable/index.html.

180 **"have gained $51,000 more"** "Home Values 77 Percent Higher," Re-
altytrac.

180 **increasingly expensive, and segregated, communities** As parents
gain access to increasing amounts of data about school quality, affluent
parents—who, given the wealth disparity in the United States, are
predominantly white—use that information to seek out neighborhoods with schools that earn the highest ratings, thus increasing segregation and driving up housing prices even further. For instance, a
recent study that examined 9,400 zip codes in nineteen states found
that once school ratings were published online by a nonprofit called
GreatSchools.org, the effect was, essentially, more segregation: "accelerated divergence in housing values, income distributions, education
levels, as well as the racial and ethnic composition across communities." (Ironically, this was the opposite of what the people behind
GreatSchools.org had intended, which was to provide low-income parents with information that could help them choose schools for their
kids.) Shariq Hasan and Anuj Kumar, "Digitization and Divergence:
Online School Ratings and Segregation in America," July 23, 2019,
p. 1, SSRN, http://dx.doi.org/10.2139/ssrn.3265316. Another study
found that once a school district receives an "A" grade, home values increase by 6.7 percent over a three-year period over areas with grade
"B" schools. David N. Figlio and Cecilia Elena Rouse, "Do Accountability and Voucher Threats Improve Low-Performing Schools?" *Journal of Public Economics* 90, nos. 1–2 (January 2006): 239–55.

181 **Compared to students** Except where noted, data points in the para-
graph are from Genevieve Siegel-Hawley, "How Non-Minority
Students Also Benefit from Racially Diverse Schools," Brief No. 8,
October 2012, National Coalition on School Diversity, https://www
.school-diversity.org/pdf/DiversityResearchBriefNo8.pdf.

181 **spend about eight billion dollars a year** "Focusing on What Works
for Workplace Diversity," McKinsey and Company, April 2017,
https://www.mckinsey.com/featured-insights/gender-equality/
focusing-on-what-works-for-workplace-diversity.

181 **can produce better citizens** Siegel-Hawley, "How Non-Minority Students."

181 **Holoien cites several studies** But there's a caveat, she warns: while
white students gain from the presence of even one student of color,
people of color (and women) benefit the most when a diverse environment enables them to interact with others from their own group.

When a college student finds herself the only person of color in a classroom, the need to steel herself against bias may prevent her from benefiting optimally from the class itself. Deborah Son Holoien, "Do Differences Make a Difference? The Effects of Diversity on Learning, Intergroup Outcomes, and Civic Engagement," Princeton University, September 2013, https://inclusive.princeton.edu/sites/inclusive/ files/pu-report-diversity-outcomes.pdf.

182     **It was a strategy** Richard Kluger, *Simple Justice: The History of Brown v. Board of Education and Black America's Struggle for Equality* (New York: Alfred A. Knopf, 1975); and Robert L. Carter, "Review: 'The NAACP's Legal Strategy Against Segregated Education, 1925– 1950,' by Mark Tushnet," *Michigan Law Review* 86, no. 6 (May 1988): 1085, https://www.jstor.org/stable/1289155.

182     **Thirty-two experts submitted an appendix** "The Effects of Segregation and the Consequences of Desegregation: A Social Science Statement," in *Brown v. Board of Education*, 347 U.S. 483 (1954), http:// www.naacpldf.org/document/social-scientists-appendix-petitioners -brief-brown-v-board-education.

183     **"confusion, conflict, moral cynicism"** "The Effects of Segregation," 6.

183     **"I believe that we must"** Sherrilyn Ifill, "Brown Decision's Legacy Should Include White Children," CNN, May 17, 2016, https://edition .cnn.com/2016/05/17/opinions/brown-v-board-anniv-sherrilyn-ifill/ index.html.

183     **"No one is born hating"** Barack Obama (@BarackObama), Twitter, August 12, 2017, https://twitter.com/barackobama/status/ 896523232098078720?lang=en.

184     **Instead, they'll come up with** See, for example, Rebecca A. Dore et al., "Children's Racial Bias in Perceptions of Others' Pain," *British Journal of Developmental Psychology* 32, no. 2 (June 2014): 218–31, https://doi.org/10.1111/bjdp.12038; "How Kids Learn About Race," *EmbraceRace* (blog), January 22, 2019, https://www.embracerace .org/blog/how-children-learn-about-race.

184     **"The most profound message"** DiAngelo, *What Does It Mean to Be White?*, 190.

185     **"The 1928 Austin city plan segregated"** "Austin's '1928 Master Plan' Unleashed Forces Which Still Shape Austin Today," https://www .austintexas.gov/sites/default/files/files/City-Council/Houston/CM _OH_1928_Op-Ed.pdf.

189     **nearly 90 percent white Catholic school** "Students at Our Lady of Lourdes High School," Niche, n.d., https://www.niche.com/k12/our -lady-of-lourdes-high-school-poughkeepsie-ny/students.

189    **Spackenkill successfully sued** Sue Books, "The Politics of School
       Districting: A Case Study in Upstate New York," *Educational Founda-
       tions* 20, no. 3–4 (Summer–Fall 2006): 15–33, https://eric.ed.gov/
       ?id=EJ794730.

189    **One can find similar stories** "White districts enroll just over 1,500
       students—half the size of the national average, and nonwhite districts
       serve over 10,000 students—three times more than that average," in
       "23 Billion," full report, EdBuild, February 2019, p. 3, https://edbuild
       .org/content/23-billion/full-report.pdf.

189    **Fiona, is now in college** "Drexel University Undergraduate Ethnic
       Diversity Breakdown," College Factual, n.d., https://www.college
       factual.com/colleges/drexel-university/student-life/diversity/chart
       -ethnic-diversity.html.

## Chapter Eight: The Same Sky

193    **WE HAVE 12 YEARS** Jonathan Watts, "We Have 12 Years to Limit Cli-
       mate Change Catastrophe, Warns UN," *Guardian*, October 8, 2018,
       https://www.theguardian.com/environment/2018/oct/08/global
       -warming-must-not-exceed-15c-warns-landmark-un-report.

193    **Climate change caused by manmade pollution** For eight hundred
       thousand years of measurable time on Earth, the amount of carbon in
       the atmosphere fluctuated but never surpassed three hundred parts
       per million; since 1950, it has shot up to over four hundred. See graph
       at NASA, "Climate Change: How Do We Know?" Global Climate
       Change, n.d., https://climate.nasa.gov/evidence.

194    **Cold spells have decreased** Sophie Lewis, "Sure, Winter Felt Chilly,
       but Australia Is Setting New Heat Records at 12 Times the Rate of
       Cold Ones," *The Conversation* (blog), September 9, 2015, https://
       theconversation.com/sure-winter-felt-chilly-but-australia-is-setting
       -new-heat-records-at-12-times-the-rate-of-cold-ones-35607.

194    **droughts and wildfires** Jason Daley, "Climate Change Has Made
       Droughts More Frequent Since 1900," Smithsonian, May 2, 2019,
       https://www.smithsonianmag.com/smart-news/climate-change-has
       -made-droughts-more-frequent-1900-180972087; Ellen Gray and Jes-
       sica Merzdorf, "Earth's Freshwater Future: Extremes of Flood and
       Drought," *Global Climate Change* (blog), NASA, June 13, 2019,
       https://climate.nasa.gov/news/2881/earths-freshwater-future
       -extremes-of-flood-and-drought.

194    **Sheets of ice are rapidly melting** "Is Sea Level Rising?," Ocean
       Facts, National Ocean Service, NOAA, updated October 19, 2019,
       https://oceanservice.noaa.gov/facts/sealevel.html.

194     **The impact on human life** Daisy Dunne, "Impact of Climate Change on Health Is 'the Major Threat of 21st Century,'" Carbon Brief, October 30, 2017, https://www.carbonbrief.org/impact-climate-change-health-is-major-threat-21st-century.

194     **declines in mental health** Nick Obradovich et al., "Empirical Evidence of Mental Health Risks Posed by Climate Change," PNAS, October 23, 2018, https://doi.org/10.1073/pnas.1801528115.

194     **nearly half the average annual growth** "The Economic Case for Climate Action in the US," Universal Ecological Fund, September 2017, https://feu-us.org/case-for-climate-action-us.

194     **"habitat destruction, overhunting"** Damian Carrington, "Earth's Sixth Mass Extinction Event Under Way, Scientists Warn," *Guardian*, July 10, 2017, https://www.theguardian.com/environment/2017/jul/10/earths-sixth-mass-extinction-event-already-underway-scientists-warn.

194     **often cheaper than higher-pollution fuels** James Ellsmoor, "Renewable Energy Is Now the Cheapest Option—Even Without Subsidies," *Forbes*, June 15, 2019, https://www.forbes.com/sites/jamesellsmoor/2019/06/15/renewable-energy-is-now-the-cheapest-option-even-without-subsidies.

195     **invented the solar cell** Using sun for energy dates back to antiquity, but Bell Labs researchers produced the first practical silicon-based photovoltaic cell in 1954. See "April 25, 1954: Bell Labs Demonstrates the First Practical Silicon Solar Cell," *APS News* 18, no. 4 (April 2009), https://www.aps.org/publications/apsnews/200904/physics history.cfm; "The History of Solar," Energy Efficiency and Renewable Energy, U.S. Department of Energy, https://www1.eere.energy.gov/solar/pdfs/solar_timeline.pdf.

195     **biggest carbon polluter in history** The United States is responsible for 25 percent of cumulative carbon emissions; the current biggest annual emitter is China, but the cumulative impact from China has been just 13 percent. (Also, much of China's emissions production comes from the role it plays manufacturing goods for multinational companies for Western markets and American companies.) The United States is also second in emissions per capita, behind Saudi Arabia. Justin Gillis and Nadja Popovich, "The U.S. Is the Biggest Carbon Polluter in History. It Just Walked Away from the Paris Climate Deal," *New York Times*, June 1, 2017, https://www.nytimes.com/interactive/2017/06/01/climate/us-biggest-carbon-polluter-in-history-will-it-walk-away-from-the-paris-climate-deal.html; and Jeff Toleffson, "The Hard Truths of Climate Change—By the Numbers," *Nature*, September 18, 2019, https://www.nature.com/immersive/d41586-019-02711-4/index.html.

195   **In our peer countries** Sondre Båtstrand, "More than Markets: A
Comparative Study of Nine Conservative Parties on Climate Change,"
*Politics & Policy* 43, no. 4 (August 2015): 538–61.

195   **with very few exceptions** Two Florida members of the U.S. House of
Representatives launched a bipartisan Climate Solutions Caucus (CSC)
in 2016, with a Senate version in 2019. However, in 2018, only four of
the House CSC members voted against H. Con. Res. 199, a nonbinding
resolution that called pricing carbon detrimental, engendering skepti-
cism about whether the CSC could meaningfully change the antiscience behavior even of the Republicans within it. See Roll Call 363,
on H Res. 119, 115th Cong., 2nd sess., July 19, 2018, https://clerk
.house.gov/Votes/2018363; "The Climate Solutions Caucus Just Failed
to Vote for Our Climate Solutions," Protect Our Winters, https://
protectourwinters.org/the-climate-solutions-caucus-just-failed-to-vote
-for-climate-solutions.

195   **the primary reason the United States** There are also Democrats
from fossil fuel industry–reliant states who have opposed some forms
of climate change regulation; however, the near-universal rejection of
climate policy from Republican lawmakers has made it impossible to
legislate solutions that would address the problem.

196   **"saddest day"** "This Is the Saddest Day of My Legislative Life," *Portland Tribune*, June 20, 2019, https://pamplinmedia.com/pt/431699
-340535-this-is-the-saddest-day-of-my-legislative-life.

196   **"Send bachelors"** Sarah Zimmerman, " 'Send Bachelors and Come
Heavily Armed': GOP State Senator Responds to Gov. Brown's Police
Threat," KGW, June 19, 2019, https://www.kgw.com/article/news/
local/send-bachelors-and-come-heavily-armed-gop-state-senator
-responds-to-gov-browns-police-threat/283-a8ccf820-32e4-44df-b81c
-2f8df92919ff.

196   **logging is the state's biggest source** "Editorial: Republican Walkout
Ignores Progress in Cap-and-Trade Bill," *Oregonian*, March 1, 2020,
https://www.oregonlive.com/opinion/2020/03/editorial-republican
-walkout-ignores-progress-in-cap-and-trade-bill.html; Matthew
Koehler, "Oregon Climate Bill Leaves Out Big Timber—State's Largest
Polluter—and Instead Rewards It with More Subsidies," *The Smokey
Wire: National Forest News and Views*, June 19, 2019, https://forest
policypub.com/2019/06/19/oregon-climate-bill-leaves-out-big-timber
-states-largest-polluter-and-instead-rewards-it-with-more-subsidies.

196   **Baertschiger Jr. simply disbelieves** Jeff Mapes, "Oregon Senate GOP
Leader Questions Whether Human Activity Is Causing Global Warming," OPB, October 3, 2019, https://www.opb.org/news/article/
oregon-senate-gop-leader-carbon-emissions-climate-change-global
-warming.

196     **only three were passed** Connor Radnovich, "2020 Oregon Legislature's Final Tally: 3 Bills Passed, 255 Abandoned," *Register Guard,*
March 9, 2020, https://www.registerguard.com/news/20200309/
2020-oregon-legislatures-final-tally-3-bills-passed-255-abandoned.

198     **According to the Yale Project** Matthew Ballew et al., "Which
Racial/Ethnic Groups Care Most About Climate Change?," Yale Program
on Climate Change Communication, April 16, 2020, https://climate
communication.yale.edu/publications/race-and-climate-change.

199     **"and the patriarchy"** Aaron M. McCright and Chenyang Xiao, "Gender and Environmental Concern: Insights from Recent Work and for
Future Research," *Society & Natural Resources* 27, no. 10 (2014):
1109–13, https://doi.org/10.1080/08941920.2014.918235.

199     **more likely to be white, male** *Global Warming's Six Americas 2009:
An Audience Segmentation Analysis,* Yale Project on Climate Change
and George Mason University Center for Climate Change Communication, https://climatecommunication.yale.edu/wp-content/uploads/
2016/02/2009_05_Global-Warmings-Six-Americas.pdf.

199     **"made explicit associations to Obama"** Salil D. Benegal, "The Spillover of Race and Racial Attitudes into Public Opinion About Climate," *Environmental Politics* 27, no. 4 (2018): 738, https://doi.org/10
.1080/09644016.2018.1457287.

199     **covertly supported** Jane Mayer, "Covert Operations," *The New
Yorker,* August 30, 2010, https://www.newyorker.com/magazine/
2010/08/30/covert-operations.

199     **coal miner had become a symbol** Thomas Blake Earle, "No White
Man Left Behind," *Washington Post,* October 27, 2017, https://www
.washingtonpost.com/news/made-by-history/wp/2017/10/27/no
-white-man-left-behind.

200     **"a general orientation toward blacks"** Adam M. Enders and Jamil S.
Scott, "The Increasing Racialization of American Electoral Politics,
1988–2016," *American Politics Research* 47, no. 2 (2019): 276, https://
doi.org/10.1177/1532673X18755654.

200     **"Asking respondents if they agree"** Enders and Scott, "Increasing
Racialization," 748.

200     **white men were much more likely** Aaron M. McCright and Riley E.
Dunlap, "Cool Dudes: The Denial of Climate Change Among Conservative White Males in the United States," *Global Environmental
Change* 21, no. 4 (October 2011): 1163–72, https://doi.org/10.1016/
j.gloenvcha.2011.06.003.

204     **a mostly homogenous "demos"** Peter S. Goodman, "The Nordic
Model May Be the Best Cushion Against Capitalism. Can It Survive
Immigration?," *New York Times,* July 11, 2019, https://www.nytimes
.com/2019/07/11/business/sweden-economy-immigration.html.

205    **weakened the New Deal in 1938** Andrew E. Busch, "The New Deal
       Comes to a Screeching Halt in 1938," Ashbrook Center at Ashland
       University, May 2006, https://ashbrook.org/publications/oped-busch
       -06-1938.

205    **kill national healthcare in 1948** Daniel Prinz, "National Health
       Insurance—A Brief History of Reform Efforts in the U.S.," KFF, Sep-
       tember 26, 2015, https://scholar.harvard.edu/files/dprinz/files/kff_
       national_health_insurance.pdf.

205    **threatened by more frequent droughts** "The Economic Case for Cli-
       mate Action in the US," Universal Ecological Fund, September 2017,
       https://feu-us.org/case-for-climate-action-us.

207    **Commission for Racial Justice** "Environmental Justice History," Of-
       fice of Legacy Management, U.S. Department of Energy, https://
       www.energy.gov/lm/services/environmental-justice/environmental
       -justice-history.

207    **three out of five** Benjamin F. Chavis Jr. and Charles Lee, "Toxic
       Wastes and Race in the United States" (1987), Commission for Racial
       Justice, United Church of Christ, http://uccfiles.com/pdf/Toxic
       Wastes&Race.pdf.

207    **1.5 times more likely** Ihab Mikati et al., "Disparities in Distribution
       of Particulate Matter Emission Sources by Race and Poverty Status,"
       *American Journal of Public Health* 108, no. 4 (April 2018): 480–85,
       https://doi.org/10.2105/AJPH.2017.304297; Maura Allaire et al.,
       "National Trends in Water Quality Violations," *PNAS* 115, no. 9 (Feb-
       ruary 2018): 2078–83, https://doi.org/10.1073/pnas.1719805115.

207    **thirteen times as many** Jane Kay and Cheryl Katz, "Pollution, Pov-
       erty and People of Color: Living with Industry," *Scientific American*,
       June 4, 2012, https://www.scientificamerican.com/article/pollution
       -poverty-people-color-living-industry.

208    **government quickly created twenty-four thousand units** The hous-
       ing for the mostly black workers of color was cheaply built, temporary,
       and located close to the shipyards and Standard Oil refinery. The
       white public housing was farther inland and had better construction.
       Marilynne S. Johnson, "Urban Arsenals: War Housing and Social
       Change in Richmond and Oakland, California, 1941–1945," *Pacific
       Historical Review* 60, no. 3 (August 1991): 283–308.

208    **"live within a ring of five"** Kay and Katz, "Pollution, Poverty."

209    **97 percent black, Latino, or Asian** Demographic data according to
       the 2010 decennial Census figures, https://www.city-data.com/city/
       North-Richmond-California.html.

209    **still unincorporated** Area leaders have proposed annexing North
       Richmond into the city that entirely surrounds it, Richmond, but neg-
       ative perceptions about crime and poverty in North Richmond have

contributed to lack of action by the Richmond City Council. See "North Richmond Annexation Information," Contra Costa Board of Supervisors, n.d., https://www.contracosta.ca.gov/6812/North -Richmond-Annexation-information.

209   **one of the first Laotian refugees** The United States' "secret war" in Laos during the Vietnam War made Laos the most heavily bombed country per capita in world history. (The United States dropped the equivalent of a planeload of bombs on the mostly rural country every eight minutes, twenty-four hours a day, for nine straight years.) "Secret War in Laos," Legacies of War, n.d., http://legaciesofwar.org/ about-laos/secret-war-laos.

210   **Henry Clark, the veteran organizer** Sara Bernard, "Henry Clark and Three Decades of Environmental Justice," *Richmond Confidential*, December 6, 2012, https://richmondconfidential.org/2012/12/06/ henry-clark-and-three-decades-of-environmental-justice.

210   **won a long battle to close** The Ortho pesticide incinerator agreed to close in 1996 and did so in 1997. Jacob Soiffer, "Emergence of Environmental Justice in Richmond: Historical Essay," FoundSF, 2015, http://www.foundsf.org/index.php?title=Emergence_of _Environmental_Justice_in_Richmond.

210   **at almost twice the rate** *Measuring What Matters: Neighborhood Research for Economic and Environmental Health and Justice in Richmond, North Richmond, and San Pablo,* Pacific Institute, May 2009, p. 11, https://pacinst.org/wp-content/uploads/2009/06/measuring -what-matters.pdf.

210   **research increasingly demonstrates a significant link** "Indoor Air Quality in High Performance Schools," U.S. Environmental Protection Agency, https://www.epa.gov/iaq-schools/indoor-air-quality-high -performance-schools; "Air Pollution Near Michigan Schools Linked to Poorer Student Health, Academic Performance," Institute for Social Research, University of Michigan, n.d., https://isr.umich.edu/news -events/insights-newsletter/article/air-pollution-near-michigan -schools-linked-to-poorer-student-health-academic-performance.

210   **ninety-ninth percentile for asthma rates** Susie Cagle, "Richmond v Chevron: The California City Taking On Its Most Powerful Polluter," *Guardian*, October 9, 2019, https://www.theguardian.com/ environment/2019/oct/09/richmond-chevron-california-city-polluter -fossil-fuel.

211   **leading to *more* toxic evaporation** Gar Smith, "Toxic Tour," *Earth Island Journal* (Autumn 2005), https://www.earthisland.org/journal/ index.php/magazine/entry/toxic_tour. On scientific support for color mattering, see M. Farzaneh-Gord, "Effects of Outer Surface Paint

Color on Crude Oil Evaporative Loss from the Khark Island Storage
Tanks," *Brazilian Journal of Petroleum and Gas* 5, no. 3 (2011): 123–
37, https://pdfs.semanticscholar.org/d947/ea1cccb5bd367ddad
9400439be64acdc60a2.pdf.

211   **a thousand pounds of chemicals** A total of 575,669 pounds of chemicals per year, per 2010 data. Jane Kay and Cheryl Katz, "Pollution,
Poverty and People of Color: Living with Industry," *Scientific American*, June 4, 2012, https://www.scientificamerican.com/article/
pollution-poverty-people-color-living-industry.

211   **went unheeded for nearly a decade** "Final Investigation Report:
Chevron Richmond Refinery Pipe Rupture and Fire," Report
#2012-03-I-CA, U.S. Chemical Safety and Hazard Investigation Board,
January 2015, p. 7, https://www.csb.gov/chevron-refinery-fire.

211   **fifteen thousand people sickened** "Final Investigation Report," 32.

212   **$816,000 in 2020** "Point Richmond Home Prices & Values," Zillow,
n.d., https://www.zillow.com/point-richmond-richmond-ca/home
-values.

213   **wasn't much difference between the three** "Analysis of Data from
Richmond Community Air Monitoring Program 2016–2017," https://
static1.squarespace.com/static/581b7ec43e00bed6261bc168/t/
5b7b4425cd8366741a97de08/1534805035391/Analysis+of+RCAMP
+Data+Extended.pdf.

214   **"It just wouldn't be that expensive"** When you measure improved
health, life expectancy, and productivity, the societal benefits of clean
air and water rules significantly dwarf the costs, but even the
pollution-control costs that companies must pay are often overesti-
mated during the debates about imposing them, by industry and even
the government. See "Progress Cleaning the Air and Improving People's Health," Clean Air Act Overview, U.S. Environmental Protection
Agency, https://www.epa.gov/clean-air-act-overview/progress
-cleaning-air-and-improving-peoples-health; "Industry Opposition to
Government Regulation," Pew Environment Group, March 2011,
https://www.pewtrusts.org/~/media/assets/2011/03/industry-clean
-energy-factsheet.pdf. For example, during the Obama administration,
automakers and conservative think tanks warned that requiring vehicles to be more fuel-efficient would make cars prohibitively expensive,
but car prices were actually lower in real terms after the new standards, and the benefits ended up outweighing even those lower costs
by three to one. See Eric Junga, "Fuel Economy Is Going Up. Vehicle
Prices Are Holding Steady," American Council for an Energy-Efficient
Economy, November 16, 2017, https://www.aceee.org/blog/2017/11/
fuel-economy-going-vehicle-prices-are; "Do Environmental Regula-

tions Cost as Much as We Think They Do?," Smart Prosperity Institute, December 2018, pp. 8-9, https://institute.smartprosperity.ca/sites/default/files/regulations-2018december-10.pdf.

215    **The solar array was built with** "MCE Solar One Ribbon Cutting," MCE, April 18, 2018, https://www.mcecleanenergy.org/news/press-releases/mce-solar-one-thinking-globally-building-locally.

217    **more energy and alignment** David Roberts, "At Last, a Climate Policy Platform that Can Unite the Left," *Vox*, July 9, 2020, https://www.vox.com/energy-and-environment/21252892/climate-change-democrats-joe-biden-renewable-energy-unions-environmental-justice.

218    **59 percent of the population** "Memo: U.S. Voters Strongly Support Bold Climate Solutions," Data for Progress, March 19, 2019, https://www.dataforprogress.org/the-green-new-deal-is-popular.

218    **California, New Mexico, New York, and Washington** Phil McKenna, "Washington Commits to 100% Clean Energy and Other States May Follow Suit," *Inside Climate News*, May 7, 2019, https://insideclimatenews.org/news/07052019/100-percent-clean-energy-map-inslee-washington-california-puerto-rico.

## Chapter Nine: The Hidden Wound

221    *"Stony the road we trod"* James Weldon Johnson, lyrics, "Lift Ev'ry Voice and Sing," 1900.

222    **privilege of being born** The privilege of being on the heroes' side in a tragic tale is double-edged. Even my role (or white people's conception of my role) in this well-intentioned narrative would mark me as a victim, a designation used against black Americans to suggest our pathology and dependency.

222    **what they were doing was morally right** For example, in 2002, white St. Louisan Roland Erbar recalled taking part in the anti-black violence during the Fairground Park Riot over pool integration, saying, "Everybody was thinking they were doing the right thing at the time, you know." Eddie Silva, "The Longest Day," *Riverfront Times*, March 20, 2002, https://www.riverfronttimes.com/stlouis/the-longest-day/Content?oid=2469321.

223    **truth-and-reconciliation process** See, for example, Olúfẹ́mi Táíwò, "The Best Way to Respond to Our History of Racism? A Truth and Reconciliation Commission," *Washington Post*, June 30, 2020, https://www.washingtonpost.com/opinions/2020/06/30/best-way-respond-our-history-racism-truth-reconciliation-commission. See also Truth, Racial Healing & Transformation, a project of the W. K. Kellogg Foundation, at healourcommunities.org.

225    **Life After Hate** The mission of the organization is stated on its website: "Life After Hate is committed to helping people leave the violent
far-right to connect with humanity and lead compassionate lives. Our
vision is a world that allows people to change and contribute to a society without violence," in "About Us," Life After Hate, n.d., https://
www.lifeafterhate.org/about-us-1.

226    **"In some parts of the country"** Erin Durkin, "Laura Ingraham Condemned After Saying Immigrants Destroy 'the America We Love,' "
*Guardian*, August 9, 2018, https://www.theguardian.com/media/
2018/aug/09/laura-ingraham-fox-news-attacks-immigrants.

226    **Tucker Carlson raged** *Tucker Carlson Tonight*, December 13, 2018,
https://www.mediamatters.org/white-nationalism/tucker-carlson
-baselessly-accuses-immigrants-making-potomac-dirty.

226    **anti-immigrant sentiment has shifted our politics** See "Polling Update: American Attitudes on Immigration Steady, but Showing More
Partisan Divides," National Immigration Forum, April 17, 2019,
https://immigrationforum.org/article/american-attitudes-on
-immigration-steady-but-showing-more-partisan-divides; "Americans'
Immigration Policy Priorities: Divisions Between and Within the Two
Parties," Fact Tank, Pew Research Center, November 12, 2019,
https://www.pewresearch.org/fact-tank/2019/11/12/americans
-immigration-policy-priorities-divisions-between-and-within-the-two
-parties.

226    **"Therefore love the stranger"** Deuteronomy 10:19 (King James version).

226    **" 'Give me your tired, your poor' "** Emma Lazarus, "The New Colos-
sus" (1883), at Poetry Foundation, https://www.poetryfoundation
.org/poems/46550/the-new-colossus.

228    **that sight triggers your ingrained associations** Tiffany A. Ito and
Bruce B. Bartholow, "The Neural Correlates of Race," *Trends in Cog-
nitive Sciences* 13, no. 12 (December 2009): 524–31, https://www.ncbi
.nlm.nih.gov/pmc/articles/PMC2796452.

228    **If those prejudices about** Rich Morin, "Exploring Racial Bias
Among Biracial and Single-Race Adults: The IAT," Pew Research
Center, August 19, 2015, https://www.pewsocialtrends.org/2015/08/
19/exploring-racial-bias-among-biracial-and-single-race-adults-the
-iat.

228    **We now know that color blindness** Megan R. Underhill, "White
Parents Teach Their Children to Be Colorblind. Here's Why That's
Bad for Everyone," *Washington Post*, October 5, 2018, https://www
.washingtonpost.com/nation/2018/10/05/white-parents-teach-their
-children-be-colorblind-heres-why-thats-bad-everyone; Adia Harvey-
Wingfield, "Color-Blindness Is Counterproductive," *The Atlantic*, Sep-

tember 13, 2015, https://www.theatlantic.com/politics/archive/
2015/09/color-blindness-is-counterproductive/405037.

229 **"explains contemporary racial inequality"** Eduardo Bonilla-Silva, *Racism Without Racists: Color-Blind Racism and the Persistence of Racial Inequality in America* (Lanham, MD: Rowman and Littlefield, 2014), 2, 302.

229 **"reactionary color blindness"** Ian F. Haney López, "A Nation of Minorities: Race, Ethnicity, and Reactionary Colorblindness," *Stanford Law Review* 59, no. 4 (February 2007): 985–1063, https://www.jstor.org/stable/40040347.

229 **Racial conservatives on the Supreme Court** Theodore R. Johnson, "How Conservatives Turned the 'Color-Blind Constitution' Against Racial Progress," *The Atlantic,* November 19, 2019, https://www.theatlantic.com/ideas/archive/2019/11/colorblind-constitution/602221.

230 **Well-funded political groups mount campaigns** See, for example, an overview of Ward Connerly's initiatives in Phil Wilayto, "Ward Connerly & the American Civil Rights Institute," Media Transparency, 2000, https://web.archive.org/web/20090212085006/http://www.mediatransparency.org/personprofile.php?personID=13.

230 **Wellesley College professor Jennifer Chudy's** Jennifer Chudy, "Racial Sympathy and Its Political Consequences," *The Journal of Politics* (September 2020), https://doi.org/10.1086/708953.

230 **"a process of knowing designed"** Jennifer C. Mueller, "Producing Colorblindness: Everyday Mechanisms of White Ignorance," *Social Problems* 64, no. 2 (May 2017): 219–38, https://academic.oup.com/socpro/article-abstract/64/2/219/3058571.

231 **Kentuckians for the Commonwealth** Kentuckians for the Commonwealth (KFTC) is a grassroots organization founded in 1981 that uses community organizing and direct action to work for "a fair economy, a healthy environment, new safe energy, and an honest democracy." Priorities in 2020 included to expand voting rights; protect the land from the predations of coal mining and other extractive industries; ensure local communities and workers have a voice and economic opportunities in the transition from fossil fuel to renewable energy; and advance racial and economic justice. See Kentuckians for the Commonwealth, https://kftc.org.

231 **"wishful insinuation that we have done"** Wendell Berry, *The Hidden Wound* (Berkeley, CA: Counterpoint, 1989), 14–15.

231 **"the anguish implicit in their racism"** Berry, *Hidden Wound,* 8.

231 **"What they see is a disastrous"** James Baldwin, "White Man's Guilt," *Black on White: Black Writers on What It Means to Be White,*

ed. David R. Roediger (New York: Schocken Books, 1998), 321–22, originally printed in a special issue of *Ebony* in 1965.

231   **"you begin to awaken to"** Berry, *Hidden Wound*, 6.

232   **"I have borne it"** Berry, *Hidden Wound*, 4.

232   **"I think white folks are terribly"** Karen Grigsby Bates, "The Whiteness Project: Facing Race in a Changing America," *Code Switch*, NPR, December 21, 2014, http://www.npr.org/2014/12/21/371679777/the-whiteness-project-facing-race-in-a-changing-america.

232   **"Americans, on average, systematically overestimate"** Michael W. Krause, Julia M. Rucker, and Jennifer Richeson, "Americans Misperceive Racial Economic Equality," *Proceedings of the National Academy of Sciences of the United States* 114, no. 39 (September 2017): 10324–31, http://www.pnas.org/content/114/39/10324.

232   **In a 2019 public opinion survey** Juliana Menasce Horowitz, Anna Brown, and Kiana Cox, "Race in America 2019," Pew Research Center, April 9, 2019, https://www.pewsocialtrends.org/2019/04/09/race-in-america-2019.

233   **both resent affirmative action and imagine** Richard Sanger and Stuart Taylor Jr., "The Painful Truth About Affirmative Action," *The Atlantic*, October 2, 2012, https://www.theatlantic.com/national/archive/2012/10/the-painful-truth-about-affirmative-action/263122; Nikki Graf, "Most Americans Say Colleges Should Not Consider Race or Ethnicity in Admissions," Fact Tank, Pew Research Center, February 25, 2019, https://www.pewresearch.org/fact-tank/2019/02/25/most-americans-say-colleges-should-not-consider-race-or-ethnicity-in-admissions.

233   **actually declined over thirty-five years** Jeremy Ashkenas, Haeyoun Park, and Adam Pearce, "Even With Affirmative Action, Blacks and Hispanics Are More Underrepresented at Top Colleges Than 35 Years Ago," *New York Times*, August 24, 2017, https://www.nytimes.com/interactive/2017/08/24/us/affirmative-action.html.

233   **students admitted to Harvard** Peter Arcidiacono, Josh Kinsler, and Tyler Ransom, "Legacy and Athlete Preferences at Harvard," June 3, 2020, http://public.econ.duke.edu/~psarcidi/legacyathlete.pdf.

233   **Meanwhile, according to a 2016 study** See Brad Tuttle, "The Cost of Being Black: 33 Facts About the Wealth Gap and Racial Economic Justice," CNN Money, June 19, 2020, https://money.com/wealth-gap-race-economic-justice.

233   **"I think affirmative action was nice"** "Ronald," Whiteness Project, http://whitenessproject.org/checkbox/ronald. The Whiteness Project is an interactive investigation into how Americans who identify as white, or partially white, understand and experience their race.

234 **outlawed in 1978 by the Supreme Court** *Regents of University of California v. Bakke* 438 US 265 (1978). See the summary in Alex McBride, "Regents of University of California v. Bakke (1978)," *The Supreme Court*, Thirteen/WNET New York, December 2006, https://www.thirteen.org/wnet/supremecourt/rights/landmark_regents.html.

234 **Although 1.3 times more likely** See Mapping Police Violence, https://mappingpoliceviolence.org.

234 **Indigenous Americans are killed by police** Elise Hansen, "The Forgotten Minority in Police Shootings," CNN, November 13, 2017, https://www.cnn.com/2017/11/10/us/native-lives-matter/index.html; Olugbenga Ajilore, "Native Americans Deserve More Attention in the Police Violence Conversation," Crime and Justice, *Urban Wire* (blog), Urban Institute, December 4, 2017, https://www.urban.org/urban-wire/native-americans-deserve-more-attention-police-violence-conversation.

235 **An estimated 15 to 26 million people** Larry Buchanan, Quoctrung Bui, and Jugal K. Patel, "Black Lives Matter May Be the Largest Movement in U.S. History," *New York Times*, July 3, 2020, https://www.nytimes.com/interactive/2020/07/03/us/george-floyd-protests-crowd-size.html. See also Orion Rummier, "The Major Police Reforms Enacted Since George Floyd's Death," Axios, September 8, 2020, https://www.axios.com/police-reform-george-floyd-protest-2150b2dd-a6dc-4a0c-a1fb-62c2e999a03a.html.

235 **Stephon Clark** Cynthia Hubert and Benjy Egel, "He Has Become a Hashtag and a Movement for Change. But Who Was the Real Stephon Clark?" *Sacramento Bee*, April 8, 2018, https://www.sacbee.com/news/local/article208051604.html.

235 **Yet the officers faced no criminal** Jose A. Del Real, "No Charges in Sacramento Police Shooting of Stephon Clark," *New York Times*, March 2, 2019, https://www.nytimes.com/2019/03/02/us/stephon-clark-police-shooting-sacramento.html.

236 **"Scared of what? Don't be scared"** Maureen O'Leary, "What Color Is Your Tiki Torch?," blog post, August 13, 2017, https://maureenolearyauthor.com/2017/08/13/what-color-is-your-tiki-torch.

236 **In one year, white people called** "To the Next 'BBQ Becky': Don't Call 911. Call 1-844-WYT-FEAR," *New York Times*, October 22, 2018, https://www.nytimes.com/2018/10/22/opinion/calling-police-racism-wyt-fear.html.

236 **in 2020, Christian Cooper was bird-watching** Troy Closson, "Amy Cooper's 911 Call, and What's Happened Since," *New York Times*, July 8, 2020, https://www.nytimes.com/2020/07/08/nyregion/amy-cooper-false-report-charge.html.

237    **Among those in the United States arrested** "Estimated Number of Arrests by Offense and Race, 2018," Statistical Briefing Book, Office of Juvenile Justice and Delinquency Prevention, U.S. Department of Justice, released on October 31, 2019, https://www.ojjdp.gov/ojstatbb/crime/ucr.asp?table_in=2.

237    **only about 28 percent** Travis L. Dixon, "A Dangerous Distortion of Our Families," Color of Change, January 2017, https://colorofchange .org/dangerousdistortion/#key_findings.

237    **Yes, violent crime rates** "Persons in poor households at or below the Federal Poverty Level (FPL) (39.8 per 1,000) had more than double the rate of violent victimization as persons in high-income households (16.9 per 1,000). Poor persons living in urban areas (43.9 per 1,000) had violent victimization rates similar to poor persons living in rural areas (38.8 per 1,000). Poor urban blacks (51.3 per 1,000) had rates of violence similar to poor urban whites (56.4 per 1,000). Violence against persons in poor (51%) and low-income (50%) households was more likely to be reported to police than violence against persons in mid- (43%) and high-income (45%) households." Erika Harrell, PhD, and Lynn Langton, PhD, BJS Statisticians, Marcus Berzofsky, Dr.P.H., Lance Couzens, and Hope Smiley-McDonald, PhD, RTI International, "Special Report: Household Poverty and Nonfatal Violent Victimization, 2008–2012," United States Department of Justice Bureau of Justice Statistics, p. 1, https://www.bjs.gov/content/pub/pdf/hpnvv0812.pdf.

238    **"I am pretty moderate"** Avalanche, "Federal Law Enforcement: Confidential Polling Memo," August 2020, on file with author.

238    **93 percent of the events** Tim Craig, " 'The United States Is in Crisis': Report Tracks Thousands of Summer Protests, Most Nonviolent," *Washington Post,* September 3, 2020, https://www.washingtonpost .com/national/the-united-states-is-in-crisis-report-tracks-thousands -of-summer-protests-most-nonviolent/2020/09/03/b43c359a-edec -11ea-99a1-71343d03bc29_story.html.

238    **45 percent in the aftermath of George Floyd's death** Michael Tesler, "Support for Black Lives Matter Surged During Protests, but Is Waning Among White Americans," FiveThirtyEight, August 19, 2020, https://fivethirtyeight.com/features/support-for-black-lives -matter-surged-during-protests-but-is-waning-among-white -americans.

238    **four in ten adults live** Lydia Saad, "What Percentage of Americans Own Guns?," Gallup, August 14, 2019, https://news.gallup.com/poll/ 264932/percentage-americans-own-guns.aspx.

238    **"They have to make Americans afraid"** Laura Reston, "The NRA's

New Scare Tactics," *New Republic*, October 3, 2017, https://newre-public.com/article/145001/nra-new-scare-tactic-gun-lobby-remaking-itself-arm-alt-right.

239 **era of record-low crime rates** John Gramlich, "5 Facts About Crime in the U.S.," Fact Tank, Pew Research Center, October 17, 2019, https://www.pewresearch.org/fact-tank/2019/10/17/facts-about--crime-in-the-u-s.

239 **three-quarters of the gun suicide** Jonathan Metzl, "White Men Keep Killing Themselves with Guns. The NRA Is Making It Worse," *Vice*, July 3, 2019, https://www.vice.com/en_us/article/7xg3zd/white-men-keep-killing-themselves-with-guns-the-nra-is-making-it-worse.

239 **"In order for the concept"** Richard Thompson Ford, "Urban Space and the Color Line: The Consequences of Demarcation and Disorientation in the Postmodern Metropolis," *Harvard Blackletter Journal* 9 (January 1992): 117.

240 **"a world turned upside down"** Abraham Lateiner, "Grief and the White Void," Medium, March 7, 2016, https://medium.com/@abelateiner/grieving-the-white-void-48c410fdd7f3.

243 **Fox News is the most-watched cable news** Tara Lachapelle, "The New Fox Shows What Outrage Is Worth," Bloomberg, March 28, 2019, https://www.bloomberg.com/opinion/articles/2019-03-28/fox-news-shows-what-outrage-is-worth.

244 **progressive policies but for basic societal norms** Fox News–watching Republicans are more conservative than other Republicans on a host of progressive policies, from a wealth tax to green jobs, and they express more support for drug testing welfare recipients and the idea that skin color does not give white people societal advantages. John Ray, "The Fox News Bubble," Data for Progress (blog), March 24, 2019, https://www.dataforprogress.org/blog/2019/3/23/the-fox-news-bubble. Researchers in 2020 found that Fox News viewership significantly impacted noncompliance on stay-at-home orders. Andrey Simonov, Szymon K. Sacher, Jean-Pierre H. Dubé, and Shirsho Biswas, "The Persuasive Effect of Fox News: Non-Compliance with Social Distancing During the Covid-19 Pandemic," National Bureau of Economic Research Working Paper, May 2020, https://www.nber.org/papers/w27237.

244 **Facebook, where content from conservative** Kevin Roose, "Social Media Giants Support Racial Justice. Their Products Undermine It," *New York Times*, June 19, 2020, https://www.nytimes.com/2020/06/19/technology/facebook-youtube-twitter-black-lives-matter.html.

244    **"none addresses how the ideology"** Kate Shuster, *Teaching Hard History: American Slavery*, Teaching Tolerance, Southern Poverty Law Center, 2018, https://www.tolerance.org/sites/default/files/ 2018-02/TT-Teaching-Hard-History-American-Slavery-Report-WEB -February2018.pdf.

247    **"I am sorry that your statement"** Dr. Martin Luther King Jr., "Letter from a Birmingham Jail," *Atlantic Monthly*, August 1963, 78–88.

248    **"So, we said they weren't"** In the colonial era, slavers sought to bend the Bible to fit their economic imperative, and they succeeded. In 1667, the colonial Virginia Assembly, composed of Anglican men, passed a law to settle a pressing controversy: If an enslaved African or [*sic*] Indian became a Christian, could they still be a slave? The Virginians decided that the answer was yes: baptism conferred Christianity, not freedom. Other colonial legislatures reached similar decisions. Craving further confirmation, clergymen sought and, in 1729, received formal declarations from both the solicitor general and attorney general of Britain, who came to the same reassuring conclusion: baptizing enslaved people set them free only metaphorically. Saving their souls did nothing to change their earthly condition as chattel. See Michael O. Emerson and Christian Smith, *Divided by Faith: Evangelical Religion and the Problem of Race in America* (New York: Oxford University Press, 2000), 23.

248    **30 percentage points more** For example, 85 percent of white evangelical Protestants consider the Confederate flag not to be a symbol of racism; only 41 percent of religiously unaffiliated white Americans agree. There's a 26 percentage point gap between white Christians and religiously unaffiliated white people on the idea that police killings of unarmed black people are isolated incidents, and a 38 percentage point gap on the idea that football players should be required to stand for the national anthem rather than protest police brutality. Jones's analysis included a battery of "racial resentment" questions and revealed that "more than six in ten white Christians overall *disagree* with this basic statement: 'Generations of slavery and discrimination have created conditions that make it difficult for blacks to work their way out of the lower class.'" Among religiously unaffiliated white people, only 40 percent disagree. Robert P. Jones, *White Too Long: The Legacy of White Supremacy in American Christianity* (New York: Simon & Schuster, 2020), 159–61.

248    **"The unsettling truth"** Jones, *White Too Long*, 6, 20. Also, the psychologists Simon Howard and Samuel Sommers found that exposure to a white-skinned representation of Jesus Christ increased white anti-black attitudes. "White Religious Iconography Increases Anti-Black

Attitudes," *Psychology of Religion and Spirituality* 11, no. 4 (2019): 382–91, https://doi.org/10.1037/rel0000144.

250   **Many of the leading lawyers, philanthropists** See, for example, Debra L. Schulz, *Going South: Jewish Women in the Civil Rights Movement* (New York: New York University Press, 2001); current-day anti-racist and anti–family separation activism by Jewish social justice organizations including Bend the Arc; Rebecca Tan, "In D.C., New York and Beyond, Jews Mark Annual Day of Mourning by Protesting Trump Immigration Policies," *Washington Post*, August 11, 2019, https://www.washingtonpost.com/local/immigration/in-dc-new-york-and-beyond-jews-mark-annual-day-of-mourning-by-protesting-trump-immigration-policies/2019/08/11/16975ec2-bc70-11e9-b873-63ace636af08_story.html; for an interrogation of the dominant narrative about blacks and Jews in the movement and today, see Marc Dollinger, *Black Power, Jewish Politics: Reinventing the Alliance in the 1960s* (Waltham, MA: Brandeis University Press, 2018).

250   **12 to 15 percent of American Jews** Ari Y. Kelman et al., "Counting Inconsistencies: An Analysis of American Jewish Population Studies, with a Focus on Jews of Color," Stanford University and University of San Francisco, May 2019, https://jewsofcolorfieldbuilding.org/wp-content/uploads/2019/05/Counting-Inconsistencies-052119.pdf.

251   **source of solidarity with antiracist struggles** Sanya Mansoor, "'At the Intersection of Two Criminalized Identities': Black and Non-Black Muslims Confront a Complicated Relationship with Policing and Anti-Blackness," *Time*, September 15, 2020, https://time.com/5884176/islam-black-lives-matter-policing-muslims.

251   **"we . . . made you into nations"** Quran 49:13.

252   **"We can rebuild a building"** Amelia Nierenberg, "Their Minneapolis Restaurant Burned, but They Back the Protest," *New York Times*, May 29, 2020, https://www.nytimes.com/2020/05/29/dining/minnesota-restaurant-fire-protests.html.

252   **For all the differences among the world's major religions** For my research, I also spoke with people practicing and leading faith communities rooted in Hinduism, Buddhism, and Indigenous American spiritual traditions.

253   **"If white people have suffered"** Berry, *Hidden Wound*, 3.


## Chapter Ten: The Solidarity Dividend

255   **oldest population in the country** David Johnson, "These Are the Youngest States in America," *Time*, November 6, 2017, https://time.com/5000792/youngest-oldest-us-states.

255    **least likely in the country** Darren Fishell, "White Maine Students Are Least Likely in Nation to See Kids of Another Race at School," *Bangor Daily News*, December 6, 2017, https://bangordailynews.com/2017/12/06/mainefocus/white-maine-students-are-least-likely-in-nation-to-see-kids-of-another-race-at-school.

255    **among the top ten in opioid** "Opioid Summaries by State," National Institute on Drug Abuse, https://www.drugabuse.gov/drug-topics/opioids/opioid-summaries-by-state.

256    **"D-Money, Smoothie, Shifty"** Randy Billings, "LePage in Spotlight for Saying Drug Dealers Impregnate 'White Girls,' " *Portland Press-Herald*, January 7, 2016, https://www.pressherald.com/2016/01/07/lepage-accused-of-making-racist-comment-at-bridgton-meeting/.

258    **many other African refugees** Cynthia Anderson, "Refugees Poured into My State. Here's How It Changed Me," *Christian Science Monitor*, October 28, 2019, https://www.csmonitor.com/USA/2019/1028/Refugees-poured-into-my-state.-Here-s-how-it-changed-me.

259    **A bipartisan think tank calculated** New American Economy, "Map the Impact," Taxes and Spending Power, January 31, 2020, https://www.newamericaneconomy.org/locations/.

259    **introduced by his new Muslim name** Harvey Araton, "The Night the Ali-Liston Fight Came to Lewiston," *New York Times*, May 19, 2015, https://www.nytimes.com/2015/05/20/sports/the-night-the-ali-liston-fight-came-to-lewiston.html.

259    **Kennett Square, Pennsylvania** Araton, "The Night the Ali-Liston Fight."

259    **90 percent children of color** Art Cullen, "Help Wanted: Rural America Needs Immigrants," *Washington Post*, February 12, 2019, https://www.washingtonpost.com/opinions/2019/02/12/help-wanted-rural-america-needs-immigrants/?utm_term=.57c0d68b736a.

260    **Dalhart grew by 7 percent** Gus Bova and Christopher Collins, "These Rural Panhandle Towns Should Be Shrinking, but Thanks to Immigrants, They're Booming," *Texas Observer*, January 3, 2019, https://www.texasobserver.org/these-rural-panhandle-towns-should-be-shrinking-but-thanks-to-immigrants-theyre-booming.

260    **one in five owes the entirety** Silva Mathema, Nicole Prchal Svajlenka, and Anneliese Hermann, "Revival and Opportunity: Immigrants in Rural America," Center for American Progress, September 2, 2018, https://www.americanprogress.org/issues/immigration/reports/2018/09/02/455269/revival-and-opportunity.

260    **nearly 83 percent of the growth** Kenneth M. Johnson, "Rural Demographic Change in the New Century: Slower Growth, Increased Di-

versity," Carsey School of Public Policy, Issue Brief no. 44 (Winter 2012), https://scholars.unh.edu/carsey/159.

260   **"Asians and Africans and Latinos"** Cullen, "Help Wanted."

260   **These small-town success stories** Mathema, Svajlenka, and Hermann, "Revival and Opportunity"; Cullen, "Help Wanted."

260   **A quarter of Maine citizens** U.S. Census Bureau American Community Survey 2012–2016.

261   **Social isolation** Julianne Holt-Lunstad, Timothy B. Smith, and J. Bradley Layton, "Social Relationships and Mortality Risk: A Meta-analytic Review," *PLoS Medicine* 7, no. 7 (July 2010), doi:10.1371/journal.pmed.1000316.

265   **three years of state championships** They were state champions in 2015, 2017, and 2018. "Lewiston High School: Team Championships," Lewiston Blue Devils Athletics, http://lhsathletics.lewistonpublic schools.org/lhs-athletic-success-championships. Six countries reported on in Scott Stump and Josh Weiner, "How This High School Soccer Coach Brought a Divided Town Together," *Today*, February 27, 2018, https://www.today.com/news/how-high-school-soccer-coach-brought -immigrant-town-maine-town-t123948.

265   **Raymond Jr. wrote an open letter** Katharine Q. Seelye, "Mayoral Race in Maine Could Help Define City's Future amid Demographic Shift," *New York Times*, December 6, 2015, https://www.nytimes .com/2015/12/07/us/mayoral-race-in-maine-could-help-define-citys -future-amid-demographic-shift.html.

267   **"to make sure Lewiston"** Maine People's Alliance, "Ben Chin Breaks State Fundraising Record in Race for Lewiston Mayor," *Maine Beacon*, September 1, 2015, https://mainebeacon.com/ben-chin-breaks-- state-fundraising-record-in-race-for-lewiston-mayor.

267   **coming within 600 votes** Andrew Rice, "Lewiston's Ben Chin Announces Bid for Mayor," *Sun Journal*, February 23, 2017, https://www .sunjournal.com/2017/02/23/lewistons-ben-chin-announces-bid-for -mayor.

268   **Ben's first opponent, Mayor Macdonald, proposed** "Lewiston Mayor Says Asylum Seekers Cost Too Much Money," WGME, January 31, 2017, https://wgme.com/news/local/lewiston-mayor-says-asylum -seekers-cost-too-much-money.

268   **almost 10 percent** "Maine Summary, 2019," Annual Report, America's Health Rankings, United Health Foundation, https://www .americashealthrankings.org/explore/annual/measure/Health Insurance/state/ME.

268   **11.5 percent of them** "Poverty in Maine: Lack of Progress and New Threats Ahead," Coalition on Human Needs and Maine Equal Justice

Partners, November 17, 2017, p. 2, https://www.chn.org/wp-content/uploads/2019/02/Poverty-in-Maine-Lack-of-Progress-and-New-Threats-Ahead.pdf. The state has roughly 60,000 people of color and 1.2 million white people, 11 percent in poverty. See "Quick Facts: Maine," United States Census Bureau, https://www.census.gov/quickfacts/ME.

269    **sixty thousand Mainers winning access** "As of 09/03/20, 61,539 people were enrolled through MaineCare expansion, including 51,505 adults without children and 10,034 parents and caretaker relatives." State of Maine Department of Human Services, "MaineCare (Medicaid) Update: September 3, 2020," https://www.maine.gov/dhhs/data-reports/mainecare-expansion.

270    **a slate of progressive school board candidates** Dan Neumann, "Progressives Running for School Boards Across Maine Focus On Racial Equity," *Maine Beacon*, October 14, 2020, https://mainebeacon.com/progressives-running-for-school-boards-across-maine-focus-on-racial-equity/.

270    **"All my jokes are quite racist"** Lindsay Tice, "Lewiston Mayor's Texts Reveal Racist Comment Before Election," *Sun Journal*, March 7, 2019, https://www.sunjournal.com/2019/03/07/lewiston-mayors-texts-reveal-racist-comment-before-election.

270    **largest Ku Klux Klan** Donna Stuart, "Gentleman's Agreement," *Portland Monthly*, Feb/March 2009, https://www.portlandmonthly.com/portmag/2017/08/gentlemans-agreement/.

272    **than the wealthiest 1 percent** Isabel V. Sawhill and Christopher Pulliam, "Six Facts About Wealth in the United States," Up Front, Brookings Institution, Tuesday, June 25, 2019, https://www.brookings.edu/blog/up-front/2019/06/25/six-facts-about-wealth-in-the-united-states.

272    **There's a growing body of literature** Andrew Berg and Jonathan Ostry, "Equality and Efficiency," *Finance and Development* 48, no. 3 (September 2011), https://www.imf.org/external/pubs/ft/fandd/2011/09/Berg.htm.

274    **were still waiting months later** Eli Rosenberg, "Workers Are Pushed to Brink as They Continue to Wait for Delayed Unemployment Payments," *Washington Post*, July 13, 2020, https://www.washingtonpost.com/business/2020/07/13/unemployment-payment-delays.

274    **due to technicalities** Ninety-nine percent of 2018–19 public service loan forgiveness applications were denied. Government Accountability Office, "Public Service Loan Forgiveness Improving the Temporary Expanded Process Could Help Reduce Borrower Confusion," GAO-19-595, September 2019.

274    **An analysis Demos did** Philip Harvey, "Back to Work: A Public Jobs

Proposal for Economic Recovery," Demos, March 7, 2011, https://www.demos.org/research/back-work-public-jobs-proposal-economic-recovery.

275 **Angela Glover Blackwell calls this** Angela Glover Blackwell, "The Curb-Cut Effect," *Stanford Social Innovation Review* (Winter 2017), ssir.org/articles/entry/the_curb_cut_effect.

275 **about 15 percent of the GDP** "Housing's Contribution to Gross Domestic Product," National Association of Home Builders, https://www.nahb.org/research/housing-economics/housings-economic-impact/housings-contribution-to-gross-domestic-product-gdp.aspx.

275 **by more than 30 percent** Amy Traub et al., "The Racial Wealth Gap: Why Policy Matters," Demos, June 21, 2016, https://www.demos.org/research/racial-wealth-gap-why-policy-matters.

276 **largest benefits on the richest people** "The deduction has always been regressive, and the 2017 tax changes made it more so. In 2018 almost 17% of the benefits will go to the top 1% of households, and 80% of the benefits will go to households in the top 20% of the income distribution. Only 4% will accrue to households in the middle income quintile." William W. Gale, "Chipping Away at the Mortgage Interest Deduction," *Wall Street Journal*, April 9, 2019, https://www.brookings.edu/opinions/chipping-away-at-the-mortgage-deduction/.

276 **inheritances from previous generations** Darrick Hamilton and William Darity Jr., "Can 'Baby Bonds' Eliminate the Racial Wealth Gap in Putative Post-Racial America?," *The Review of Black Political Economy* 37, no. 3–4 (2010), https://doi.org/10.1007/s12114-010-9063-1.

276 **Kamala Harris and Elizabeth Warren** Maggie Astor, "Kamala Harris and Elizabeth Warren Introduce Racial Equity Plans," *New York Times*, July 6, 2019, https://www.nytimes.com/2019/07/06/us/politics/harris-essence-festival-2020-democrats.html; Team Warren, "My Housing Plan for America," Medium, March 16, 2019, https://medium.com/@teamwarren/my-housing-plan-for-america-20038e19dc26.

276 **eight trillion dollars larger in 2050** "Nine million potential jobs would be created if people of color owned businesses at rates comparable to Whites . . . Better jobs, health and education would spark an additional $109 billion of food purchases each year, $286 billion on housing, $147 billion on transportation, $44 billion on entertainment and $30 billion on clothing and apparel. Federal tax revenues would increase by $450 billion annually and state and local tax revenues would increase by $100 billion." "Updated Study Outlines Potential Gains to U.S. Economy and a Pathway for Economic Growth,"

W. K. Kellogg Foundation, April 24, 2018, https://www.wkkf.org/
news-and-media/article/2018/04/updated-study-outlines-potential
-gains-to-us-economy-and-a-pathway-for-economic-growth.

277    **wealth gap is growing** Lisa J. Dettling, Joanne W. Hsu, Lindsay
       Jacobs, Kevin B. Moore, and Jeffrey P. Thompson, "Recent Trends in
       Wealth-Holding by Race and Ethnicity: Evidence from the Survey of
       Consumer Finances," Federal Reserve, September 27, 2017, https://
       www.federalreserve.gov/econres/notes/feds-notes/recent-trends-in
       -wealth-holding-by-race-and-ethnicity-evidence-from-the-survey-of
       -consumer-finances-20170927.htm; Jennifer Cheeseman Day, "Black
       High School Attainment Nearly on Par with National Average," U.S.
       Census Bureau, June 10, 2020, https://www.census.gov/library/
       stories/2020/06/black-high-school-attainment-nearly-on-par-with
       -national-average.html.

277    **the descendants of a stolen people** These inventors are Dr. Shirley
       Jackson, Dr. Lewis Latimer, Charles Drew, Garrett Morgan, Alice H.
       Parker, Dr. Daniel Hale Williams, and Katherine Johnson.

277    **A 2020 Citigroup report** Dana M. Peterson and Catherine L. Mann,
       "Closing the Racial Inequality Gaps: The Economic Cost of Black In-
       equality in the U.S." Citi GPS: Global Perspectives & Solutions, Sep-
       tember 2020, https://www.citivelocity.com/citigps/closing-the-racial
       -inequality-gaps/.

278    **multiple times more likely** "COVID-19 Hospitalization and Death by
       Race/Ethnicity," Cases, Data & Surveillance, Coronavirus Disease
       2019 (COVID-19), Centers for Disease Control and Prevention, up-
       dated August 18, 2020, https://www.cdc.gov/coronavirus/2019-ncov/
       covid-data/investigations-discovery/hospitalization-death-by-race
       -ethnicity.html.

278    **study modeling COVID-19 transmission routes** Phillip Atiba Goff,
       Amelia M. Haviland, Tracey Lloyd, Mikaela Meyer, and Rachel War-
       ren, "How Racism Amplifies Covid-19 Risk for Everyone," *Vox*, Octo-
       ber 26, 2020, https://www.vox.com/2020/10/26/21529323/
       police-covid-19-risk-race-racial-disparities.

278    **decades of cuts to public hospitals** "This history of cuts has led to
       the United States having just 2.9 hospital beds per 1,000 people, com-
       pared to 3.1 for Italy, 4.3 for China and 13 for Japan." George Au-
       moithe, "The Racist History that Explains Why Some Communities
       Don't Have Enough ICU Beds," *Washington Post*, September 16, 2020,
       https://www.washingtonpost.com/outlook/2020/09/16/racist
       -history-that-explains-why-some-communities-dont-have-enough-icu
       -beds.

278    **half of low-income areas without** Genevieve P. Kanter, Andrea G.

Segal, and Peter W. Groeneveld, "Income Disparities in Access to Critical Care Services," *Health Affairs* 39, no. 8 (August 2020), https://doi.org/10.1377/hlthaff.2020.00581.

278     **In my hometown of Chicago** Duaa Eldib et al., "The First 100: COVID-19 Took Black Lives First. It Didn't Have To," *ProPublica,* May 9, 2020, https://features.propublica.org/chicago-first-deaths/covid-coronavirus-took-black-lives-first.

279     **"How precisely is diversity"** Carla Herreria Russo, "Tucker Carlson Has No Idea How Diversity Strengthens America," *HuffPost,* September 8, 2018, https://www.huffpost.com/entry/tucker-carlson-diversity_n_5b91d170e4b0511db3e0b3e8.

280     **"Members of a homogeneous group"** Katherine W. Phillips, "How Diversity Makes Us Smarter," *Scientific American,* October 1, 2014, https://www.scientificamerican.com/article/how-diversity-makes-us-smarter.

281     **Samuel Sommers borrowed real jurors** Samuel R. Sommers, "On Racial Diversity and Group Decision Making: Identifying Multiple Effects of Racial Composition on Jury Deliberations," *Journal of Personality and Social Psychology* 90, no. 4 (2006): 597–612, quote at 606.

282     **Truth, Racial Healing and Transformation (TRHT)** "TRHT is a national effort and throughout the next two to five years there will be place-based TRHT processes in 14 communities, including: (1) State of Alaska; (2) Baton Rouge and (3) New Orleans, Louisiana; (4) Buffalo, New York; (5) Chicago, Illinois; (6) Dallas, Texas; (7) Los Angeles, California; (8) Richmond, Virginia; (9) Selma, Alabama; (10) Saint Paul, Minnesota; and (11) Battle Creek, (12) Flint, (13) Kalamazoo and (14) Lansing, Michigan." See "Where Is TRHT Happening?," Frequently Asked Questions, *Truth, Racial Healing, & Transformation,* W. K. Kellogg Foundation, accessed September 22, 2020, https://healourcommunities.org.

282     **"To reconcile"** See "Is the TRHT the same as a Truth and Reconciliation Commission (TRC)?," Frequently Asked Questions, Truth, Racial Healing, & Transformation, W. K. Kellogg Foundation, https://healourcommunities.org.

284     **I almost turned the page** Jerry Hawkins et al., "A New Community Vision for Dallas: 2019 Report," Dallas Truth, Racial Healing, and Transformation, p. 23, https://dallastrht.org/wp-content/uploads/2019/05/DTRHT-Report.pdf.

284     **a photo of a smiling twelve-year-old** Jerry Hawkins et al., "A New Community Vision," 24.

285     **"Marsha Jackson and the Shingle Mountain"** Michelle Aslam, "What Is Shingle Mountain?," *Daily Campus,* Southern Methodist

University, November 21, 2019, https://www.smudailycampus.com/
news/the-mountain-of-toxic-shingles-in-south-dallas; Robert Wilon-
sky, "Here's How Shingle Mountain Was Born—And Why Dallas
Won't Pay to Destroy the 70,000-Ton Monster," *Dallas Morning News,*
February 14, 2020, https://www.dallasnews.com/news/commentary/
2020/02/14/heres-how-shingle-mountain-was-born-and-why-dallas
-wont-pay-to-destroy-the-70000-ton-monster.

286 **After a white policewoman mistakenly walked into** Erik Ortiz and
Alex Johnson, "Amber Guyger Sentenced to 10 Years for Murdering
Neighbor Botham Jean," NBC News, October 2, 2019, https://www
.nbcnews.com/news/crime-courts/amber-guyger-sentencing-resumes
-after-murder-conviction-death-botham-jean-n1061146; Joel Shannon,
"Lawyer: Police Seized Pot to Smear Botham Jean After He Was Shot
in His Own Apartment," *USA Today,* September 13, 2018, https://
www.usatoday.com/story/news/nation-now/2018/09/13/lawyer
-claims-police-seized-pot-smear-botham-jean/1297225002.

## Afterword

291 **"Have you heard of the new Child Tax Credit?"** Annie Lowery,
"Cash for Kids Comes to the United States," *The Atlantic,* July 14,
2021, https://www.theatlantic.com/politics/archive/2021/07/cash
-kids-child-tax-credit-biden/619439.

291 **highest child poverty rates** The twenty-five-country OECD average
for relative child poverty (children in households falling below half
the national median income) was less than 12 percent in 2019; the
United States' rate was over 20 percent. See "Poverty Facts and
Myths," Fact 4, Confronting Poverty, https://confrontingpoverty.org/
poverty-facts-and-myths/americas-poor-are-worse-off-than-elsewhere.

292 **The American Rescue Plan was popular with nearly 80 percent of
voters** Politico Morning Consult poll via "Transcript: *All In with Chris
Hayes,* 3/3/21," MSNBC, March 3, 2021, https://www.msnbc.com/
transcripts/transcript-all-chris-hayes-3-3-21-n1260940.

292 **In fact, when voters learned that the infrastructure plan** Morgan
Sperry and Ethan Winter, "Voters Want Infrastructure Paid for by
Corporate Tax Increases, Not the Gas Tax or Pandemic Funding,"
Data for Progress, June 16, 2021, https://www.dataforprogress.org/
blog/6/16/infrastructure-corporate-tax-increases.

293 **"political prisoners"** "Representative Madison Cawthorn of North
Carolina cast those arrested after the riot as 'political prisoners' and
suggested he wanted to 'try and bust them out.' . . . Representative
Paul Gosar of Arizona accused law enforcement of 'harassing peaceful

patriots' and 'law-abiding U.S. citizens.' " David Leonhardt and Ian Prasad Philbrick, "Valorizing Jan. 6," *New York Times*, September 17, 2021, https://www.nytimes.com/2021/09/17/briefing/january-6 -capitol-riot-rally.html.

293    **50 million people** Lois Beckett, "Millions of Americans Think the Election Was Stolen. How Worried Should We Be About More Violence?," *Guardian*, April 16, 2021, https://www.theguardian.com/ us-news/2021/apr/16/americans-republicans-stolen-election- violence-trump.

293    **The iconic photo from January 6** Maria Cramer, "Confederate Flag an Unnerving Sight in Capitol," *New York Times*, January 9, 2021, https://www.nytimes.com/2021/01/09/us/politics/confederate-flag -capitol.html.

294    **the filibuster, a Jim Crow–era relic** Rashad Robinson, "The Senate Filibuster Has a Racist Past and Present. End It So America Can Move Forward," *USA Today*, March 1, 2021, https://www.usatoday.com/ story/opinion/2021/03/01/end-filibuster-make-progress-race-voting -guns-health-care-column/6779720002.

294    **created in 1806 because of a drafting error** Sarah A. Binder, "The History of the Filibuster," Brookings Institution, April 22, 2010, https://www.brookings.edu/testimonies/the-history-of-the-filibuster.

294    **The lead story of the week** Aaron Rupar, "Why Fox News Is Having a Day-Long Meltdown over Dr. Seuss," *Vox*, March 2, 2021, https:// www.vox.com/2021/3/2/22309176/fox-news-dr-seuss-cancel-culture -fox-news-biden.

294    **"That's the only play they've got left"** "Transcript: *All In with Chris Hayes*, 3/3/21," MSNBC, March 3, 2021, https://www.msnbc.com/ transcripts/transcript-all-chris-hayes-3-3-21-n1260940.

295    **the Lost Cause, the multigeneration campaign** David W. Blight, "Europe in 1989, America in 2020, and the Death of the Lost Cause," *New Yorker*, July 1, 2020, https://www.newyorker.com/culture/ cultural-comment/europe-in-1989-america-in-2020-and-the-death -of-the-lost-cause.

295    **"made white students in the class feel uncomfortable"** Eesha Pendharkar, "A $5 Million Fine for Classroom Discussions on Race? In Tennessee, This Is the New Reality," *Education Week*, August 3, 2021, https://www.edweek.org/leadership/a-5-million-fine-for-classroom -discussions-on-race-in-tennessee-this-is-the-new-reality/2021/08.

295    **The same secret-money groups** Alyce McFadden, "Secretive 'Dark Money' Network Launches Anti–Critical Race Theory Campaign," Open Secrets, June 30, 2021, https://www.opensecrets.org/news/2021/ 06/secretive-dark-money-network-anti-critical-race-theory.

296    **The suburbs would seem to be difficult ground** Geoffrey Skelley, Elena Mejía, Amelia Thomson-DeVeaux, and Laura Bronner, "Why the Suburbs Have Shifted Blue," FiveThirtyEight, December 16, 2020, https://fivethirtyeight.com/features/why-the-suburbs-have-shifted-blue.

297    **In Rhode Island, a woman sent in more than two hundred public records requests** Linda Borg, "S. Kingstown School Committee Will Not Pursue Lawsuit over 'Race Theory' Records Requests," *Providence Journal*, June 3, 2021, https://www.providencejournal.com/story/news/education/2021/06/03/ri-school-committee-not-file-lawsuit-over-race-theory-requests/7523819002.

297    **the words "Black Lives Matter" or "equity"** Linda Borg, "Westerly Is Latest Town Where Teaching of Racism Is Under Fire," *Providence Journal*, June 9, 2021, https://www.providencejournal.com/story/news/education/2021/06/09/westerly-becomes-latest-community-subject-sweeping-public-records-request-teaching-race-schools/7621728002.

297    **Timothy Ryan, executive director** Tyler Kingkade, Brandy Zadrozny, and Ben Collins, "Critical Race Theory Battle Invades School Boards—with Help from Conservative Groups," NBC News, June 15, 2021, https://www.nbcnews.com/news/us-news/critical-race-theory-invades-school-boards-help-conservative-groups-n1270794.

297    **A record number of school board recall petitions** Ballotpedia data from NBC News via "Uncovering Who Is Driving the Fight Against Critical Race Theory in Schools," *Fresh Air*, June 24, 2021, https://www.npr.org/2021/06/24/1009839021/uncovering-who-is-driving-the-fight-against-critical-race-theory-in-schools.

297    **Activists have taken aim at public libraries** Kelly Jensen, "Demolishing Public Libraries from the Inside: Niles Public Library Is a Warning," *Book Riot*, July 15, 2021, https://bookriot.com/niles-public-library; Eleanor J. Bader, "Right-Wingers Are Taking Over Library Boards to Remove Books on Racism," Truthout, July 13, 2021, https://truthout.org/articles/right-wingers-are-taking-over-library-boards-to-remove-books-on-racism; Neil Steinberg, "If It Gets Cut, Where Do the Kids Go?," *Chicago Sun-Times*, July 18, 2021, https://chicago.suntimes.com/columnists/2021/7/18/22582356/niles-maine-library-budget-cuts.

297    **Generous public benefits** Jason DeParle, "Pandemic Aid Programs Spur a Record Drop in Poverty," *New York Times*, July 28, 2021, https://www.nytimes.com/2021/07/28/us/politics/covid-poverty-aid-programs.html.

297    **Upon taking office, the new administration announced a set of**

**plans** Sarah Ewall-Wice, "Biden's American Jobs Plan and American Families Plan: What's in Them and Where the Funding Will Come From," CBS News, May 1, 2021, https://www.cbsnews.com/news/ biden-american-jobs-families-plans.

298    **For the first time, the U.S. Transportation Department** Ian Duncan, "A Woman Called for a Highway's Removal in a Black Neighborhood. The White House Singled It Out in Its Infrastructure Plan," *Washington Post,* April 1, 2021, https://www.washingtonpost.com/local/ trafficandcommuting/highway-removal-infrastructure/2021/03/31/ effd6a26-9234-11eb-a74e-1f4cf89fd948_story.html.

299    **"For too long, we've allowed a narrow, cramped view"** "Remarks by President Biden at Signing of an Executive Order on Racial Equity," January 26, 2021, https://www.whitehouse.gov/briefing-room/ speeches-remarks/2021/01/26/remarks-by-president-biden-at -signing-of-an-executive-order-on-racial-equity.

# List of Interviews

Natalia Abrams, September 2020

Zaheer Ali, June 2020

Michael Ash, September 2019

May Boeve, August 2018, February and August 2020

Dr. Robert Bullard, January 2020

Melanie Bush, May 2019

Sanchioni Butler, August 2017

Mike Calhoun, April 2020

Ben Chin, June 2017, May 2018, and June 2020

Dr. Gail Christopher, June 2020

Robin DiAngelo, April 2019

David Donnelly, January 2019

Lisa Donner, April 2020

Errika Y. Flood-Moultrie, May 2020

George Goehl, February 2019

Debby Goldberg, March 2018

Ginny Goldman, April 2020

Jerry Hawkins, May 2020

Daniel Hill, November 2019

Bridget Hughes, June 2019

Julie Christine Johnson, August 2017 and June 2020

Kirsti M. Jylhä, January 2020

Angela King, June and August, 2017

Nancy MacLean, February 2019

Mal Maynard, June 2020

Don McBeath, April 2020

Yavilah McCoy, August 2019

Rachel Morello-Frosch, February 2020

Phil Nadeau, May 2018

Coral Nichols, May 2020

Nissan workers at Canton, Mississippi,
    Worker Center, August 2017

Bruce Noddin, July 2017

Torm Nompraseurt, March and April 2020

Michael Norton, August 2017

Marisa Novara, May 2019

Nathan Nunn, January 2019

Susan Parrish, May 2018

Ron Pollack, April 2020

Amy Rogers, July 2018

Jim Rokakis, April 2020

Said Mohamed, June 2017

Rabbi Felicia Sol, June 2019

Samuel Sommers, August 2017

Ali Takata, March 2019 and August 2020

Cecile Thornton, August 2017

Isaiah and Janice Tomlin, June 2020

Rachel Vindman, June 2021

Jim Vitarello, May 2018

Jim Wallis, June 2019

Maureen Wanket, April 2019

Terrence Wise, June 2019

Gavin Wright, August 2017

Tracy Wright-Mauer, May 2019

Miya Yoshitani, February 2020

# Index

# THE SUM OF US
## Heather McGhee

### Discussion Guide

**Zero-sum theory:** Many white Americans view race as a zero-sum game: there's an us and a them, and what's good for them is bad for us. This rationale animates our public policies even today, when those who benefit from our country's drastic economic inequality sell the zero-sum story to block public support for any collective action that could benefit all of us, from universal healthcare to living wages.

1.    How do we create spaces that encourage solidarity, given that we often engage in cultural practices and support institutions that can reinforce a zero-sum mentality?

2.    Considering what you've recently learned, what would you want to tell your younger self about the history of the United States and why its social reality looks the way it does?

3.    How does McGhee's background in economics influence her thinking about matters of race? How does she use her background to show us a new way into, and out of, a centuries-long problem?

4.    McGhee uses the example of public pools to illustrate how racism caused people to destroy something that could have benefited all of us. What are other "pools"—public goods that you see America

going without—and how do you now think differently about the role racism might have played in this dynamic?

5. Why would laborers like the white autoworkers McGhee describes refuse to unionize? How does this enhance your understanding of the "mystery" of people who vote against their own interests?

6. Let's talk about the way "the drained pool," to use McGhee's metaphor, has led to the student debt crisis—and how it is influencing generations of black *and* white college graduates.

7. If you lived through the financial crisis and the Great Recession, what was your impression of the causes of the crash and the political debate afterward? How did reading chapter 4, "Ignoring the Canary," change your narrative about what happened?

8. McGhee writes that white people are the most segregated people in America. What are some of the costs of continuing to segregate like this? What are the benefits of integration—both culturally *and* economically?

9. McGhee coined the phrase "Solidarity Dividend" to describe Americans reaching across racial lines to work together for the common good—and securing better lives for all of us. Discuss some of the examples she shares where such solidarity has been achieved, and offer others you've observed. If you have no real-life examples, what do you think impeded coalition building in your community or institution?

10. What's one thing you can do this week to work toward solidarity?

11. After sharing a memory of a white classmate proudly stating that she's fiscally conservative and socially liberal, McGhee challenges the morality of advocating fiscal conservatism when we could afford to eliminate poverty. Do you agree or disagree with this?

12. What are some ways white people can work to challenge zero-sum thinking?

HEATHER McGHEE designs and promotes solutions to inequality in America. The former president of the inequality-focused think tank Demos, McGhee has drafted legislation, testified before Congress, advised presidential candidates, and contributed regularly to news shows, including NBC's *Meet the Press*. She chairs the board of Color of Change, the nation's largest online racial justice organization. McGhee holds a BA in American studies from Yale University and a JD from the University of California, Berkeley, School of Law. She lives in Brooklyn with her husband and son.

heathermcghee.com
Facebook.com/HeatherCMcGhee
Instagram: @HeatherCMcGhee
Twitter: @hmcghee

## ABOUT THE TYPE

This book was set in Walbaum, a typeface designed in 1810 by German punch cutter J. E. (Justus Erich) Walbaum (1768–1839). Walbaum's type is more French than German in appearance. Like Bodoni, it is a classical typeface, yet its openness and slight irregularities give it a human quality.

## ABOUT THE ILLUSTRATOR

FRANCES TULK-HART is a visual artist and photographer. Raised in London, England, she moved to New York City following her graduation from Chelsea College of Art and Design. During the span of her almost twenty-five-year-long career, Tulk-Hart has traveled the world photographing and documenting people and their stories. In 2018, in protest of family separation at the U.S.-Mexico border, Tulk-Hart embarked on a massive project titled *2000 Taken*, where each day she would draw some of the thousands of children taken from their parents. Other notable projects include a bimonthly zine, a multiplatform interview series titled "Five Minutes with Franny," and, most recently, "The Corona Diaries," which focuses on the lives of people worldwide during the COVID-19 pandemic. She lives in New England with her husband and two daughters. Her work can be followed on Instagram @francestulkhart.

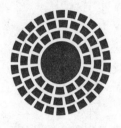

# ONE WORLD

One World, an imprint of Random House,
is a home for authors—novelists, essayists,
memoirists, poets, journalists, thinkers,
activists, and creative artists, all unconstrained
by genre—who give us new language for
understanding our past, present, and future.

**Discover other One World books
and sign up for our e-newsletter:**

**oneworldlit.com**

**Follow us:**
Instagram: @oneworldbooks
Twitter: @oneworldlit